DELOREAN

The rise and fall of a dream-maker

DELOREAN

The rise and fall of a dream-maker

———————

by

IVAN FALLON
and
JAMES SRODES

HAMISH HAMILTON
LONDON

To Sue, Tania, Lara and Robert Fallon

and

Louise and Cecile Srodes

First published in Great Britain 1983
by Hamish Hamilton Ltd
Garden House 57–59 Long Acre London WC2E 9JZ

Copyright © 1983 by Ivan Fallon and James Srodes

British Library Cataloguing in Publication Data
Fallon, Ivan
    DeLorean: the rise and fall of a dream maker.
    1. DeLorean, John   2. Automobile industry and
    trade – United States – Biography
    I. Title   2. Srodes, James
    338.7'6292222'0924   HD9710.U6
    ISBN 0-241-11087-4

Typeset by Rowland Phototypesetting Ltd, Bury St Edmunds, Suffolk
Printed and bound in Great Britain by
Richard Clay (The Chaucer Press) Ltd, Bungay, Suffolk

CONTENTS

	List of illustrations	vii
	Acknowledgements	ix
	The main characters	xii
	Prologue	1
1	Happy Childhood – Unhappy Home	5
2	The General Motors Years	20
3	Dream Car	57
4	The DeLorean Motor Company	81
5	Puerto Rico and Ireland	98
6	Northern Ireland	114
7	GPD	144
8	The Dream Takes a Dark Shape	183
9	Crisis and Confusion	209
10	DeLorean's Pen	228
11	A Day in the Life	246
12	Delays and Indecision	255
13	Bobby Sands	279
14	Marian Gibson	301
15	Scoop	315
16	The Storm	330
17	The Money Runs Out	347
18	Receivership	365
19	You have the Right to Remain Silent	387
	Epilogue	413

ILLUSTRATIONS

Between pages 178 and 179

1a DeLorean plays the clarinet in the Lawrence Tech band (*From the 1942 L-book*)
1b 1968: a chubby DeLorean poses with the Pontiac Grand Prix (*Detroit Free Press*)
2a 1973: a new style DeLorean (*Detroit Free Press*)
2b DeLorean as laid back tycoon (*Detroit Free Press*)
2c With his second wife, Kelly Harmon (*Detroit Free Press*)
3a The ranch at Pauma Valley (*Glasheen Graphics*)
3b With his third wife, Cristina Ferrare (*Detroit Free Press*)
4a and b and 5 The factory at Belfast
6 Colin Chapman (*Keystone*)
7a and c The designs
7b The competition (*Detroit Free Press*)
8a The interior (*DeLorean Motor Co.*)
8b The chassis
9a and b The finished DMC-12
10a Roy Mason with DeLorean and Don Concannon
10b Adam Butler with Shaun Harte
11 On the stand at Earl's Court: DeLorean and Prince Michael of Kent
12 The team in Belfast (*Telegraph colour library*)
13 The team in New York
14a Cristina visits the Belfast factory
14b Unwanted cars pile up at the Belfast docks
15 Cristina outside the court room (*Syndication International*)
16 John DeLorean in handcuffs (*UPI*)

ACKNOWLEDGEMENTS

This book is the result of an enormous research programme which never could have been accomplished by two men working alone on opposite sides of the Atlantic Ocean. We were blessed with a team of colleagues who were unstinting reporters and editors and encouraging friends as well.

A special note of thanks goes to Stella Shamoon of the *Sunday Telegraph*, whose early discoveries about John DeLorean were the spark to our own efforts. Dr. Philip Beresford, also of the *Sunday Telegraph*, contributed a uniquely expert insight into the tangled tragedy that is Northern Ireland; indeed all on the *Sunday Telegraph*, from Editor J. W. M. Thompson to Deputy City Editor Ian Watson and the City staff, gave generously of their support.

Sue Fallon and Christine Tierney proved adept and unstoppable interviewers and researchers. Maritsa Blackman in London and Maryse Rhein in Washington kept us both on time and on track. Irene Goldstein checked and queried and edited through the avalanche of manuscript and notes we generated. And Christine Jennings typed it all, at least once, and always on deadline. Thanks, too, to John Cushman, our agent, whose good counsel was as invaluable as his faith, and to Richard Sykes, our peerless legal adviser. Authors should always be grateful to publishers such as Phyllis Grann of G. P. Putnam's Sons in New York and Penelope Hoare of Hamish Hamilton in London, who put their support behind us early when it really counted. Nor would we be authors at all if it were not for Putnam's superb editor, Christine Schillig, who combined enthusiasm and professionalism to make it all happen.

Finally, there is a debt owed to the scores of men and women who were interviewed or who provided us with documentation or expert advice during the nearly two years of our investigation. These ex-DMC employees, relatives of our subject, friends, enemies, attorneys, bankers and automobile executives, as well as the officials of the governments of the U.S., U.K., Northern Ireland, the Republic of Ireland and the Commonwealth of Puerto Rico, brought invaluable perspectives to our research. Many had to relive painful personal episodes; others risked jobs and even prosecution to help. Some are named in the chapters that follow, many are not. However we know who they are and hope that our efforts repay them for their contributions.

We conducted numerous interviews in the preparation of this book. Quotations cited throughout the text and descriptions of scenes witnessed by them are based on personal communications from the following individuals:

Barrie Askew	William Haddad
Humphrey Atkins	Shaun Harte
Peter Avrea	Michael Hayes
Robin Bailie	Clark Higley
John Banham	Robert Holberg
Charles Bennington	Tony Hopkins
Alan Blair	Clarence Jones
C. R. Brown	Arvid Jouppi
Kenneth Bunker	Peter Kalikow
Frederick Bushell	Michael Kimberley
Adam Butler	Semon Knudson
George Clarke	Kurt Kuennecke
William Collins	Richard Kuntz
Alan Curtis	Gary Laughlin
Kenneth Dahlinger	Michael Loasby
David E. Davis	Carl Ludwigson
Charles DeLorean	Brendan Macken
George DeLorean	Bruce McWilliams
John DeLorean	Rupert Murdoch
Robert Dewey	Tony O'Reilly
Harry DeWitt	Colin Pinn
Manuel Dubon	Jim Prior
John Freeman	Sir Lindsay Ring
Nathan Gantcher	John Simpson
Marian Gibson	Colin Spooner

Walter Strycker	Barrie Wills
John Thomas	Nicholas Winterton
Alejandro Vallecillo	Jacques Wittmer
James Wangers	J. Patrick Wright
Alan Watson	

We have also talked to a number of politicians, officials, former executives, lawyers and advisers who have greatly contributed to the information in this book but for a variety of reasons preferred to remain anonymous. We have also made extensive use of letters, memos, company files, board minutes and other documents.

Information in Chapters 1 and 2 concerning John DeLorean's early life and years at General Motors was taken from *On a Clear Day You Can See General Motors* by J. Patrick Wright (Wright Publishing, Chicago, 1979). Material on the history and organization of the automotive industry included in Chapters 1 and 2 was provided by *American Automobile Manufacturers* by John B. Rae (Chilton Company, Radnor, Pennsylvania, 1959).

Much of the information contained in Chapters 6 through 19 regarding events in Northern Ireland and the United Kingdom, came from confidential interviews, public staff-level documents and other records pertaining to the Northern Ireland Development Authority and Her Majesty's Government's Department of Commerce.

IVAN FALLON
London
JAMES SRODES
Washington, D.C.

Publisher's note on spelling: Since this book is a collaboration between an American writer and an Irish writer, it contains a mixture of American and British usages. On the whole, the narrative is spelled in the British manner, while material quoted from American sources remains American in style.

Throughout, the name DeLorean is spelled as one word, although John DeLorean himself used it both ways, for himself and for different companies. His early records show it as one word, as does his current driving licence.

THE MAIN CHARACTERS

DeLorean Motor Company – New York/Detroit

John Z. DeLorean – chairman
Eugene Cafiero – president, 1979–81
Thomas Kimmerly – general counsel
C. R. (Dick) Brown – marketing
William Collins – engineering, 1975–79
Robert Dewey – chief financial officer, 1975–79
Walter Strycker – chief financial officer, 1979–80
James Stark – chief financial officer, 1980–81
William Haddad – public relations, 1979–81
Joseph H. "Buck" Penrose – corporate development
Marian Gibson – secretary/office manager
Mike Knepper – public relations
James Season – financial
Bruce McWilliams – marketing
George Hayward – legal
Henry Bushkin – Johnny Carson representative
Alex Fetherston – NIDA representative
James Sim – NIDA representative
Roy Nesseth –

The Belfast Team – DeLorean Motor Cars Limited (DMCL)

C. R. "Chuck" Bennington – managing director, 1979–80
Don Lander – managing director, 1980–82
Barrie Wills – purchasing
Myron Stylianides – personnel
Michael Loasby – engineering
Joe Daly – finance
George Broomfield – manufacturing
Shaun Harte – planning/PR
Dixon Hollinshead – construction
Brian Beharrell – organization
Robert Donnell – traffic
Ted Chapman – engineer
Peter Allinson – engineer
Joe Hillebrande – engineer
Ken Bunker – engineer
Colin Pinn – engineer

British government ministers

Roy Mason (Lab) – N.I. Secretary of State 1976–79
Don Concannon (Lab) – Minister of State 1976–79
Humphrey Atkins (Con) – Secretary of State 1979–81
Giles Shaw – Minister of State 1979–80
Jim Prior – Secretary of State 1981–?
Adam Butler – Minister of State 1981–?

NIDA

Dennis Faulkner – chairman
John Freeman – deputy chairman
Ronnie Henderson – chief executive 1977–79
Tony Hopkins – chief executive 1979–?
Shaun Harte – 1978/79 (see DMCL)
Gil Wilson –

Department of Commerce

George Quigley – Permanent Secretary, 1976–79
Frank Mais – Permanent Secretary, 1979–80
Ken Bloomfield – Permanent Secretary, 1980–?
Bryan Lytlle –
Frank McCann –

Lotus

Colin Chapman – chairman
Fred Bushell – finance
Mike Kimberley – managing director
Colin Spooner – chief engineer
Tony Rudd – senior engineer

Others

Robin Bailie – Belfast solicitor
Nicholas Winterton – Conservative MP for Macclesfield
Dick Measelle – auditor, Detroit
Alan Cohen – New York lawyer
Mike Hayes – Oppenheimer
Alejandro Vallecillo – Puerto Rican official
Manuel Dubon – Puerto Rican official
Michael Killeen – managing director IDA in Dublin
Sir Kenneth Cork – joint Receiver
Paul Shewell – joint Receiver

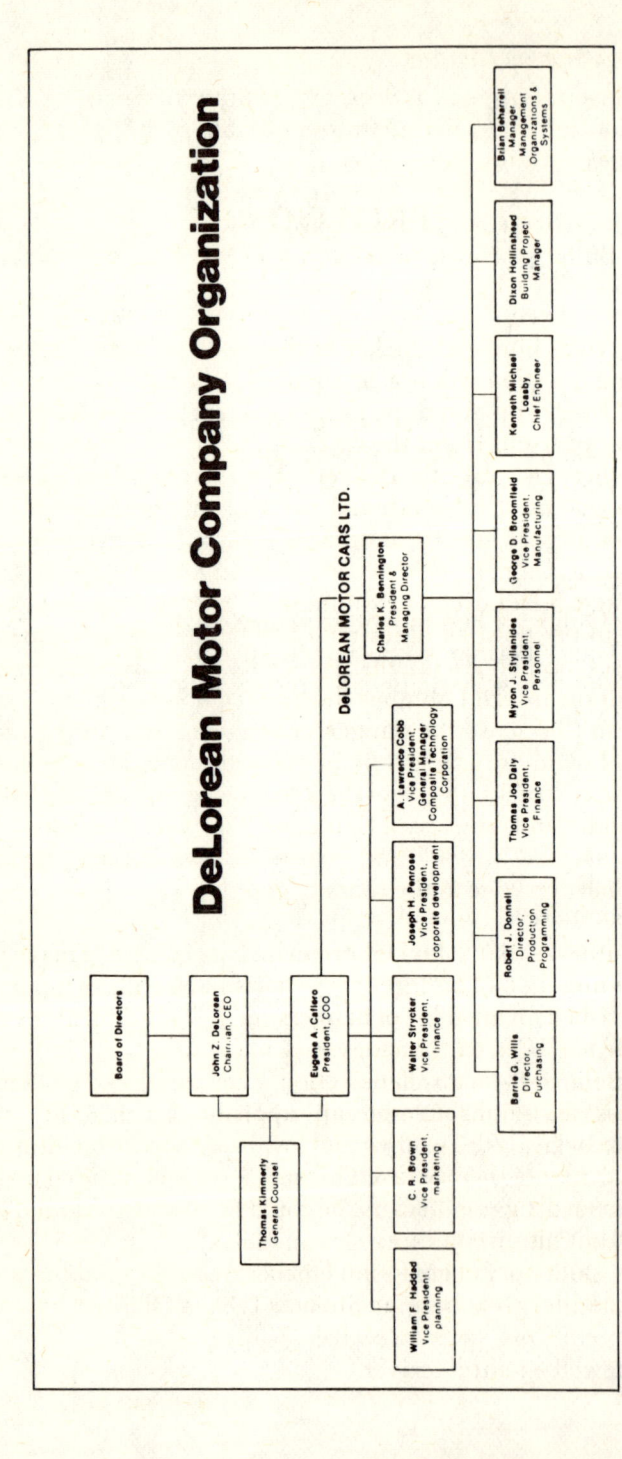

PROLOGUE

In the cold, blue-grey flicker of the video monitor screen, the nagging question will not be silenced. What is that guy doing there? Every cop and dope pusher knows the rule: never make the buy yourself. Hand the cash over – but have someone else, somewhere else, take the delivery. But there is John DeLorean, media celebrity, international car tycoon, standing in a Los Angeles airport hotel room that is so wired for sound it could generate a magnetic field.

What can DeLorean be thinking of? He says something that is lost in the noise of other men moving around and opening suitcases. Somebody laughs. Why not? It's a law enforcement convention and DeLorean is the guest of honour.

Doesn't he sense the danger? There is tension in the room, but DeLorean appears to be in good humour. He moves to a suitcase and picks up one of the kilo bags of cocaine. He hefts it with both hands the way a farmer would a sack of wheat.

'It's as good as gold, and just in the nick of time,' he says. This time everyone in the room chuckles.

The truth was that John DeLorean had no one else to make that buy for him. For all his legendary charisma, for all the money he had lavished on an army of hangers-on, he ended up alone that day. He had been called a maverick many times, and indeed he was – isolated from any satisfaction in his engineering talent or business accomplishments, an appealing personality who could draw beautiful women and loyal aides, but who ultimately drove most of them away. This sad, lonely man ended up in a hotel-room drug trap because he could not bear to be found out, to confront his own failure.

This is the story of how John DeLorean began a public career that promised great hope and benefit to the world and how that promise was broken. It is the story of a man who once preached the social duties of the business executive, but who ended up cheating thousands of the poorest and hundreds of the richest people in the world – from Hollywood's exclusive Bel Air to the grimy slums of Belfast – and how he dared not be unmasked.

But this also is a story about the ideals of our society, and how far we are willing to go to have our dreams fulfilled. It is about the limitations of the institutions that we have established to protect our dreams from those who would pervert them. The DeLorean story tells how one man could amass a fortune – at one time his company had as much as *$500 million* in economic clout behind it – and how nothing is left except a beautiful but empty factory in Belfast, and millions of dollars in debts.

This story is not really about the U.S. government drug charges against John Z. DeLorean or the other defendants who at the time of writing still face their day in court. Nor is it merely a breathless listing of the sex-drug-celebrity innuendoes that have fascinated the popular magazines and broadcast media.

Rather, the story began as a search for answers to a swarm of questions that surrounded the DeLorean Motor Company project in Northern Ireland. In late 1981, the future of the 'Dream Car', as the DMC-12 was called, still shone bright enough. Full production on the car had not yet been reached, but prospective buyers were offering as much as $35,000, a full $10,000 over its list price, to win an early place in the delivery line.

Yet there were troubles. There were reports of embezzled funds and of production problems that could be traced back to poor design and bad management decisions. As the company's prospects daily became more convoluted and doubtful, the search for answers generated serious questions about John DeLorean himself and the men who followed him from Detroit's top executive suites to the green fields outside Belfast, where the most modern car plant in the world would soon become an empty, rusting reminder of how greed and fraud can sour the dreams of thousands.

Other men must share the blame for the wreck of the DeLorean dream machine, but so do many of the institutions we rely on to protect us from just this kind of disaster. Because this is also a story about the failure of government watchdog agencies, the probity of our financial centres, and the credulity and dubious accuracy of our news-gathering organizations.

Finally, the DeLorean story is about a world standard of morality that places the highest value on immediate reward and pays less attention to the true worth or actual success of an enterprise. It is about world celebrity status granted on the basis of lifestyle and conspicuous consumption, but ignorance of the real character and substance of the individual.

The DeLorean story warns us to be more cautious and reluctant to entrust our dreams to others.

CHAPTER ONE

Happy Childhood – Unhappy Home

It was election day in Northern Ireland – October 20, 1982. Voters were being asked to turn out for candidates for the provincial Ulster Assembly that served as Britain's gesture of self-government for the six Irish counties under its control. It was a brisk, sunny day.

In Belfast, the good weather brought the shoppers out to wend their way through the iron turnstiles and checkpoints designed to keep the terrorists out of the main department store district. Nevertheless, bomb blasts rocked the surrounding city in unusual number as the Irish Republican Army tried to discourage voters from giving respectability to the Assembly at Stormont.

The sunny day did nothing to penetrate the gloom inside the 72-acre DeLorean Motor Company plant in the nearby suburb of Dunmurry; this was the last day the DMC-12 gull-wing sports car would be coming off the factory's assembly lines. Most of the 2,000-man workforce had already been sent home weeks before, but that day there was a finality to it all. Once a plant closes, it rarely opens its doors again – especially in Northern Ireland.

Inside the brightly lit main assembly building, the entire production process stood frozen in time. Small groups of men puttered around the various work areas, sweeping up, gathering tools, talking quietly among the piles of fibreglass bales and mattings that formed the basic outlines of the DMC-12. All along the line were large wire hampers filled with the parts that were added at various production stages, and further down were the huge mould presses that produced the top and bottom halves of the car's body shell. At the end was a line of cars, each with one gull-wing door extended into the air like an injured bird.

But for the men who were spending their last days on the job – perhaps their last job ever – there was something else to talk about. The overnight wire service reports from California had filled the morning radio programmes with little else. John Z. DeLorean had been arrested near a Los Angeles airport hotel and charged by U.S. government investigators with taking part in a plot to smuggle in 100 kilos of cocaine that could have been resold on American streets for $50 million. U.S. Justice Department officials said they believed DeLorean was making a frantic effort to raise the money he needed to save his bankrupt car company in Northern Ireland.

And why shouldn't they think that? All that the federal agents knew about John Z. DeLorean was what almost everyone else knew – what they were told by the admiring journalists who built the DeLorean myth. According to that myth, John DeLorean was the iconoclastic big businessman who had 'fired General Motors' and gone on to found a flashy, high-flying sports car company.

He was still a glamorous figure, as likely to turn up as the subject of a glowing profile in some high-fashion magazine as on the business pages of the *Wall Street Journal*. The general news media knew him as a swinger who dated movie stars and who was now married to one of the top fashion models in the world; a gifted engineer who had switched with style and grace into the world of high finance; a classy guy on the fast track of life – that was John DeLorean.

Nowhere was DeLorean's reputation better than in Northern Ireland where the 2,500 jobs provided by the car plant had injected an enormous economic boost to that desolate, strife-torn region. The men who were collecting their final pay cheques that afternoon had only seen John DeLorean on rare occasions as he regally toured the kingdom of his factory in West Belfast. But his fall was their fall, too.

Outside, a cluster of men stood in the bright sunshine having a last cigarette before going home. They watched silently as two large trucks pulled through the plant gate, each carrying six of the shining steel sports cars to the storage yard at the Port of Belfast.

Had the men heard about Mr. DeLorean's arrest? A sad thing, said one as the others nodded. He did his best for this area. It was a shame what had happened to the company, to their jobs and now to him.

'Some of the lads never had jobs before; now they stand a chance of never having another. This summer I was able to take my kids to the seaside for the first proper holiday they've ever had. Now there'll be no Christmas,' one man said, turning away toward home.

A journalist walked after him; where could he be found later on? 'Oh, you'll be able to find me all right. I'll be down on the Falls Road dole from now on.'

In London there was shocked bewilderment. But there was also some undisguised glee. By the time of his arrest, DeLorean had made powerful enemies in British government circles. For months ministers had been arguing that the government should not deal with John Z. DeLorean at all because he was a 'crook'. But they never had any real evidence, only their own hunches. Now, it was a day full of 'I told you so.'

The bewilderment was centred mostly in the office of Sir Kenneth Cork. Sir Kenneth was the British government-appointed bankruptcy receiver charged either with restructuring DeLorean Motor Cars Limited of Northern Ireland or with selling it off and settling as many of its huge debts as he could. He was a tough professional with an impeccable reputation. One London newspaper called him the 'familiar provider of a better class of financial funeral service'. For eight months he had been running DeLorean's factory and was in almost daily touch with DeLorean himself.

Cork had been on the phone most of the day before making one last try to save the factory. For months DeLorean had been telling him he had 'the head of a Middle Eastern State' or a 'friend from the West Coast' or a 'wealthy industrialist' who was going to invest $30-$50 million. Every one of them had fallen through – except one. And that last one was coming through with the money. Even the sceptical Cork was persuaded of it.

The night before, Cork received a call from Virginia, from the woman representing the bank that would transfer the money. It was all ready, she told Cork. All it needed was a signature from DeLorean, but she was not able to get hold of him – he had apparently left New York to fly to Los Angeles without signing the document. That morning a shocked Cork heard about the arrest on the seven o'clock news. A few hours later he arrived at his office to find a telex from the bank confirming the money was there. It was waiting for a simple 'John Z. DeLorean' signature. But John Z. DeLorean was not available that morning. The final hope for the Belfast factory had gone.

News reports and radio and television talk shows devoted to the arrest produced disquieting public reaction to the scandal. Such was the apparent level of cynicism in America about government and institutions that people thought of John DeLorean as a version of Robin Hood. A veteran investigative journalist, who had tracked DeLorean's long history of business vandalism, emerged shaken from one national radio show on which listeners were asked to telephone their reactions to the arrest.

'You wouldn't have believed it,' he recounted later. 'The calls ran seven or eight to one in sympathy for John. There was one poor guy called all the way from Buffalo. He'd lost his job when the factory he'd worked at for 20 years went bust and he said, "I just wish my boss had sold some cocaine or anything just to keep that plant open." That still bothers me. How can people still support him after all the harm he's done? How can they ignore what he has done to other people and then consider *him* some kind of victim?'

To be sure, there were people who did not consider John DeLorean a victim at all. To them, he had been and remained a first-hand threat.

In Phoenix, Arizona, the news of the arrest brought telephone calls from friends and relatives to the home of Pete and Shirley Avrea who had suffered through the lengthy lawsuits and threats. In 1974 Pete had relied on DeLorean to help market an invention – a device that keeps automobile radiators from boiling over and that is now on almost every car in North America. During one trial, the judge estimated that Pete Avrea had been cheated out of royalties worth $70 million. In the end Avrea had to give up his efforts to recover his losses because of his wife's deteriorating health. He took no joy in the calls about the arrest; he wished he had never heard of John DeLorean.

Across the country in the resort town of Cape Coral, Florida, Kenneth Dahlinger reacted to a radio report of DeLorean's arrest by changing the route he took to work that morning. Dahlinger was now the owner of a prosperous business, but he had once owned an even more prosperous Cadillac dealership in Wichita, Kansas. DeLorean and a henchman left Dahlinger bankrupt and the continuing threats against his life forced him to move, to keep changing his unlisted telephone number, to keep looking over his shoulder and changing his daily routine – even with John DeLorean 3,000 miles away, locked up in the Terminal Island Federal jail awaiting his bond hearing.

Houston's sprawling glass and concrete airport has an exclusive section of hangars and support buildings set aside for the private planes that wealthy Texans use to cover the frequently huge distances between home and work. Out in the parking lot, Gary Laughlin sat staring at his waiting plane, paralysed by the news he had just heard on the radio. Laughlin had wrenched his fortune out of the ground in the Texas oil patch as a wildcat driller and investor. He had trusted John DeLorean: he had invested $500,000 of his own money and convinced friends and relatives to invest still more in DeLorean's car venture.

Show business super-star Sammy Davis Jr. was even harder hit. Although Davis had earned several fortunes during his 50-year career on stage and in the movies, he had been ill-served by some early managers and was frequently in trouble over taxes and alimony. The $150,000 Davis had given John DeLorean had literally been earned by the sweat of his brow and was the entertainer's hope for winning some financial independence. 'Sammy can't come to the phone,' an aide told a sympathetic caller. 'He's really in mourning over that man DeLorean.'

DeLorean had plenty of friends in high places. And he had his inner circle of faithful supporters. The horde of journalists and television cameramen who jammed Los Angeles airport a day later to cover the arrival of DeLorean's cover-girl wife Cristina Ferrare paid no attention to the tough, heavyset man in a windbreaker who met her at the arrival gate and whisked her to a waiting car. It was Roy Nesseth, DeLorean's long-time comrade in many shady business deals. It was Nesseth who struck terror into the heart of any business associate or DeLorean employee who interfered with his desires. 'Roy enjoys hurting people,' DeLorean would boast. Threats from Nesseth caused Pete Avrea to drop his suits to regain control over his invention and forced Kenneth Dahlinger to move into hiding in another part of the country.

Thomas W. Kimmerly, a 60-ish, retiring man, had given up a thriving Detroit practice as a tax and securities lawyer to follow John DeLorean on his odyssey from the executive suite at General Motors to the ill-fated and now bankrupt car company across the Atlantic. Kimmerly was totally devoted to John DeLorean, and right to the very end remained totally loyal, and protective of the interests of his boss. It was Kimmerly who worked out the details of DeLorean's many business ventures, who plotted the securities offerings and the tax strategies that shifted funds from one enterprise to another and ultimately to DeLorean himself.

After the company crashed, former officials fell into the habit of referring to DeLorean, Nesseth and Kimmerly as one entity – an overpowering combination of drive, muscle and shrewdness. Indeed, at the end, there were those who argued that DeLorean himself had become dominated by the other two, that he was powerless to resist Kimmerly's plots and Nesseth's predations.

But the fact is that DeLorean was alone in that Los Angeles airport hotel room. Kimmerly and Nesseth were never considered suspects by the federal strike force agents.

2

John Zachary DeLorean was born on January 6, 1925, in Detroit, Michigan. He was the eldest of four sons of Zachary and Kathryn DeLorean.

It was the thirties and DeLorean's father was lucky to find any industrial work. He was an immigrant French-Alsatian whose irregular jobs at the Ford Motor Company foundry left him drinking and raging at the frustrations of his life. A gifted millwright, Zachary DeLorean was nevertheless kept to relatively menial, insecure jobs at the foundry because of his poor command of English. Furious at the snubs he endured at work, the six-foot-one, 220-pound DeLorean vented his anger in bar-room fights that only added to the family's hardship.

Kathryn DeLorean was also an immigrant, a refugee from the wreckage of the Austro-Hungarian Empire. Necessity forced her, too, onto the factory floor and, throughout most of young John's life, his mother worked as a tool assembler for the Carboloy Products Division of General Electric.

How poor were John DeLorean's family and childhood?

'You don't know what poor is until you know how poor we were. We were really poor,' he said in a recent interview.

> When I was twelve I got one of those Sears & Roebuck suits that cost about twelve bucks in those days, and I wore that suit until I got out of college to go into the service. It was the only one I had; it was bought so you could let the pants out as I grew taller and I didn't weigh anything then anyway. No, no, we were really poor.

Even if this were true, the DeLorean family was hardly an example of the grinding poverty that millions of Americans endured in the middle 1930s. Very few American boys had suits at all, or they got hand-me-downs from older brothers – an embarrassment young John did not have to endure as he grew towards his eventual six-foot-four-inch height.

No, the less dramatic truth was that, through much of his childhood, John DeLorean lived in a pleasant, if small, frame house near Six Mile Road and Dequindre on Detroit's Near East Side. He would describe it as a tough, lower-middle class neighbourhood but it was considerably better than that. There were three bedrooms and thus the four brothers had the relative privacy of sleeping two to a room. There was enough food and love. And there was enough money for school and even for music lessons for John, who used his talent in playing the clarinet to win scholarships to the better Detroit schools.

But it is also clear that the DeLorean family suffered from Zachary DeLorean's emotional flare-ups. Three times during his early years, John's parents separated and the boys were taken by Kathryn to the sanctuary of her relatives in Los Angeles. Each reconciliation lasted a year or so, through John's early teenage years. Finally in 1942, when John was 17,

Kathryn and Zachary DeLorean divorced. After that, the boys saw little of their father and he died at the age of 61 of throat cancer.

It is hard to say how much of an imprint was made on John DeLorean by his father's frightening explosions and subsequent neglect. But it is easy to sympathize now with a new arrival in a hard land at a hard time. Perhaps Zachary DeLorean could have done better for his family, yet he took care of them for as long as he could and prophetically installed in his sons a familiarity with and love of the automobile. Like every other mechanic in Detroit, the elder DeLorean tinkered with cars at home when he wasn't building them at work. One of John's earliest memories, he later recalled, was helping to put cylinder heads on Ford Model A's in his father's backyard workshop.

There are two themes that characterize John DeLorean's childhood: his disappointment in and lack of respect for his father's perceived weakness, and his own embarrassment at coming from a factory-class background. In his own words:

> Kids are inherently happy if you give them half a chance, and I thought we had a pretty happy childhood. Part of the reason is that while we had the humble surroundings that come with lower-middle class existence, we didn't know we were being deprived of some of the great fruits of American life because we didn't have the means of instant communication then as we do today. So while we didn't have a lot, we also weren't aware of what other people had. That comfortable picture was *shattered* [italics added] one day when I was about 13, and two classmates, a brother and sister, at Nolan Intermediate School asked me to their house for dinner. They lived in a very plush area known as Palmer Woods, at Woodward and Seven Mile Road. And while their house wasn't the biggest in the area, it was the largest I'd ever been in. I remember feeling awkward at dinner, not sure of how to act or eat. The conversation covered some things I'd never heard of, *like going to summer camp and traveling on vacations* [italics added]. Vacations, for the most part, when I was young, meant getting out of school and playing around the house for three months. The experience opened a new vista

for me. I began to realize what things were possible and available in America.

Palmer Woods, where Detroit's Municipal Golf Course is located, is a very pleasant neighbourhood, to be sure. But on Detroit's grid system of streets and neighbourhoods, the Six Mile Road (now called McNichols) and Dequindre neighbourhood where the DeLoreans lived was less than a mile away from his schoolmates, and that was scarcely the impenetrable class barrier he would later portray it to be. If school holidays did not mean summer camps for young John DeLorean, neither did they mean summer jobs to help the family make ends meet.

The point is that John DeLorean plainly felt ashamed of his family and background. This is a common enough story in the families of new immigrants. Some families stick together in tight units and work their way to a better life for all. In others, individual members abhor the embarrassment of the old ties to old ways. They seek their success through education and advancement.

Young John DeLorean was to take full advantage of the open American public school system as it existed in those days. After the family's last return from Los Angeles to reconciliation, John went to Cash Tech, Detroit's High School for honour students. There he qualified for a music scholarship to the Lawrence Institute of Technology, the top-flight training school that turned out the army of draughtsmen and designers for the region's manufacturing complex.

At Lawrence, DeLorean specialized in industrial engineering studies and was good enough to be elected to the school's Honor Society. He also played in the school dance band, and wrote for the school newspaper, the *Tech News*. He ran for the presidency of Lawrence's Student Council organization in 1947, but lost.

Photographs show a tall, slender American teenager: a soft and dreamy-eyed boy. He pushed hard at his studies – but that was why the boys were at Lawrence Tech: to get ahead. He was brash and slightly self-promoting – but his classmates and teachers also remember him as being willing to help less gifted students with tough engineering problems. He also showed a barbed sense of humour in his newspaper writings and often sank a shaft or two into himself.

World War II interrupted DeLorean's studies at Lawrence Tech, as it did for millions of other Americans. He returned to Detroit after his three-year hitch and got a job with the city's Lighting Commission until he had enough money to re-enroll at Lawrence. During his final two years there, he worked part-time in a Chrysler plant (a job arranged by an uncle) and at a neighbourhood body and fender shop.

Early in 1947, he was still young and self-confident enough to risk writing the following discourse for *Tech News* on the topic, *Know You What It Is To Be An Engineer?*

> It is to have a dream without being conscious you are dreaming lest the dream break, it is to be trapped in a terrible tower of pure science.
>
> It is to live in a mean, bare prison cell and regard yourself the sovereign of limitless space; it is to turn failure into success, mice into men, rags into riches, stone into buildings, steel into bridges, for each engineer has a magician in his soul . . .
>
> It is to give imagination full play, to accept the inventions of nature, to tell stories born of silence that fill the world with wonder . . .
>
> It is to be a conquerer and a coward, a king and a captive, a savior and a slave, it is to be good unto seeming Godlike while contrasting evil incarnate; it is to suffer a throne alone in your terrible temple of science while companions roam the city streets making carefree carnival . . .

When DeLorean graduated from Lawrence in 1948, his first jobs were as an insurance salesman and as a salesman for the Factory Equipment Company, a concern that made machine tools. He was quite successful, and won a trip to Bermuda for selling the rather considerable sum, for the late 1940s, of $850,000 in insurance policy coverage.

But DeLorean's restlessness and unwillingness to focus were becoming evident even at that early time. A relative helped him get a job at the Chrysler Institute, a post-graduate facility run by the car company to train higher level engineers. In 1952 he graduated with a Master's Degree in Automotive Engineering and went to work at Chrysler while pushing on to earn the credits necessary for a Master's Degree in Business Administration from the University of Michigan.

It was during this time that two other patterns emerged in John DeLorean's persona. One was his recognizable skill as an automotive engineer. He would be comfortable with that skill, secure in his ability for the rest of his life. He also developed the patterns of diligent, hard work that brought him advancement and promotion throughout his career.

Chrysler soon bored DeLorean and he shifted over to a job with the legendary Forest McFarland, the head of Research and Development for the Packard Motor Company. DeLorean was assigned to work on the new central hydraulic systems and the innovative 'ultramatic' transmission system. These were important formative years for his professional life, for they imbued him with the spirit of Detroit's classic auto engineers and set him firmly on the career path he would follow for the rest of his life.

Up to this point, there was very little that would set John Z. DeLorean apart from any other young man trying to get a foothold on life in the years immediately after World War II. He was middle class, had a decent education, had served his country honourably during the war. Afterwards, he worked hard to finish his training and had moved from job to job trying to better himself. He was not above using the help of relatives to find jobs and he was ambitious enough to move on if the opportunities looked better elsewhere. Like millions of others, DeLorean also married. His wife was the former Elizabeth Higgins, a secretary. He continued to play his clarinet as a pickup addition to the jazz bands that played in Detroit's interracial black-and-tan clubs, but even that was more for enjoyment than for the money it brought in.

The discontented aimlessness that re-emerged later in DeLorean's life disappeared at least temporarily when he joined McFarland's design shop at Packard. Here was something that absorbed his interest, something he could respect and even aspire to.

3

The automobile industry is one of the key expressions of that personal yearning that has turned into cliché as the American dream. Central to the American experience from the time the first settlers arrived in the New World are the themes of personal mobility and individual independence and enterprise. If times are hard, move on. Go west. Go somewhere.

In the early 20th century, the automobile ceased being just a convenience for the rich and emerged as an engine of true social change. The car itself became an object of fantasy and speculation. Exploration of the innards of the internal combustion engine became a rite of passage for most American boys – John DeLorean and his brothers were no exceptions – so much so that few American adult males have ever really outgrown the fascination and romance.

And why should they? A man could grow rich by building a better automobile. Indeed the entire nation profited by the unprecedented development of the automobile. General Motors Chairman Charles W. ('Engine Charlie') Wilson never said, 'What's good for General Motors is good for America.' What he did say that fateful day in 1952 at a U.S. Senate hearing was, 'I have always believed that what was good for America was good for General Motors and vice versa.'

Since World War II, car production has been far and away the largest manufacturing enterprise in America. That explosive growth has fuelled thousands of other business enterprises, provided employment for millions and valuable mobility and convenience to all.

The present-day car is essentially the same product it was by the early 1920s. All technological changes from the Ford Model-T to the DMC-12 have been refinements and improvements rather than drastic innovation. Moreover, by the 1920s, the supply of automobiles in America had caught up with the demand for them. The industry could produce more cars than there were buyers. The increased competition led the U.S. car industry steadily away from its entrepreneurial founding days and inexorably onward to the consolidations and increasingly complex corporate organizations that were forged to survive.

By the 1920s, the old myth of the genius mechanic in his

modest workshop was being replaced. Henry Ford, Ransom Olds, David Dunbar Buick, Louis Chevrolet and even the five Studebaker brothers had been shirt-sleeve inventors. And it is a little known fact that these men – even the stiff, reclusive Henry Ford – raced their cars against each other. That was how they proved an auto's worth: they built it, then hauled it out to some county fair dirt track and raced it until someone won or the engine blew up.

But these same men, to the varying degrees that they were successes, were also pioneer industrialists. They invented the manufacturing techniques that would make their particular cars sell profitably. The real revolution of the 1920s was the consolidation of management controls and decision making into one group of senior executives, often under the leadership of a single man.

At the base of this change was a revolutionary idea: the offering of a variety of products to suit broader market tastes. Henry Ford had become rich making a car that the average American could buy for $500. Other men had varying successes selling luxury cars to the very rich. But by the middle of the First World War, William C. Durant was busily putting together the structure of General Motors from the disparate parts of Buick, Oldsmobile, Cadillac and Oakland. Into his conglomerate he folded other autos whose names now read like a museum of old cars – the Carter, the Elmore, Ewing, Marquette, Rapid, Reliance and Welsh.

Durant's strategy was sharply rejected by Henry Ford at the time. Durant reasoned that, if a company offered a model to fit every definable market category, then that very variety was insurance against the total company failing because one product line had hit a slump. Ford, on the other hand, argued for most of his life that one should do only what one did well; that the complexities of making so many kinds of cars would ultimately drag such a conglomeration down.

In the end, Billy Durant died a penniless failure. But the trends he set in motion became part of the folkways of the industry. Where Durant stumbled, other men pushed ahead, many of them set on their way by the old conglomerator himself.

Alfred Sloan, W. S. 'Billy' Knudsen and other General

Motors chief executives would take Durant's philosophy and refine it over the next 30 years. Sloan set up the lines of organization and decision making that last to this day. Knudsen contributed his own emphasis on product development and improvement. He guided Chevrolet to its rivalry with Ford by the simple principle of trying to offer the buyer a visibly better product than Ford, even if the price was just noticeably higher.

It is important to remember that these now-mythic figures of the American automobile industry were still alive and functioning when young John DeLorean was beginning his career. Their theories and achievements would be among the lessons DeLorean absorbed along with his technical training.

4

For now John DeLorean was learning valuable technical skills at the Packard design shop. Packard was one of the independent luxury car holdovers from before World War II. It was justifiably proud of its precisely engineered heavy-weight engines and was now trying to design its way back to profitability with innovations in its power train and transmission.

Because Packard lagged behind in meeting the public's quick-changing tastes for style in the middle 1950s, the company's fortunes never recovered. But while he was there, DeLorean benefited from access to both the assembly shops and the production facilities where Packard designers worked side by side with the toolwrights.

Packard also had an institutional pride that attracted DeLorean: it was a bit old-fashioned and stuffy; its pride was the pride of the individual craftsmen, with the inherent disdain that such men hold for any mass-produced products.

In 1956, four years after joining Packard, DeLorean succeeded Forest McFarland, who moved to Buick as Assistant Research Engineer. DeLorean was now in charge of a small research and development operation at a fatally troubled firm.

His reputation was good enough to win a call from the newly appointed chief of General Motors' Pontiac Car Division. Semon E. 'Bunkie' Knudsen was a true prince of the Motor City. He was the son of GM's former president and was himself an MIT-trained automotive engineer who had nevertheless retained his father's predilection for getting his hands dirty building cars that others would buy. Knudsen needed new engineering talent to revive Pontiac.

He hired Elliott 'Pete' Estes as Chief Engineer and DeLorean as his assistant for advanced design work.

CHAPTER TWO

The General Motors Years

There were two of them. This other fellow and John, and the other guy right away started asking me about benefits and raises and things like that. John just wanted to know about the job. The other fellow was gone in a week.

In those days John was a bit on the heavy side, about 190 pounds. And like everyone else back then, he didn't dress with much style, and he had the short hair. But he worked hard enough.

Semon Emil Knudsen is now 70 but looks as if he's in his mid-50s. His immaculate suits and reserved manner mask the fact that he feels equally at home in the executive suites of Detroit and in the pits at a race track. These days, Knudsen is in partnership with American racing's super mechanic, Smokey Yunik, in the development of a high-compression, low-pollution, fuel-efficient engine that produces the same horsepower with two cylinders that most engines do with four. Until April 1982, Yunik and Knudsen were being actively courted by John DeLorean, who wanted the design for his 1985 model DMC-12 car.

William S. 'Big Bill' Knudsen had emigrated from Denmark to Buffalo where he married and where young Semon ('Bunkie') was born in 1912. The boy was an only son with three younger sisters. By 1926, the elder Knudsen had become Vice President of the Chevrolet division at General Motors; and that year he gave his 14-year-old son a new Chevy, completely unassembled. Bunkie was told that the car would be his if he could put together the 1,000 or more parts unaided. It took him two months to complete the task.

Bunkie graduated from MIT as a fledgling automotive engineer. Instead of taking a plush GM post, as might have been expected, he got a job at a machine shop and then went to work in a rollerbearing plant that turned out 100,000 units a day, so he could have the experience with mass production. When finally he did join GM, it was to tour the outposts of the giant corporation, working in the plants that produced engines for aircraft and for the diesels. By 1956, at the age of 43, Bunkie Knudsen would be 'the youngest man ever to head one of GM's five automobile divisions'. He was made General Manager of Pontiac.

A common belief around Detroit is that 'Bunkie Knudsen was the father John DeLorean never had'. In an uncharacteristic acknowledgement, DeLorean recalled later in his book: '(I was) a naive, rough-edged engineer . . . (when) I came under the tutelage and into the friendship . . . of Bunkie Knudsen. He showed me another side of his life I never knew existed.' Knudsen, for his part, has the kind of sober regret one has for an old comrade-in-arms who has fallen on hard times. John DeLorean may well have been some kind of surrogate son to Bunkie Knudsen but the older man was never blind to John's flaws.

John DeLorean came along just as Knudsen was setting off on his campaign to match his own father's legend – to become President of General Motors. You never wish ill of someone who was there at the beginning, so Bunkie still has a fondness for the man who began the march with him.

In that summer of 1956 when Knudsen entered the lists with John DeLorean among his squires, Detroit was just becoming the engineering backwater it is today among other U.S. industries. Perhaps World War II and the Korean War were to blame. Other industry groups (aerospace, chemicals, communications, for example) all received enormous technological boosts during wartime that were immediately translated into improved commercial products in peacetime, just as our high technology industries of today are still feeding off the advances of the space programme. What the wars and the space programme have in common is that they force companies to solve problems and improve products well in advance of market demand – indeed, they create the demand for products that are unknown to the consumer until then.

The automobile emerged from the war years in a form almost

indistinguishable from its prewar predecessors. It was still a box on four wheels powered by an internal combustion engine. Ironically, not even the advances in engine development had been all that useful because they emphasized speed rather than efficiency. Tooling and manufacturing costs placed limits on just how fast a mass-produced car could go and, besides, even speed-happy Americans have little use for a car that can exceed 200 mph, then or now. So, Detroit settled for making its cars prettier or more novel in appearance. For a while, it was a seller's market as pent-up demand outstripped everyone's ability to put new cars into dealer lots fast enough. By 1956, however, the industry was being steadily nudged to pay more attention to how popular taste could be motivated and manipulated.

This is where men like Bunkie Knudsen and John DeLorean represented a break with Detroit's tradition of shirt-sleeve engineers and managers. They had an eye for fashion and public taste.

There would be differences between the two men as they evolved over the years. Knudsen never ended his love affair with the car. Recently, he told with pride of how he failed to get the dealer who had sold him a new Ventura to fix some complicated ignition problem. Finally, Knudsen took the afternoon off, grabbed his toolbox and solved the problem himself. DeLorean, on the other hand, lost that enthusiasm as his increasing cynicism overwhelmed even the one talent that everyone agreed he possessed, his engineering skill. But at the beginning, he and Bunkie Knudsen had more in common. They were both good engineers and the future in Detroit beckoned to them both.

2

We are encumbered with myths about the way things are done in America. One of the more pervasive is about the way top management is chosen for the biggest American corporations. Cartoonists have relied for years on the image of callow Junior being inserted into a top vice-presidency of Dad's firm over the heads of senior, more qualified people. Another myth is the conspiracy theory that envisions a web stretching from the Ivy

League business schools to Wall Street and out across the land to the executive suites of 2,000 major corporations.

The truth is that the business school graduate has only recently become a major component of the management pool for big firms. The tradition of most heavy industries has been to select chief executives and senior officers from the ranks and to put a premium on men who have the greatest experience on the manufacturing side of the enterprise, sometimes to the exclusion of colleagues who come from backgrounds in research, marketing or even administration. The prejudice of management to replace itself with men 'who know how to make what we sell' over men known as 'bean counters' is still remarkably strong, even in the 1980s.

John DeLorean became scornful of this tradition. To him, it smacked of stagnating conformity; it put a premium on men who could mask their lack of ability by wearing the same clothing styles and by adopting the same attitudes as their mentors and judges. He believed that the later generation of General Motors executives – his bosses – were poor inheritors of the industry's traditions.

> As I grew in General Motors it became apparent that objective criteria were not always used to evaluate an executive's performance. Many times the work record of a man who was promoted was far inferior to the records of others around him who were not promoted. It was quite obvious that something different than job performance was being used to rate these men.
>
> That something different was a very subjective criterion which encompassed style, appearance, personality and, most importantly, personal loyalty to the man (or men) who was the promoter, and to the system which brought this all about. These were rules of this fraternity of management at GM. Those pledges (initiates) willing to obey the rules were promoted. In the vernacular they were the company's 'team players'. Those who didn't fit into the mold of a manger, who didn't adhere to the rules because they thought they were silly, generally weren't promoted. 'He's not a team player,' was the frequent, and many times only, objection to an executive in line for promotion. It didn't mean he was doing a

poor job. It meant he didn't fit neatly into a stereotype of style, appearance and manner. He didn't display blind loyalty to the system of management, to the man or men doing the promoting. He rocked the boat. He took unpopular stands on products or policy which contradicted the prevailing attitude of top management.

At General Motors, good appearance meant conservative dress. In my very first meeting as a GM employee in 1956 at Pontiac, half the session was taken up in discussion about some vice-president downtown at headquarters who was sent home that morning for wearing a brown suit. Only blue or black suits were tolerated then. I remember thinking that was silly. But in those days I followed the rules closely.

What DeLorean did not say was that the men who ran Motor City, when he was beginning his career, were men who had spent those careers adjusting to a depression and a global war that forced tremendous dislocations and accommodations on them and their industry. They were conservative, of course. But, however conformist it was in its dress code, General Motors was then and is now a place of sharp-elbowed, aggressive personalities. Like many of its sister industrial centres, Detroit has always been a tough town and the scramble to survive reaches from its streets and factory floors to the panelled offices of senior management.

It is possible that DeLorean never quite realized how tough these older men could be – and when he found that out it was too late.

No senior management group or individual chief executive is ever so secure that he can fill a line of succession with clones of himself. This was doubly so at General Motors where the average tour of duty as president or chairman of the board was less than five years.

The pressure on young executives in those days was that they 'make their numbers' – that is, they achieve the goals or quotas set out for them by the demands of profitability and productivity set by senior managers. Personal style had very little to do with it. There, DeLorean was right: dullness was endemic. But, what he apparently never accepted was that your reward depended on success with immediate goals, not on attractive promise nor even in being right over the long haul in spite of being wrong today. You made today's numbers today and collected today's reward. To get tomorrow's reward, you kept on succeeding.

3

In 1956 Bunkie Knudsen was the hottest young engineer-manager in Detroit. But he had learned several lessons from his father's career, one of them being that you are only as good as the team of people working for you.

For Knudsen, that team was John DeLorean and Pete Estes. Estes was the man Bunkie Knudsen needed most. He was 41 and the hot engine wizard at GM. Like other boys of his day, he had begun 'fooling around' with cars at an early age and was skilled enough to make repairs on his father's Flying Cloud. At 14, he attached a one-cylinder engine to his coaster wagon to make it self-propelled. He had worked his way through the General Motors Institute, that company's farm system for draughtsmen. In 1946, Estes moved over to GM's Oldsmobile division. It was the time of the post-war buying frenzy – Americans were rushing to buy any car at all at first, just to replace their old, deteriorated models. But a new sales environment was already on the horizon.

Old brand loyalties counted for nothing with the millions of young men who were returning from war. They were making money in their new civilian jobs; they were getting married; a new car was more important than a new home in those days. It offered mobility, privacy, excitement; but more than anything, having a new car symbolized to the world that the interruption caused by the war was over.

Styling counted for much in this new market – styling and speed. Estes' design for the Olds rocket-88, the world's first high-compression V-8, captured the fancy of that coming-home generation. By 1949, the medium-priced Olds outsold every other car in America except the cheaper Ford and Chevy models. By 1954, Estes was chief engineer at Oldsmobile; and by 1956, he was looking for other challenges. In joining Knudsen at Pontiac, Estes lined up with a man who complemented his own engineering bent, and gained the opportunity to learn the management skills he would need to rise up the ladder.

Pontiacs had turned into 'old ladies' cars'. Heavy metal, stolid models, Pontiacs were still being turned out according to the diehard Detroit vision of an America where both the men and women who drove their cars wore hats and so needed large box-like car bodies to accommodate their headgear in comfort.

So, too, the Pontiac had clung to its old hood ornament with a fierceness that took one back to the 1930s, when every motor car had its own readily identifiable hood ornament signature, recognized by every schoolboy and prospective customer. In Pontiac's case, it was the profile of the Indian chief Pontiac and, in the last years, the old warrior was sometimes even made of plastic and lit from within so that at night his grim visage stared into the dark road ahead.

Knudsen and Estes were under direct orders to turn Pontiac around fast, to change the car's image completely. They set to work rounding up a support team and trying to make the maximum impact in the minimum amount of time. As *Motor Trend* magazine said in February 1965, 'Estes . . . bought, borrowed and stole some of the best engineering brains in Detroit.'

It's important to realize how little time there was to make major changes in the car. DeLorean joined the team in September 1956, even as the 1957 models were going into production. As a symbolic gesture more than anything else, Knudsen chopped off the Chief Pontiac hood ornament and removed the chrome side strips that had been the model's concession to modernity.

DeLorean's task was to begin advance planning both for the styling and power train changes that would push the model into top sales contention. The next five years were perhaps the happiest and certainly the most productive period in DeLorean's engineering career. It was the start of more than 200 innovations, from power trains to recessed windshield wipers, that would be patented in his name.

Critical to Knudsen's broader campaign was a strategy which was novel then, but which is considered standard practice today. He took the Bill Durant notion of using various product lines as an insurance against failures and applied it to the Pontiac division. Pontiac, by tradition, had been a single identity car, a metal behemoth that conveyed assurance and stability to the driver.

But America was growing younger as it grew more affluent. Increasing numbers of teenagers and college-age customers were entering the new car market. Tastes were varied. Small imported sports cars were a popular novelty. Bigger, more powerful cars with flashy designs also offered new sales opportunities. Knudsen decided that Pontiac would compete at both ends of the market.

Dirt-track racing had long been Detroit's design proving ground. And Knudsen had made himself a fair reputation as a driver when the sport was revived in the early 1950s, both as entertainment and as a magnet for the growing number of independent car customizers and stylists. These independents – often no more than garage mechanics working in their spare time – took Detroit's boringly standard models and turned them into sleek, growling, power mills.

It was an exciting time in racing. It was the early days of the Don Garlitz dragster shop and the early Daytona stock car races in Florida, of Fireball Roberts and Junior Johnson in the Carolinas; and it was a time when the body and engine customizers of California were chopping and channelling chunky Fords and Chevys into pink-candy-striped muscle cars for the long boulevard racecourses of suburban Los Angeles.

The first thing the new Pontiac team did in early 1958 was to sponsor field racing teams at the major stock car races around the country. Pontiac sponsored Joe Weatherby and Fireball Roberts to punch around dirt track circuits the models that would later be refined into designs for the LeMans and the Catalina. Much of the important testing of new ideas and designs was done by Knudsen, Estes and DeLorean.

'Let the car tell you,' was an Estes motto.

Under Knudsen's leadership, engineers and design executives were encouraged to put innovative designs or bits of test equipment on standard models and drive them home each night. Woodward Avenue, which slashes north to the wooded Bloomfield Hills area, where top Detroit executives live, became a unique part of the street drag racing scene. Detroit's grid system of streets created one-mile stretches of three-lane highway between intersections and stop lights – an ideal length for drag racing. So Detroit's teenagers became used to having their home-made hot rods challenged by older men (in their 40s), pulling up at traffic lights in dull-looking standard sedans. There they would be, the kids with their tailpipes grumbling from backyard tinkering, goosing and backing off, goosing and backing off as the light went from red to green. But, as the months went by, word began to spread: these old dudes in their square cars could fool you. There was this little car they were driving. It didn't look like anything recognizable, and there was no brand name on it. But it could move! It was fast and light; and, from stop light to stop light, it was hard to beat.

The key to the new Pontiac Tempest's success was an innovative 225 horsepower engine created by Estes that featured an overhead cam designed by DeLorean. In fact, the entire drive train for the Tempest was put together by DeLorean's advance planning staff.

When the Tempest was introduced in 1959, it became the most popular of America's compact cars. By 1961, it was voted Car of the Year by *Motor Trend* magazine's poll; and it helped boost the sales of the Pontiac division from sixth place to third behind Chevrolet and Ford. The 1960 model year was Knudsen's year of triumph at Pontiac. Not only did the Tempest catch on among the new generation of economy-minded buyers, but the Estes-DeLorean engineers also unveiled the Grand Prix sports car as well as the luxury-market LeMans, an important addition to the Pontiac arsenal.

But if 1960 and 1961 were hot years for Pontiac, they were down years for Detroit in general. Chevrolet, in particular, was giving GM problems. Its basic design had not been changed since the classic 1956 model, which had become stale and boring.

In 1961, GM's top management predictably moved Knudsen to the post of General Manager of the Chevrolet division and, at his suggestion, made Estes his successor as General Manager of Pontiac. DeLorean, who had been promoted to Assistant Chief Engineer in 1959, was named Chief Engineer to succeed Estes on November 7, 1961.

What kind of man was DeLorean at that time?

'He was very secure as an engineer; and so he was fairly easy to get along with. You could test out an idea of his and go to him and say, "John, this just doesn't work." He would say, "Well, you're the one who tested it so you know best. Let's try something else,"' recalls one of his original design team.

'He could be tough to work for though; everyone worked hard in those days and you didn't expect to go home at 5 o'clock and get ahead, not with Knudsen and Estes around either. But while Pete Estes was a pleasant man with a good sense of humor, John wasn't much with the jokes and the friendly approach. People liked and respected Pete. They respected John, and worked for him, even when they didn't like him a lot. I can't think of any single thing that stands out, except that John never really cultivated close ties to anyone. He didn't have friends among the younger engineers, and he didn't really cultivate his bosses either.'

As chief engineer of the division, DeLorean's life changed dramatically. Before, he could bury himself in his work and leave the administrative duties to Estes, while Knudsen did the politicking. Now, he had to take on an increasing share of both the administrative and corporate manoeuvring. He did not do well at it; not surprisingly, he did not like it.

Another GM engineer who followed DeLorean's career from a few steps behind noted, 'He was a great engineer. The word genius is overused but he was certainly at the top of his profession in those years. He had a sense of what the public wanted, even if it didn't know what it wanted already. He could create style, and that is a precious commodity. But he was a godawful administrator.

'So when he took Estes' job, he formed a small cadre of people he trusted implicitly and shut everybody out. If you were in with John, you were in; and anything you said was okay with him. If you were out, he would walk all over you; he would shut you out.

'The worst thing was for a man to be imposed or inserted into John's shop by upstairs management. Then John walked all over the poor bastard; he never had a chance. John began to develop a very hard attitude to people, but at the time, you could excuse it as being the price you pay to get ahead.'

And times were competitive, both within the car industry and within GM itself. The sixties boom was underway. It was the time of new fashions, of the Kennedys and their informal but elegant style. America was repudiating the fifties dullness and looking for exciting things.

But, coming out of the recession of 1959-60, Detroit was still feeling cash poor; budgets for research and development were cut. For Estes and Pontiac that meant no more new model experiments. In mid-1963, the company pulled Pontiac's racing team off the stock car circuit as a cost-cutting measure; this robbed Estes of an immediate way of testing engine and body designs. His response was to look for a new body style and image that could be built around the wide-track LeMans. The result was the Pontiac GTO, named after the Ferrari coupé, Gran Turisimo Omologato. It was a car that would symbolize a generation, and it was the root of the John DeLorean myth.

The myth was that John DeLorean single-handedly came up with a design for the GTO which was so successful that it rescued a troubled division of General Motors and set the American automobile scene on its ear for years.

The truth was something else.

'In the sense that John worked on the Tempest, he can take credit for the GTO, because the Tempest was just a small GTO. But by that same sense, you should give credit to Ronnie and the Daytonas,' says David E. Davis, who was part of the public relations and advertising team that helped boom the GTO into America's consciousness.

Burly and now bearded, Dave Davis, a former race car driver, had a unique vantage point from which to watch DeLorean's GM career. Davis became one of DeLorean's inner circle – to his discomfort – at the Campbell and Ewald agency, which for 50 years had held the $100 million annual advertising budget for Chevrolet. As a veteran writer for *Car & Driver*, before he joined Campbell and Ewald, he has since returned and made that trade publication into the most outspoken and independent magazine for car enthusiasts all over the world.

'To go back to the beginning, Knudsen started the original four-cylinder Tempest, and as did all of those compact cars of that period, it grew and got a V-8 engine. Then it became the LeMans. Then later, when GM cracked down, all they had to do was drop in a great big engine, put on different wheels and tires and they had a GTO. They were able to take off the LeMans name and just make it a GTO, and it was easy to do within the corporate structure because it wasn't a new car by any stretch of the imagination. It was just a model spun off an existing line of cars,' Davis explains.

'But to be absolutely scrupulously honest, if you want to name the man who came up with the *concept* of the GTO, you have to name Jim Wangers. It was Wangers who was the wild-eyed drag-racing enthusiast – he was very much tuned to the street racing crowd of the sixties – and he had a lot of latitude when Knudsen was running Pontiac,' Davis adds.

At that time, Jim Wangers was the product sales promotion specialist for the Pontiac division's outside advertising agency. The GTO, which actually came out in 1962, had been doing well enough around the country, but in early 1964 sales of the car went from good to spectacular. Again, industry insiders credit Wangers with coming up with the sales pitch that caught on.

'There was this singing group, Ronnie and the Daytonas; and they came to GM with a song about the GTO. They were pretty damn good. They had a California surfin' sound, much like the Beach Boys. It got recorded and we bought thousands of copies to send to our dealers. The record went on to sell a million copies and reached third place in the top-40 charts. It was nothing but a two and a half minute commercial for the Pontiac GTO,' Wangers says.

The version of the GTO story put about by DeLorean was that he had come up with the concept of the car because of his close contact with the world of the teenage dragster.

'These rock stations, the things they say, what they discuss, that's what counts. It's the cheapest education you can get,' he told *Newsweek* in September 1968.

In another version published by *Current Biography* in 1976:

> When the management of General Motors prohibited its divisions from racing their new models in 1963, DeLorean introduced the sporty GTO . . . to attract and hold racing enthusiasts. To promote the new car, he backed a massive publicity campaign that included T-shirts, emblems and the

hit recording, 'Little G.T.O.,' as well as more traditional advertising techniques. By the end of the model year, the entire run of 31,000 G.T.O.'s had been exhausted. Within two years, G.T.O. sales nearly tripled.

DeLorean had good reason to push himself forward. Knudsen was now making his play for a berth on the 14th floor top executive suite at GM and Estes was rumoured to be his successor at Chevrolet. DeLorean could move into the management track behind Estes. He was making his numbers, and so he pushed for his reward.

Moreover, the ever-energetic DeLorean had burnished his credentials for promotion. What time he hadn't spent working for Estes and the design team over the last 18 months, he'd spent working on a masters degree in business administration from the University of Michigan in nearby Ann Arbor. There was even time for a course on business law at the Detroit College of Law. DeLorean was also an active joiner of all the professional engineering and automotive societies and industry trade associations.

While John was a joiner, he was not much of a success in the social circuit to which he had been elevated. He and his wife Liz now lived in Bloomfield Hills, the hilly, wooded enclave for the city's elite that was just north of central Detroit. Appearances at the Bloomfield Golf and Country Club were now a weekend ritual. So was dinner out at the Kingsway Hotel dining room on Woodward Avenue, the restaurant of choice of the motor industry social set.

'Liz loved it. She was beautiful and blonde – really a dish – and very lively. John hated it. Even then, he didn't drink to speak of. He had no small talk. But at the same time he sometimes couldn't keep his mouth shut. He would name-drop or tell really bad jokes. Some of his stuff was really teenage dirty joke humor. But people excused it. They liked Liz because she was so enthusiastic, and I guess they figured John would grow out of it in time,' remembers a long-time social friend.

'It was really strange. At a big party John would just stand there with one drink, shifting from one foot to another while Liz danced and had fun. At a small dinner party, he would try to dominate, telling those awful, coarse jokes and name-dropping, name-dropping all the time. So-and-so had said his design of something was the best he'd ever seen. That sort of thing,' another recalls.

But social clumsiness had never been a bar to promotion at General Motors. Far from it. Detroit's upper management was a reflection of the American tastes of the upper middle class. Pete Estes complained that his elevation to the managership of Pontiac forced him to travel overseas. He hated the unfamiliar food, the uncomfortable strangeness of foreign language barriers and chilly hotel rooms. A thick charcoaled steak at the Kingsway and a few bourbons at the country club – with the obligatory turn around the dance floor to keep the wife happy – that was how these men relaxed on Saturday night. Real fun was a round of golf on Saturday afternoons (after a morning in the office) and a few beers in the locker room. John DeLorean took up golf, too.

On July 1, 1965, it all paid off. Knudsen had been elevated to head of GM's North American car and truck vice presidency. Estes was named General Manager of the all-important Chevrolet division. And John Zachary DeLorean was named General Manager for the Pontiac motor division.

One long-time journalist who had covered Detroit for more than 20 years recalls:

'I'll never forget John DeLorean's first press conference as General Manager of Pontiac. Most of us had only seen him once or twice as an engineer, so we really didn't know what to expect. So here is the automobile industry press corps all ready to meet this guy and he starts off the conference with a joke. I've never forgotten the joke, either.

'It seems there were two guys who were in a big city on some convention and they went to a whore house. And one of the conventioneers says to the madam, "Look, lady. We've been here three days already so we're a little jaded. Can you fix me up with something special?" "Sure," says the madam, "I have a girl you'll like. She's half-French, half-Chinese." So the guy goes upstairs and comes down a little bit later. His friend asks him, "What was it like?" And the conventioneer says, "Really strange. She ate my laundry."

'None of us knew what to do, we were so embarrassed for him. It was such a dumb, juvenile joke and it was also clear that he thought it was enormously funny. Some gave him a break and wrote it off to being nervous and young, and nobody wrote about it. But I've always remembered it.'

DeLorean's announcement noted that 'at 40, he is the youngest man to ever become general manager of one of General Motors' ten main divisions.'

The press releases for both Knudsen and Estes had said the same of them.

The promotion took DeLorean away from hands-on engineering, which he liked, and involved him more in the tedious but nonetheless crucial tasks of management and planning. There were committee meetings to attend if you wanted something. DeLorean had learned to his vexation that you did not just ask for something and get it; you had to campaign and convince and even fight for a larger share of corporate resources if your division was to prosper within the GM family.

'John didn't like to politic for things. And he began to get frustrated with the way things are done at GM much too early in the game,' Knudsen later would recall.

There were other distractions, too, now. The marriage with Liz was becoming increasingly troubled. She was an office secretary for a small Detroit firm when she met John. They were unable to have children and that always distressed her. So she devoted herself to the life of a Bloomfield Hills housewife.

Like other bored wives, she concentrated on decorating their home and on planning what their life would be as John worked his way further up the GM ladder and eventually into retirement, either in Palm Beach, Florida, or Palm Springs, California, or some other fashionable haven for the burned-out executives of America.

But John had other ideas. Turning 40 reminded him forcefully that he had a great deal of distance to travel before he could fulfill his still vague ambitions. One good thing about being Pontiac General Manager was that it got him away from Detroit. John revelled in his newly won celebrity and the power that came with it.

From Knudsen and Estes he had learned the importance of the division's network of car dealers and how critical it was to pay attention to the advertising campaign that supported the cars he was trying to sell. Both tasks required getting on the road for extended periods of time. Liz never enjoyed the noisy dealer conventions and was a comparatively drab companion when her husband made his initial forays to California's glitter and glamour world. In time, he began to resent her demands on his time at home. Who wanted Bloomfield Hills after seeing Beverly Hills for the first time?

It was not an uncommon problem among Detroit management families. The generally prescribed remedy of the sympathetic wives of Bloomfield Hills was patience. Wait until he's had his fling and then he'll come home. Sometimes it worked, sometimes it didn't.

4

November 1967 was the turning point in Bunkie Knudsen's GM career. Detroit had been in turmoil for much of the two previous years as changing public tastes led to growing public and government criticism of the safety of some of the hot-off-the-drawingboard designs.

It was also a period of changing management styles. Conglomerates were the buzz-word of the day and the intuitive Wall Street gunfighter was the glamour figure.

The middle-1960s saw even staid corporations become unsettled by the advent of 'the professional manager', the man who was equally at home running a conglomerate or any one of its diverse constituent parts. The art of management, with its supposedly arcane superiority in accounting and controls, was deemed more important than knowledge of production techniques or abilities on the factory floor. The engineer-executive might deride these newcomers as 'bean counters', but he made way for them nevertheless.

James Roche was a 'bean counter'. But he was a superb 'bean counter'. In 1965, the 14th floor was shocked to find him becoming President of GM and also taking over the roles of Chief Operating Officer and Head of the GM administration committee. But that was also the year of the Corvair controversy, and the publication of Ralph Nader's *Unsafe at Any Speed*, an attack on the design dangers of a number of major automobile brands put out by Detroit. The industry was also just struggling back onto its feet from a disastrous strike in which Roche had played an active role as negotiator.

The situation at GM did not improve at all during 1966. First-half sales were bumped down by nearly 7 percent to 2.1 million units. The Nader controversy spread like a brushfire as the book became a bestseller – the Bible of the newly formed American consumer movement.

In March 1966, Nader charged before a Senate hearing in Washington that he was the target of a concentrated campaign to intimidate him. Private detectives hired by GM were harassing him and his friends and a smear campaign could be traced back to the 14th floor. It was Roche who went to Washington to apologize.

Aside from the blow to GM's public image, the Nader affair had a serious impact on sales. Worse, the scandal and sales slump produced chaos within 14th floor management circles and the other executives waited with increasing impatience for Roche to take a hand and turn things round. What alarmed the executives most of all was growing conviction that quality control was poor throughout the company – that Nader had been right.

Then GM internal estimates projected that the 1966 profits slump would sag even further in 1967. Roche had to go. GM's experiment with a 'bean counter' had been judged a failure.

So it had to be a 'production man' who would succeed Roche. But who? Bunkie Knudsen would be taking a chance if he tried to step over the two or three men ahead of him in seniority. The man just ahead of him in line, Edward N. Cole, was perhaps a more adroit politician than Knudsen. Cole was also the father of the Corvair, the rear engine compact, which hit the market to applause in 1960. He had used the success to lever himself onto GM's board and in 1965 into the executive vice presidency in charge of research, engineering, manufacturing and marketing plus public relations. And when the Corvairs of 1961 and 1963 developed appalling suspension problems, Cole was far away from the chain of responsibility.

More to the point, in that spring of 1967, Cole campaigned hard for the presidency. He had a platform: GM management must be centralized. Cole's philosophy was an important break with Detroit's longstanding tradition of separate product lines and management teams which made independent decisions. At its best, the old way had allowed men fully to explore technological frontiers and to come up with innovative designs. It was a system that put maximum responsibility on individuals.

But now it was obvious that the damage that could be caused by the failure of one man or a small design team could have dangerous impact on the whole corporation. Look at the uproar caused by the Corvair. There were too many men out there who were off on their own schemes and dreams. Bunkie Knudsen's attitude was to let them continue, as long as they made their numbers. Ed Cole argued more persuasively that the senior management should have more control. Projects should be conceived for the entire company, not one division competing against another.

With good reason John DeLorean could consider Ed Cole's campaign a direct attack at his own personal management style; not a few of his worries came from his close identification as a Knudsen protégé.

In November, 1967, by a tiny margin, Ed Cole made it into the president's chair and Roche was kicked upstairs to the chairmanship.

On January 31, 1968, Bunkie Knudsen resigned his $182,000-a-year job. Less than a week later, Knudsen was president of Ford, just 45 years after his father had quit Ford to go to GM.

Henry Ford II had paid Knudsen stock bonuses valued at $750,000 and guaranteed him a base annual salary of $200,000 for five years. Knudsen stayed with the mercurial Ford until he, in turn, was replaced by another ambitious hard charger named Lee Iacocca. During the late 1970s, Knudsen added to his reputation by taking control of and rescuing the faltering White Motor Corporation, which specializes in tractors and heavy equipment. On his retirement from corporate life, he had built a personal fortune of more than $30 million.

But even in those hectic mid-1960s, Bunkie Knudsen had not lost track of John DeLorean.

'I had made a point, and so had Pete Estes, of getting John out on the road to the dealers' meetings. You have to listen to them because they are our front line troops. They hear what the buyer says, and they are quick to pick up on why a buyer buys one kind of car in preference to another. By the time John became manager at Pontiac, though, I was well away from that division so I have no idea how he arranged his management of the division, except that he appeared to travel a lot, which I thought was a good thing at the time,' Knudsen explains.

'The trouble with being a manager of a major automobile division is the sudden celebrity that goes with the job. I remember that, when I took over Chevrolet, I got a call my first day on the job from Dinah Shore and she wanted me to come out to Hollywood that weekend for a party that she was going to give for me. Gregory Peck and a lot of other stars were going to be there.

'Now you have to remember that the Dinah Shore Show was the biggest show on television in those days. Campbell and Ewald, our advertising agency for Chevrolet had a $100 million budget that was one of the biggest in advertising; so the general manager of Chevrolet was very much a show business celebrity whether he wanted to be or not. That *See the U.S.A. in your Chevrolet* song she sang was important. But I had very strong feelings about that sort of thing and I said, "Miss Shore, I enjoy your program very much, and I thank you for your kindness. But it might be in the best interest of Chevrolet for me to fire you some day, and I wouldn't want our social friendship to get in the way of such a decision. So I'll do my job, and you keep doing yours."'

But John DeLorean did not see it that way.

'No, John was on the first plane to Hollywood he could get,' Knudsen recalls. 'He got in with that crowd and went through all sorts of changes.'

If the rest of General Motors was in turmoil just after John DeLorean's appointment as General Manager at Pontiac, his division at least continued to build sales, not only on the firm popularity of the GTO, but with the other spin-off lines – the Bonneville, Firebird and Catalina.

DeLorean continued to press his design team for new stylings and features. Vertically stacked headlights, split grilles and passenger compartments that resembled airplane cockpits were all part of the DeLorean search for the next generation of popularity.

But success with new designs that would fuel Pontiac's popularity was slowed by DeLorean's increasingly chaotic administrative practices and his penchant for centralizing the responsibility for all key decisions within a tight circle of trusted aides – without regard to whether or not they had been assigned to those tasks by General Motors senior management.

'He was probably one of the worst administrators that ever lived. Not because he didn't have the skills, but because he had such contempt for the administrative arts. He believed that was all bullshit and that you handled the staff work by bypassing the people officially in charge and finding some bright young guy who would be knocked out by your charisma. Then he would go straight to that guy and get answers from him, leaving the superior off in limbo, wondering what had happened to them,' recalls David E. Davis.

'He was a curiously complex guy. He was extraordinarily talented, a really good engineer. There was absolutely no question in the mind of anybody who worked closely with him that he was a good engineer. But his organization was just nightmarish because John would take a dislike to a guy and cut him out of the decision-making process whether he really knew anything or not.

'In fact, that's how I got to work with John later on. I joined Campbell & Ewald, Chevrolet's advertising agency, because he announced that everyone there was an old fart and he would only talk to me. He had known me when I worked on the magazine back when he was doing research at Pontiac.

'So there was John, the head of Pontiac, building his little coterie, freaking out the people he didn't like. There is really nothing so very wrong about that except that the people who surrounded John tended to echo his own tastes. And that was where John started to leave the rails. When Knudsen and Estes and Wangers – all real racing enthusiasts – were there, Pontiac was well in tune with the market that was developing.'

Davis says, 'By the mid-term of his period at Pontiac, John had bought the entire California package of the youth culture – being intuitive, letting your feelings hang out, that sort of thing.

'So, in 1968, he directed a promotional film that is still

famous in the advertising group, and it was what everyone was supposed to look at to learn "where John is coming from" so it would guide us in dealing with him. It was a nicely photographed job showing beautiful cars smoking down the road with gorgeous young people at the wheel. The background music was the theme, or something like it, from the French film, *A Man and A Woman*. Everything was soft and oh, so California. John had seen *A Man and A Woman* and went nuts over the picture.

'So there was a constant fight at Pontiac about any effort to put content into advertising. It embarrassed John to think that an institution like Pontiac had to reach out and really provide potential customers with hard information about how to go and buy the car, or to convince them that they should want to buy it. And remember, in the late sixties, coming out of that sales jolt GM had just had, people needed to be convinced about the product all over again.

'Instead, John said the best you could hope to do is leave a nice impression. You did that with nice music, beautiful pictures of the most beautiful young people with a nice warm feeling, and they would go for it. But don't try to tell them how big it is or what it weighs or about gas mileage. "Who cares about that?" he would ask. "Nobody wants to know that bullshit," he said, "That's Detroit talking."

'John was wrong about the advertising. Certainly, the traditional Detroit advertising of the day wasn't very good; but John wanted to eliminate any useful information from the traditional message so that it became, if anything, worse. Somebody once described John's vision as being like peeing in your pants – all you get is a nice warm feeling.'

In California, DeLorean was meeting a new kind of businessman. What an enormous contrast it must have been to match up the blue-suited, plain spoken, pens-in-shirt-pockets engineers of Detroit against the laid-back, California wheeler-dealers who did their business by poolside or in a restaurant and not on the top floor of some box-like office complex.

The man who caught John's imagination was James T. Aubrey, the whiz-kid of broadcasting and movie production of the late 1960s and early 70s. Seven years older than DeLorean,

Aubrey was already a mega-celebrity. He was called 'The Silver Fox' for his ruthless management techniques.

Aubrey was the man who had the instinct for 'instant pop', that indefinable quality about a performer or programme that would catch the public's fancy in a big way. At ABC, he had churned out such hits as *The Real McCoys, Maverick, The Donna Reed Show, 77 Sunset Strip* and *The Rifleman*.

After boosting ABC into contention as the third network, Aubrey joined the Columbia Broadcasting System as vice president for creative services and put his 'instant pop' vision to work with a mixture of low comedy and adventure sit-coms including *Mr. Ed, Gomer Pyle, Route 66,* and *The Munsters*.

But in 1965, the year John DeLorean took over at Pontiac, Jim Aubrey's luck appeared to have run out. Several of his production efforts bombed. Viewer ratings fell and advertising revenues fell with them. In his heyday, Aubrey's imperious manner, his image as the original swinging jet setter and his casual sense of business ethics had been overlooked. But after the failures began to build, Aubrey's enemies came out of the woodwork. Finally, without specifying why, CBS President Frank Stanton sacked Aubrey.

Down but not out, Aubrey walked away from the sacking with millions of dollars worth of CBS stock options which he exercised. He plunged immediately into the red-hot Los Angeles real estate market and into the equally hot Wall Street stock market. He set up an import-export firm that specialized in pearls and, with his production company, sold series ideas to Screen Gems, which in turn had contracts with half the studios in Hollywood.

Tall and lean, a health and exercise fanatic, Aubrey continued his high profile, jet-set escapades; always impeccably dressed in the informal but studied fashions of the West Coast, always putting in heroic working hours, always sniffing ahead to the trends and shifts in taste that would lift his career back on track.

John DeLorean was fascinated. And Aubrey enjoyed the unabashed admiration of his protégé. He helped introduce the new Pontiac boss around to other media chiefs, to advertising 'creative' specialists, to wealthy men whose money came from deliberately vague sources.

'Aubrey was probably the closest thing to a friend John had out in California. Neither of them drank much, and Aubrey nagged John into losing weight and shaping up his clothes,' a former Pontiac official who had been based in Los Angeles at the time would recall later.

By 1969 Aubrey was riding high again. He was back on top of the heap at MGM. Jacqueline Susann modelled her sex-obsessed anti-hero in *The Love Machine* after Aubrey and some of his apocryphal sexual adventures.

And he took John DeLorean along for the ride, introducing him to still more important people. DeLorean met Herb Siegel who later became the chairman of Chris-Craft. Dave Mahoney, the chairman of Avis, became a friend, as did a host of show business stars including Sammy Davis, Jr., Englebert Humperdink and Johnny Carson, who was in the process of moving his popular late-night talk show from New York City to Hollywood.

And there were the girls. Aubrey collected willing females without effort, and there were more than enough to go round for a friend.

Although DeLorean's marriage to Liz was over, for a time, at least, he was simply too busy to get a divorce. Too busy grappling with control over Pontiac, too busy exploring a new life style, a new business style in California.

Everybody in California loved John DeLorean's classy cars. 'They ought to have loved that car. He gave away enough of them,' an ex-Pontiac executive asserts. 'After John shifted over to Chevrolet, there were dozens, and I mean dozens of cars in the California inventory that nobody could find. John had just given them away to various girlfriends, golf pros and business buddies out there.'

Why wasn't there an investigation? A recently retired GM corporate counsel, who refused to be identified, explains. 'From the time John DeLorean took over at Pontiac until the time he left, we had to deal with a whole string of shabby business practices that he got involved in. I never trusted him from the beginning; and the more I saw of him, well, nothing I saw ever changed my mind.'

But why didn't GM management come down on DeLorean at that early date? Or, if early warnings failed, why wasn't he fired? 'Remember the time. We'd had all the scandals we needed in those days. Pontiac was doing well enough, and the rest of the company had plenty of problems. Also, DeLorean was getting tremendous publicity and quite a few people in top management in those days saw John as a comer – a bit rough around the edges, but too valuable a property to lose just over a few cars he had given away.'

The retired corporation counsel also notes, 'Make sure you understand that no one ever accused John of stealing those cars. It was never brought to us on that basis. It was never brought to us formally at all. In any event, we had other things that John was doing that worried me more.'

Indeed, General Motors executives had plenty to worry about. The consumer movement sparked by Ralph Nader showed no signs of going away, the company's union problems were worsening and the profitability of several key product lines was slipping alarmingly.

But Cole's victory strengthened the prestige of the engineers over the 'bean counters' and Pontiac had its best year in 1968. The Division sold 877,000 cars, almost 200,000 cars more than in 1964.

Cole, too, was something of a swinger. On taking over Chevrolet in 1952, he had, as Knudsen described it, 'gone Hollywood'. An active, hearty sort, he became entangled with Hollywood movie starlet Monique Van Vooren in the early 1960s. There was a minor scandal when, just after the Detroit Business District Association voted him 'Father of the Year' in early 1963, he divorced his wife of 30 years.

Cole had sense enough to scramble back across the undrawn line between propriety and excess. In 1964, he married the vivacious Dollie McVey, a divorcee who owned and operated her own line of women's designer clothes. Dollie Cole quickly installed herself as a major figure among the Bloomfield Hills wives and helped push her husband's career forward again.

Cole had reason to look at John DeLorean as a promising young executive well worth cultivating. Both were engineers; both shared in that secret fraternity of disdain for hypocritical moral standards. The two also shared two other affinities – a fascination with rear-mounted engines and an instinct for consolidation of power.

DeLorean and Liz agreed to divorce in January 1969. There was someone else – Kelly Harmon, a 20-year-old, honey-blonde, blue-eyed beauty who was a prototype of the California look that Bo Derek made world-famous a decade later. The marriage of Kelly and John DeLorean was later portrayed as having rocked Detroit's staid society to the core. It was considerably less an event than that.

At first, the executives and their wives had watched with amusement as DeLorean embarked on a crash programme of weight loss late in 1967. John had gone 'Grecian' – that is, he had begun touching up the greying sideburns of his black hair with a well-known preparation, Grecian Formula 16.

Then there was the 'minor car accident' in California early in 1968 that kept DeLorean out of the Detroit offices for several weeks. When he returned, Bunkie Knudsen bluntly asked DeLorean what was wrong with his face.

'John mumbled something about getting some cuts in the accident; but it was a face lift, all right,' Knudsen recalls.

Shortly afterward, DeLorean was playing golf at the posh Bel Air Country Club in California in a foursome with Tom Harmon, the CBS sports broadcaster and former University of Michigan all-American halfback of the 1930s. Harmon invited DeLorean home for dinner.

It was love at first sight for John and Kelly Harmon. Kelly was immediately attracted to the six-foot-four DeLorean's carefully maintained good looks; but she was even more impressed by the fact that DeLorean took her seriously, listened to her opinions and treated her as an adult. 'It was his sincerity. I could recognize it right away. John's a very deep thinking man. He's real. And a very strong man,' she told the *Detroit Free Press* shortly after their wedding.

What Kelly offered DeLorean was the youth, beauty and the fashionability – indeed, the respectability – he felt was lacking from his own life. The Harmons, after all, were more than national celebrities. Tom Harmon's exploits on the gridiron with the 1939 and 1940 University of Michigan football teams made him a permanent idol for any teenage boy growing up in Detroit. He went on to fashion a life that dreams are made of. When World War II broke out, Harmon became an Army Air Corps pilot and was shot down over China. He returned safely to the United States and married movie star Elyse Knox in a ceremony at the University of Michigan chapel that made the front pages of every newspaper in the country. The bride's dress was given special attention – it was made from the silk parachute Harmon had used to escape from his damaged plane.

So the Harmons were a much-loved family in Detroit; the prospect of the 44-year-old DeLorean being married to a daughter of Tommy Harmon was accorded curiosity and a little snickering, but hardly stony-faced shock. DeLorean came in for good-natured ribbing, such as this 'blind-item' comment from a *Detroit Free Press* gossip column in May 1970:

> Model D: It's not easy to be 45 and look like the Pepsi Generation. Even a radiant new young wife, imported from Hollywood, can't have that kind of influence on a man. The real youth miracle can only be obtained medically. Word has it that John Z. DeLorean, Chevrolet division Vice President and General Manager, has done more than pushups to retain his young image. Bloomfield Hills neighbors say the sudden development of DeLorean's manly jawline in 1968 was due to cosmetic surgery – the insertion of a foamlike material – not to the medical reconstruction of a disintegrating infected jawbone. [John's explanation at the time.]
>
> Toward the end of the recovery from a serious automobile accident, but preceding DeLorean's divorce from his first wife, certain members of the automobile elite wondered about some newly accrued scars.
>
> This particular location of the scars around the ear and hairline, which John tells everyone in sight he suffered from going through the windshield in the car crack-up, reminds one strangely of a certain Swiss surgeon's style of facelifting.

Detroit had also devoured the press reports from Los Angeles as DeLorean was first divorced from Liz in January, then ordered to pay her $370,000 in alimony over 15 years. Then there was the news that John had bought Kelly a six-carat diamond ring for her visit to Detroit on a modelling job.

On February 4, Ed Cole reshuffled his second layer of management and moved Pete Estes to Car and Truck and DeLorean to

Chevrolet as general manager. DeLorean's orders were specific. He was to oversee the launching of the new Chevy Vega which would be the division's entry into the compact car sweepstakes. And he was also to supervise the remodelling of the Camaro and Corvette for the 1970 model year.

Cole also exacted a promise from DeLorean as a condition of the move. It was a simple enough request. DeLorean had been spending an increasing amount of his time overseeing his private investments – large minority stakes in the San Diego Chargers football team and the New York Yankees baseball club – while on Pontiac trips. Doing private business on company time had to stop, Cole said.

'Ed was no saint. He told John he didn't care where he was playing around or who he was screwing. But Chevy was having troubles, and he wanted those new lines turned out fast. John promised he would buckle down, and he had lots of quick ideas about doing this and that. He agreed to the condition,' a GM official recalls.

On May 31, DeLorean and Kelly were married in a civil ceremony at the Bel Air Country Club in Brentwood Hills overlooking Los Angeles. The Mitchell Boys Choir, dressed in white robes, provided the music, and Kelly was described in rapturous terms by the newspaper reporters. Her matron of honour was her sister Kris, who was married to rock star Ricky Nelson. The guests were an uneasy mixture of Harmon's broadcasting industry friends, some General Motors officials and John's new California friends. Bunkie Knudsen flew in to be best man.

But even as the champagne flowed and the flash bulbs popped, the festivities were chilled. A long-time DeLorean aide remembers: 'Tom Harmon put the stopper in it. John was standing there talking to Bunkie Knudsen and Tom Adams, the head of the Campbell Ewald Agency, when Tom walked up to him in the middle of the celebration and said, "If you ever hurt her, you'll have to answer to me." No quiet chat in the library – just the open threat. John didn't know what to do, so he just smiled.'

DeLorean had little to smile about when he returned to Detroit with Kelly. By early summer it was clear that a number of design changes DeLorean had ordered could not be accomplished in time for the traditional September introduction date for the 1970 model year. This put DeLorean in the embarrassing position of having publicly to cancel the 1970 models and announce that his division 'would continue to meet the backlog of demand for the 1969 cars until we can push ahead into production of all new designs for both which we had planned for 1971'.

The trouble was that there were no such new designs on the drafting tables, and the motor industry press knew it. DeLorean's credibility – and that of GM's – took a whacking. Unabashed, he pushed ahead that summer, trying to make a name for himself as the iconoclastic superexecutive. If he couldn't talk GM management into a scheme, he went public with it to the Detroit press corps, which was always eager for stories to feed out onto the national news wires.

'You had to wonder whether John didn't have a suicide wish or something. He went so far out of his way to insult people who didn't fawn over him or approve of everything he did,' the long-time aide says.

There was, for example, DeLorean's legendary falling-out with Dollie Cole, the wife of the man who had elevated him. At a number of private dinner parties and club dances, DeLorean repeatedly teased Dollie about having married her husband on the rebound from his Hollywood fling.

'Maybe it was John's way of saying that they weren't any better than he was, having married Kelly. Anyway, Dollie didn't like it and finally told him never to mention Monique Van Vooren again. Well, Dollie loved to give costume parties for Ed's birthday, and it was his 60th birthday or some special occasion and everybody was to dress up in costume for a real bash,' the ex-aide recalls.

'John and Kelly arrived late, and John had a huge wrapped-up present for Ed. He said in a loud voice that Ed should open the present later and not do it in front of everyone; so needless to say, Dollie got all curious and made Ed open the present. It was a painting of Monique Von Vooren in the nude. John stood there laughing and laughing and laughing. And that was it! Dollie never forgave him, and it just confirmed in Ed Cole's mind that he had made a mistake in pulling John up the ladder.'

Early in 1970 DeLorean resumed his forays out to California again, frequently leaving Kelly to visit her family in Bel Air or back in Detroit. Later in the year, they bought the Pine Creek ranch near the Snake River in Idaho, as his response to her increasing involvement with disadvantaged youth groups. The ranch was to be a summer holiday camp for inner city kids, and for a while John was very taken with the notion of being the father figure, providing holidays for the new generation of ghetto children with whom he identified. DeLorean also had his own ranch and groves in Pauma Valley near San Diego which he had bought at the same time he was investing in the football team. Here he would take frequent refuge from the turmoil at Chevrolet and the troubling realization that he had made a mistake marrying someone as young as Kelly. He began to increase his weekend visits to the ranch of a neighbour, Fletcher Jones, the millionaire founder of Computer Science Corporation. Jones had gone into forced retirement from CSC for tax reasons, but he was still an active dabbler in real estate, car dealerships and various investment schemes that interested DeLorean as well. By this time, his $200,000 salary plus $400,000 or so in annual bonuses were causing DeLorean to seek out increasingly venturesome tax shelters. Besides, Jones shared DeLorean's taste for young beautiful girls, especially Hollywood starlets.

Jones would hire pilot William Morgan Hetrick to fly a planeload of girls and other friends to San Diego for the weekend. A regular visitor was Jones' special girlfriend, a starlet named Cristina Ferrare, whose distinction among the other girls was that she had actually starred in a movie, *The Impossible Years*, with David Niven. There were rumours that Cristina would marry Jones. Also present at the parties was another neighbour, John Timothy Hoffman. Hoffman's name will surface again in the course of DeLorean's story.

Drugs of all varieties were plentiful, although there is no evidence that either Jones or DeLorean were more than casual users. They had more important things to do with their time – talk business, chat up the girls and, for John, relax from a Detroit world that was becoming increasingly hostile.

It became obvious to DeLorean that he had to build up his independence so that, if the worst should happen at General

Motors, he could still walk away with financial security for the rest of his life. An easy way to do that was to use his position as the head of one of the largest corporations in the world – for Chevrolet by itself certainly was – to do business with men who could be of help to him later on.

'The schemes that he came up with were a constant bother to us. The one that caused us the most trouble was his proposal that Chevrolet franchise service centers to various gas stations with a separate franchise organization that he would head. The dealers went stark, raving mad when they heard about that. Here they had gone to the expense of setting up shops to make our cars ready for delivery and we were going to give the repair business to any gas station owner who could put up the money to John,' the GM lawyer remembers.

'That caused a lot of damage within the company. His other stunts were just as off the wall. He decided that Chevy salesmen were too ignorant to give the complicated sales pitch about the variety of models the division was selling, so he forced through a plan for dealers to buy these little theaters and prospective buyers would first be shown a movie about the new line of cars with all the advertising promo built in. Of course, he owned a piece of that action, but he got that one by us,' he adds. 'The obvious thing to do was to go to video-tape; but John came out of left field with an incredibly stupid super-eight-millimeter projector arrangement that was at the very end of the line of super-eight technology. But John rammed his plan through. Only later did we find out that a Hollywood television producer friend of his owned the company.'

Also involved in the mini-theatre company was a new friend of DeLorean's – California car dealer Roy W. Nesseth. In a state where car dealers are the acknowledged zero-sum standard of dishonesty, Nesseth was something of a rarity even in that profession. He had been convicted in the early 1950s on fraud charges involving forged car sale documents.

When DeLorean met him, Nesseth was the manager of the largest Chevrolet dealership in California (in Norwalk); and the GM executive was attracted by the older man's hard attitude and tough business talk.

Through 1970 and 1971 DeLorean used Chevrolet's promotion budget as his own privy purse. To save money for more grandiose projects, DeLorean cancelled Chevrolet's historic commitment of funds to the National Soapbox Derby in Akron, Ohio. This national televized event brought boys and girls from all over North America to compete in a series of downhill races in their home-made, unpowered car models.

But DeLorean needed the money for other things: for lavish television productions from Las Vegas, shows sold to Chevrolet and Campbell and Ewald by Aubrey and other producers. The trouble was that the shows never achieved the kind of audience that made the expense appear worthwhile. Rumours began to circulate that John was demanding kickbacks from advertisers.

GM officials began to worry about leaving DeLorean in charge of their single most important division. His erratic behaviour worsened. Executives who prized DeLorean's undeniable engineering skills conflicted with those who worried about the increasingly public controversy he was stirring up.

The Vega had finally shaped up and boosted Chevrolet sales. 1971 was the first year that a General Motors division ever achieved sales of 3 million cars and trucks. Furthermore, DeLorean was successful in slashing scores of production duplications from within the division's lines. In one instance, he cut the possible dashboard option combinations in the Camaro line from 2,700 to 96. Within a year of his taking over, Chevrolet was running just 200,000 cars behind Ford's total U.S. output.

But for every success, there was more than one failure. DeLorean campaigned hard to build a compact version of each of the Chevy division's mid-range lines: the Nova, Camaro and Ventura. He also enraged union officials by demanding that styling and tooling changes be done at night or on weekends in order to cut lost production time. Both efforts were countermanded by senior management.

His attempts to use GM for his own personal gain enraged others among the management group. And his attempts to make internal company matters public, through Detroit's always credulous press corps, also helped turn the tide against him.

From 1972 a number of highly secret internal discussions had been finding their way into print in the Detroit newspapers and automotive industry periodicals. The information being leaked to the press was too detailed not to be coming from someone privy to the innermost workings of GM management.

DeLorean was moved up to the 14th floor and became vice president car and truck production. It was a promotion. But it was also a test.

DeLorean's marriage to Kelly was widely rumoured to be on the rocks, despite their decision to adopt a baby son named Zachary. The kick upstairs was his last chance to survive at GM, provided that he buckle down and stay out of trouble for a while.

But DeLorean stepped up his public criticism of the company. By now, his public image was complete. He was six-foot-four John Z. DeLorean – the hip, socially-conscious, business wizard. He was a fashion plate with a heart. He was at home with Hollywood swingers, ghetto kids and big businessmen. He was saving General Motors from itself. He was going to succeed Ed Cole as president.

Arvid Jouppi, Wall Street's leading auto industry analyst, remembers the time.

'John DeLorean was the most exciting thing going in Detroit. Folks thought he was the greatest thing since Billy Durant, and he was the new generation of engineer-executive the industry needed. After all, he was projecting this image of being pro-civil rights, pro-consumer, pro-safety and fuel efficiency; and yet, he was making his numbers. The stuff with the clothes and sideburns and the dyed hair didn't count against him with those people. If you want to know how John got away with it, ask the people at GM who knew better but kept promoting him.'

DeLorean by now had an international press following for his public speeches and writings on various social issues. Late in 1969, he met William F. Haddad, a former John F. Kennedy speech writer and liberal activist journalist. Haddad was compiling a book on the economic struggle of the blacks in the United States, featuring chapters written by major business executives. DeLorean had an introductory chapter whipped up for the book by GM's publicity shop, in which he urged the white business establishment to make a greater commitment to the promotion of black business enterprise in the United States.

Much of what he had to say needed saying, yet those closest to him felt his beliefs were as carefully tailored as the new European fashions he wore.

Much, much later, a disillusioned Haddad (who served as the public relations director for the ill-fated DeLorean Motor Car effort in Northern Ireland) would discover, 'John was a racist. He really was afraid of black people; and the sad irony was that he positively hated the Irish, the very people he was supposed to be trying to save.'

Another crisis came in September 1972. The three year marriage to Kelly came to an end. Kelly left and filed for legal separation in Los Angeles. She moved in with her parents, taking the adopted son Zachary.

'We're trying to do it like a lady and a gentleman, the best we can. I'm trying to keep Zachary with me, but I guess it's up to the adoption agency and the court,' Kelly told a *Detroit Free Press* reporter at the time.

But she had not reckoned on DeLorean's capacity for anger at what he felt was a desire to embarrass him in public. Through his attorney, John Noonan, DeLorean mounted a campaign in the courts to take Zachary away from Kelly. Private detectives were called in to investigate Kelly's life before and during the marriage. It threatened to be a long, public and bloody affair.

Finally, Tom Harmon and his attorneys stepped in and negotiated an out-of-court settlement and kept it out of the newspapers. For a $500,000 settlement spread over 15 years, Kelly Harmon gave back Zachary and disappeared from DeLorean's life. She did not know it, but she was one of the lucky ones.

The divorce proceedings were still in the wrangling stage when DeLorean began appearing around Detroit in early 1973 with a new date: Fletcher Jones's girlfriend Christina Ferrare. Jones had been killed late in 1972 in a plane crash on his own property.

DeLorean was being carefully discreet about the affair since he was intent on not losing the war with Kelly's lawyers by default. By that time Cristina was a fast-rising fashion model.

Her trips to Detroit were covered by stories about a forthcoming General Motors advertising campaign.

David Davis was frequently used as a stooge for the happy couple.

'I remember one time, the idea was we were supposed to be discussing a film that we were going to do for Chevrolet. That way, John could be seen publicly with Cristina. So my wife and I and all these people from California were dragged along while John sat with his nose stuck in her ear all night. My wife said right then that was the last time she would be a beard for John DeLorean.

'John was in his image hey-day at that time. His hair was jet black, and he wore smart, very dark blue suits. They were three-piece suits, but he always wore the vest unbuttoned, and he had those shirts with the long collar points – really good linen, really good neckties. But it was always this enforced casualness. "I'm wearing a $600 suit, but I can't be bothered to button the vest." That sort of thing. So he would swoop into a room. He was tall, and his clothes would swirl around him because of all the flapping; but after five minutes, you had to get him out of the meeting because he would initially impress people for about that long and then he would begin to turn them off.

'Because enough was never enough for John. If we were successfully pushing a product line or cooling down the dealers, John would turn everyone off again by bringing up something else, by bragging about something, by name-dropping. He never really bothered to learn how to deal with people,' Davis says.

By now, it was probably past the time when John DeLorean could have talked his way out of his internal problems at GM. The leaks of corporate secrets to the press were increasing. It was March 1973.

Every three years, the top levels of General Motors management journeyed to the Greenbriar Hotel in White Sulphur Springs, West Virginia. There, over a long weekend, top executives played golf, drank whiskey and relaxed. More importantly, they plotted long-term strategy for the mammoth corporation. The meeting was held in the strictest secrecy, and no minutes of the morning and afternoon discussion sessions were kept.

Many American corporations have similar rituals. At the root of the struggle to climb the corporate ladder in the United States is the universally-held belief that the ladder is worth climbing, not just in terms of personal gain, but because the company is worth fighting for, that its products are useful and beneficial. These secret conferences – where board chairmen play golf with division managers, where young analysts speak freely to senior vice-presidents – are part of the bonding process that gives American management its sense of continuity and purpose.

The Greenbriar meetings had been held without interruption since the 1930s. The 1973 meeting was especially important because Ed Cole was convinced that GM had to make some fundamental changes in its production and marketing strategies if it was to prosper in the 1970s.

John DeLorean was asked to submit a future planning paper. The topic was product quality and a critique on whether American car buyers were getting what they wanted. Cole told DeLorean to make the criticism as forceful as possible in order to spark the maximum discussion at the conference. It would be one of the key presentations at the meeting. It might even be the first step on the long road back to rehabilitation for DeLorean, who had been effectively isolated from any real work on the 14th floor for nearly a year now.

On Thursday March 17, the day before the executives were scheduled to embark on their weekend at the resort, Robert W. Irvin, the leading automobile writer for *Automotive News*, the authoritative trade daily, carried a detailed advance story on DeLorean's speech, including quotes of some of the more controversial attacks – ranging from the assertion that Detroit was deliberately selling substandard transportation designs to the consumer to charges that General Motors' design capability was mediocre. What intrigued the GM management was that the script Irvin had obtained was clearly a copy of an earlier draft that DeLorean had circulated among the most senior management for comment prior to the conference.

Cole ordered that a private investigator be hired to check the leak since he could not even trust the company's own in-house security personnel to do the job. Within a month, the report from the private detective was delivered. The trail led to one person in particular, much to the investigators' surprise: DeLorean himself. Moreover, the detective reported evidence of irregularities in DeLorean's personal life, which could only be overlooked at GM's peril. Specific allegations about his more outré sexual preferences were pinpointed to gossip stemming from Dollie Cole and Liz DeLorean.

Cole ordered the report suppressed and destroyed.

In early April, DeLorean was sent for and told he would have to resign. At first he resisted, threatening to release still more damaging documents on GM product safety standards, on its poor minority hiring record and other scandals. A deal was finally struck.

He would be given a Cadillac dealer franchise in Florida that was worth at least $1 million. Better still, Gerstenberg, who was that year's chairman of the National Alliance of Businessmen, would see to it that DeLorean was named president to head an effort to find employment for disadvantaged young people. And DeLorean's salary of $200,000 was to be continued that year.

On April 18, DeLorean flew to Gerstenberg's New York office and agreed to the final details in a meeting presided over by Cole. It was a low-key affair – no shouting or recriminations. Cole later recalled that DeLorean even appeared uninterested and somewhat distracted.

The resignation was announced to the press, to become effective May 31. 'I want to do things in the social area. I have to do them; and unfortunately, the nature of our business just didn't permit me to do as much as I wanted,' DeLorean told newsmen. A week later, his appointment to the business-jobs coalition was announced with a flattering comment from Gerstenberg.

Before his time was officially up at GM, DeLorean had two opportunities to make Detroit sit up and notice him.

On May 8, 1973, he and Cristina were married in a civil ceremony in Detroit and then flew to Washington, D.C. for a reception.

A few weeks later General Motors top management and wives turned out in force for the retirement dinner that he had insisted be part of his separation package. Pete Estes had derided these affairs for the false sentimentality that pervaded. 'You work your life off for the company and all they give you is a dinner and some damned pickle plate or other gee-gaw,' he had quipped, and the name had stuck.

'You wouldn't have believed John's pickle plate dinner,' an eyewitness recalls. 'The place was packed because all the wives wanted a good look at Cristina – the men too for that matter. But we all knew that John had been pushed out so it was awkward at the beginning. But not for old John; he got up and gave us all hell for half an hour. He had been the one who warned us about this and that, he had tried to do this and that and the management wouldn't let him. He named names and raised specific complaints. We would all be sorry after he was gone. And what was amazing was that everyone sat there and took it. It was the damndest thing I've ever seen, before or since.'

So, no matter that he had been pushed, John DeLorean had made sure it was he who slammed the door as he left.

CHAPTER THREE

Dream Car

The October 1973 OPEC-led oil embargo did more than rattle the oil industry and unsettle Wall Street; it changed forever the assumptions under which millions of Americans had lived their lives. The all-day lines at the petrol pumps, the economic shock and inflation that followed are now memories. But the diminished hopes and limited realities that spread through the industrialized and developing nations of the world are the legacy of that autumn upheaval a decade ago.

The embargo provided John DeLorean with instant 'issue focus'. He became the ex-General Motors executive who had warned his employers to do something about fuel economy before it was too late. The hip and socially sympathetic big businessman took on a new aura. DeLorean was *right*. He was a prophet with honour.

Not that he had been languishing. As president of the National Alliance of Businessmen (an appointment for one year only), he had been visible and busy. Since the 1968 summer riots raged through frustrated black neighbourhoods, the NAB had waged a campaign to convince the public that American big business was sympathetic to the problems of the growing army of hard-to-train disadvantaged urban black and Hispanic youths. His job was to tour industrial cities that had high unemployment rates and express the desire of the big corporations to help. His speeches were DeLorean at his best, uplifting messages followed by entertainingly caustic press conferences where he needled Detroit for its shabby products and constipated management techniques.

The general newspapers and magazines around the United States took their cue about DeLorean from the automotive industry press corps. There was a tacit acknowledgment that perhaps DeLorean *had* been fired, but the consensus was that GM's management had been intolerant of his flashy clothes and jet-set lifestyle and not a little jealous of his engineering skills.

Automotive News set the tone, comparing DeLorean's ouster with the resignation of a talented Ford executive vice president named William Innes who had retired at the early age of 51 a few weeks previously. On April 23, 1973, *AN*'s editors wondered aloud whether or not a trend against innovative young executives was endemic in the car industry.

> The auto industry has thrived on the accomplishments of individuals. Men like Henry Ford, Walter Chrysler and the Fisher brothers are only a few whose style and manner set them apart from the crowd in terms of accomplishments and goals . . . . Today more than ever before, it is important for corporations to continue to nurture the climate for executives who do not always fit into the corporate mold. In a society that is fast becoming more and more impersonal, it seems so important that individuals be encouraged to speak up, even if their voices do not always echo the corporate line.
>
> John Z. DeLorean has quit General Motors. He left for a number of reasons, but one thing is sure: the industry will miss him. Now, more than ever before, the industry needs the color and style of a DeLorean. His most important attribute is, simply, credibility. People believe him – his co-workers, his dealers and his suppliers . . . perhaps even government and the consumer, too . . . . If his style set a pattern for the future, the auto business will be better off. If he is one of a kind, the auto industry has lost more than it realizes.

Moreover DeLorean was cleaning up his act, toning down the swinger-jet-set image, stressing the solid business executive image. His marriage to Cristina Ferrare was an instant success.

Even though she was 23, just a year older than Kelly Harmon, Cristina had a sharp-edged sense of reality. Born in Los Angeles, the daughter of a supermarket butcher, she had managed to survive the dead-end of the starlet scene and make the jump to high fashion modelling. She had started out as a child model and had endured the exploitation of the movie studio system of the 1960s, even to the point of turning her luxuriant black hair blonde. But now her modelling career was on an upswing and covers for *Harpers Bazaar*, *Vogue* and a host of women's magazines came thick and fast. Unlike Kelly, who lived in a protected dream world where she was the benevolent, laid-back helper of poor children, Cristina knew exactly who she was and what she was getting in the 48-year-old John DeLorean.

She assured her family that the much older, twice divorced DeLorean would make a good husband. Together they would get that life at the top that was their shared hunger.

At work, John DeLorean was invariably serious, concentrated, always pushing. The early years of his marriage to Cristina, by contrast, brought out a latent sense of fun which friends had never seen in either of his first two marriages. It was as if he had experienced a sudden release from the constraints of a first marriage, which had settled in the sort of dull routine norm that he hated, and, a second marriage which had led him into areas which he had explored and had eventually been equally bored by.

DeLorean's friends were delighted by Cristina; she was not only beautiful but warm and witty. She loved her home and, although it would be several years before she bore John DeLorean his daughter, she concentrated on providing not only DeLorean himself with the home-life he wanted, but young Zachary, too.

Like any good Italian mother, she loved cooking – and was unquestionably a good cook. Although her husband was a faddy eater, Cristina produced from the kitchen a plethora of dishes, mostly Italian – enormous salads, lasagna, spaghetti. 'She'd make a mess out of the kitchen and she didn't mind cleaning it up herself,' recalls a friend.

Through it all ran that bubbling sense of fun which infected the often over-serious John DeLorean. Detroit business promoter Sonny Van Arnem, who was a neighbour and social friend of DeLorean, remembers one incident from the early days of that marriage in an interview with the *Detroit Free Press* in October 1982:

> She would make great cakes – and sometimes they weren't so great. The last time we had a big dinner, John complained about this banana-fruit cake she made. It looked terrible. It

had fallen down in the oven and she stuck a little candle in it. John made fun of it, so she stuck it in his face. We had a cake fight. We were all dressed up and going out and it got real messy.

Van Arnhem says he had 'never seen people love each other the way they did.' They were he reckons 'the most fun people I've ever been with'.

Cristina joined in the more serious conversations, too. DeLorean could talk for hours into the evenings with friends about raising money for computer projects or for automotive projects, for revitalizing America's railroads, grandiose schemes for moving vast masses of people or food around the world. These conversations would take place at the DeLorean home, with friends coming in for one of Cristina's huge meals. The DeLoreans seldom wanted to go out, a feature of their marriage which never changed. Neither of them enjoyed the party set, certainly not in Detroit where DeLorean was contemptuous of the conversational level, but not much in California nor in New York later, either. His marriage to Cristina brought a permanent change to John DeLorean's way of life.

The changeover to the stay-at-home husband from the Hollywood swinger was not as difficult as it might have been. DeLorean had never been an enthusiastic party-goer, he had no taste for alcohol and was indifferent to gourmet cooking because of his fixation with diets and health.

While he had been publicly linked in the show business press with many of the most beautiful women in the film colony, many of the 'dates' were public relations affairs arranged by studios or industry friends to provide both the woman and DeLorean with sufficiently prominent companions for some public function or other. His fetish for health and weight control won the interest for a while of Candice Bergen, herself a food faddist. And he was also photographed with Nancy Sinatra and Ursula Andress. In most cases, there would be a date or two, a dinner party or a film premiere, but no real romance.

'The fact is, that John at a dinner party is pretty dull company. He has no small talk whatsoever. He picks at his food and he doesn't really enjoy drinking. Usually he would try to find some excuse to get on his host's telephone and talk business with somebody somewhere else,' a social friend from Los Angeles recalls.

DeLorean was uncomfortable around women he viewed as aggressive or opinionated. His response was to become equally aggressive and to retaliate with coarse derisive humour. For intimate relaxation during his sprees with his Hollywood friends, he preferred the more pliant, submissive girls that were procured for him.

'John felt bad when Kelly left him, he felt betrayed somehow. And he really did miss the boy until he got him back. But he went out to California one weekend and came back all elated. He told me a wild tale about how Jim Aubrey and Milt Scott had hired three prostitutes who looked a lot like Kelly – that same California-girl face and body. So they got these girls all made up with their hair and make-up just like Kelly's so they really looked like her, all three of them. And then they put the girls in a house at Malibu and packed it full of booze and threw John in the middle of it for the weekend. His friends were saying to him, "Don't worry, there are more like her anytime you want." John thought it was great. He said it was the *classiest* thing anyone had ever done for him – that was his phrase, classy. And he said it could only have happened out there in California, that no one in Detroit would have enough class to pull off something like that. I guess he was right about that,' says a Detroit business associate and long-time friend.

But all that was over with now. He was getting the esteem he needed from the public and the love he wanted from Cristina. And she was proving to be a definite business plus, providing real assistance with the job he held with the National Alliance of Businessmen. The NAB was based in Washington, D.C. and the couple threw themselves into the social whirl of a city just settling down to the second Nixon term in the White House; it was a Washington still unruffled by the gathering Watergate stormclouds.

The DeLoreans were a success in Washington. There were gushing comparisons between the dashing Detroit business executive with the Hollywood past and Henry Kissinger, the swinging Secretary of State. Cristina drew approving reviews for her New York-chic clothes and her ability to prop John up at interminable receptions with her gift for small talk. He too won admirers for his willingness to speak against the car industry. His jeers fitted in with the mood in official Washington that the industry should be more closely regulated in the wake of the energy crisis. DeLorean went further and began speaking out in favour of a heavy tax on gasoline to force energy conservation and to help finance an expanded drive to find alternative energy sources.

But his year with the NAB would soon be over and with it the $200,000 annual stipend continued by General Motors. There would be more payments from GM over the next few years, but most of them were payoffs from bonuses and stock options. At his peak earning period over the five previous years, DeLorean had been piling up bonuses at roughly $400,000 a year, but those were meant to be taken after retirement when the tax bite would be less. DeLorean was well-heeled; but not wealthy enough to support the life he and Cristina were determined to maintain. It appeared that most of the private investments he had made over the last few years were turning into big money losers. Being strapped for cash was unendurable to John DeLorean. It was something he could not even discuss with Cristina, whose own six-figure income from modelling was scrupulously segregated in her own accounts.

The hard truth that DeLorean had to face in early 1974 was that he needed to get back to work in a big way. His stakes in the New York Yankees and the San Diego Chargers were not turning out the profits his higher-flying friends had promised. Another upset was the growing squabble between DeLorean and his brother Chuck over a venture they had started with other partners several years before – Grand Prix of America Inc. The firm tried to franchise reduced-to-scale replicas of famous Grand Prix racing circuit tracks. The idea was a variation on the concept of the miniature golf course. Customers could rent reduced models of famous Formula One race cars and test their skills at the banks and turns of the mini-tracks.

Grand Prix was one of the business interests that DeLorean promised Ed Cole he would soft-pedal during one of the final confrontations at Chevrolet. At the time, what jolted GM management was DeLorean's publicized decision to power the mini-cars with the Wankel rotary engine, which was also used in the Mazda, the newly arrived Japanese entry in the U.S. motor car sweepstakes. It just didn't look right, Cole insisted. It didn't really matter, though. The franchises did not sell well and DeLorean lost interest.

In 1974 Grand Prix of America filed for bankruptcy and one brother, Jack Z. DeLorean, sued to recover his lost funds. Another brother, Chuck, threatened to sue unless his losses were covered in his suit, Jack DeLorean alleged that John had illegally used proxies to shift needed capital into other De-Lorean ventures that involved Roy Nesseth. The suit was later settled out of court.

Although he disputes it, Jack DeLorean was among the first victims of a Nesseth-DeLorean corporate looting pattern that ranged across the country for the next eight years. 'John repaid me. It took a while but he finally did. Look, we've always been close brothers, John has always been a good businessman, a hard fighter.'

And Roy Nesseth? 'Well, that's a sensitive area. Roy Nesseth is a hard driving, very shrewd negotiating businessman. I would say this: If I were dealing with some of the people that John was dealing with under the circumstances, I would have been very pleased to have a man of Mr. Nesseth's capabilities representing my interests. There are instances where John has really been taken to the cleaners by people who later claimed that he was unfair to them. In one case, a real estate deal, John turned it around with Nesseth's aid and got the guy back instead,' Jack DeLorean argues.

But John DeLorean needed something bigger than a failing go-kart franchise or a couple of football teams to put him back on top. There were reports every few weeks that one major corporation or another was considering him for a top post, but somehow firm offers never came. DeLorean began to complain that GM was on an 'SOS' campaign. That decoded into putting 'Shit On his Shoes'.

2

The seeds for the dream car had been sown while DeLorean was still running Pontiac. He had watched the foreign sports car craze build-up during the mid-1960s. From England had come the Triumph Spitfire and Austin-Healey Sprite–tiny two-seaters with few luxuries, but tough, zippy and economical little cars. The Fiat 124 and the Datsun 240Z had soon joined the ranks.

Why not build something to beat them?

Back at Pontiac DeLorean had his team put together a small, low-priced two-seater with the Pontiac overhead cam, a six-cylinder engine (the foreign cars had four) and a fibreglass body. The project excited DeLorean. He presented it enthusiastically to General Motors' engineering policy group, but they turned it down. The GM executives wanted to keep the Chevrolet Corvette as their only product in the low-price sports car market; they wanted no competition, not even from Pontiac.

When DeLorean left GM in 1973, he had no reason to speak publicly about any plans he might have to build his own car. But at the back of his mind the idea for that Pontiac sports car lay simmering.

'The easiest car to build is a sports car,' Bunkie Knudsen was fond of saying, 'because you can do exciting things with the design.'

DeLorean's own much-quoted quip about his final days at GM was: 'We quit designing cars and started designing committees.'

In April 1974, DeLorean addressed a meeting of the Texas Christian University management alumni association in Dallas. He had just completed his year at the NAB, and the next stage of his career – whatever it was to be – was about to unfold. What would he do?

In the previous year, he told his audience, he had designed a couple of little cars – one, similar to the Pontiac, was a two-seater sports job. The other was a mini-commuter car with a foreign engine.

At that point it was the commuter car that sparked DeLorean's enthusiasm. 'Initially it will run on gasoline,' he told the excited alumni group, 'but down the line it will be a multi-fuel vehicle.' Hydrogen was a possible fuel, he said. He could be in production within 18 months to two years.

DeLorean was deliberately enigmatic. He was putting his toe in the water to gauge the temperature. In March, DeLorean had received nationwide publicity with a speech in Chicago in which he had forecast that Detroit would have to abandon the 'grotesque monsters of the 1960s and 1970s'. Consumers, he had predicted, were going to demand smaller cars with less weight, better fuel economy and adequate room for a family. 'By 1980, less than 1,500 working days away, the largest car sold in any quantity in America will be little bigger than today's Chevy Nova.'

The public response had been warmly positive. Now he was going on to the next stage in Dallas, hinting that he himself might build such a car: perhaps 350,000 cars a year, a truck line to be added later with its own production run of 200,000. What would the auto industry think of that? he wondered.

Automotive News soon told him. 'We think it would be a stroke of luck for the industry and consumer alike if DeLorean would return to the auto business and build the sort of car he says will be king of the road by 1980. We're ready, John. C'mon home.'

On that April day in Dallas, DeLorean talked about his deeper ambitions. 'The ideal thing I would like to do with my life right now would be to build the American equivalent of the Mercedes-Benz,' he said, 'A car with high quality, where you wouldn't have to worry about the price, just build the best car you could.'

But it would take enormous sums of money.

Earlier that April, DeLorean had been telephoned by Walter 'Pete' Avrea, a Phoenix inventor who was beset by serious business problems in marketing two extremely valuable automotive patents. DeLorean reacted quickly; he flew at once to Phoenix to meet Avrea and his brother Bill, who had helped form the small stockholders' company, Saf-Guard Products, that sold licences to manufacture and market the inventions.

Pete Avrea is a self-taught mechanic turned inventor. He freely admits that his goal was to be left alone in his workshop with his projects. He wanted other people to navigate the frighteningly complex world of patent development and sales. His two main inventions were genuine winners; both helped prevent car and truck engines from boiling away their radiator coolant and guarded against the risk of burned out engines. One device helped recover vaporized coolant; the other was a radiator cap that prevented blow-outs.

But it is just not enough to be able to prove that one has invented a product or some unique device. Even after the patent is granted the owner must vigilantly pursue pirates who run into the marketplace with quickly copied versions. The only way to survive as an independent inventor is aggressively to use lawyers and the court system to recover royalty monies collected by pirates and to block them from future exploitation.

Pete Avrea's two inventions were worth hundreds of millions of dollars in potential sales and scores of millions of dollars in potential royalty payments. As he recalls now, 'After we had been sent back from the U.S. Supreme Court to the District Court here, the judge ruled that we had valid patents and that they had been infringed on by all the major car manufacturers in the world.' At that point in 1980, the judge ruled that, for every single one of the Avrea units made by companies without valid licences, the major manufacturers owed Avrea $11.30.

Avrea never came close to collecting that. The original Saf-Guard Products firm spent hundreds of thousands of dollars in suits against the big auto parts manufacturers but the court cases dragged on and on, first in the trial courts to establish the patents, then to determine that the patents were being stolen, and finally to establish the amount of money due to Saf-Guard in pirated royalties. The inevitable appeals and delays finally put Saf-Guard into bankruptcy in 1974 and that is when the call for help went out to DeLorean. Would he provide his name, his heavy Detroit reputation and some of his expertise to recapture some of the lost royalties? Could he market the kits to new companies and work out profitable licensing deals with other auto parts manufacturers?

'Norm Bernier, who was president of Saf-Guard Products, called John DeLorean on a Tuesday or Wednesday. On Friday, John arrived here and after a brief talk he said he wanted to take over our company and that he could do for us what we wanted done. Norm and I just stood around in awe. He was just like they said he was in the magazines. He was such a success it was fantastic.'

What Avrea and his family could not know was that John DeLorean was already familiar with the coolant recovery device. It had been put on the production run of the Vega while he was at Chevrolet. There were also hints that DeLorean had learned that General Motors was planning to order 167,000 more units shortly after he entered into contracts with Avrea to set up a new company – Saf-Guard Systems Inc. The new GM order would have been worth $1.8 million.

Saf-Guard Systems was the corporate vehicle under which DeLorean was supposed to be conducting Pete Avrea's business, but it was only a corporate shell. All the business – that is, all the purchasing, borrowing, licensing and shifting of capital – was done through the corpse of Saf-Guard Products, a legally bankrupt firm with no direct ties to John DeLorean.

'He never had the phone changed, nor the building lease changed. He took no responsibility under the name of Saf-Guard Systems until the day the door closed. All the purchase orders and all the cheques still continued to be in the name of Saf-Guard Products. He didn't even tell Ford or General Motors, who were using the kits under license, that there was a company name change because he would have had to pass their quality control standards all over again,' Avrea recounts.

In the meantime, Avrea was visited by Roy Nesseth, who introduced himself as DeLorean's nominee to run Saf-Guard.

'Our first meeting was so unpleasant that I went to the phone with my attorney on the line and called DeLorean and told him that if this was the man he was putting in here, we had no deal. And he said, "Okay, I'll get him out of town. Put him on the phone and I'll tell him to get out of town and I will send another man in,"' Avrea says.

'And Nesseth did go away and another man came in as president of Saf-Guard, but Roy would come through town periodically and make a point to see me and tell me about the big wheelings and dealings he was handling for DeLorean.'

While the inventor fretted over Nesseth's boorishness, DeLorean moved quickly to extract as much money as possible. Royalties that had been coming regularly into the company dried up. Firms that were suspected of using Avrea coolant kits without licences were sold licence at cut-rate royalties without notification to Avrea. The Celanese Corporation loaned DeLorean $200,000 for the development of the radiator cap but the loan was shifted over as a debt of Saf-Guard Products while the capital vanished.

Pete Avrea went back to his workshop, unaware of what was going on.

That summer DeLorean discovered gull-wing doors and forgot about his commuter car.

Gull-wing doors, hinged in the roof, were by no means new. The famous Mercedes 300SL, the glamour car of the 1950s, featured them. So did the ill-fated Bricklin, the private car venture that was about to go belly-up in a few months.

DeLorean wanted his car to be different. He loved Mercedes cars – at that time he drove a Mercedes 300SEL and Cristina had a 450. He also owned a Cadillac, a Monte Carlo and a Corvette, plus six trucks on his California ranch. He had always been adroit at taking the ideas of others and translating them – often brilliantly – into his production cars at Pontiac and Chevrolet. Now he decided to adopt the Mercedes gull-wing doors. He also decided, finally, that the easiest route was to build a sports car. It would fit with his image of the dashing former GM executive. The car could be produced in smaller numbers and sold at higher prices than a standard sedan. It would not require the huge fortune needed to compete in the mass markets.

'We can't play in the same concert halls as GM,' he quipped to newsmen. 'They play on the keys and we have to play on the cracks.'

There was another attraction, too. DeLorean had commissioned surveys at GM that showed that sports cars were a 'growth area'. But, most important of all, he realized they offered him the best chance of winning government subsidies. 'To qualify for government financing, you need a statement from the U.S. Department of Labor confirming that your project would not displace Americans in similar employment. Well, the sports car market was mostly imported cars,' he would recall later. At that time he began thinking about building his car in Pennsylvania or Texas, or so he told the press.

Now he needed someone to put it together for him. DeLorean was an undeniably fine engineer and knew that side of the business very well. But if he was going to launch his own company, he needed someone else to take care of the mass of detailed design work that would lead to the prototype state and on to production. He began to look around.

William T. Collins was a lanky, quietly intense project manager at General Motors. He wore a large handlebar moustache that flourished or disappeared whenever whim dictated. Collins created an air of professional calm and proficiency; he knew what he was doing and liked doing it well. He was a good man to have on any team. He served six years as assistant chief engineer at Pontiac and in the corporation was dubbed the 'godfather of the Grand Am.'

In 1974 Collins was project manager of the 1977 model B Car for GM. This was to be the first down-sized car the company made. The B Car was also the first car produced at a GM 'project centre' where a chief engineer was in charge, put there by a vote of other car division chief engineers. The new model would start its life in styling, after which different divisions would take responsibility for designing and producing specific parts or systems. Buick might have the brakes and Pontiac the rear suspension. These divisions were spread geographically throughout the state of Michigan but the parts would be monitored at the design centre where the project would be pulled together. Collins' B Car project was a success and he found himself sought after by GM's rivals.

Collins had worked on DeLorean's two-passenger sports car experiment at Pontiac and was still irked by the way the idea had been killed off. He had stayed in touch with DeLorean.

But, now in the summer of 1974, Collins was being head-hunted. American Motors wanted him and offered him more money and a promotion. He leaned towards making the break. One of the references he gave was John DeLorean. Within days of the job interview with American, Collins received a phone call from Miami Airport. (DeLorean could not resist making phone calls from airports.)

He had finally decided to make a two-seater sports car, DeLorean told Collins. It would have gull-wing doors and lots of new safety innovations – safety would be the theme. DeLorean ticked off the features he planned. New plastic process, very strong, very light. Everything rust-proof – use plastics and stainless steel. Get one of those flashy Italian designers to come up with a body line that was really ritzy. Get government money to build it in the United States. And get the dealers to put up the money in advance.

'Bill, I want you to be in charge of the whole thing,' DeLorean promised.

Collins did not resist long. 'Hell,' he would say later, 'I guess the concept of any engineer who loves cars is to be able to do your own car.' He compared his dull task of coordinating the 1977 B Car with a chance to build a sports car for which he would be totally in control. DeLorean was promising good salaries to start with and the lure of a large fortune for everyone once the car was off the ground.

Collins knew what he was giving up at General Motors – bonuses were paid out over five years, and if he left he could forfeit them. He decided to go ahead and 'throw off the golden handcuffs'.

Having made up his mind, he had to tell GM. Pete Estes had taken over from Ed Cole and it was to him that Collins offered his resignation. In the president's office on the 14th floor, Collins explained to Estes what he was doing and why.

'Geez, I wish you'd stay,' Estes responded after a pause. 'John is flaky, you know,' he warned Collins. 'He has just plain flipped out.'

Collins himself observed some years later, 'I am not sure if any of us understand what we all go through in our lives, but some people do have something that happens to them in their early forties.' This is a theme that recurs when people, who knew John DeLorean from the early days, ponder his subsequent fate. It might be Bunkie Knudsen's euphemistic 'gone Hollywood', or David Davis's quip: 'DeLorean and John Glenn both have been out into outer space. John DeLorean's problem is that he lost a few tiles on re-entry.'

In September 1974 Bill Collins joined DeLorean in the offices of the John Z. DeLorean Corporation in Bloomfield Hills, Michigan.

The concept had begun to take firmer shape in DeLorean's mind. The Corvette was selling nearly 50,000 cars a year, priced around $12,000. It was no longer exclusive. DeLorean figured he could sell 20,000 of a more exciting car at a price pitched $1,500 more than the Corvette. That was the market he would shoot for. Why, even Porsche was selling nearly 20,000 cars a year.

That autumn, DeLorean and Collins flew to Italy for the Torino Motor Show in search of a designer. They looked at the

Maseratis and the Farina designs. They spent some time talking to a man named Giorgetto Giugiaro.

Giugiaro had earned a reputation as one of the most adventurous automotive stylists of the Torino school. He had worked as Bertone's chief stylist on the Lamborghini, one of the world's most dramatic sports cars. Then he founded his own Ital Design, and performed some of the work on the new generation of highly successful Volkswagen cars that succeeded the Beetle. He had also worked on Lancias, Audis and Alfa Romeos. Most intriguing of all, he did the styling work for a small British sports car maker – Lotus.

DeLorean and Collins decided Giugiaro was the man for them. DeLorean explained to the designer what he wanted: the stainless steel shell and the gull-wings. DeLorean wanted the engine behind the driver. 'It's more sporty – that's where it is on the Indianapolis and Grand Prix cars.' That configuration demanded a wedge-shaped body design, which Giugiaro also liked.

By February 1975, Giugiaro had his design ready and Collins had produced the seating and chassis parameters to go into it. Collins and DeLorean went to Italy again and fitted the two together. It all looked glamorous enough, even for John DeLorean. Giugiaro had come up with a sleek, low-slung, silver beauty.

By March 1975 DeLorean and Giugiaro had signed a deal. Over the next five years, Giugiaro would tweak the design here and there, but basically the silhouette produced that spring was the same one that DeLorean would send into production. And while it was later to be criticized for many other reasons, its looks were undeniably eye-catching.

By the end of July, before Giugiaro's workers went off on the traditional month-long August break, the design was complete. DeLorean's dream now had a shape. His own contribution had been less than crucial.

'He would occasionally make sketches,' Collins recalls. 'Not to scale though, so we never had anything workable. He had a favorite concept he came up with that I called, "Zachary's Greenhouse". He kept showing this little guy – like his son – sitting behind the front seat and if you bulged out the rear window, supposedly little Zachary could sit back there. And I kept showing John that to scale you can't do it. It wouldn't work. And finally the idea went away. Occasionally he made sketches of areas he was interested in, but the basic engineering and all the basic design was work that I did. All the suspension parameters, the ground clearance, the seating dimensions were all put together by me.'

The first Giugiaro-designed drawings and models featured the initials 'DSV' on the front panel – it stood for 'DeLorean Safety Vehicle'. That was never intended to be the car's name, but it produced the image DeLorean sought. The safety, and the car's special lightness and strength, were to be provided by a new plastic wonder material called 'Elastic Reservoir Molding' or ERM. It was not a widely known process in the United States, although it had been in use for a short time in European cars. As John DeLorean originally conceived it, ERM was the secret key to his dream – the ingredient to make his car something special. In the end it was used only for a few non-essential parts.

The ERM method was a fibreglass process originally developed by Royal Dutch Shell. DeLorean set up a company called Composite Technology Corporation (CTC), separate from his personal investment company, John Z. DeLorean Corporation, and through CTC bought an option on the licence to the product for the motor industry. CTC rented a 25,000 square foot factory near Troy, Michigan, and DeLorean hired Peter H. Hofer as CTC's director of research and development.

Collins was enthusiastic about the process. 'Based on what I know so far,' he reported in July 1975, 'the weight of a car body would be almost as light as if it were made entirely out of aluminum.'

But it was also expected to have another important characteristic. Collins estimated that it could be used to design one of the safest cars ever built. 'You could vary the (composition),' he told *Automotive News* in July, 'to achieve energy management during a high-speed crash.' He hoped he might even be able to achieve 'barrier survivability' at 40 to 50 miles an hour, which meant that a passenger would crawl out unhurt from a head-on crash at those speeds.

The idea Collins and DeLorean worked out was based on a

one-piece body moulded from ERM. Over this shell would be placed a skin of stainless steel, thus avoiding the need for paint. The engine would either be in the middle of the car or in the rear, 'so the entire front end can be devoted to energy management in a crash'. The light weight of the plastic also meant the car would meet DeLorean's ambitious goals for fuel economy, which were now defined as 30 miles per gallon on the highway and 20 mpg at city streets speeds. It also meant lower tooling costs – 'fewer holes,' said Collins happily, 'a lot less nuts and bolts.'

On August 18, *Automotive News* presented to the world the first glimpse of the dream car. It was just a frontal flash, with a large 'DSV' on the front. The gull-wings were not in evidence – they were still on the 'secret' list. But in the same issue, DeLorean's broader strategy was revealed. Although he was not quoted directly in the article, he had written down his thoughts for Collins to ascribe to him in the interview. In view of later events, it makes for ironic reading.

> One word, to me, describes our car's concept and that is responsible – no gimmicks and no compromises. It must demonstrate a responsibility for conservation of energy, human life and human resources. Responsibility also implies recognizing the customer's desires and needs, not only in the product but also in service after the sale.
>
> Quality in all aspects, combined with durability and serviceability are paramount. I do not feel any of these needs compromise a vehicle and force it to be either unattractive or undesirable, but quite the contrary . . .
>
> Today's technology will allow, even encourage, all of these if you decide on your goal. Further, we feel in a position to provide an enlightened response to the needs of society without being encumbered by numerous constraints.

So there it was, spelled out for the first time. John DeLorean's dream car was to be safe, beautiful, economical, and what the customer wanted.

Late in 1974, Allstate Insurance Corporation, the insurance subsidiary of the giant Sears & Roebuck merchandizing chain, commissioned the John Z. DeLorean Corporation to prepare a study on car safety standards for the future.

Like other insurance companies, Allstate was alarmed that the post-oil-embargo rush toward fuel economy might have the unhappy side effect of reducing car safety standards. DeLorean's early findings confirmed Allstate's fears. But, DeLorean argued, there were things that could be done. Cars could be designed for more fuel efficiency in ways that did not sacrifice safety in the race to reduce vehicle weight. Airbags could be installed in the front seats of all new cars. He went further; his research showed that a delay of just three years in making air-bags standard equipment in U.S. cars would cost $18.8 billion in 'societal loss' due to injuries and fatalities.

But with airbags and other safety-oriented design features, it was within the technological reach of the U.S. motor industry to produce a car that not only was fuel-efficient and affordable, but could also be run into a brick wall at 40 mph with no serious harm to its occupants. Here it was then, another case of DeLorean billing the possible as an almost certainty.

Allstate was so pleased with the early DeLorean work and the press coverage of his safety remarks that they commissioned him further to do the design work on the very elements that might be included in such a safety vehicle.

'It was a cooperative program,' an Allstate spokesman said after a recent search through the records. 'Between us and the DeLorean Corporation, in the construction of an advanced concept two-passenger safety car.'

In Allstate's now dusty and forgotten files, the joint project targeted a car 'for a 2,200 pound weight class with fuel economy in the range of 30 miles per gallon. It would have increased protection in those side, rear and low-speed front end accident situations. The fuel tank would be centrally located. A rear-mounted engine is planned. They fulfilled the contract with a design that met our agreed-upon goals and the design was used as our proof that such a safe car could be produced right then in 1975.'

The cost to Allstate was a reasonable $50,000; in return, it got several batches of creative designs for seating and structural alternatives. Allstate would not own the designs; rather, they would be able to show them off and claim credit for helping fund the concept should some future manufacturer – Ford, Chrysler, yes even General Motors itself – agree to take any or all of the innovations.

But John DeLorean now had those innovations and Allstate had in fact paid the overhead on his design work.

In November 1975 DeLorean leaked more of the details of the new safety car he was going to put into production under his own name:

. The car would weigh around 2,200 pounds;

. Fuel economy would be 30 MPG on the highway and 20 MPG in the city;

. It would have an integral body construction based on a new advanced ERM plastic technique;

. The car would have solid barrier protection for crashes at speeds exceeding minimum federal government standards;

. There would be airbags for driver and front-seat passenger.

. Front-end structure would be solely devoted to 'energy management' of head-on collisions which, according to the statement, represent about 30 per cent of serious road crashes;

. Foam-filled rear structure would offer similar crash protection;

. Centrally located fuel tank would be a design feature;

. The windshield would be located well in front of the occupants.

Later that November, Bill Collins announced that Allstate had provided another $500,000 grant for the building of three 'safety car' prototypes: real metal, glass and plastic full-sized cars to be tested against the realities of the wind-tunnel, the test track and public taste.

But, even with Allstate inadvertently footing the bills for the initial design work, DeLorean was short of money. Grand Prix of America had gone bankrupt and several of his Detroit friends (not to mention his brother) had been burned in the deal.

DeLorean turned to his hulking friend Roy Nesseth.

Men like Roy W. Nesseth pockmark the business landscape of all countries; they skirt along the edge of the law, preferring the fruitful shallows of the grey areas of legality. But they are always willing, for a reward equal to the risk, to dart over into outright lawlessness provided they can get back quickly to the other side.

By the late summer of 1975, DeLorean had worked out a business and personal relationship with Roy Nesseth that was a variation of the classic Tom-and-Jerry, good-guy/bad-guy routine used by many skilled manipulators.

In 1954 Nesseth had been convicted of forgery and fraud in car sales to two elderly couples. An affable six-footer, he had just the mix of charm and chutzpah, when he wanted to show it, that DeLorean lacked. Roy could establish rapport. By the time the two were introduced through the General Motors dealers' network, Nesseth had become the manager of the largest Chevrolet dealership in America, the Williams Chevrolet firm of Norwalk, California.

In one of the many suits filed against him, Nesseth was described as 'the best auto salesman and closer in the field'; the last a tribute to his ability to get reluctant or undecided prospects to close the deal and buy.

In 1968 he had convinced a wealthy widow, Hazel Upton Dean, to put him in charge of her extensive properties which included a redwood sawmill, a ranch, a thoroughbred horse farm, a large art collection, a home in Palm Springs, California and an apartment in Beverly Hills. Mrs. Dean had had a heart attack and she wanted to rest at her Palm Springs home undisturbed.

But Hazel Dean soon suspected something was wrong, that Nesseth was selling off her properties without her knowledge and pocketing the proceeds. He had taken over her Beverly Hills apartment and was using it as a party place; among the guests who had stayed at the apartment, she learned later, was

John DeLorean. She sued, charging that Nesseth had defrauded her of property worth several million dollars; at one point she went and stole back one of her horses that had been spirited away to another farm. She still maintains that the grand piano from her apartment is in Nesseth's Huntington Beach, California, home. Since 1980, that same home has been listed as the property of John Z. DeLorean.

John Thomas, of La Jolla, California, an attorney who has made something of a career of representing Mrs. Dean and other people defrauded by Roy Nesseth, says, 'He has no assets listed, titled or recorded in his name. This makes him virtually litigation proof, or rather he is recovery proof, penalty proof. Yet, he enjoys a high standard of living and I allege upon information and belief that he earns very large amounts of money and has significant assets, all of which are deeply hidden from his creditors.'

In the early summer of 1975, DeLorean transferred control of the Delaware Corporation that owned the Pine Creek Ranch near Salmon, Idaho to Roy Nesseth. The ranch was the thousand-acre property he had bought for Kelly Harmon to turn into a holiday camp for ghetto kids.

Nesseth scouted the region until he found a likely prospect to buy the ranch. Clark Higley and his wife were plain-spoken farm folks who had turned a small homestead claim into a 500-acre potato farm. With their profits they had already bought a $125,000 house on the Snake River and two boutiques.

As Higley tells it, 'We wanted to consolidate and find some place big enough so that my two boys and their families could come and work it with me and make a living for us all. I was getting on in years and wanted something that did not take every waking minute to take care of.

'DeLorean and Nesseth, they mesmerize you. They told me everything I wanted to hear. When we first started talking, they would take us to dinner and treat us super-good,' he recalls.

What Higley did not know was that Nesseth already had sold off some of the cattle and that DeLorean had secured a $1 million mortgage on the ranch from the Metropolitan Life Insurance Company. As an aside, the local Metropolitan representatives recommended that the property be valued for purposes of the loan for only $800,000, still half a million dollars more than DeLorean had paid for it five years before. But DeLorean was skilled at using his old ties to GM when he could; Metropolitan was a major health and life insurer at the car company, so a quick call to the head office helped boost the value of the loan on the Pine Creek Ranch.

With Nesseth rapidly quoting figures from past deals as confirmation, DeLorean suggested a way that Higley and he could construct a deal so as to minimize the tax consequences of the sale. Perhaps more importantly, although Higley would only realize this later, the DeLorean deal also did away with the necessity to do the normal title search that would have revealed the Metropolitan mortgage.

The deal worked like this: Higley was to rent the ranch with an option to buy. DeLorean was to take possession of Higley's potato farm (which he subsequently sold in 1981 for $800,000). DeLorean was also to receive a $300,000 cash payment from Higley for 1,100 head of cattle and various ranch equipment. Higley paid $375,000 in rent for two years during which time the light slowly dawned that he was being taken for a very long ride by DeLorean and Nesseth.

First of all, the cattle and farm equipment – like the ranch itself – already were security against DeLorean borrowings. In the case of the cows and machinery, DeLorean had borrowed $300,000 from the First National Bank of Idaho. Instead of using the $300,000 in cash which Higley had paid him to pay off the loan, DeLorean gave the money to Nesseth so that he and a brother could open a Chevrolet dealership in Lewiston, Idaho. The dealership had its franchise yanked two years later by General Motors, 'for no longer serving the sales and service needs of customers'.

Ultimately Higley, during one of his many court actions (most still pending), did get back most of the $300,000 he had paid after the bank collected it from DeLorean. But he was not so lucky with Metropolitan, which foreclosed because DeLorean never made a payment on the outstanding mortgage loan. Higley and his wife were finally forced off the Pine Creek Ranch in 1980; later that year, DeLorean repurchased it for $1.7 million from Metropolitan, thereby settling the mortgage against him. And a few months after that he sold the ranch again for $2.1 million.

The immediate yield of $1 million from Metropolitan's loan, plus the $300,000 cash that went to Nesseth, plus the regular monthly payments Higley made, all served to ease DeLorean's ravenous appetite for cash. For the moment.

The Higleys and DeLorean and Nesseth are still tied up in Idaho courts but there is little hope now that the Idaho farmer will ever recover his losses.

'It just ruined us. He and Roy changed lawyers on us all the time and that kept the court from pushing the trial ahead. They would not pay their lawyers and the next thing you knew there was a new set of them asking for delays,' Higley says.

'I will say Mrs. DeLorean was nice. When she was out, she and I would talk many times. I don't think she knew what all was going on with him. She told one of our friends that if I didn't get that Pine Creek ranch, DeLorean would never go to heaven. Well, I never got that ranch.'

By the beginning of 1976, DeLorean was talking about production being 'less than two years away'. Over the winter the first prototype was built. The body was tested at the Torino Polytechnic and Caltech windtunnels. Collins used a computer to do a body stiffness analysis, tire and suspension analysis and simulations of what would happen to passengers during a head-on crash of up to 40 miles per hour. He also used a computer program to work out the four-wheel independent suspension.

This prototype was powered by a transversely mounted Citroen Powerplant engine. It also featured a high door sill, which was said to provide extra side protection, but in fact was a largely structural necessity. The car had no main chassis, but two sub-chassis – front and rear. DeLorean was relying heavily on the strength of his new plastic material to keep the car rigid on the road.

The prototype also featured an on-board computer with a digital read out. Few of these features were to survive development into the production car, but the basic size and shape changed only marginally. The prototype was 165.1 inches long and 72.7 inches wide – the production car was 166 inches long and exactly 6 feet wide. The final version ended up just one inch higher than the original 46 inches. And 2.2 inches were chopped off the wheelbase to leave it at 95 inches.

As for the all-important weight of the car, the prototype was designed to weigh a light 2,200 pounds, compared with the 3,541 pound Corvette. The production car was to weigh in at 2,844 pounds as ERM faded from the scene and the engineers installed an all-steel backbone chassis.

True, all cars change between the prototype and production models. It would be unreasonable to expect that DeLorean's hastily put together designs would not be amended considerably – why else build prototypes? The significance of the changes to the DeLorean car, however, is that he was openly boasting about its 'uniqueness', with every individual feature specifically designed for safety and durability.

John DeLorean had accused General Motors and the whole auto industry of pulling a great con job on the American public by selling it the same car for 20 years with nothing more than a minor facelift each year. His car was going to be revolutionary: an ethical car.

Over the next four years, there was a steady series of compromises on feature after feature. Each so-called 'unique' element dropped away.

What hit the American market in June 1981 was a car that was not at all bad; it looked good, behaved relatively well, and had some useful safety features. But it was just an ordinary car. It was the 'stainless steel Lotus' that not even the Lotus people were very excited about.

CHAPTER FOUR

The DeLorean Motor Company

Thomas W. Kimmerly was a partner in the three-man law firm of Kimmerly, Gans and Shaler.

He was the son of a well-known Detroit business executive with the Burroughs Corporation. A quiet, diffident man, he had been frankly swept off his feet by the glamour and purpose in DeLorean's manner. Above all, Kimmerly loved cars.

Kimmerly had done a few minor bits of legal work for DeLorean and, when DeLorean was looking for an office for his fledgling company, he suggested that he take space in his building in Long Lake Road, Bloomfield Hills. Soon DeLorean used him more and more – talking deals and talking cars. But it was one day, as they were both standing at the urinals, that (as Kimmerly later recalled) DeLorean suddenly said: "Let's start a car company."

DeLorean turned over to Kimmerly the complex task of raising the money needed to keep the car venture going and to provide him with the cash flow he had to have to live like a man at the top.

Kimmerly's first act was to create the DeLorean Motor Company (DMC). In January 1974, DeLorean had founded his own personal corporation, the John Z. DeLorean Corporation, which was known by the acronym JZDC. In April 1975, JZDC had formed Composite Technology Corporation to take a licence for the ERM process, but the rights to that licence, while held by CTC, were also held by JZDC. In one of the few traceable instances where John DeLorean can be said to have invested any of his own money, JZDC was capitalized at $20,000 and he had loaned the company another $350,000 from his own resources.

In October 1975, Kimmerly incorporated DMC and transferred to its capital stock from JZDC all the design work done by Collins and his staff (and paid for by Allstate) and the rights to the ERM licences – all assigned a value of $3.5 million.

At the end of the month, Kimmerly moved to set up yet another corporate structure for the purposes of raising money. The shift of assets out of JZDC and into DMC had accomplished one important purpose: John DeLorean still retained total control over the assets but now there was an intervening corporate layer between those assets and the public, not to mention the law.

By creating the DeLorean Sports Car Partnership (DSCP) in December 1975, Kimmerly created a vehicle into which outside investors could contribute large sums of money to help with testing and research on the project. Once it was set up, DeLorean again transferred the ERM method and car design work, with their established worth of $3.5 million, to DSCP where they would be matched by cash investments worth just a shade more than $3.5 million. DeLorean retained a 49.9 percent interest in DSCP, which gave him unchallenged control.

The attraction to investors, who were being asked to put up minimum amounts of $100,000, was that, as a research and development project, every dollar of investment reduced one's taxable income that year by one dollar. For an investor caught in the 70 percent tax bracket that then prevailed, the opportunity meant he could use only 30 cents of his own cash and 70 cents of money that would have been taxed away by Washington, to buy something with a nominal worth of one dollar, multiplied of course by $100,000. Plus the fact that there was an option to buy shares in future stages of the venture at preferred prices, and also the romance of an exciting car development project. The money came in easily: some Merrill Lynch Fenner and Smith traders formed a special group and invested $450,000 in one chunk.

So now DeLorean had $3.5 million at his command. Indeed the project was acquiring a breathless momentum of its own. People whom John DeLorean had never heard of volunteered enthusiastic support; others wanted to give him money, almost on a no-questions-asked basis. His preaching about the evils of big business and the need for an ethical car had struck nerves all over America.

But, if a car was going to be built, as much as $70 million to

$90 million would have to be raised. The project would have 'to go public', to offer stock on the open market and to attract a large number of cash-rich investors.

For all his corporate skills, Kimmerly could not alone handle the flotation of a national public stock offering. He needed legal help. Detroit attorney Malcolm Gushee was brought in.

DMC also needed an expert financial planner and strategist. Robert W. Dewey had been in financial management with General Motors and during 1974 and 1975 DeLorean had frequently turned to him for advice. He recalls:

'John would call me up every once in a while and say, "Are you having fun, Bob?" and I would say, "Well, I'm working here." And he'd say, "Why don't you swing by some Saturday morning or on the way home from work and see what I'm doing." And it was right on my way home, so I'd drop in from time to time and he'd bring me up to speed on how the project was coming. He said he was looking for a chief financial officer and at the appropriate time he'd like me to consider it.'

When he finally came aboard, Dewey immediately buckled down to the backbreaking task of getting ready to launch DMC's fund-raising effort for the kind of seed money that would make the company a serious manufacturing contender. For Dewey, the lure of being chief financial officer of an exciting new company overcame any personal misgivings he may have had about DeLorean.

'No, I didn't like him personally. Not many people did. But it was a chance to do something, to do it the way it should be done – at least I thought it could be at the time – and I couldn't pass it up,' Dewey says.

John DeLorean paid himself $125,000 a year, but he also paid his top executives very well with the promise of more. Dewey got $70,000 a year, plus stock options, as secretary-treasurer of DMC.

The next man DeLorean recruited to the team was C. R. 'Dick' Brown, a solid, quiet man who had been the U.S. chief executive of the Mazda Motor Company of Japan when it located an assembly plant in California in the early 1970s. He was hired as vice president for operations at $100,000 a year. He not only played an important rôle lining up potential investors, but he would be in charge of planning the early phases of manufacturing and marketing through dealers.

'This is a very self-serving remark, but I didn't joint because I thought John DeLorean could do it. I felt *I* could do it. Then why do it with him? Because he had a stronger, more international name – a General Motors name if you will. And it was his concept. I didn't really care that much for him, he was a braggart and a loudmouth and as time went on I never saw a shred of evidence of this engineering genius he was supposed to have. He may have had it, but he never spent any of it, or any time, on the car project's design – that was Bill Collins. Dewey was the financial man. What I could provide for him was the know-how of putting the mechanics of a car company together and to establish the dealer organization,' Brown recalls.

So, early in 1976, the core of the DeLorean car executive team was in place: Brown, Collins and Dewey, with Kimmerly helping from the sidelines. There were 15 employees now in the Long Lake Road offices.

In the meantime, Roy Nesseth had been busy elsewhere.

Gerald Dahlinger was a Wichita, Kansas businessman who was an early investor in the Pizza Hut fast-food chain. He pulled out a $450,000 profit and in 1974 reinvested it in a Pontiac dealership in his small town. Later, he added a Cadillac franchise to the dealership and for a few months was doing all right. But the 1974-1975 recession really bit into car sales and, by early 1976, Dahlinger had run up a dangerous level of debt at the Kansas State Bank and Trust.

In May 1976, bank officials presented Dahlinger with an unusual restructuring plan to keep his company in business and their loans secure. John DeLorean, the well-known ex-GM executive, was interested in taking over the dealership, investing new capital. He would put in his own man, Roy Nesseth, as president, but Dahlinger's name would remain on the franchise and he could stay on as vice president.

Dahlinger was initially surprised at the deal, even though he accepted DeLorean's demand for anonymity on the grounds that he was still 'a controversial figure at GM'. The bank accepted Nesseth as the front man, too.

J. V. Lentell, the president of Kansas State Bank, says, 'DeLorean didn't want his name on the franchise because the

GM people were not too friendly. Nesseth and DeLorean were both very impressive.'

Dahlinger agrees, and he still calls Nesseth 'Mr. Personality', in a rueful way. 'He was the best charmer I've ever seen.'

The terms of the deal were that Dahlinger was to collect $80,000 for his interest in $4,000 monthly instalments. He was also to look after the dealership in Nesseth's absence.

It turned sour at once. Nesseth ordered up an American Express card in the dealership's name. He ran up thousands of dollars worth of champagne and hotel bills in Wichita, all of which were duly paid for by Dahlinger Pontiac-Cadillac.

Worse still was the rush of cheques in and out of the dealership's accounts. More than $1 million in cheques were written to Saf-Guard Systems (not Saf-Guard Products, where the actual work was going on) and cheques from Saf-Guard Systems were coming back. When the final litigation ended, years later, the Kansas Bank was to recover $300,000 from the Saf-Guard cheque-kiting scheme alone. In the final accounting, there were even cheques to Clark Higley in Idaho, as Nesseth and DeLorean kept draining funds out of the dealership.

Cash was not the only thing that Dahlinger lost. In plusher times, Dahlinger had restored a classic 1956 Mercedes 300 SL, a design unique for its use of gull-wing doors. To cut considerable insurance on the car, it was registered to the dealership and when DeLorean borrowed it, ostensibly to help promote the DMC-12, Dahlinger never saw the car again.

After six months of trying to persuade credulous bank officials that something terrible was going on, Dahlinger literally walked away from his dealership and moved to Wichita. Later he sued Nesseth and collected $80,000.

But for three years, at least, the Dahlinger dealership remained a plentiful cash cow that DeLorean and his henchmen milked with great regularity.

In the meantime, the finishing touches had been put on the DeLorean Sports Car Partnership fund-raising effort. Brown, who had valuable connections with car dealers and potential investors all over the country, had rounded up many of them. There were several early-warning signals that Brown now recognizes he should have heeded.

'I gave one presentation to a group in Palm Springs and a dealer there, I knew the guy real well, came up to me later and said he had been involved with DeLorean in something called Grand Prix of America three years before. The guy said, "I went through all this with that guy and I wouldn't touch him with a ten-foot pole again."'

Another signal, symptomatic of DeLorean's attitude toward money – other people's money – came when the full $3.5 million had been raised for the DSCP. DeLorean took a $200,000 consulting fee off the top.

For the project to succeed, DeLorean now had to get four elements in place. There was the design for the car, and under Bill Collins that was now coming along well. Then there was the money for it – a bigger problem but not insurmountable. Third were the dealership networks and Dick Brown was working full time on them now that the DSCP had been fully funded.

The fourth factor was a location where he could build his car. He needed a factory – a large, new one built specially for him. Initially he had left this problem on the back-burner and tackled the other elements. But the day was fast coming when he would have to give this problem his full attention.

2

As the months passed during 1976 and into early 1977 the new DeLorean team members worked on crash schedules. DeLorean was making increasingly frequent commuting trips to New York City. The idea was that he would meet prospective clients and keep up his media contacts. His friend Herb Siegel let DeLorean and a small staff set up housekeeping at the Chris-Craft headquarters there.

DeLorean was stepping up his lifestyle and spending. Without any formal discussion with the others, he decided to locate his own headquarters in New York. He and Cristina moved into a duplex about to be sold by Johnny Carson. The superstar had moved his programme to Hollywood and his marriage to second wife Joanne had broken up. The negotiations over the apartment caused Carson and the DeLoreans to become fast friends. It was to be an expensive friendship for the entertainer.

At the same time an interesting pattern was developing in the relationship between DeLorean and the team of Brown, Dewey and Collins. Increasingly each of the three sought to isolate DeLorean from contact or interference; each felt strongly that DeLorean had little to contribute and in some cases was a dangerous liability when he suddenly took an interest in the task at hand.

Collins had the least trouble because DeLorean was most secure around engineers and had confidence in his designer. But Collins also came to feel that DeLorean really was not very interested in the crucial drudgery of the design sequence. Indeed, the suspicion grew that DeLorean was diffident about the details of his own car now that its basic shape and configuration had been determined.

Bob Dewey, however, took special pains to keep DeLorean away from the delicate negotiations he was conducting. In December 1975 and January 1976 the DeLorean Sports Car Partnership (DSCP) had attracted $3.5 million from various investor friends of Dick Brown. But that amount would soon be spent and another, and this time public, stock offering would have to be made.

In order to make a stock offering, one must first 'register' it with the U.S. Securities & Exchange Commission in Washington. While the agency takes no stand on the potential profits or losses of an investment opportunity, it will not register a stock offering for sale to the American public unless it meets certain standards of fair dealings on the part of the company offering the stock for sale. An SEC attorney who followed the DeLorean case file explained later, 'The registration statement is exhaustive. A stock issuer has to list everything from the pay of the president to the kind of widgets they are going to manufacture. Those statements are usually handled by examiners and our [legal] office rarely sees them unless there is a problem.

'Now our office became involved in DeLorean before the first registration statement was filed because there were a number of previous private financings and the [DSCP] partnership. There was a technical question in our minds as to whether we should consider the previous private financings as part of this upcoming public offering.'

But even after the initial slow start and confusion, Kimmerly and attorney Malcolm Gushee were able to submit a proper registration statement for filing in the spring of 1976. What happens next, in SEC parlance, is known as the quiet period. This is the interval between the time the company submits its stock sale plan to the SEC for registration and when the agency clears the plan so the company can actually get out there and sell the stock to the waiting public. During this quiet time the company may not do anything that can be seen as a promotion of its upcoming share offering.

It was during this critical period that DeLorean got a break. The National Automobile Dealers Association was slated to hold its annual convention and car show in New Orleans that June. DeLorean had not only booked an exhibitor's booth at the show, but he also planned to have one of the DMC-12 prototypes on display and to use a special mini-theatre to show a promotional film to potential dealer-investors who might later become part of the nationwide DeLorean network that was so vital to the car's marketing success. But wouldn't all this violate the SEC regulations?

'We let them go to the convention and perhaps in hindsight we can be criticized for being too liberal. But after all, the SEC is not here to *prevent* stock offerings. Our mandate from Congress is to *help* companies issue shares to the public that meet standards of adequate disclosure.

'Also you should keep in mind that we had no knowledge and no way to know about Mr. DeLorean's legal problems, nor did we examine the reorganization of the company prior to the registration statement. Perhaps we should have. Perhaps we *would* have, but again no one came forward to tell us about these potential problems and we have no investigative facilities to go out and search every potential stock seller in America.'

The SEC attorney was referring to an occurrence that might have clouded investor enthusiasm – not to mention the agency's cooperative attitude – had it been widely known at the time. In February 1976, Pete Avrea had had enough and filed suit against John DeLorean and Roy Nesseth, alleging fraudulent behaviour and demanding the return of ownership of his patents.

Throughout the winter of 1975-6, his complaints about the fall-off in royalty revenue and disturbing rumours of cheap licence sales by DeLorean had come to a head. Roy Nesseth returned to Phoenix with the news that he had purchased control of Saf-Guard Systems from John DeLorean for $1. 'From now on you're not dealing with Mr. DeLorean anymore, you're dealing with me.'

Had Avrea known what he was in for, he might have walked away from Saf-Guard right then. It would take him four years of tedious on-again, off-again court struggles and $250,000 in legal fees and deposition costs to reach a dead end. In the meantime there were the threats and harassment.

'I can't prove who it was but my wife believes it was Roy Nesseth who would call the house and tell her to tell me to drop the suits. If I were sure it was he, if I had heard the calls myself I would know what to do about it,' Avrea says today. 'But it hurt her health, she became afraid to go out and start the car in case it was a bomb meant for me. I had to do something.'

And in the end, Pete Avrea gave up. He paid $400,000 to DeLorean for the return of his patents and thereby released another $250,000 in royalties that had been impounded by the courts – royalties that were immediately turned over to the John Z. DeLorean Corporation, not to the official owner of record, Roy Nesseth. In the meantime, during most of 1976 and 1977 the rush of kited cheques reached a flood tide between Saf-Guard and Dahlinger Pontiac-Cadillac. As much as $1 million in meaningless cheques may have been generated among the various DeLorean enterprises, with as much as $250,000 from just the car dealership and Saf-Guard disappearing in the process. It may have been 'quiet time' for the SEC, but it was business as usual for Nesseth and DeLorean.

On June 29, 1977, the SEC finally permitted registration of the DeLorean Motor Company share offering. The offering sought to attract 400 investors who also wanted to be DMC-12 dealers, to contribute $10 million in capital to the project. The minimum $25,000 investment not only bought 5,000 shares of DeLorean Motor Company stock (at $5 a share) but it also secured a franchise as a dealer. The investor was presumed to be an existing operating car dealer – this was important since it provided the showroom and service facilities so necessary to successful automobile marketing, as well as the kind of local name identification for the DMC-12 that is equally important to sales. The dealer-investor was also committed to sell between 100 and 150 (depending on the size of his dealership volume) of the DMC-12s during the first two years of the company's production run. Although this part of the investment agreement could not be enforced it served its purpose to support DeLorean's claim that two years' production run had been sold out before the factory was built.

In the year that followed, the stock offering would be only moderately successful; 206 dealers instead of the needed 400 came forward and the $5.16 million in capital inflow from them, however welcome, was not enough to put the project over the top.

Part of the problem lay in the ambitious nature of the sales and investment plan cooked up by Brown, Dewey and Kimmerly. The DMC-12 could only be an instant success if it could plug into an already existing network of dealers, and, more importantly, the best dealers who sold only the most prestigious models in every town across the United States and Canada. What that meant was that the DeLorean Motor Company had to sell shares on a nationwide basis and it had to attract dealers the same way. Normally, attempts to raise money through public stock offerings concentrate on those regions of the United States where heavy investment capital is found in the greatest abundance, or in the home state where the company will do business. The SEC registration statement clears the way for the stock issuers to seek the permission of the various state regulatory agencies where the shares will actually be sold.

Recalls financial officer Dewey, 'It was a unique offering in that we went to all 50 states. Very, very few stocks are sold in every state in the union but we had to because we wanted a dealer network in every state. Normally you don't do it that way because each state has its standards.'

And some states have what are known as 'blue-sky laws'. These impose a stricter standard of fairness than the federal standard. Under blue-sky laws it is not enough just to disclose the facts in an adequate and candid manner. While you may be able to sell shares easily in Nevada and Georgia, you come up against a very tough standard indeed in states such as Texas, Wisconsin and California.

Richard Kuntz, executive director of the Texas Securities &

Exchange Commission, handled the negotiations that followed when Dewey and Kimmerly arrived in Austin in January 1978 to file their offering there. Texas was important – there were plenty of wealthy high-rollers there and the rich markets of Dallas, Houston and Fort Worth.

'Under blue sky laws such as we have here, we can say no, this business is not fair, you cannot do this to the investors in this state. Because we feel that even if you have adequate disclosure, the complex language of securities law is such that the layman can get lost in the underbrush and the investor is not protected,' Kuntz explains.

They raised plenty of objections in Texas, and the record of those objections and similar complaints raised in Wisconsin, California and the other tough blue sky states should have been ample public warning for future investors and backers – had they cared to look. The objections raised in Texas alone should have been enough.

'First off we had problems with the cheap stock. But what we really fought over was the dilution of the stock he was trying to sell down here. He had his own shares that he had paid nothing for, and the officers of the company had options on other shares – about 650,000 – at about 10 cents apiece and here he was charging $5 for a share to our people,' Kuntz recalls.

'Dilution' is one of those rare legal-financial descriptions that can be taken literally; an investor who pays money for a share of stock has that investment's value 'diluted' by every share that is issued for free or at less than he paid for his shares. The percentage of dilution – or loss of equity and value – can be precisely measured by the number of shares issued and their respective prices.

'When you work it out, as we did, a Texas investor or any investor was paying $5 a share that was immediately worth only 30 cents as soon as he bought it. The remaining $4.70 of value accrued to Mr. DeLorean personally – or to his officers in the future – by virtue of their cheap stock. That's a dilution of value that runs somewhere between 80 to 90 percent by my unofficial calculations at the moment. Under our laws we get worried when a share offering here gets diluted by 20 percent or thereabouts; so we were *really* worried by the DeLorean offering.

'What we ended up doing was letting them have their registration here but on a limited basis. We ruled that we would allow it on the basis that the shares could not be sold to the general public. We let them sell shares only to people who wanted to go into the dealership,' Kuntz says. 'That, finally, was the best we could do.'

The objections in Texas and the other states kept Dewey, Kimmerly and the others flitting between Detroit, Austin, Sacramento and other state capitals for most of that summer and autumn of 1977.

Money came in from other states and, in August of 1977, Johnny Carson bought 250,000 shares at $2 a share, in a placement that was treated separately by most of the state securities regulators. In October the Canadian brokerage house of Wood Gundy Company, Ltd. came in with another $500,000, prompted by a young senior partner, Edward King, who was impressed by DeLorean and his venture.

For their large single investments, two seats on the DMC board were also included. King represented Wood Gundy while Johnny Carson's attorney Henry Bushkin became a director. Carson had a special interest in the car project by now. One of the objectives of his major commitment to the DMC-12 was the promise that he would become the advertising symbol, the official spokesman for the car when it was up and running. While these separate placements caused some worries about dilution among the state regulators, this did not slow the flow of money into the DMC coffers.

'Restricting us to dealers-only offerings as they did in Texas really was to our advantage, it added a little zip to our deal. This wasn't something for just anybody,' Dewey the financial officer says now. 'And it was a good proposition for a dealer. His entrance fee was $25,000 and for this he got not only 5,000 shares but the opportunity to sell the cars. On the price mark-up for the car, which was going to run $4,000 or so, all a dealer had to do was sell the first six or eight cars and he had recovered the cost of his investment plus he had the ownership of the shares and the franchise. So it was a pretty attractive deal in its own right.'

But the deal did not stand still. Sometime earlier, in 1975, John DeLorean had created DeLorean Manufacturing Company and transferred into it the assets of JZDC. In October 1977, Kimmerly restructured the entire corporate alignment to strengthen John's personal control over the growing assets. First off, DeLorean Motor Company paid 300,000 of its shares which were valued at $5 each – or $1.5 million total – to DeLorean Manufacturing Company, for ownership of Composite Technology Corporation (CTC) and for the non-automotive development rights to the ERM plastic resin process. Over the years to come DeLorean Motor Company paid another $1.5 million in billings to CTC, its own wholly-owned subsidiary, for various engineering and design jobs, money that somehow vanished from that company's coffers. In 1982, when CTC went into bankruptcy liquidation, the bankruptcy trustees were able to win bids of only $250,000 for its assets and net worth.

But the reshuffling was even more ambitious than a sell-off of questionable subsidiaries from one company to another. In another part of the restructuring, DMC *reacquired* the rights to the development of the DMC-12 car and the automotive use of the ERM method from the DSCP partnership by issuing each of the three dozen partners part of a total issue of 99,995 new shares of DMC's $8 cumulative dividend convertible preferred stock.

'This was a very attractive thing on paper for the partners. They were coming into DeLorean Motor Company with preferred stock with a conversion right downstream if they wanted to, into common stock. And their dividends were accumulating, a preferred $8 a share dividend that was piling up at a rate of about $1.6 million a year. So in theory if the company had gotten off and running they would have had quite a windfall of dividends and they were not being diluted since there was no other preferred stock in the company. Plus of course their original partnership investment of $100,000 had had its tax write off consequences,' Dewey notes.

Of course, all of this was in theory. The immediate effect was that DeLorean regained control of the assets he had put into DSCP – the car development work and the ERM process. He had spent the $3.5 million the partners had invested and he had rolled them into DeLorean Motor Company as preferred shareholders at no dollar cost to himself. The DSCP partners also had the option to become DeLorean car dealers without putting up the $25,000 entrance fee required of the later dealer-investors.

The box score at this point looked like this. John DeLorean had sold Johnny Carson half a million dollars worth of DMC stock, 125,000 shares of which had come out of his own holdings. Thus he had picked up $250,000 in cash that had been meant for the company. Then DMC gave him 300,000 new shares for ownership of CTC. This left DeLorean owning a 64 percent interest in DeLorean Motor, since the DSCP partnership was now dissolved and the remaining partners had been rolled into DMC through the preferred stock gambit. He now had firm control of the $6.1 million in new capital that the early dealers, Carson and Wood Gundy, had pumped in and it had cost him nothing. Not even the personal effort to sell the shares.

By this time, as Dick Brown would note, 'we felt we could build a car company in spite of John DeLorean. I was seeing quite a bit of him during this period. He was pompous and loud. He would get on an airplane and start talking business in a loud voice, or if we were in a restaurant he would talk loud enough to make sure everyone heard him and recognized him. But he really didn't do anything and he wasn't responsible for either conceiving of or recruiting the dealer-investor network.'

Brown and a former Mazda associate Robert Holberg had recruited many of the dealers for the DSCP partnership and it was they who were now coming up with the bulk of the 400 dealer-investors that was set as the target.

'We wanted the dealers to invest because we wanted to retain their interest and the only way to do that was to give them equity participation. And we had a solid no-nonsense presentation worked out that would appeal to the kind of sophisticated investor we wanted. After the first two presentations in Dallas and Houston we agreed that we had to keep John out of it, otherwise he would blow the whole deal then and there.'

Holberg recalls, 'The original idea was that we would make the presentation and then John would come into the room for the closing remarks. He exaggerated so much that people lost confidence in our presentation and you could see the prospects falling off right away. He didn't just talk about the car, he bragged about how he was already moving on to bigger and better things. He confused them with claims that he was going to build this and invest in that when he hadn't really won their support yet for the car project.'

And all the while, as the money flowed in from 1977 through early 1978, DeLorean's level of spending rose to meet it.

'I really had not anticipated that he would be so reckless and self-serving with other people's money. I was stunned by it. I criticized John for it to his face and his response was to tell me that I didn't understand, that I really wasn't participating in the management of the company there in New York. He was right about that, I was way far away in California. So he put me off," says Brown.

'The thing about John was that in many ways he was like a child who had never had any discipline. He tried to see how far he could go with a thing and if you yelled about it, often he retreated. He'd say, "Well, you're right about that, we won't do that anymore." He sent Nesseth around and Nesseth tried to take over one of the promotional meetings – one in Las Vegas, I think – and I called John and said, "Get this guy out of here or I leave" And John said, "No don't do that," and he yanked Roy right away.

'But John never stopped trying things. I guess I thought that, as the organization took shape, the corporate organization itself would provide the discipline on John DeLorean. We had a public offering with the dealers and we were registered with the SEC; I figured the SEC regulations alone would provide some kind of limits on him. After that I hoped the British government was not going to give him all that money without the necessary controls. But I was wrong,' Brown now says.

In May, the Kansas State Bank filed suit against DeLorean and ultimately against Nesseth. The previous September the bank had demanded and got a meeting with Kimmerly to discuss its loans. General Motors informed the bank that it was pulling both the Pontiac and Cadillac franchises out unless Nesseth was replaced by another buyer. When the buyer was located, Kimmerly talked the bank into negotiating a debt consolidation. Poor Dahlinger was out of it, he had left town anyway. So the bank took all the previous financings and put them together into one $1.3 million loan to DeLorean who used the proceeds to buy the land under the dealership. The idea was that the new dealer would pay enough rent to pay off the majority of the debt. The remainder of the debt was to come from a massive sell-off of the used car branch of Dahlinger Motors. DeLorean signed a personal guarantee for that part of the loan since the rest was secured by the mortgage on the land.

From September 1977 through May 1978, Nesseth used all his powers as a salesman to unload the used Cadillacs and Pontiacs from the Dahlinger lot. The proceeds of the sale disappeared, however, and in some cases the buyers of the cars had their property seized by the county government because the money that was supposed to go for taxes and licence plates had been appropriated by Nesseth. Although the litigation took three years and involved appeals to the courts of both California and Kansas, Nesseth ended up having to return $130,000 from this scam and DeLorean himself had to put back nearly $300,000 more.

DeLorean looked over three potential sites for his factory in Pennsylvania and even took an option on one. He was genuinely interested in Pennsylvania, but not in the financial package the state offered. It was not enough. Bob Dewey and his financial team had been working out how much was needed, and they estimated that approximately $75 million for a factory, machinery, tooling and working capital would see the vehicle through to pilot production.

DeLorean gave up on Pennsylvania, but not on getting that money. Who in 1978 had the most money in the world? The Saudi Arabians, of course. DeLorean found himself a Saudi and turned on his charm. He could offer an almost irresistible package. At the time, the Saudis were being blamed for wrecking the world economy, and the auto industry in particular, by increasing the oil price six-fold in the previous two years. The world financing system also had a new problem: how to recycle the $60 billion surplus that OPEC had piled up? Arab money at the time had assumed a special quality. And what better venture was there for a rich Saudi to invest in during the mid-1970s than a new, ethical, economical car, creating jobs and prosperity? DeLorean's negotiations with the Saudi were handled by the First Boston Corporation, which was keen on both John and his dealings with their friendly Saudi. The Saudi was also keen on having the project go to a third world country. But like many Arabs, this particular Saudi wanted anonymity.

His name was Ojjeh Akram.

CHAPTER FIVE

Puerto Rico and Ireland

At various times DeLorean had disclosed promises of financial support from Maine, Ohio, Rhode Island and 'two Canadian provinces'. He had also hinted that Spanish industrial sources had offered to provide capital and facilities.

In 1977 while press attention centred on Pennsylvania, DeLorean was discovering the Caribbean island of Puerto Rico. It was First Boston that brought Puerto Rico into the picture. The bank had a subsidiary there and was alerted by their man on the scene that the Puerto Rico Economic Development Administration, or Fomento as it preferred to be known, was offering large, generous aid packages to potential investors, particularly to foreign firms, which would provide both jobs and prestige. A DeLorean car plant would offer both.

Early in 1977, John flew to San Juan and drove the 80 miles to the northwest corner of the island. At Borinquen there was the old, abandoned Ramey U.S. Air Force Base that Fomento planned to turn into an industrial zone. Nearby was the town of Aquadilla, one of Puerto Rico's larger cities, where the necessary labour could come from. There were few trained people but labour was cheap, and the Puerto Ricans were very enthusiastic. So was DeLorean.

Through February and into March they negotiated. By March 23, there was a written offer. A week later, Fomento set out the agreed-upon deal in a memorandum of understanding. John had had his first experience at serious negotiation with a government and had acquitted himself well. However, he made one major mistake, which he was later to kick himself for: he agreed to put $25 million up front. He was still a novice at these negotiations; by the time it came to Northern Ireland he would be a master.

The DeLorean team consisted of Collins, Dewey, Brown and

Terry Werrell, a production man who DeLorean had hired from GM. They did some calculation and estimated that they needed a 500,000 square-foot factory, plus 50,000 of administrative space. They would also need a test track and storage space for the finished cars. Puerto Rico was a long way from the component makers, which were mostly grouped around the big three in Detroit. But there were 185 acres of space at Ramey, an airstrip they could use and reasonable shipping facilities.

The memorandum of understanding, dated April 4, 1977, was the basis of an agreement that was to be argued over for the next year. Besides the initial equity of John DeLorean ($3.5 million based on his rights in the DMC-12) and the partnership (their matching $3.5 million), DMC was expected to raise not less than $25 million 'additional equity capital'. It was reiterated again and again that the whole package hinged on this. DeLorean had convinced Fomento he would have the money within weeks, that his Saudi – Ojjeh Akram – was very excited about the project. He had still not signed a single dealer and would not be able to until he had updated the prospectus to take account of the plant site in Puerto Rico, but he had claimed that he would raise a minimum of $3,750,000 from 150 dealers and a maximum of $10 million from 400 dealers.

The memorandum went on: 'DMC expects to raise the balance of the equity from private investors which will be evidenced by commitments acceptable to Fomento by April 15, 1977' – only 11 days away.

Alejandro Vallecillo, then the Administrator of the Puerto Rico Economic Development Administration, signed the memorandum and sent it off to DeLorean for his signature. DeLorean hesitated. Suddenly that Arab money was not so assured. A few days later, First Boston told him the bad news: Ojjeh had pulled out.

De Lorean was to claim afterwards that Ojjeh did so because U.S. securities laws would have required that his identity be publicly revealed and he feared that members of his family might be kidnapped and held for ransom. The true story of his defection at this crucial time was more mundane and vastly more significant.

Ojjeh Akram was born in Syria and only became a naturalized Saudi in 1950. Since then he had built one of that country's leading industrial companies, Technique d'Avant Garde Finance, which specialized in high-quality prefabricated building construction projects. The car project had initially appealed to Ojjeh. His son Mansour was a student at UCLA and a fan of DeLorean, and Ojjeh himself was attracted to the concept of an 'ethical car' that also would be constructed in a Third World economy – as Puerto Rico certainly was.

But Ojjeh was not just going to take the word of John DeLorean, nor the recommendations of First Boston, without doing some checking on his own. He asked his principal American bank, a leading institution outside New York, to do a top-secret, for-his-eyes-only investigation. The bank hired experts, including the leading motor car engineering specialist in Detroit, Zora Duntov.

Given that Ojjeh was openly enthusiastic about the deal, the bank could have satisfied its important customer by whipping up a report that endorsed his wishes. Instead the report turned out to be the best analysis of the DeLorean project ever done. Scrupulous to the point of keeping its investigators anonymous – Duntov was referred to throughout as 'Mr. X' – it put forth an astonishing array of arguments and proof against Ojjeh's participation in the project.

No one reading this analysis would put a penny into John DeLorean's dream car. In the light of history, one cannot but speculate what would have happened if the Northern Ireland and British officials had done the same kind of exercise a year or two later.

The bank's analysts told Ojjeh that DeLorean's car might have been viable before the OPEC oil crisis, but it no longer was. The whole market had changed and John DeLorean had not caught up with it. He was still back in his GM days, an entirely different era. The U.S. sports car market was no longer a growth area, and a so-called 'ethical car' could not easily be reconciled with building a sports car that would only be bought by the idle rich in the first place. Glamour was out; utilitarianism was in. The report went on to state that the only group of people who would still buy a high performance sports car would have to earn more than $75,000 a year; and they would prefer a Mercedes, Porsche or Jaguar.

In addition to 'Mr. X's' scathing comments about the car's design and capabilities (he had driven the prototype DMC-12s on a regular basis), the analysis also noted that the overall market for sports cars was in sharp decline in America; it had once been a 30,000-cars-a-year sales environment, but it no longer was. And it was certainly not the 200,000-car market that John DeLorean had told Ojjeh it would be.

Competition in the sports car market was going to get ferocious. A new model Corvette was to be introduced in 1979, and GM had a completely new version, freshly engineered, already on the shelf ready for launch in 1981. If DeLorean's car began to see even 10,000 units of sales, and that seemed unlikely, GM would bring out its new version even sooner. There was the fox box series from Ford, and Honda was said to have a new sports car ready for the spring of 1979. These would all be priced at under $10,000. The DMC-12 was now priced at a probable $11,000-plus, which made it too expensive.

Then there was the colour, which the analysis saw as a major flaw. For instance, only one-third of the Corvettes sold were silver grey because many Corvette owners liked to have their own distinctive colour. No DMC-12 owner could have that. 'The more cars DeLorean sells, the more common the product will become and, thus, the less attractive it will be to the prospective buyer.'

Since the 55-mph speed limit had been imposed, sports car owners tended to compensate by cruising with the top off. This would be impossible in the gull-wing DeLorean.

The product was wrong: too highly priced and not exceptional enough for the new market conditions. It might have been right for the market of four or five years earlier when the typical sports car buff, a male between 25 and 40, wanted performance, styling and exclusivity. Now they wanted safety, quality and value for their money. Producing the DMC-12 in Puerto Rico would 'definitely have a negative impact on its quality image'. It was no use trying to make a unique feature out of the air-bag: either it would be compulsory, and all cars would have it, or it would not be allowed.

The report went on to say that DeLorean was 'considered an

outstanding automotive engineer and his successes at GM are attributable to his certain charisma'.

There was more, much more; but the basic conclusion was brisk enough: 'We can envision a situation where production is delayed for one year, first year sales volume is in the area of 5-7,000 units, unit costs exceeding forecast, price increases ruled out by competitive pressures, and warranty costs running $500 a car. Under this set of circumstances, shareholders equity would show a deficit of the order of $20-25 million calling into question the company's continued economic viability and/or the requirement of substantial additional capital.'

That was remarkably prescient, except that the delay was two years rather than one and the deficit correspondingly larger.

Ojjeh was warned he might well find he was the only source of new capital. And because the company would be public, the Saudi would face the same responsibilities – and exposure – as any other director. (The bank felt obliged to enclose a special appendix setting out the responsibilities of a director.) Finally, and this was perhaps a crucial point, Ojjeh would be a second class shareholder, in the same way the dealers were, with his investment made at a much higher cost than DeLorean himself or the other early investors, including Johnny Carson.

At the end of April, Ojjeh said: No, thanks, and walked away.

Ojjeh Akram easily found another place to invest his money. Later in 1977 he became a world celebrity when he bought the luxury ocean liner, *France*, for roughly $20 million. A week later he was back in the headlines when he paid another $20 million for a superb 202-piece collection of French furniture, the unique Wildenstein collection. The furniture would grace the soon-to-be-refurbished luxury liner, Akram told the press, as part of his plan to turn it into 'a little travelling French city'.

But while Ojjeh Akram could blithely walk away from his near-folly, his departure left John DeLorean in a very deep hole. He had to have that money to get his Puerto Rico deal off the ground. He had absolutely counted on it. The Puerto Ricans were adamant on that $25 million of new equity before they would budge.

For the next year, DeLorean tried everything he knew to raise that money. He could not sign up a single dealer until the SEC had given its approval for the prospectus and that approval would not be given until it was amended to allow for the proposed location in Puerto Rico. But there was no Puerto Rico deal until he had his $25 million. It was a vicious circle that left him bitter against Ojjeh in particular and, later, all Arabs in general. 'You just have lots of cups of tea with them. You sit, you talk and nothing happens,' he once remarked. 'Back in the Sixties,' he told the *Detroit Free Press*, 'any moron with an idea could raise capital. Now it's impossible. If you want to know what raising venture capital is like; well, most people say it's impossible. If it's accomplished, it will be the most incredible accomplishment of the last 100 years!'

DeLorean was forced to extend his agreement with Puerto Rico until October 31, by which stage he had to have his minimum 150 dealers. He made that one, but he was still a long way from the requirement of 400. By the end of the year he had signed up 177 dealers, but he had wasted a full year; his whole programme was now getting even further behind his original target.

Then, as 1978 opened, things livened up again. A new location was emerging right under his Bloomfield Hills nose: Detroit, itself – his own home town!

On December 15, a story broke in the *Detroit Free Press*,

> Detroit officials are quietly trying to assemble a financial package sweet enough to lure General Motors executive John Z. DeLorean into locating his planned $90 million sports car company in the city.

DeLorean was learning the art of bargaining for development aid money. He could toss Spain into a conversation with the Puerto Ricans, saying he had an offer to go there, and watch them sweat. Now he would do the same with Detroit. He was also at pains to point out that Detroit was pursuing him, not the other way around. John had met Detroit's Mayor Young a number of times, impressing him with the possibility of a plant employing 2,000 people, with an annual payroll of over $35 million and the extra jobs that would be created. Said Anthony

Devito, Detroit's planning director, 'We're pursuing him . . . We have to convince him.' The Detroit officials planned to tap some of the $300 million assigned under the federal government's new Urban Development Action Grant Program which would come into effect on January 1, 1978. This programme was specifically earmarked for distressed cities with high unemployment and a need for development.

DeLorean delayed the filing of his prospectus with the SEC while waiting to see if Detroit could come up with an attractive package. He had already been trying for nearly a year and had not been able to raise the money the Puerto Ricans required. They again extended the deadline, until January 31, but were showing obvious signs of impatience and annoyance that he was talking to Detroit as well.

On January 22, the Detroit City Council unanimously approved a financing plan, stepping up the pressure still further. The city held two weeks of open discussion on the project, including a public hearing at a school near the proposed site just south of Jefferson to the west of the Conner Creek Power Plant. There was, reported the *Free Press*, 'only modest opposition'.

Egged on by the Puerto Rican proposals, the Detroit City Council was coming up with an astonishingly attractive package for a city that was already heavily industrialized. Even Kenneth V. Cockrel, the one reluctant councilman, supported DeLorean in the vote. 'There was no real alternative if the city wanted jobs,' he said. 'That's really the bottom line.'

But DeLorean still had to find that extra $25 million. Now, however, there was new hope. Oppenheimer and Company, the Wall Street firm, was working on it for him.

So DeLorean had two offers and could play one off against the other. It was Detroit versus Puerto Rico.

2

Then, one day early in 1978, a young man called Liam Keilthy happened to be driving through Michigan. Keilthy was the Irish Development Authority's (IDA) man in Chicago; his job was to attract American companies to go to Ireland and build factories, create jobs and exports and wealth for a nation which, until ten years before, was essentially a poor farming country.

Keilthy listened idly to the car radio tuned to the local Detroit station. Then he suddenly stiffened. The Detroit City Council, said a news announcer, had confirmed reports that it had approved a financing plan to lure former General Motors vice president John DeLorean to build an auto plant there. A similar offer from Puerto Rico expired on January 31, just a few days off. Keilthy was driving from Chicago to Detroit. Now he stopped long enough to make a phone call, checked a Bloomfield Hills address, and headed north past the huge Ford plants at Dearborn. By early afternoon he was in Bob Dewey's office.

At first Dewey and Collins did not take him too seriously. Mentally, they were focused on Puerto Rico. But they sat down with the Irishman and spent two hours going over the project with him. In turn, Keilthy told them about the industrial prospects for Ireland: it now had the highest economic growth rate in the whole of Europe and was even ahead of Japan; it was emerging into the industrial world rapidly; there was plenty of labour, much of it trained; thousands of Irishmen had gone to the English midlands to get jobs in the car plants there – and many had drifted back again. Would DeLorean Motor Company consider an approach from the Industrial Development Authority of Ireland?

'By then,' says Bob Dewey, 'we had people coming through the door all the time who wanted to tell us about their state or country and all their attributes. The only ones that really had any substance were Texas and Pennsylvania – I spent many days trying to put deals together there. And I spent many days in Puerto Rico. But there was also Kansas, Georgia, Detroit. And we had to go through it with each one because we never knew who the real one would be.' Dewey becomes almost anguished as he recalls the amount of work he put in on potential sites for the factory. 'I had Louisiana, I had Maine, Spain – I couldn't name them all. Spain was always John's great fall-back but I had a notion they wanted a large piece of John. There was this Spanish priest that used to come over and explain it and John would say, "Do you understand it?" and I'd say, "No, John, I don't understand it. I hope you do." It was gobbledygook to me.'

At the end of February, however, Puerto Rico finally seemed to have won the battle to build John DeLorean's dream car. It had more money to spend than Detroit and, although Detroit still hoped to win DeLorean over, most officials privately accepted the fact that the plant would be built in the Caribbean. On February 16, with tempers fraying and irritation openly showing, the Puerto Rican Council in Washington had finally got DeLorean to sign a new agreement prohibiting him from negotiating with anyone else for alternative plant sites. 'The agreement,' said Fomento's Alejandro Vallecillo, 'unequivocally states that the decision has been made to locate the plant in Puerto Rico. The agreement reaffirms the DeLorean Motor Company's commitment to locate its plant in Aguadilla and states that no other sites are being nor will be considered.'

The new agreement expired at the end of May. The Puerto Ricans were ecstatic. They had won: Detroit was out! They did not know that Ireland was now in. Nor did Oppenheimer's Mike Hayes, who was busily raising money with a prospectus that carefully assessed the abilities and working habits of the Puerto Ricans.

In Dublin, the IDA had decided it was time to speed things up. DeLorean was obviously sceptical about going to Ireland – why should he be anything else? The IDA used a tactic that it had employed before on Americans who were ignorant of the modern Ireland – they drafted one of the Irish 'mafia' of American businessmen who could invite DeLorean to dinner or lunch in a familiar American environment and persuade him that Ireland was to be taken seriously.

The man chosen for the task was Ireland's greatest star in the business world – in fact, in several other worlds, too. In his home country he was almost a legend. At 42, Tony O'Reilly had already been the president and chief operating officer of the huge H. J. Heinz Company of Pittsburgh for six years. (He is now president and chief executive officer.) To Irishmen, however, his greatest feats had been on the rugby field where he was arguably the greatest player the country had produced since the war. A tall, dashing figure with flaming red hair, he had run the Heinz operation in Britain and then moved to Pittsburgh where, by the time he was 36, he was that worldwide company's head. He still had substantial interests in

Ireland, and was already a wealthy man. Not even DeLorean, with his notorious contempt for almost everyone else, could look down on O'Reilly – physically or in any other way.

In Pittsburgh O'Reilly had a call from the New York director of the IDA, who explained the situation and said, 'Look, would you mind meeting with Mr. DeLorean?' O'Reilly instantly agreed – he was quite looking forward to it. So the IDA set up a dinner at the Plaza Hotel in Pittsburgh.

O'Reilly talked to DeLorean about the problems, perils and potential of Ireland. O'Reilly knew Puerto Rico well. Heinz has a large tuna and pet food plant in Miaguez and is one of the three biggest employers on the island. He knew the grant structure, the problems, the advantages of Puerto Rico far better than DeLorean did. It gave his support for his native Ireland that extra degree of credibility.

O'Reilly offered to host a dinner party at his Pittsburgh home, get together a group of Irish-American businessmen, and have DeLorean along to meet Dr. Martin O'Donohue, the Irish Minister for Economic Planning and Development, who was due in the United States soon.

A few weeks later, the dinner party took place. O'Reilly had organized it well – he had some leading business dignitaries including Krome George, chairman and chief executive of Alcoa, which is also based in Pittsburgh.

DeLorean arrived after the others and started straight away on a monologue. He was barely civil.

O'Reilly was not offended, and nor were the others. 'At the end of the meal DeLorean sort of stood up and started to phone his wife and friends, without any reference to the host. Now Irish dinner parties often have a character of their own, so I wasn't alarmed at it, but I was a little dismayed because I didn't think he was winning friends and influencing people like that. Martin O'Donohue had come a long way and he is an extremely intelligent, well-versed economist. There was a lot he could have told DeLorean about the Irish economy. And it is not that I felt like he was not being treated with proper reverence, but I just felt that as an evening, although it was very pleasant socially, it seemed to proceed on the assumption that whoever got the DeLorean car company would be extremely fortunate. By removing himself from the dinner almost before it had finished, there was some surprise. I think of that marvellous line "delusion of grandeur is the curse of the Celt". I think he was suffering from the curse of the Celt that night.'

In March, DeLorean sent Bill Collins off to Ireland to assess the working habits of the Irish and to inspect what the Irish had in mind for the DeLorean factory – a new plant in Limerick built by the IDA for the Dutch firm Akzo. Then in April, it was DeLorean's turn to go. 'It takes a lot for John to go away for four or five days,' says Dewey. 'You don't get him to spend that amount of time anywhere unless there is a pretty good chance he's going to get a good deal.' The deal was beginning to take shape, and it looked highly promising. DeLorean was stalling Puerto Rico, keeping Ireland secret for the moment.

In Dublin, the Irish Industry Minister Desmond O'Malley hosted a dinner for him. Despite himself, DeLorean had responded to the place, and he was impressed with the businesslike way the IDA went about its affairs. He turned his full charm and persuasive power on O'Malley.

For the Irish Minister it was riveting stuff. DeLorean's reputation had preceded him. Every Irish schoolboy knows that General Motors is the biggest company in the world. Here was the man who had nearly got to the top of it. The Irish, too, have an almost mythical respect for Americans, particularly tall, well-groomed, tanned and obviously wealthy Americans.

DeLorean outlined his thesis on the decline and fall of the American automobile industry and General Motors in particular, and how it could be saved if people stopped designing committees and started designing cars again.

In Ireland, DeLorean said, he wanted to build a car to the same standards as Porsche or Mercedes. He had plans for a sedan after the sports car, new revolutionary cars that would be built with materials that would last. There would not just be 2,000 jobs, but 5,000 – maybe ten. He had an idea for a bus – America didn't build buses. Everyone wanted his factory: Puerto Rico, Detroit, Spain. He had rich backers behind him, Middle Eastern money that would come in.

O'Malley was impressed. 'He's what we want here,' he told a colleague. DeLorean sensed it, and he had discovered something else that day: the proposed factory was in O'Malley's own constituency. There had to be a lever here that no one had yet thought of, and he, John DeLorean, was going to use it. When he did, he found he had misjudged his men.

At Oppenheimer, the team, including Mike Hayes, had completed their analysis of Puerto Rico. They were getting ready to close. By April 22, they would have $22 million ready to go into the DeLorean project. They had sold $150,000 unit shares in a limited partnership to be called, simply, the DeLorean Research Limited Partnership. The partners would put up 20 percent of the new company's capital and, in return, could write off 99 percent of the company's losses against their own income. It meant that effectively they were investing '30 cent dollars' – they were all in the 70 percent tax bracket, and through Oppenheimer's clever scheme they would get tax relief on their investment. Or so they thought at the time. If the project succeeded, they would be able to take either royalties or stock. At last, at long last, John DeLorean was about to get his money. However, there was one little problem. DeLorean hadn't yet told Oppenheimer that he was thinking of going to Ireland, and they hadn't told their clients. As far as everyone was concerned, it was Puerto Rico. After all, John had signed an exclusive agreement with them, had he not?

Mike Hayes had done most of the donkey work, often taking DeLorean with him to meet the potential investors, travelling widely with him around the country. The two had become good friends, and Hayes had decided to invest his own money in the project. But he had been working flat out on it for six months and needed a vacation. With everything now complete, he took his family to Virginia Beach, a small resort near Norfolk, Virginia.

Hayes, for no reason he could fathom, suddenly felt a stir of unease. He had learned that John DeLorean was secretive, difficult to get information from. Hayes trusted what DeLorean did give him, but felt he had to drag it out. John never volunteered anything. There was only one phone Hayes could use in Virginia Beach, and he called the lawyers, Javits and Javits, in New York. How was the closing going? Everything being signed okay? No, it was not! 'DeLorean's delaying it,' the lawyer told him. 'There is something wrong.'

The phone was in an Italian delicatessen, and Hayes spent the next seven hours on it, with the proprietor ready to kill him. He soon discovered what was wrong. The Governor of Puerto Rico had made a statement. DeLorean was breaking his agreement and negotiating with the Irish.

Oppenheimer had a number of men still down in Puerto Rico working on the details. They had spent weeks on the island. Now, the anger of the Puerto Ricans could almost be felt in New York. The team had to telephone all their investors saying, 'It's not Puerto Rico any more. It's the Republic of Ireland.' They did not even know what the wage rates were there, had not assessed the transportation situation, the package itself. The long, detailed analysis they had done on Puerto Rico was now a waste of time.

Oppenheimer would earn a $2 million fee for putting the partnership together and another $1.8 million over five years for running it; but if there was no deal – and that was the way it looked – then there was no fee.

It was a gloomy Hayes who drove back to New York to start work on a new fact sheet and analysis of building the car in Limerick. He had one interested investor in Des Moines whom he called to advise that the vehicle was going to be built in Ireland. 'Then, I'm out of the deal,' said his client. 'I'm not putting a cent in. You can't manufacture anything there. I had a little company there and couldn't make any money. There were labor problems and all kinds of other problems. I'm out.' Enough investors stayed in, however, to make it still workable. Instead of $22 million, Oppenheimer now had about $20 million.

By late April the Irish package was basically in place. The IDA would put up $13 million equity, which would consist of the factory. Then there would be $22 million in grants, which would have to be repaid if the company failed within ten years. There would be no taxes, no royalties to pay. Worked out over the period of the project, it was roughly in line with the Puerto Rican deal, although with less cash. With the Oppenheimer money, it was enough.

But DeLorean now asked for more, believing he had O'Malley hooked. He said he wanted more Irish government money by way of training or employment grants. He wanted to put in less himself. Control would be from DMC in New York, which would become a large conglomerate, the Irish factory a small part of the whole. Dr. Michael Killeen, the head of the IDA, was getting suspicious. It was Killeen who had turned the IDA into the success it was and he had laid down strict vetting procedures that not even DeLorean was going to short-cut. As a result of other investigations, the Irish were doing some rethinking.

Killeen had met DeLorean only once, briefly, at a cocktail party in New York when someone had thought they should be introduced. Martin O'Donohue had not reported favourably, and O'Donohue carried a good deal of weight. But Killeen did not allow himself to get too close, leaving the direct dealings to other negotiators. In May, they were getting near to signing. The lawyers were drawing up the papers, supervised by Dewey and Walter Strycker, a San Francisco financial consultant who had recently joined the team.

The change in the Irish stance began to come through during those final days of negotiation. 'We felt somewhere during the course of that week,' says Dewey, 'that they were starting to play games with us and that there was something else going on. We weren't getting a true reading about whether the Republic was really going to fulfill all the promises, or whether there were people up the hierarchy who were throwing cold water on it. We didn't quite understand what was going on. It became a mystery when you didn't get to sit down and talk with the top people.'

Then what had already been going sour turned even more so. At a meeting between the two teams, DeLorean suddenly opened up about his huge dreams. 'It was a sort of Global Motors – he was envisioning this huge conglomerate as only he can do. All you have to do is encourage John a little bit and he will start puffing and puffing and puffing and going into his dreams,' says Dewey. 'And these people were sitting there, visualizing this man going on and acquiring General Motors and some day making a tender offer. And they got really blown out of proportion and everybody became very alarmed. I felt that the Irish became very alarmed about whether they weren't just a stepping stone in a huge pyramid. And the whole deal just started crumbling.'

Afterwards, Walter Strycker described the reactions of the IDA people and the Irish officials: 'Their jaws just kind of dropped and their eyes got big, and then they recessed for a special meeting. And then they came back and said they wanted absolute control over the management of the company for seven years.' DeLorean, of course, would not accept that.

'They had already started changing the deal on us,' says Dewey. 'And then I think the thing was really lost when we started discussing constraints on John, and he was playing hardball. It was all over.'

DeLorean still believed he had O'Malley on his side and that would swing the deal his way.

Instead, Killeen called his team together for his own meeting at the IDA. They reviewed the project. There were technical doubts – the car had no clearance on emissions, on safety or, indeed, on anything else. One member of the team, John Kerrigan, believed the DMC-12 was too expensive at over $11,000 – too close to the Porsche and too far above the Corvette. The surveys showed the market was very price-sensitive. He didn't believe the costing figures either; and there was no provision in the financing plan for new models. But above all, it was DeLorean's character and behaviour they were all worried about. Like the Saudi, the Irish could see themselves as the only source of funds if things went bad. 'It could be a huge gobbler of money,' someone remarked. They were also disturbed by DeLorean's unshakeable and unreal optimism. He simply would not admit that there were any circumstances, no matter how bad, under which the project could fail. 'The minister's keen on it,' one of the IDA men said. They all knew that by now and had come to resent very much the way DeLorean was trading on O'Malley's enthusiasm, but they also knew something DeLorean had not bothered to find out: the minister did not make the decisions at IDA.

Killeen decided to reject John DeLorean. He picked up the phone and asked for Desmond O'Malley. The minister accepted it without argument.

Back in New York, Mike Hayes and his team began telephoning their clients again. 'That DeLorean project – well, it's not Ireland after all. We're back in Puerto Rico.'

'Okay,' said the investor in Des Moines. 'I'll go back in. I'll reinvest.'

In fact they were not back in Puerto Rico. The Republic of Ireland may have gone, but there was another part of Ireland: richer, less critical, and desperate for jobs. John DeLorean was going to Belfast.

CHAPTER SIX

Northern Ireland

For centuries, Northern Ireland had been the only part of Ireland that could boast any real industry. For 100 years it led the world in fine linen, was a major shipbuilder and producer of complex and sturdy textile machinery. Its Harland and Wolff shipyard had built the unsinkable *Titanic*, not perhaps its proudest achievement, but it was no fault of the craftsmen who lived in the rows of terraced houses huddled around the huge shipyard that she hit an iceberg on her maiden voyage.

In the 60 years since Ireland was divided between the 26 counties of the South and the six 'Loyalist' counties of the North, Ulster had modernized much more rapidly than its neighbour, producing man-made fibres, motor industry components and aircraft. The Short Brothers plant in East Belfast turned out small, box-shaped, commuter aircraft and guided missiles.

But for all that, it remained the poorest, most neglected part of the United Kingdom. And, for a brief spell, the Irish Republic enjoyed the fastest growth rate in Western Europe. Killeen's organization was attracting foreign investment to Ireland that the Belfast officials felt should have gone there; and in 1978, competition between the two was considerable. But Killeen, in Dublin, had to be sparing and careful with his money. Because of the violent reputation of the North, the policy was to take greater risk, offer more money.

In 1976, Dr. George Quigley, a senior civil servant, prepared a report on the Province's economic and industrial strategy. His conclusions had not been encouraging. 'The Northern Ireland economy is in serious difficulty, and if no measures are taken, the outlook is grim,' he wrote. 'The wide gap between average income per head of population here and in Great Britain must, at best, endure and, at worst, enlarge.' This report was especially concerned with the growing division in the population, not just between Catholic and Protestant, although there was that too, but between the haves and the have-nots. The haves, essentially, were those with jobs; the have-nots, the growing population of the unemployed.

For the recession had hit Ulster hard, harder than any other part of Europe. Its shipyard could still boast the largest crane in Europe, dominating the Belfast skyline, but each of its 7,000 workers cost the state a subsidy of about $8,000 a year. In 1950, the shipyard employed 20,000 people; now, it was a third of that. Belfast's textile industry had declined by two-thirds in 25 years. Man-made fibres were in massive world over-supply. The car industry in mainland Britain was apparently in terminal trouble, causing cutbacks in Ulster's engineering firms.

Male unemployment of 50 percent in towns such as Strabane, Newry, Fermanagh and West Belfast meant they were breeding grounds for violence. It was there that the IRA could recruit at will, feeding on the festering hatred of the Catholic population who, for generations past, had seen themselves as a disadvantaged people, still fighting the ancient enemy across the Irish Sea.

In his report, Dr. Quigley recommended a reorganization and beefing up of the inducements to encourage 'blue chip' overseas companies (particularly American) to come and invest in Northern Ireland. Against the reputation of the place for bombings and outrage, it was an uphill task. But by the time DeLorean came along, Quigley's plan was winning.

Northern Ireland now offered 40 to 50 percent capital grants, plus employment grants, interest relief grants, grants toward houses for key foreign employees and even rent grants. The Department of Commerce had soft loans, loan guarantees and hard loans. There were experts and factories and factory sites – anything and everything the prospective investor could desire if he would just come to Northern Ireland and create jobs. For jobs and prosperity were the one answer the politicians could agree on as a possible solution to the violence. 'Jobs, homes and hope – that's the way to beat the IRA,' said Roy Mason, Secretary of State for Northern Ireland.

John DeLorean was about to become part of the battle against the IRA.

2

Roy Mason was squat, thick-set and beetle-browed – a rough, tough-looking man, pale from too many late sittings in the House of Commons and the gruelling schedule that all ministers have to put up with. Beside him, John DeLorean appeared extra tall and thinner than ever, his mass of grey hair and his white shirt setting off his California tan. Mason looked the Barnsley coal miner he once was, while DeLorean seemed to be straight off a Hollywood set.

They sat in front of the microphones and the gathered press to give the world the glad tidings on August 3, 1978. Northern Ireland and DeLorean had signed a deal. A 550,000 square foot factory would be constructed on a 72-acre site on the Twinbrook industrial estate at Dunmurry, six miles to the southwest of the city. It was, said Mason, a tremendous breakthrough for the government. An initial 800 jobs would be created immediately just to build the factory; 600 permanent jobs after 1979; 1,500 more after that as the company hit its full stride of 30,000 cars a year.

DeLorean was enjoying himself. 'We aim to move from cow pasture to production within 18 months,' he told the press conference. His audience laughed appreciatively.

'But isn't it a rather high-risk venture?' asked a reporter.

'We have orders as of now for 30,000 cars,' said DeLorean smoothly. 'That is $300 million worth of business. Of course, there are going to be difficulties, a lot of hard work and many taxing problems. There always are. But I cannot agree with the description of this as a high-risk venture.'

Although he did not say it, the risk was now mostly taken by the British government. John DeLorean had talked Mason into giving him £54 million in grants, equity and loans. More importantly, DeLorean himself did not have to put in a penny. He could afford to be magnanimous. One of the reasons he had settled on Northern Ireland was, he said, because – of all the places which were chasing him – it had the most highly motivated, stable and dedicated work force. The financial incentives, he added off-handedly, were attractive, but not compelling. They were, in fact, approximately three times as attractive as the Dublin offer and twice those in the

Puerto Rican deal. For John DeLorean, that was a lot of compulsion.

As the news from Belfast flashed round the world, however, there were some who did not find it compelling at all – Governor Carlos Romero-Barcelo of Puerto Rico, for example. The Governor had put up with a great deal from DeLorean and had pulled out all the stops to get that plant at Aguadilla. Months of tortured negotiations had finally ended. He had even gone to New York to sign a deal with DeLorean. Now, there was no deal. He had some choice words to say about DeLorean in private and, in public, accused him of 'an open violation of good faith', 'duplicity', and of going 'behind our back'. He would be suing, he added venomously.

In the Wall Street office of Oppenheimer and Company, there was some discomfort, too. The DeLorean team had to telephone its whole list of prospective investors yet again with the third change of location. Mike Hayes got through to his man in Des Moines. 'Surprise, surprise! Remember we were going to Southern Ireland? Well, as you know, it's not Southern Ireland, but it's not Puerto Rico, either. It's – wait for it – Northern Ireland!' The phone exploded in his ear. 'Are you guys crazy? Do you know what you're doing? I'm going to get in my car, drive to New York, come up to your office and beat the shit out of you. You're torturing me. Go anywhere in the world! Go to hell! It beats calling me up and telling me you're going to Southern or Northern Ireland.' The phone slammed down. The man in Des Moines did not invest.

John DeLorean had played cat-and-mouse with the Puerto Ricans for 18 months. The IDA in Dublin took five months to vet his project and turn him down. In Northern Ireland, from first approach to the final signing on August 3, 1978, it took only 45 days. Mason was to say later that the project had been subjected to a very thorough evaluation. Yet few of the details in this book, which surely would have caused them to run from the project, were uncovered or even suspected. The Northern Ireland ministers saw and heard mostly what John DeLorean wanted them to.

3

It had been late evening on Sunday, June 18, when the DeLorean team had gathered in Belfast. It had been only the previous Wednesday that Killeen, after an IDA board meeting in Dublin, had telexed the news: the IDA was withdrawing its offer. Strycker had been expecting it. DeLorean, because of O'Malley's position, had not. He had still clung to his belief that the Ferenka factory had had a special rôle in the deal, and that Killeen had been bluffing. However he had been quick to recover when John Plaxton of Wood Gundy's London office had announced he had made contact with NIDA in Belfast – and they sounded keen.

DeLorean himself was not keen to stay overnight in Belfast. He had heard too many stories about it. He would be joining the others the next morning, flying overnight from New York, changing planes at London in time for nine o'clock shuttle to Belfast. He was due to join them the next morning at the offices of the Department of Commerce in Chichester Street, in the centre of Belfast, about 10.30. Walter Strycker and Al Cohen of the New York lawyers Paul, Weiss, Rifkind, Wharton & Garrison, booked into the battle-scarred Europa Hotel in the centre of Belfast. Plaxton joined them. Belfast was never the most lively of places. On a Sunday night it could be deadly – in more ways than one. While the three men checked in, the province was experiencing business as usual.

The day before, a police patrol had been ambushed by the provisional IRA (the Provos) near Bessbrook in South Armagh. One policeman was killed and his partner abducted. In retaliation that morning, the extremist Protestant group, the Ulster Freedom Fighters, kidnapped a Catholic priest. As DeLorean and his colleagues were settling in to their evening meal, the Protestant extremists released him. The Provos announced their victim had been 'executed'. The policeman's body did not turn up for three weeks; and then, a post-mortem established that he had died in the ambush. The 'abduction' was simply a tactic of the IRA to tie down the security forces.

None of the DeLorean team had had very high hopes of Northern Ireland at the beginning, particularly after their setback in the South. But Plaxton assured them there was money there – Wood Gundy was to get a large finder's fee – and DeLorean had been convinced enough to make the trip at short notice.

At nine the next morning Strycker took his team to the Department of Commerce offices where they began gentle preliminaries. Everyone was waiting for the arrival of DeLorean, a fabled figure. They were delighted the negotiations had failed in Dublin, although they assumed (and continued to assume) that it had been DeLorean who had pulled out, preferring Puerto Rico. Strycker did nothing to disillusion them. As they settled down, the news came that DeLorean was going to be late. Two hours out of Kennedy his plane had had to turn back with engine trouble. He had been immediately transferred to another plane but that put him more than four hours late. It would be early afternoon before he got in – and, after a flight like that, he would not be in much shape for a hard negotiating session. But they decided to press ahead with the schedule anyway.

A couple of hours later they left the Commerce offices to drive east out of the city's centre, past the towering cranes of the Harland and Wolff shipyard, and onto the sweeping four-lane motorway that runs past the Short Brothers plant and landing strip, along the coast to Holywood, an exclusive suburb of Belfast where the wealthy businessmen, civil servants and executives live well away from the violence. Here it was another world: fine houses overlooking the sparkling bay, the countryside lushly green in mid-summer, army patrols and armoured cars left well behind in the city centre.

Out here, loosely grouped around the bulk of Stormont Castle, were a series of government offices. Among them, on 100 Belfast Road, was the modern building which housed NIDA.

It was here that John DeLorean finally caught up with them. He had been travelling nearly 20 hours and had probably worked through the previous day as well. Yet he looked remarkably fresh. The officials were impressed. DeLorean insisted on going through the formalities again, introducing his team and setting out his objectives.

The next few days were to be the most fruitful in John DeLorean's career. By the end of it he would have a rough agreement for a deal and a plant in Northern Ireland. He himself however only stayed a couple of hours in Belfast that day. By late afternoon he was aloft again, flying back to London and on to Paris to talk to Renault about engines. It was Walter Strycker who would do the deal.

Back in Detroit, the others were only too happy it was that way. 'We've got to keep John out of it,' said Brown. 'He'll blow the deal for sure.' Brown was already experiencing problems with DeLorean at his investor meetings as he attempted to persuade the dealers to join. He usually did a carefully prepared presentation; then DeLorean would take questions. 'He comes in with these closing remarks, and you can tell there's an immediate falling off in the results,' he told the others. 'He exaggerates so much that people just lose interest.' Strycker had seen that in Dublin. Here, it was up to him, at least for the next few crucial days.

By now, Strycker, still only employed as a consultant by DeLorean, had the figures and presentation at his fingertips. The tall, slim Californian was low-key, sincere, persuasive. He had an attractive, educated voice. At that stage, he believed the DeLorean dream was going to work; and the officials were visibly impressed that DeLorean was represented by such a man.

He showed them a business plan prepared for Puerto Rico by Booz Allen and Company. He had a summary of it ready, projecting sales of 20,960 cars in 1980, producing revenues of $195 million and a profit of $6.8 million. By 1984, the projections showed sales of $280 million and profits of $45 million. There were some even healthier balance sheet projects: the company would have cash of $152 million in the bank within five years. The manufacturing project they were planning to build would cost around $85 million, and although the company hoped to raise approximately $40 million from dealers and other sources, that would be needed for development work on the car and for the distribution network. Unfortunately, there was a possibility that because the plan had now switched from the Irish Republic to the North, the Oppenheimer Limited Partnership would not go ahead. Would NIDA be prepared to fill that gap if necessary?

Strycker was able to inject a certain amount of urgency into the talks. Puerto Rico still had an offer on the table. They were being pressed to sign. There was a time limit on it. And, because of the abortive Dublin talks, time was running out.

By the end of the first day, there was already a rough deal. On Tuesday morning, NIDA had a special board meeting – it normally met the last Wednesday in every month at 10 in the morning. The operation looked very promising. The Department of Commerce seemed happy to come in for $55 million – $16 million to pay for the factory itself and another $35 million in grant assistance. That left NIDA to find $30 million, and it seemed possible. The Board nodded approval. Then Dennis Faulkner, NIDA chairman, Belfast businessman, colonel in the part-time Ulster Defence Regiment and brother of Northern Ireland's former prime minister, went into a huddle with the Commerce officials. He took with him Londonderry businessman Sean O'Dwyer, a Catholic businessman on the NIDA Board, and the deputy chief executive Tony Hopkins, and went to see Dr. Quigley, permanent secretary at the Department of Commerce.

Both the agency and the Commerce Department were in agreement. It was well worth pursuing, particularly if they could agree on a site in West Belfast, the constituency of Gerry Fitt, for many years Northern Ireland's leading Catholic politician. The assumption (one of the more naive ones, as things turned out) was that a Wall Street investment house would be no bad judge of the risk involved. Oppenheimer's senior partner, Jack Nash, was investing his own $150,000, and another Oppenheimer company, Sisyphus, was investing $300,000. If a Wall Street firm was willing to stake its own money and reputation, and if Northern Ireland could get in on the same basis, surely it couldn't be bad.

By Tuesday evening, after numerous meetings, there was an initial agreement: NIDA was to invest $17.5 million (£9.5 million) in a new Northern Ireland company identified for the moment as DeLorean Motor Company Northern Ireland. Because of Britain's exchange controls at the time, NIDA could not invest in DMC itself, so its investment in the new Belfast subsidiary would be linked to the value of DMC shares. That already weakened its position, and it was to be doubly unfortunate – exchange controls were abandoned by Mrs. Thatcher's government a year later.

On top of this there would be another $11.5 million (£6.3 million) for ten years, with no repayments for three years. The exchange rate being used was $1.825, although the pound, having been down to $1.53 at one stage at the end of 1976, was now starting to rise rapidly against the dollar. NIDA's shares, linked to the value of DMC's shares, could be bought by DMC if NIDA required it. On the other hand, in order to encourage DeLorean to get the project going quickly, DMC had the option for four years to buy out NIDA at cost plus 15 percent annual rate of interest.

Already the basis was being laid for the events which would haunt the enterprise over the next two-and-a-half years. The officials in Northern Ireland were used to dealing with major multi-nationals such as Du Pont or GM itself which had already invested in Northern Ireland. Their negotiating position in those days was at least partly based on the view that DeLorean, like all American investors that had come to them, was a major United States corporation which could guarantee the debts and problems of this new venture. It never seemed to occur to them that DeLorean Motor Corporation was nothing more than a shell company with scarcely a dozen and a half employees.

The result was that, even at these early stages, the fatal pattern was set. NIDA's money would be in the subsidiary, for which it would put up 94.5 percent of the capital but get 5.5 percent of the votes. Including the Commerce Department's $55 million, the Northern Ireland authorities were already at this early stage agreeing to invest $99 million, or £54 million, while DeLorean's contribution was to be exactly $1 million, or £546,000. DMC would have an exclusive licence to sell the cars made in Belfast, effectively weakening control by the Belfast authorities.

On Wednesday, the officials drew up the agreement. The preamble read:

> Based on the tripartite discussions held on 19 and 20 June 1978, the following assistance will, subject to the approval of the Secretary of State for Northern Ireland, be offered by the

Department of Commerce and the Northern Ireland Development Agency respectively to the company to be formed in Northern Ireland by the DeLorean Motor Company.

On three pages it then laid out the terms: the grants and loans from the Commerce Department, and the lease of the factory at Twinbrook at £1,000 a year for three years plus another 50,000 square foot factory free for five years. It went on to NIDA's contribution, including the right to appoint one director to the board of DMC and to the new Northern Ireland company. Then there were a few general conditions: that DeLorean would use its 'best endeavours' to employ 600 people when production started, 1,000 after a year and 2,000 after five years. A fourth condition related to the Oppenheimer money and would soon cause a major reworking of the arrangement. It stated that DMC would 'complete a satisfactory agreement in respect to the formation and financing' of the new Limited Partnership on the basis of the prospectus dated March 14, 1978. Although Strycker had hinted there might be problems, everyone assumed the Oppenheimer money was on the way.

The agreement was dated June 21, 1978 and was signed first by Walter P. Strycker with a flowing elegant hand. Next, Brian Lyttle signed for the Department of Commerce; finally, it was signed by Ronnie Henderson, NIDA's chief executive. Less than three days after opening negotiations in Belfast, the DeLorean team had a deal, signed and on the table. It was far from a final deal, of course. It was subject to checks, searches and investigations, but the broad terms had been set – Strycker's job was done. He rang John DeLorean in New York.

In the Oppenheimer office at One New York Plaza there was no great joy, however.

'That was when we found out what John was like,' said an Oppenheimer man later. 'He would just go off in his own way, and you couldn't find out what the hell he was doing. He wasn't reachable or whatever. Of course, our problem was that our investors wanted to know what the hell was going on and we couldn't provide them with the information because we didn't know. At this point we were shell-shocked.'

Oppenheimer, in fact, was so annoyed that it decided it

would not invest in Northern Ireland. It would forfeit its huge fee, but in the heat of the moment that seemed a small price to pay. The Limited Partnership it was attempting was already extremely delicate and difficult. They had tapped their own friends, DeLorean's friends, clients, anybody they thought was a high rate taxpayer interested in either cars or John DeLorean, anyone who had $150,000 to spare. Sammy Davis Jr. had agreed to invest that amount. So had the country singer Roy Clark; Amon G. Carter, the publisher from Fort Worth; author Ira Levin; the Craig Corporation, which made the stereo equipment for the DMC-12; and DeLorean's old friends Herb Siegel of Chris-Craft Industries (from whose office on Madison Avenue DeLorean was still working) and Gary B. Laughlin from Fort Worth. Laughlin's former wife Vivienne Wilson was also in for another $150,000.

Oppenheimer had nearly $20 million on the table. Now it decided it would not use it – not for Northern Ireland!

On Monday, June 26, the DeLorean negotiating team was back at NIDA. By now it consisted only of John Plaxton of Wood Gundy, who had flown in from his base in London. Plaxton announced himself as the negotiating link between the agency and Mr. DeLorean. DeLorean was handling the negotiations personally – but wasn't there. He was in New York, available by phone.

Faulkner was away, and so was Tony Hopkins. The NIDA negotiating team that morning consisted of two men: John Freeman, a shrewd moderate trade union leader, skilled in negotiating deals for his members but with no experience of the type of negotiation he was now thrown in to; and the chief executive Ronnie Henderson, not the strongest of personalities. Freeman, deputy chairman of NIDA, soon took charge and in the circumstances acquitted himself creditably although it would have taken a Henry Kissinger to bargain successfully with John DeLorean that day.

There was no Oppenheimer money, announced Plaxton. They would not invest if the project was going to Northern Ireland. So would NIDA fill the gap? What was the gap? Oppenheimer was raising $20 million, but that was only $18 million after its fat fee; so they were looking for another $18 million. Fine so far. But on what terms? Freeman was intent on getting the government's money in on the same terms as the Oppenheimer investors, and wanted all $18 million extra on that basis. DeLorean threw that back with a definite no. Freeman offered $12 million on the Oppenheimer basis, $6 million on loan.

For several hours the negotiations bounced back and forth. DeLorean was sitting in his office in the Chris-Craft building on Madison Avenue, doodling on his pad, tracing out artistic shapes as he habitually did, all the time playing with the numbers coming over the phone from Belfast. He began to throw figures in which wholly confused the two NIDA men. At one point Plaxton came back from a phone call to announce DeLorean's latest proposals: $47 million in equity, including the $17.5 million already promised. In return DMC would pay NIDA a royalty of $600 per car up to a maximum of $80 million, at which stage DMC would have the right to buy out the original equity for a nominal $5 million. No, said Freeman – but he was beginning to feel uneasy. This was not his scene, although he was learning fast. DeLorean seemed to be escalating the amounts all the time, and in trade union bargaining terms, he knew what that meant. He began digging in his heels. Henderson became worried for other reasons: he thought Freeman was going to blow the deal altogether.

DeLorean's next proposal was just as cavalier and audacious: $23.5 million equity to be repaid on a royalty basis with a return of 15 percent, plus $11.5 million in loans, and another $12 million to be repaid at $267 a car.

Freeman and Henderson by now were becoming anxious. George Quigley had suggested they try to fill the gap left by Oppenheimer – and that they should go for the same terms being offered to those investors. What they seemed to be arriving at was something vastly different – DeLorean was asking for more money, giving no concessions himself. Finally Freeman decided to try an old trade union negotiating tactic.

'Well, we're sorry,' he said to Plaxton. 'I'd like those jobs in West Belfast as much as anybody, probably more. But we don't seem to be getting anywhere. Unless you can persuade your principal to give way, there'll be no deal.'

Plaxton went again into Ronnie Henderson's office where he

was using the telephone. A few minutes later he emerged. 'I've just learned that the Governor of Puerto Rico has arrived in Washington within the past hour,' he announced. The Governor, DeLorean had told him, had come to sign an agreement with DeLorean. Unless they could agree with Northern Ireland tonight, the factory would be going to Puerto Rico.

Henderson paled; Freeman sensed the type of negotiating escalation he had seen often with employers. He decided to take a risk.

'Well, that's it then,' he said. 'I was very interested in the project, but I have to tell you I'm not happy with these financial arrangements. I regret it. But there we are. With the greatest of reluctance, we have to tell you we can't agree your terms. You'll have to sign with Puerto Rico.'

Henderson hadn't expected Freeman to take that line, at least not so strongly. Plaxton, too, was taken aback. There was a long silence while Freeman's words, delivered in his heavy Northern Ireland accent which made his formal language sound almost incongruous, hung heavily in the room. Then Plaxton yielded. He too had his orders. He probably had no idea how much better this deal was than Puerto Rico's although Vallecillo's Memorandum of Understanding had been freely passed around among the Northern Irish officials during the negotiations. 'Well,' he said finally, 'I'll just make one more phone call.'

When the door had closed behind him, Henderson wheeled on Freeman. He had gone quite white. 'Jesus, John, we're going to lose it!' 'It's brinkmanship that's being played here,' returned Freeman. 'If we lose it, we lose it. But I don't think we will.'

It was a long twenty minutes before Plaxton finally came back. 'We'd be prepared to offer the same conditions for $3 million out of the $18 million gap,' he announced. Freeman was overjoyed. 'Now we're negotiating,' he said warmly. Beside him, Henderson breathed a loud sigh of relief. The deal was still alive.

The two men, however, had already decided this was getting too big for them. They needed to take it to higher authority. At 5.30 they called it a day with Plaxton. They then drove up to Stormont Castle where Quigley and his senior official involved,

Brian Lyttle, were waiting, equally anxiously. Freeman outlined what had happened, adding his own view that public money should not be put in at any greater risk than the private Oppenheimer investors had been offered. If DeLorean was prepared to make concessions for private money, why should he not do it for government money too?

Quigley, however, was more concerned about a broader point. To him the principal attraction of DeLorean, apart from the immediate jobs it would create, was that it might be a trailblazer for bigger and better companies to come to Northern Ireland. It fitted into the policy guidelines he himself had laid down for attracting foreign investment. Why therefore was Oppenheimer not investing? Why was a major Wall Street house saying it would not invest in Northern Ireland, when it had been prepared to invest in both Puerto Rico and in the Irish Republic? Freeman and Henderson could not answer.

Quigley was perturbed. He would make further enquiries, he decided. In the meantime he thought Freeman had better brief the Secretary of State himself on the progress. If the Governor of Puerto Rico really was about to sign, then the next move had to be up to Roy Mason who had been pushing this project on the officials since he first heard of it.

A quick telephone call to the Secretary of State's office. No, he was not at his desk at Stormont. He was already at Hillsborough Castle, giving a dinner party in honour of his Labour Cabinet colleague Roy Hattersley who happened to be visiting Northern Ireland. Quigley made the arrangements with Mason's civil servants the other end: Mason would give John Freeman five minutes at 8.30.

It was still bright when the trade union leader and NIDA's chief executive arrived at Hillsborough. They waited in the study until Mason appeared. Freeman did the talking, laying out, blow by blow, his final confrontation with Plaxton. Mason listened attentively. 'That's quite good, John, that's good negotiating,' said Mason, who had been a trade union official himself. 'But for Christ-sake sign it. It'll be a great psychological boost for Ulster.' He went back into his dinner party.

Mason from the first had left no-one in any doubt that he wanted the DeLorean factory for Ulster. Everyone at the negotiating table had been made aware of that. DeLorean, with his own keen nose, had picked it up, probably on that first day. It coloured the whole negotiation on both sides, each party knowing there would be an agreement, the only points to be decided being the conditions and amounts. Later Mason would say: 'West Belfast, a Catholic community, is like an enclave of the Third World within the United Kingdom; appalling unemployment, awful housing conditions, a community in despair and without hope. The Labour government, at my personal request, recognized their needs and aspirations.'

That night, however, when the negotiations had hit their first serious difficulty, Mason set a new stance: 'Sign it.' That was the word which the two NIDA men took back, and which John DeLorean, 3,000 miles away, soon picked up.

The next day the negotiations moved at a swifter pace. First, however, Quigley telexed the British Consul General's office in New York and asked Gordon Booth to telephone Howard Phillips at Oppenheimer to establish why the firm was reluctant to invest in Belfast. He was somewhat reassured. No, Belfast didn't smell. But the banking house had done its investigative work on Puerto Rico, and then all of a sudden found itself doing the same work on the Irish Republic. Then it was back to Puerto Rico and, just as it was getting its investors settled down again, John DeLorean had gone to Belfast. None of them knew much about Northern Ireland, although Mike Hayes could claim Irish ancestry and Colin Keith, also on the DeLorean team, was British. They just couldn't seek investors for a project in a country they had not vetted, had not worked out the sums on comparative wage rates, productivity, work records and all the rest of it. Besides which, although Phillips refrained from saying so, they were furious with John DeLorean.

Booth telexed the news back to Quigley, adding that Oppenheimer now said that it would, if asked by John DeLorean, seek investors for Northern Ireland but only after it had done a proper study. 'Being a bank of high repute,' Booth put in drily, Oppenheimer would not go ahead without the figures. Booth added something else in this telex. 'The Limited Partnership was a device by which high income earners in the United States could use a tax haven country such as Puerto Rico or the Republic of Ireland to invest with large benefits to their own personal tax position,' he added. Northern Ireland did not offer those advantages, Oppenheimer had told him.

This struck the Northern Ireland officials as nothing more than excuse, as indeed it was. Within weeks, seeing its fee slipping away, Oppenheimer was clamouring to get aboard again.

Back again to the negotiations, Plaxton still acting as DeLorean's messenger; the master himself in New York; Henderson and Freeman holding the NIDA fort. NIDA now changed the mix of its $18 million offer, but insisted on altering the voting structure too. DeLorean gave way on that, coming down from his initial 94.5 percent of the votes to 73.5 percent (which is where it stayed). He could afford to do so – he still remained in more than effective control of the Belfast subsidiary which was all he needed.

It was agreed. The Oppenheimer gap had been filled, with John DeLorean offered a far cheaper $18 million than Oppenheimer proposed. There was now no need for that Oppenheimer money at all. Yet while the negotiations were taking place in Belfast, DeLorean was quietly asking Oppenheimer to revive its scheme. For reasons then known only to himself, he still wanted that Oppenheimer money.

Two days later, the NIDA board met again at Holywood, this time for the regular board meeting. If they were going to take it further (and they all decided they would), then it was time for the process of 'due diligence'. Someone would have to go to the United States, see that the company had title to the things it said it did, that there was a car at all, look at the offices, talk to the complete management team, check with the auditors, lawyers, consultants and so forth. Who to send?

Tony Hopkins, the obvious candidate, was on holiday. But there was a new man who had joined the staff two weeks before: Shaun Harte, a loquacious, dark-haired accountant. He was given the job and so was Gil Wilson, another NIDA official. The Department of Commerce was to send Frank McCann and Robin Bailie, a local Belfast solicitor who had done a lot of work for the agency recently, was to go also. Bailie was something of a Belfast whiz-kid. He had already been minister of commerce in the Brian Faulkner government in the early 1970s and now had a thriving practice in Belfast. On this trip he would represent NIDA.

On Thursday June 29, the team of Harte, Wilson, McCann and Bailie flew to London and then caught a plane to Detroit. In Bloomfield Hills, however, they were not overpoweringly welcomed by the chief financial officer Bob Dewey. 'I thought Puerto Rico looked good, and I didn't want to be all the way over in Northern Ireland.'

Dewey afterwards recalled that he was 'not very cordial'. The visitors never noticed. Collins was his usual bluff, enthusiastic self. Strycker was there. So was Brown. They made a good team: experienced, capable, friendly but businesslike.

At this time, the whole DeLorean empire consisted of only 14 professional men. In addition to Collins, Brown, Dewey and Strycker, who was a consultant, there was A. Lawrence Cobb who enjoyed the title of 'General Manager' although there was little to manage. He had come from Rockwell International in February. Harry DeWitt was an old hand, although he was only 28. He had been there since the end of 1976, helping Dewey in general accounting. Collins had a couple of people to help him: Alan Cross who had worked on the ill-fated Bricklin (the only man to work on both the Bricklin and the DeLorean) was doing development work on the chassis; Robert Manion, from Chrysler, was in charge of electrical. Then, there was the team of Terry Werrell and Marshall Zaun who had been involved in the new Chevrolet Vega plant at Lordstown, Ohio – a two million-square-foot plant built in 15 months, employing 5,000 people and turning out 60 cars an hour. They were standing by to build the DeLorean factory.

Dick Brown had brought his own team from Mazda: James Fearer, Louis O. Glasgow and William A. Morgan. Tom Kimmerly did not officially join until later, although his law firm had a well-established relationship with the company. His vanguard was Jeffrey B. Levine, who became a full-time employee in April 1978, hired from Kimmerly's law firm.

And that was all. The British government was considering an investment of more than $100 million in it.

Bob Dewey had another reason for not welcoming the Irishmen. He had made a momentous decision: he would leave John

DeLorean just as soon as he possibly could – the first member of the team to go. He had nearly quit in May, but he knew that would have 'put up many red flags', and there would be no project. And he did not want to kill it, merely get away from it. He was increasingly concerned at the way money was going out of the window faster than it was raised.

Since he had joined, more than $8 million had been spent (most, in his view, senselessly and wastefully), with little to show for it. Much of the money seemed to be going for John's private projects and on his lifestyle. The original sports car Limited Partnership had put in $3.5 million, and that was gone. Wood Gundy had invested $500,000, and that was gone. Johnny Carson's $500,000 was gone. The dealers, to date, had invested $3.7 million, and that was almost gone. DeLorean was flying round the world with teams of people, spending money like water on consultants and legal fees without any visible objective or plan, taking up projects and dropping them again. But it was DeLorean's company – he owned 84 percent of the common stock – and Dewey could not argue. But there were minority shareholders, and Dewey knew what his fiduciary responsibility as chief financial officer was, and he was worried by it. Through 1978, he said, he had spent more and more time minding the till.

Now he was spending his July Fourth holiday weekend showing the Irish team the books, resenting them and resenting DeLorean even more. They split the team up. Brown, Collins and Dewey each took a day in the office, and Strycker was there too. DeLorean was 'available by telephone', but no one bothered him. They met the DeLorean auditor, Dick Measelle from the accounting firm of Arthur Andersen in Detroit, and he supported their already favourable impressions and also laid out in more detail why the Oppenheimer Limited Partnership was no longer available.

Then Gil Wilson went down to California, taking Shaun Harte's camera to photograph the prototype, as someone remarked 'to prove there really is a car after all this'. The others went to New York, where Ronnie Henderson joined them from Germany.

In New York, they tried to see the Oppenheimer people, who were still annoyed, and refused. But on Monday, they finally saw DeLorean at his office in the Chris-Craft building. It was still the holiday weekend, and there was no one about. They had seen the investors' prospectus and were impressed by that. If it was good enough for the SEC to pass and to get through the 'blue skies' regulations of various states, then that was another major plus. Not a bad first trip, they decided, as they flew back across the Atlantic.

But something more detailed, more substantial, was needed, and there was now a great hurry. The British Cabinet would have its last full meeting at the end of July, at which stage Parliament would go into recess and even the Prime Minister would go on holiday. If they missed that (and the project was going to require full Cabinet approval), then it would have to wait until September.

The end of July was also the final, final, final signing date given by the Puerto Ricans. The head of Fomento in San Juan, Manuel Dubon, who had recently replaced Vallecillo and who opposed the project, had been pressing to get on or get out of the project and Governor Romero agreed with him. Now they indicated that unless the deal was signed by August 2 at the latest, the offer would be irrevocably withdrawn.

On Friday, July 7, the Department of Commerce asked the consulting firm of McKinsey to investigate. In Britain, McKinsey is something of an institution in financial consultancy. It has reorganized such institutions as the Bank of England and the island of Hong Kong.

It was John Banham, a McKinsey consultant who had prepared detailed reports on both Northern Ireland and the car industry, who prepared the report. It was not favourable.

In that first report, Banham did not advise against investment in the DeLorean project, but within a week he had spotted most of the weak points and laid them out for the Commerce civil servants in Belfast.

'The project is very risky, and it is not difficult to see why Mr. DeLorean has found it hard to raise private risk capital. High risk projects require higher returns.'

Quigley asked Banham to do some more detailed research and let them have a written report – when could he do that? Banham gulped and promised it for the following Tuesday.

On July 18, Banham turned up with his final McKinsey report. It was even more critical than his verbal one but still did not definitely come down against the investment. He had only seen the DeLorean corporate plan two days before. Banham could point to lots of reasons for not going ahead with the project, but the Northern Ireland politicians palpably wanted it so he started by looking on the bright side, stating why it might be attractive, 'if the formidable odds against its success can be overcome'. He underlined the 'if'.

There were all those jobs, and in West Belfast, too. The project would be a morale booster for the Province and help keep up the impetus generated by the announcements that both General Motors and Michelin were to invest in Ulster. 'The DMC investment would further strengthen the local automotive industry, particularly since the luxury and sports car segments of that industry are less sensitive to business cycles as a whole,' he went on.

In his efforts to find good points at the beginning, Banham then went over the top:

> The project itself would be an attractive advertisement for the Province in terms of its quality and the technical innovation involved. (Porsche is also researching the possibilities of a 20-year car.) Many of the likely purchasers could be in a position at some stage in their careers to influence U.S. investment overseas. The Ulster operation would not be marginal to DMC success and, thus, vulnerable to closure in a recession. On the contrary, the plant would be essential to the whole venture; so the Province would be acquiring high quality managerial talent. Finally, Mr. DeLorean himself would be a very effective ambassador to the U.S. industry for the Province. As the press clippings demonstrate, DeLorean is well known and highly regarded in industrial circles in the United States and had an impressive record during his career at General Motors. Moreover, he is likely to be familiar with the Washington scene, which could be important if anti-dumping actions are brought against the DeLorean Motor Company in Northern Ireland.

Now perhaps it is unfair to subject that paragraph to the test of hindsight. But, instead of an 'attractive advertisement' for Ulster, the DeLorean project turned into the worst possible publicity. There was no technical innovation worth speaking of in the car and to compare it with Porsche's idea of a 20-year car was nonsense. The 'likely purchasers' did not become fans of DeLorean and Ulster. The car had so many problems in the United States that the opposite was true. The Ulster operation was never intended to be central to John DeLorean's corporate schemes. On the contrary, it was only part of his plan for a General Motors-type conglomerate, which so scared the Dublin officials and greatly worried his fellow directors. In fact, a month or so after the deal was signed, DeLorean shook some of his colleagues by suddenly saying, 'I don't think we'll ever build the car in Northern Ireland; the IRA will blow it up.'

Then there was that final point of Banham's: that DeLorean would be a good ambassador for the Province and that he knew Washington well. None of his executives recall DeLorean saying anything favourable about Northern Ireland. Brown's father was a Northern Ireland Protestant and he still had family there. He became very upset with DeLorean, who characterized the Northern Irish as 'dummies', 'morons', 'incompetents', and worse. Nor did DeLorean know much of the politics of Washington and he remained extraordinarily naive about them.

Banham, however, was on surer ground in assessing the risks in the project and he now listed them in detail. For a start, he did not believe the sales targets. DeLorean was projecting sales of 20,000 cars a year immediately, rising to 30,000. Yet the sales of the Porsche 924, priced below the DeLorean, were only 13,657 in 1977. The Porsche 911 had sold only 5,709 and the Lancia Beta Scorpion, which McKinsey reckoned was also a competitor, a mere 1,375. The entire Lotus line managed fewer than 1,000 cars world-wide in 1977, Banham added. Part of that Lotus line was designed by Giorgetto Giugiaro, just like the DMC-12, and Banham had clippings from the magazine *Road and Track* that indicated that Giugiaro saw the DeLorean design as little more than one of the family of cars he designed for manufacturers all over the world.

Banham also worried about the colour problem. Chevrolet,

his report pointed out, had so many potential colours that each of its 42,000 Corvette owners could have been unique – and liked to imagine themselves so. With DeLorean, you only got stainless steel. There was no allowance for competition. If his car really sold well, the others would react fast enough; and DeLorean was planning to capture 15 percent of the market.

The report was dubious about the ERM plastic process, pointing out that, if it could not be used, the plant and equipment budget would have to be increased by $29 million, the extra money to be found presumably from the British taxpayer. Then there was the time involved. DeLorean was promising to do it all in 18 months. Yet the standard time for developing a new car with an established company and experienced management was three years. Porsche took seven or eight.

In general, there were too many optimistic assumptions, no margin for error, all estimates and projections worked out on the basis that nothing could go wrong, that the whole set-up from day one would click into top gear, be as efficient as General Motors or Porsche or BMW, 'which had literally generations of accumulated experience in the automotive industry'. DeLorean was blithely assuming that with untried management, a new distribution network, new suppliers, new work force, new location and a new car using new and untested technology, he would not just match 'but be able to exceed the best industry practice'. This section summed up forebodingly: 'On the face of it, these projections seem hazardous.'

There was some gentle irony in the report. Banham wrote:

> Labour productivity is assumed at North American rates – that is, the Northern Ireland unit labour cost is based on standard hours per unit developed for a possible site in Pennsylvania and adjusted for Belfast labour rates. If this can be achieved, it will be a remarkable performance, and one that has eluded the management of Ford, Chrysler and GM in the United Kingdom – not to mention British Leyland.

Then there was a section headed 'Undue dependence on one man'. The man, of course, was John DeLorean and this was by no means all negative. 'One of the (few) reassuring aspects of this project is that Mr. DeLorean's personal reputation depends on its personal success, and that he also stands to gain substantially if the odds can be overcome. Under the latest proposals he would retain a 34 percent interest in DMC and its subsidiaries – and his equity stake could be worth $60 million.'

On the other hand, the project would be threatened if anything happened to him, and that was possible 'given the nature of the project and the location of the plant'. Banham suggested that an insurance policy could be taken out, although the premiums 'will almost certainly be quite significant.'

He then got to the crux of the matter:

> In summary, the Department is being asked to fund an extraordinarily risky venture. The combination of DOC grants and NIDA equity investment will mean that a large proportion of the financial risk ($116 million out of a total funds requirement to April 1, 1980 of $118.1 million) will be carried by the U.K. taxpayer in return for a 22 percent stake (after conversion) in the company if it can succeed in overcoming the odds. Moreover, by the nature of the investment, most of the funds have to be committed at the front end: working capital amounts to less than £9 million [about $16.2 million] of the total Northern Ireland investment of £61 million [about $109 million].

Banham didn't know it, but of course Puerto Rico had insisted that not a penny of government money went in until DeLorean had spent $25 million.

Banham's final paragraph was not exactly reassuring. His analysis, he said, suggested that the chances of the project succeeding as planned were 'remote'. Analysis was not everything, he then admitted.

> The odds can be beaten, even though this may seem unlikely. Mr. DeLorean has a formidable record behind him, and he has committed his personal reputation, not to mention $3.5 million of his personal funds, to the project. He has persuaded some competent people to join him, and they also appear to believe in the project's viability.

To justify investing in the high risk DeLorean venture, said Banham, 'the political and image benefits . . . will have to be very substantial and the opportunity costs to NIDA . . . will have to be low.'

Except for that one naive and uninformed paragraph at the beginning, it was a remarkably prescient and penetrating report for 11 days' work.

It was Tuesday, July 18, when Quigley got the report. It went down like a lead balloon.

In the Commerce Department, Frank McCann was apparently enthusiastic for the project. Quigley wanted it, too, but not at any price, and he was worried. At NIDA, chief executive Ronnie Henderson was enthusiastic; so was Shaun Harte. Tony Hopkins, who had been on holiday with his family in Donegal in the early stages, had now taken over from Harte and was deeply involved with the figures. He was in favour, too, but was already worried by it.

McKinsey had raised some serious questions. What were the answers? More frantic telexes flew between Belfast and Detroit, but it seemed only reasonable that the DeLorean team in Detroit should have the report in its entirety.

Banham's office was in St. James's Street in London. The next day Buck Penrose, a new DeLorean executive who had joined DMC from Booz Allen a week before, collected a copy of the report from Banham's office and flew straight back to Detroit with it. Three days later, on Saturday, he wrote Quigley a 15-page reply. The Commerce officials were meeting on Tuesday 25, and time was now precious. By Monday the Penrose letter was in Dr. Quigley's hands. It attempted to deal with McKinsey's criticisms and doubts with a mixture of condescension and obfuscation.

McKinsey, Penrose implied, just didn't understand what he was talking about. The analysis was drawn from its 'extensive and highly regarded experience' of the U.K. and EEC automotive industry, but a critique 'which does not include U.S. perspective may not be balanced or objective'. The new DeLorean company was 'lean, hungry and aggressive' and should not be compared with the stodgy, old companies such as Porsche or BMW. 'Digital Equipment Corporation,' added

Penrose by way of example, 'has achieved annual sales of more than $1 billion by pursuing market opportunities that IBM ignored.' DeLorean, he implied, could achieve something similar by penetrating markets that General Motors ignored. The DMC management had 276 man-months invested in the programme. How could McKinsey analyse it even better than they in 11 days?

Perhaps the most interesting point to emerge from this letter was the reaction to McKinsey's worry about the dependence of the project on one man. Obviously, acknowledged Penrose, John could suffer a heart attack, an airplane crash or even an 'act of terrorism', so the company had taken out a 'key man' life insurance policy from Prudential. The sum: $10 million. 'Management believes that this amount will be more than sufficient to offset any loss in program momentum which may result from Mr. DeLorean's demise.'

Tuesday, July 25: Four days to go before the master agreement was due to be signed and just over a week before Mason, himself, would be there for the grand ceremony, which was now scheduled for August 2, the press conference to be held a day later. The news was beginning to leak. Mason had bumped into Gerry Fitt in the House of Commons and had indicated that he had something special to announce soon for West Belfast. He did not say what it was, but there had been teams of people out looking at the Twinbrook estate.

Everyone knew there were Americans in town, and Belfast is a small place. The *Belfast Telegraph* carried a story indicating that NIDA had something major on the way that would offer thousands of jobs. Mason was busy priming the Cabinet, preparing the ministers through their permanent secretaries. He already knew there would be opposition.

By now, the basic framework of the deal had been settled. The last major issue, an inflation clause, had been sorted out the week before.

'What allowance are you making for inflation in your projections?' had asked one of the Commerce people of DeLorean.

Neatly, DeLorean had turned it back on him. 'That's up to you guys, isn't it? You're the government. It's your inflation, not ours.'

The officials had been nonplussed, but DeLorean had not let up. 'You've raised it and I think it's a good question. What do you suggest we do?'

In the end, it was agreed that inflation and movements in the pound against the dollar should be taken care of in a special clause added to the overall agreement. This stated that the Department of Commerce would 'be prepared to consider' the possibility of further financing 'if required for the satisfactory establishment of the undertaking at the factory and for the provision and maintenance of the (specified) levels of employment . . . as a result of currency fluctuations, inflation or other causes outside (limited's) control.' It was another mistake that would cost the British government dear.

Strycker was back in the Europa Hotel redoing the corporate plan originally done for Puerto Rico. With him were Buck Penrose and Harry DeWitt. DeLorean, Brown, Kimmerly, Dewey and Collins would all be there by the weekend. The officials, lawyers and accountants were burning the midnight oil, dotting the 'i's' and crossing the 't's' of the lengthy, complicated master agreement.

At One New York Plaza, Oppenheimer had had a change of mind. Times were hard on Wall Street, and $2 million was $2 million. 'We weren't going to get paid unless something really consummated itself,' recalls Hayes. 'And we put in a lot of time and effort into the project – a lot of people invested including myself, you know. We all thought he had a good idea and he could make money.'

With the deal all but done, with Northern Ireland offering approximately twice as much as Puerto Rico and three times as much as the Irish Republic and with almost no strings attached, Oppenheimer decided Belfast was the place after all. Howard Phillips booked a flight to Belfast to get him there in time for the signing.

At one stage DeLorean had called the NIDA men aside. 'Oppenheimer,' he had explained 'is being too greedy. I want you guys to help out a little here.' He himself, he had explained to Tony Hopkins and Shaun Harte, wasn't in the best position to beat them down. There then had followed the bizarre episode where Hopkins and Harte had had a furious bargaining session with Howard Phillips, whom they had already disliked in any case, but now disliked even more. The irony of it was that NIDA stood to gain little or nothing if Oppenheimer changed the terms: DeLorean stood to gain most. 'Here were these guys kicking the shit out of Oppenheimer,' recalls a NIDA man, 'to get a better deal for John DeLorean while DeLorean himself sat at the back as if it had nothing to do with him.' He meant no disrespect for his former colleagues – they were doing their best for the whole project. He was just amazed at DeLorean's ability to make others, even those who were not even working for him, do his dirty work.

By now, it seemed unstoppable. Mason was confident of enough Cabinet support to get it through, and indeed he had it. The Commerce officials were responding to his enthusiasm by pushing NIDA, although in truth there were not many critics about.

There was at least one, however. At the NIDA board meeting on Wednesday morning, the august Sir Lindsay Ring, former Lord Mayor of London and a leading financial figure, spoke up. Sir Lindsay had missed the original meeting that had agreed on the DeLorean deal. Now he had just been given a copy of the McKinsey report which, he told all the other board members, he saw as 'highly critical'. Why didn't they all have it earlier so they could study it properly?

Patiently, Faulkner pointed out that the report had been prepared for Dr. Quigley at Commerce, not for NIDA, and NIDA had it just as a matter of courtesy. But Sir Lindsay reckoned that, even without an earlier look at the report, NIDA had not been supplied with enough information to make a proper decision. How could they possibly tell, on the basis of what they had seen so far, that it was a viable proposition?

Faulkner and Henderson pointed out that there was a deadline, that it had been discussed at one monthly and four special board meetings, that they had studied three separate consultants' reports and the ones from Booz Allen and Kearney were favourable. Henderson, Hopkins and Harte had studied those reports in great detail and had concluded that, while there were certainly considerable risks, the project was worth pursuing because of the employment prospects for West Belfast and the potential morale boost to the Province.

Sir Lindsay found some support from trade union leader John Freeman who disliked the financial fortunes being gleaned off by DeLorean and various advisers. But Freeman badly wanted that project for West Belfast.

'There are people there in their 30s and 40s who have never worked in their lives, people with grown-up children who have never seen their fathers do a day's work. You have to look at those men's eyes to understand what West Belfast is about. There's no sparkle there, no hope.'

At the end of the discussion the NIDA board reaffirmed its decision to go ahead with the DeLorean project, subject now only to Cabinet committee approval. Doubts had been allayed by a revised group structure, whereby the Northern Ireland company would own the major assets.

It was another mistake. The structure under which DMC sold the cars made by the Belfast company, now called DeLorean Motor Cars Limited or simply Limited, meant that John DeLorean himself could make all decisions, concentrate profits where they were most suitable to him and make it virtually impossible for Limited to get rid of him or free itself of his control. All its cars had to be sold through him.

All that remained now was the signing and the ceremonies. DeLorean arrived with Kimmerly. Brown flew in from California; Dewey and Collins from Detroit. The master agreement was signed that Friday, July 28. DeLorean, in high glee, went off house-hunting over the weekend. He had decided to buy a castle, he said, returning in time for the big ceremony on Tuesday when Mason signed the formal agreement. (DeLorean had it framed on his office wall.)

That evening, Mason held a dinner for them in Hillsborough with speeches by himself and John. The next morning, they were ready for the press conference. John DeLorean had done the deal of his life.

That deal gave DeLorean this: equity, grants and loans totalling approximately £52,943,000. For the sake of simplicity we can convert that at a rate of £1=$2.00. The negotiations started at $1.83 but the pound was rising rapidly and did go all the way to $2.43. But let's call it $106 million.

In addition there was another $15 million loan offer (in the event not taken up) to fill the gap left by Oppenheimer. So John DeLorean had an offer from the Northern Ireland government of $121 million, which was enough, according to his own calculations and the estimates of all those involved, to build a factory, engineer a car, get it into production and see the enterprise through to the time revenues began to accrue from car sales.

The Northern Ireland cash was a complex mixture; but the key component was £17,757,000 of equity money, or risk capital. That entitled NIDA to 17,757,000 votes on the basis of one vote per share. DeLorean on the other hand contributed $1 million through DMC – and got 546,000 Class B ordinary stock, each with 90 votes. Do DMC ended up with 49,140,000 votes, or 73 percent of the total votes for an investment of $1 million.

On top of the NIDA money was £25,218,000 in non-repayable grants from the Department of Commerce. And another £10 million in loans.

So much for the money side. DeLorean also negotiated a so-called 'technical assistance' agreement, whereby DMC would be paid by the Belfast company for its managerial and technical expertise. This was a generous $1.6 million a year, or $290,000 a month, and was for the next two-and-a-half years DMC's only official source of income. Theoretically this would have been enough to support the operation in Bloomfield Hills.

Then there was a complex royalty agreement: NIDA and the Department of Commerce were entitled to £185 for each of the first 90,000 cars sold and £45 a car after that. But later the Belfast company would have to pay another $375 a car to the Oppenheimer partners.

NIDA structured its own equity involvement on the basis that it would encourage DeLorean to buy it out quickly. DeLorean had the option to purchase its £1 shares at £1 plus 15 percent a year accumulated interest, over the first four years. NIDA's desire was not to make a profit, but to create jobs – and if it could tempt DeLorean into buying it out within four years, so much the better. It would mean the operation at Dunmurry was already a success.

That in essence was the deal. DMC would have the sole distribution rights to the car in the United States. Limited in Belfast would make them; no cars would pass from one company to the other without payment being made first. DMC was not allowed to get involved in any other venture without NIDA's express approval.

CHAPTER SEVEN

GPD

Pause for a moment and consider John DeLorean's position that summer weekend in Belfast. He now had all the money he needed – more than he expected, more than an enterprise that thus far employed fewer than 20 people could ever reasonably have hoped for. There was now every prospect that, in two years, he would have a custom-built factory on that cow pasture at the far end of the Falls Road.

The car he would produce there was also advancing – Bill Collins had built two prototypes. Dick Brown had nearly completed the dealer network; each of the dealers had put up $25,000 in advance and agreed to take at least the first year's production. DeLorean's team was assembled: Collins the engineer, Dewey the finance man, Brown the marketer who would also be invaluable in building the factory, and Walt Strycker.

He had his Wall Street supporters: Oppenheimer had now agreed to put together a tax shelter scheme, having magically found a way round the problems that six weeks before had seemed insuperable.

The whole strategy was falling into place beautifully. What could go wrong?

There was one thing he had not yet arranged – John DeLorean had not yet got out of it any cash for himself. There was plenty of money around for the car and factory, but that was all tied up – or so in their innocence the money brokers thought. A method to channel some of those funds away from the car venture had not yet occurred to DeLorean.

There is no hard evidence that he set out with premeditation to divert some of those investment funds away from the car project. But there is plenty of evidence to show that, when the opportunity arose, he diverted in abundance. Some $17.87 million raised for the car venture would never be applied to it.

That story, however, lies ahead. In Belfast in early August, John DeLorean had a different problem: how to live up to his promises. He had persuaded the Northern Irish officials that his staff, slim as it was, was ready to go the instant the deal was signed. Now that he had to produce results, John DeLorean admitted privately that it could be difficult.

The man to whom he confessed was Dick Brown. After the signing he took Brown aside. 'You know, Dick, we really have nobody who knows a thing about building a plant.' Brown had built Mazda's highly successful U.S. plant. DeLorean said: 'Could you stay and get it done?' When it came to the point, DeLorean admitted that Werrell and Zaun, the men he had told NIDA would do the job, did not have the experience.

DeLorean was also talking expansively of another idea. Renault had a division, SERI, that had built car plants all over the world. SERI could do a turn-key operation on the plant, he suggested.

Brown blanched. It was several days before he could get DeLorean to see that it wouldn't work. The whole reason for the Northern Ireland government getting involved in the first place was to create jobs. 800 of those jobs would be in building the plant – immediate jobs that would last for two years.

He told DeLorean: 'We are here to develop labor for the Northern Irish, not for France.' DeLorean finally got the point.

The same day that he asked Brown to stay in Belfast, DeLorean also told him: 'We really need somebody who knows the ins and outs of the United Kingdom.'

Brown had an idea. 'Well, John, my next door neighbor has a brother who is the director of personnel and administration for Chrysler, Europe.'

The man he had in mind was Myron Stylianides, an anglicized Greek who knew his way around the car industry in Europe. Brown phoned him and the following evening, the festivities in Belfast over, he and DeLorean flew to London, where they had dinner with Stylianides.

Stylianides had some news of his own to impart in private to the two Americans. Chrysler, desperately strapped for cash, was bailing out of its European operation. There had been talks for weeks, he confided; the deal was almost complete and would be announced in a day or so. Peugeot-Citroen, France's proudest car company, would take it all over. And he, Myron Stylianides, would be out of a job. If DeLorean wanted someone to look after personnel and administration . . . DeLorean did. Stylianides became the first new recruit.

DeLorean now went home to New York, leaving the Belfast operation to Brown.

It had been his longest visit to Northern Ireland – three days. He would never be there as long again.

Dick Brown did not mind. He was enjoying himself. His father had emigrated from the Province in 1910, and Brown felt he was home again. He brought his wife, his son and daughter over and they all stayed in the Conway Hotel, a few hundred yards from the factory site. On the edge of the site there was a carpet factory, a new but small building, that he used as his headquarters. It had been built for an industry that no longer existed there – another victim of the deep recession that was hitting Northern Ireland so hard.

Brown soon hired another old friend. Dixon Hollinshead had put up the buildings for Mazda when Brown started that company in the United States. Brown phoned him in California and within a week Hollinshead was in Belfast. He, too, brought his wife with him and he became the project manager for the plant. Hollinshead would stay two years and, perhaps more than anyone else, was responsible for the factory being built almost on schedule. Brown himself would stay in Ireland two and a half months. By mid-October, the project well under way, he was back in California.

At this point, John DeLorean had to appoint a new chief financial officer. Bob Dewey had done what he said he'd do: keep the team together until the money was assured. In mid-August he left – and was soon regretting it, though for reasons he could not have foreseen.

Dick Brown explains it like this: 'When anybody leaves John DeLorean, he has an expression – at least I've heard him use it on a couple of people. "Now," he will say, "we've got to get some Shit On his Shoes."

'After Dewey left he had a couple of job offers and John was called for a reference and he told people that the reason Dewey left was because he had a nervous breakdown. Well, who is going to hire a chief financial officer who's had a nervous breakdown?'

To the others, Dewey's departure was a shock. But the company seemed to be up and running and, for the moment, it could bear it. It was perhaps the biggest shock of all to Dewey's immediate successor: Walter Strycker. Strycker turned up at the Detroit office on the first working day in September and Dewey wasn't there. There was no explanation. Eventually Strycker discovered that Dewey had left a note saying he was gone.

'John asked me to cover and I said, you know, I couldn't do that full-time because I had a bunch of other obligations and I would give him priority over what I was doing. And I covered the slot for him because I was the only one who knew what was going on. That's how I got sucked in.'

Strycker had been a $75,000-a-year consultant. In his new rôle as chief financial officer he got $100,000. Within a month Dewey had come back, effectively swapping places and salaries with Strycker, as a consultant at $75,000. It was a bad move. It was months before he realized why he had been finding it hard to get another job. And by that time, he was once again locked in with the man who would do so much damage to his career.

During August and September, DeLorean was busy doing what he continually seemed to be doing from the day he left General Motors: raising more money. He didn't need any more – not then, and not if the car could have been built to budget, which Collins, Dewey, Strycker and the company's hordes of consultants believed it could.

For reasons which only became apparent later, DeLorean decided to allow Oppenheimer back into the deal, although the money the Wall Street house was offering was far more expensive than the loan from NIDA. Oppenheimer had put together a neat tax shelter scheme which improved on the principle that out of every dollar invested, a top rate taxpayer could save 70 cents – 70 percent was the top tax rate at the time. This money was known in the trade at the time as '30 cent dollars'. The Oppenheimer financing also offered investors an opportunity for 'leverage' because they would borrow up to 50 percent of their investment from a bank with DMC paying the interest to the extent that it exceeded 5 percent. The investors could therefore claim tax deductions equal to twice the amount of their cash investment. Investors also expected to be able to repay these loans (from Chemical Bank) with royalties of $375 per car payable by DMC to the Limited Partnership.

Oppenheimer's Howard Phillips had gone to Dublin with the DeLorean team. He had also turned up again for the signing in Belfast. NIDA in Belfast had filled the financing gap left by Oppenheimer with an offer for a loan of $15 million, but in those last days of July, Phillips negotiated Oppenheimer back into the deal. If it could still put the partnership money together, NIDA would withdraw that loan offer. The amount of money DeLorean would get would be the same, but the mix would be very different. And the way it was spent would be even more different, although it was several years before anyone other than DeLorean or a few of his close colleagues knew that.

On the day of the formal signing in Belfast, DeLorean signed a separate agreement with Phillips, countersigned by Ronnie Henderson on behalf of NIDA, to indicate his agreement to the arrangement. It was effectively an amendment to DeLorean's sales agreement with Oppenheimer dated March 23, 1978. The Limited Partnership offering was officially back in business.

This same letter also clearly set out Oppenheimer's fees: $2,050,000 – $200,000 at the closing of the partnership, the rest paid at a rate of $100,000 a quarter.

After fees, the Oppenheimer money came down to a net $15.5 million. And what exactly did the DeLorean Research Limited Partnership hope to get for its money? For a start, it got the car. And it got the ERM plastic process rights. DMC contributed all its rights to the DMC car and became the sole general partner with a one percent interest in profits and losses which would have increased to 2 percent after royalties paid to the investors totalled more than twice their investment. But DMC had a much higher stake in assets of the Partnership on liquidation – the lawyers in fact would claim 36 percent interest, although that was contended. For its part the Partnership would receive either $375 in royalties for every car manufactured and sold, or – wait for it – 23.4 percent of DMC's profits.

John DeLorean accepted that extraordinarily expensive

money despite the fact that he had a signed offer for a loan for roughly the same amount from NIDA, which wouldn't require dipping into profits. Why should he agree to give away nearly a quarter of his profits when he already had the money he needed? It had made sense for Puerto Rico which had insisted on the money up front. It had made sense for Ireland, where he could not have hoped to get the project off the ground without the Oppenheimer money. But it made no sense at all now – unless John DeLorean knew that money would not end up in the car.

Bill Collins had been labouring for three years under the impression that he would lead the engineering team that would build the car. He had built the nucleus of his group and at the end of August he took his engineering colleague Alan Cross over to Britain to start work on what he assumed would be the climax to his years of work on the prototype.

There was a further factor, however, which now came to dominate John DeLorean's thinking. The car itself. DeLorean in Belfast had persuaded NIDA that his prototype could be taken to the production stage within 18 months and be on sale in the United States within two years. That was an impossibly short timetable. But DeLorean needed to meet it, or suffer huge damage both to his reputation and to his finances. The operation was now geared to the timetable that he himself had set. If he ran over it, he would run out of money. NIDA had gone along with it because he had convinced them he could do it, that his prototype was much more advanced than in reality it was. DeLorean was still a capable engineer and, while the Northern Ireland negotiations were going on, he seems to have come to the conclusion that his own team, under Bill Collins, would not be able to do it in the time available. Without telling Collins, DeLorean that summer began looking hard for someone else to do the development work.

He may have had a further reason for this. Collins and his team, even DeLorean himself, only had experience of the American auto industry. They knew the component makers grouped around Michigan intimately. They knew the working habits and the customs of Detroit. But if the car was going to be built in Europe, then it would be expensive and difficult to use American components. Collins had reckoned he could put together the team he needed basing himself on Coventry, the town in the British Midlands that most closely resembles Detroit in its car industry concentration. The British car industry was in deep recession and the takeover of Chrysler, which had been intimated by Stylianides to DeLorean and Brown, had now occurred. 'Chrysler was laying a lot of people off and I'm sure we could have put together a good engineering group right in Coventry. Well, that's what I thought John intended,' said Collins.

DeLorean however intended no such thing. His thoughts seem first to have fallen on Porsche, whose reputation he was in awe of. If DeLorean could not build a group to rival Mercedes, he would have loved to have built a Porsche, which offered its engineering skills to other businesses in the industry on a contractual basis, as well as building its own beautiful but highly priced sports cars. Porsche would have done the job. But it would have cost DeLorean $30 million, and it could not be done in 18 months – Porsche themselves took up to seven years to produce a new car. DeLorean later claimed he had also approached BMW.

Again and again, DeLorean kept coming back to a man who was already, arguably, the best designer of Grand Prix racing cars who ever lived: Colin Chapman.

Strycker, Brown, Collins and Dewey had no idea Chapman was involved at all until August. In fact DeLorean's wooing of Chapman, and his fascination with the brilliant engineer, went back to very early summer. John DeLorean wanted winners on his team – and never in the history of motor racing had there been such a dominant winner as Chapman was that season.

2

Zolder, Belgium, May 21, 1978. The Belgian Grand Prix was about to get under way. The crowds, the mechanics, the hangers-on, who swarmed around the low, flat machines all day, had gone. The drivers were now in the cars, strapped immobile in their cockpits, unrecognizable behind their helmets. In pole position on the starting grid was the black and gold JPS Lotus of Mario Andretti, the favourite and leader in the world championship, although it was still early in the season. Behind him was his teammate and second favourite, Ronnie Peterson, a Swede who was generally regarded as one of the most skilful drivers on the entire circuit. They were driving Lotuses – the two fastest cars that world racing had ever seen. Unless they had mechanical problems or made a mistake, they would be unbeatable that day.

Less than a minute later, in a tearing crescendo of noise and burning rubber, the cars leapt away, watched by 60,000 spectators and by millions more on live TV. Andretti started smoothly, taking a lead he would not lose. Peterson took up his accustomed second place behind Andretti and stayed there until the 56th lap. Then he had to change a tyre and dropped to fourth. Gilles Villeneuve chased Andretti for a while but could never really get near him.

Ten laps from the end, the excitement focused on the second Lotus when it began its fight back for second place – which Peterson regarded as his right. He overtook Jacques Lafite's Ligier and then, with some brilliant driving that had the crowd on its feet, caught and passed Villeneuve's Ferrari only four laps from the finish.

It was another one-two win for Lotus.

For Colin Chapman, founder and chairman of Lotus, 1978 was his best season ever. He had turned 50 two days before, but he was already a legend in the world of auto racing. He had won his first Grand Prix 18 years earlier when Stirling Moss drove a Coventry-Climax-powered Lotus to victory at Monaco. That day at Zolder was Chapman's 66th Grand Prix win, a record topped only by Ferrari, which had been racing much longer.

'It's difficult to know what to do for an encore,' Chapman told reporters who gathered round the winning team. 'Mario wins with the new car and Ronnie has a fantastic drive for second place after a pit stop. We have the best drivers in the world!'

It was his series of Grand Prix victories that season that drew John DeLorean to Colin Chapman like a bee to honey. Chapman had everything that DeLorean wanted: his own car company; a world reputation as a designer and engineer of genius; a beautiful, stately home in the English countryside, complete with his own airstrip and two planes; and his car factory beside it. He had wealth, reputation, respect and the comforts of life. Above all, he had done what DeLorean wanted to do – built his own car company from scratch.

Anthony Colin Bruce Chapman – the ACBC monogram was incorporated into the Lotus badge – had started from far more humble beginnings than had John DeLorean. He built his first competition car in 1948 when he was only 20 in a lock-up garage in Muswell Hill in North London. He based it on a beat-up Austin 7. It was to become the first in a long line of sports cars leading to that superb JPS machine driven by Andretti at Zolder.

Chapman borrowed £25 from his fiancée Hazel (later his wife) and set up his own business, concentrating on 'kit' cars, to be assembled by impecunious but enthusiastic sports car drivers at home. He raced at weekends, basically to advertise the Lotus name. Now in 1978 he hired the world's best drivers to do the same thing – Team Lotus advertised the wedge-shaped sports cars, which Chapman produced in his factory at Hethel, in the middle of the East Anglian countryside. Now it was a far larger – but still precariously financed – operation.

It was July when DeLorean first found his way to Chapman's head office, home and factory in the Norfolk countryside. He had already had various discussions with him but, with the Northern Ireland deal moving towards its successful outcome, his plans had crystallized – and escalated. He no longer wanted just a contract with Lotus for the development work on the car. His glimpse of Porsche had made him more ambitious than that – and what he saw in Norfolk that day confirmed it. He wanted nothing less than to take over the whole of Lotus, and use it not just to build his car but to create a mini-Porsche, offering Chapman's brilliant skills to the rest of the industry.

Lotus at the time was a depressed stock on the London stock market. The whole operation was valued at less than £3 million, which was a fraction of what Porsche had quoted for development work on the car. There was one obstacle: Colin Chapman controlled the company through a series of offshore and nominee companies. And Lotus was Chapman's brainchild, creation – and his life. DeLorean worked on a scheme which would tempt him to sell.

'John DeLorean appeared here at short notice,' recalls Fred Bushell, Lotus finance director at the time and long-time confidant of Chapman. 'And he talked to Chapman in terms of buying Chapman out of Lotus. Chapman wasn't particularly impressed but obviously when someone talks to you, you listen. Mr. DeLorean, I believe, had some fairly grandiose schemes as to how he would develop Lotus and he was enough of a psychologist to be able to present his arguments in an attractive manner – how he would want to carry on the racing team, get onto a four-door saloon, which was a dream of Chapman's anyway but which we were unlikely to have the money for. But obviously, for a man who is the founder of a company, contemplating disposing of that company is a great psychological hang-up. Once he got through all the charms and the blandishments, the hard core resolve of Colin Chapman was that this was his business and that was the way it would stay. It always had been his business, he wanted to run it his way and so much of his blood was in it. So the courting of DeLorean in terms of buying the company and imposing his own stamp on it – he made clear that was what was envisaged – didn't meet a response from Chapman and the conversation just petered out.'

Talks between DeLorean and Chapman may have gone further than Bushell knew, however. Lotus was a publicly quoted company but tended to be run as a private concern by Chapman. Chapman had organized his personal affairs in a tax-effective but complex manner, some of his holdings held through companies based in Jersey. He resented any enquiry into his corporate structure, and made elaborate arrangements to shield them from public view. His Team Lotus was run separately from Lotus Group – but critics often wondered whether the accounts of the two ever became blurred. He had other companies: building boats, an aeroplane venture which only emerged after his death. Carl Ludwigson, a private relations consultant employed by DeLorean at the time, recalls it differently. 'John told me they were down to the very fine detail on taking over Lotus. But there was one major snag, he told me. DMC which would have been doing the taking over was a public company and the details of the Lotus deal would have been subjected to U.S. Securities laws. DeLorean reckoned under those laws Colin Chapman would have been in real trouble.'

This was undoubtedly a monumental exaggeration: Lotus had auditors, a board of directors and had to satisfy the quizzical British Inland Revenue. But it probably has a point: Colin Chapman was reluctant for his elaborate tax avoidance schemes to be subjected to full scrutiny. And that could not have been avoided if DeLorean had bought Lotus.

Nevertheless, Chapman was at least interested enough in doing the development work on DeLorean's car to go to the United States.

He took with him Mike Kimberley, a six-foot-five engineer who was Lotus's managing director. The two men went to Phoenix where DeLorean still had an involvement with a test track and where some of the work on Bill Collins' prototype was being done. They wanted to look at the John DeLorean dream.It was not a reassuring experience. Mike Kimberley recalls it. 'Colin and I took the prototype out on to the freeway – and it broke down in the fast lane. There we were, stranded in this DeLorean car in the middle of Arizona. The police came along and were anything but amused. Eventually we were shunted ignominiously off into the side.' It turned out that glue had got mixed up with the petrol. But Chapman, never renowned for his sense of humour, was unamused. He was not impressed with anything on the car. He reckoned that ERM wouldn't work, that the engine had to be in the middle rather than the rear. He could see no point to the stainless steel shell. He told DeLorean that he could never get away with a car with so little luggage space.

The two Lotus engineers went home.

While DeLorean was negotiating his agreement in Belfast, Chapman's fortunes continued to rise. In July, the French Grand Prix was held at the Paul Richard Circuit near Marseilles in a blinding heat wave. Once again, it was a one-two for Andretti and Peterson.

'Just perfect,' said Andretti of his car, decked out in the gold and black colours of Chapman's sponsor, the John Player Cigarette Company.

'Just keep the winning streak going,' said Chapman. And they did. It was, said the motoring correspondents, the 'Year of the Lotus', its superiority clearer than anything in the history of Formula One car racing.

By the first week in August DeLorean had the money to build his car plant and the car itself. Those problems were at last solved. Now he switched his efforts to the wooing of Colin Chapman. He still had the option of using Bill Collins who had gone to Coventry with his assistant Alan Cross to look over the place. Porsche and BMW were not runners. It had to be Collins – or Chapman.

In August he redoubled his efforts to talk Chapman into it, but the racing man was tied up emotionally in the Grand Prix season, driving himself and everyone else harder than ever as his cars went faster and faster, his two drivers increasing their lead in the World Championship points.

Chapman, however, needed money. Fred Bushell sets the scene like this:

'Lotus is a business which is always a little fraught and one is always trying to look into the future, trying to see how a small company this size, which doesn't have any right to exist yet does exist, is going to continue. And the board, in 1977, faced with the ever higher expenditures that the engineers were demanding, decided that the best thing to do was to seek out contract work. It would enable us to retain a staff of engineers which frankly otherwise we couldn't afford. But how do you get contract work? At that time we had no one who could go and bang on people's doors, so we chose to contact a number of long-standing associates of ours, inviting them to act as a finder service to find contract work for us, particularly in the sphere where we had particular expertise: the application of what we now call our 'composite technique' and structures which involved light-weight and high efficiency engineering.'

One of the 'associates' that Lotus at that point approached was, according to Bushell, the Juhan family of Geneva whom Chapman had known for 25 years. Jaroslav, or 'Jerry', Juhan, who had been a Czech motorcycle champion after the War, emigrated to Central America, settling for a while in Guatemala. He had a brief insignificant motor racing career when in 1953 a group of Guatemalan racing enthusiasts got together and bought him a Porsche. That year he entered the Mexican Road Race – and won; and the following year he won the 1,000 Kilometre Race in Buenos Aires. He was second in both races the next season and after that was briefly on the Porsche team. He remained an enthusiast, however – and who better to be enthusiastic about than a young designer called Colin Chapman?

In the late 1950s Juhan had returned to Europe and eventually settled in Geneva. He and his wife Marie-Denise built up a series of businesses, dealing in car components, wine, watches, diamonds. At one time their Perrin Importeurs business distributed Lotus but according to Bushell that arrangement ceased in 1974. In 1976, however, Chapman and the Juhans did another deal: Chapman decided to abandon European distributors altogether since Britain had entered the Common Market and move to a single-tier system for distribution – direct from the family to the dealer. 'And we engaged the Juhans,' says Bushell, 'because they are multi-lingual and have contacts to find those dealers for us. And to organize these dealers to take cars off us. They also were very useful in organizing local technical clearances in these countries where equipment or type approval was required.' To do this for Lotus, says Bushell, the Juhans set up a company called LCI SA Distribution Automobile. It sounds as if it might stand for Lotus Cars International, but Bushell claims it stands for 'nothing particularly'.

When Lotus asked the Juhans in 1977 to find contract work for them, a new shelf company was prepared. We now switch to Panama for a moment, a country with which Juhan had some familiarity from his South American days. On August 7, 1977 ILC Inc was created by De La Guardia, Arosemena & Benedetti, described as a 'second-tier' law firm, which means that it is big and its partners come from well-to-do Panamanian families. Erasmo De La Guardia, one of the founders (although no longer a director) is a brother of a former Panamanian leader. The common practice in Panama is that thousands of little shelf companies are created each month, to be sold to 'foreign interests' to use for their own reasons, usually to do with tax or the avoidance of disclosure – or, more likely, both.

ILC Inc stood ready for the Juhans to buy it and use it – as soon as they had something to put into it. Its time was near.

By the first week in September, Chapman, although he was still adamantly refusing DeLorean's offers for the whole company, was weakening on doing the contract work on the DMC-12 sports car. Even so, he might never have accepted had it not been for a tragedy which shook him badly. The Grand Prix season was now approaching its climax. It had reached the stage where drivers were already making their arrangements for the following season, manoeuvring for places in the new teams. Ronnie Peterson was tired of playing second fiddle to Mario Andretti. He had done well – he was the only man who could overtake Andretti. Peterson, 34, was a tall, pale Swede regarded by his peers as the fastest of all Grand Prix drivers. He had finished four times in second place behind Andretti, strictly honouring his agreement to do nothing to jeopardize Andretti's chances. Now he decided to leave Lotus at the end of the season to join McLaren.

But for the Italian Grand Prix at Monza early in September, both Lotus drivers were in top form. Monza is an unpopular track with drivers. The cars start on a wide straight and then funnel into a narrow corner, unlike other tracks that are the same width throughout. Under the rules in force that day, the cars approached the starting grid from the warm-up lap. When they were all in position, a red light came on. Six seconds later it turned to green and the race was on.

The idea was to permit up to 24 cars to be spaced out in rows of two, have the cars come to rest and engage first gear. That September day, some of the cars in the rear were in third gear moving at 90 miles an hour when the light turned to green. So they jumped the start, causing the cars in front to bunch. The result was disastrous.

Peterson started from the third row. His car took off sluggishly and several rows of cars behind shot past before he got to the zig-zag turns of the chicane. James Hunt's McLaren was right on his tail. Then Hunt was rammed from behind, hit Peterson's car and caused the Lotus to slide across the track. Vittorio Brambilla's Surtees rammed it broadside. The cars crowding in from behind piled into them. Within three seconds of the start, there was a ten-car smash-up.

Peterson's car, its 55-gallon fuel tank full, was hurled into a guardrail and caught fire, the driver trapped under the twisted steering wheel. Hunt leapt from his stalled McLaren and with help ripped off Peterson's safety belt and eased him out of the flames and smoke as a track marshal sprayed foam on the wreck.

Both the Swede's legs were broken and he had suffered burns and lung damage from inhaling the fumes. At first he seemed to be recovering from emergency surgery, but complications set in. The following day he fell into a coma as clots began to block the blood and oxygen supply to his brain, kidneys and lungs. On September 11 he died.

Andretti was sixth in a re-run race that was won by Niki Lauda – and that was good enough to capture the 1978 world title. But it was a deeply distressed Chapman who returned to his headquarters in Norwich to pick up the pieces of his business.

Chapman had been there before. He had never fully got over the death at the wheel of a Lotus of his great friend Jim Clark. It was Chapman's partnership with Clark that had first established Lotus at the top of world Grand Prix Racing in the 1960s. When Clark was killed, Graham Hill took over and won the 1968 World Championship, only to die in another accident years later, when he landed his plane in fog. World Champion Jochen Rindt had also died in a Lotus – ironically at Monza as well – eight years before. He was replaced by Emerson Fittipaldi, who also became World Champion in a Lotus. Now Peterson had been killed through no fault of the driver or of the car. Tragedy was part of car racing. Drivers died, but the team went on. Chapman would bounce back, he had been a driver himself and knew the score. But it did not make it any easier.

It was at this time that he began to negotiate seriously with John DeLorean.

There is still some mystery as to how the deal was revived after its inauspicious start. Bushell's version is this: 'After a lapse, the Juhans got onto us and said they had ascertained that DeLorean was going around Europe looking for means to engineer his new car and various people were being approached. Why the hell weren't Lotus involved? We told them that we had had discussions with him regarding buying the company and that we weren't interested. And they said "Well, someone else is going to get the contract regarding the engineering work. Wouldn't this be just what you're looking for?" And again Chapman was very uninterested. He just didn't think it was going to be a viable programme. He didn't really think that DeLorean could make it. And all we knew about it at the time was what we had read in the press, a very coy statement that the British government were going to provide him with a factory in Belfast. They didn't mention any funding for the car at all.'

According to Bushell, 'The Juhans were saying, well, this work is going to go somewhere. We've spent a lot of money on your behalf in the past year looking for contracts and not got very much in return yet. At least talk to the man.'

DeLorean had gone to Lotus twice that summer, the first time in July, the second time in September. On that second occasion, recalls Bushell, 'he had already made the assumption that he'd bought Lotus. His opening comments were "Well, now that I own the place . . ."' As far as Bushell recalls, the next time Chapman and DeLorean met was in Geneva, at the invitation of the Juhans, at the end of October. Long before that, however, the deal seems to have been agreed, if not yet fully consummated.

On September 20, nine days after Ronnie Peterson died, the name of the Panama shelf company ILC Inc was changed. It had been bought from the lawyers in Panama by a group including the Juhans. Eloy Benedetti of the law firm refused to confirm who else was involved. But he did provide some information. 'This John DeLorean was part of the corporation,' he told *Automotive News*. To the *Sunday Telegraph* he confirmed that Colin Chapman was also involved. The vehicle for the two men to do business had been created.

From now on, John DeLorean had no doubts who would build his car for him. It would not be his loyal engineer Bill Collins who was now effectively out of a job. Nor would it be Porsche or BMW. It would be Colin Chapman.

Chapman was a trim, pale man with piercing blue eyes and a clipped moustache, his fair hair showing the first tinges of grey. He had a decisive, sometimes 'grumpy', air and a reputation for being difficult. 'He was not the easiest man to live with,' says

Bushell, who for 25 years was as close to him as anyone was. 'The better things went with the racing team, the harder the time Chapman gave the rest of us. When things were going well, he would get the big stick out and beat us for not matching it.' He was 'a bit of a Jekyll and Hyde'. When he left Norwich for a race meeting, they never dared even to ring him for a decision – 'No bloody way,' says Mike Kimberley. 'I couldn't live with him at a race meeting,' says Bushell. 'That's why I rarely went. Because he wasn't the man I knew. At a race meeting he was entirely different. In motor racing decisions have to be made quickly, there's no finesse, it's either yes or no, you've only got 24 hours before the flag drops. Once he got to a race meeting he just changed personalities and that was probably the secret of his success. And he would change back the minute the meeting was over.'

Despite his success and his millionaire status, Chapman was a private, almost lonely figure, with few close friends apart from his immediate family – his wife Hazel, a son and two daughters. In more recent years he had developed a weight problem, the pounds going on and off in reverse relationship to his Grand Prix fortunes.

3

Back in New York, Walter Strycker, unaware of events shaping in Europe, was getting his first taste of John DeLorean's accounting. Until the deal with Northern Ireland, there was very little money around. As Dewey had discovered, it was going out faster than it came in. In the summer of 1978, Dick Brown had to lend the company money as DeLorean kept up his expensive lifestyle.

'There were some things that came up real quick after I got exposure to the books,' said Strycker later. 'One was that John gave himself a retroactive raise back to January 1 of 1978 and I also found out that although he said he wasn't taking any compensation, in lieu of a salary he was taking a cost of living allowance for being in New York.'

That cost of living allowance was $150,000 a year. And the raise that DeLorean gave himself meant his salary went from $150,000 to $375,000.

Over the following months, Strycker was to question again and again the enormous expenses of the operation.

'I can't wait the five or six years it will take for the company to perform,' DeLorean told him bluntly. 'I want to live now.'

On October 2 John DeLorean was back in Belfast for what was scheduled to be a big day. He brought Cristina with him. Brown and Hollinshead were right on schedule. Exactly two months after the signing of the agreement with Northern Ireland, the champagne bottles popped for the ground-breaking ceremony. The Northern Ireland Minister of State Don Concannon, Roy Mason's deputy, did the honours, heading up a cast of hundreds, including the Lord Mayor of Belfast, the Mayor of the local town of Lisburn, and a host of local politicians, clergymen and dignitaries. Ten large bulldozers moved forward to begin churning up the mud. The building of John DeLorean's factory had begun.

DeLorean made a little speech. 'We have been working very hard both here and in the States the past 60 days. I must say that our experience and the accomplishments in Dunmurry thus far has only reinforced our conviction that Northern Ireland, with its highly motivated and competent workforce is the ideal place for DMC to assemble our entry into the world's prestige car market.'

Beside him, Cristina's elegance and style contrasted with the drab costumes of the local people. But it was all smiles that day. Everything was moving forward.

That day DeLorean chaired the first full board meeting of the new Northern Ireland company. Brown and Collins were both members. So was Stylianides. NIDA was represented by Shaun Harte and Ronnie Henderson. Tom Kimmerly was also a DMCL director from the beginning, although he refused DeLorean's offer to join the DMC board on grounds of professional conflict.

By now DeLorean had told his directors he was making a deal with Lotus, but no one was quite sure yet what sort of deal except perhaps for DeLorean himself (and Kimmerly). He told Strycker in New York that he was thinking of buying Lotus, that NIDA would fund it, and that he would create a new Porsche in Britain, offering engineering deals to the auto world.

NIDA was complaining that the cash withdrawal from the Agency and from the Department of Commerce was falling behind schedule. So DeLorean obliged by speeding it up.

He had already made a 10p a share cash call – £1,775,000 – immediately after the signing. Now at that day's board meeting he called for another 15p, making £4,439,250, and requested a further £1,775,700 (the pound was then approaching $2.00) by November 15. The money was rolling in very nicely.

The Lotus headquarters where John DeLorean went to negotiate that summer and autumn was very different from anything the Detroit man had ever seen, and it filled him with a desire to acquire something similar for himself. It was hidden away in the East Anglian countryside, approached either through narrow country lanes – along which tiny Lotus cars could be glimpsed hurtling round hairpin bends – or by private plane into Chapman's airstrip. DeLorean preferred to fly in – the journey by car took nearly three hours from London.

Chapman's office was in Ketteringham Hall, once an English nobleman's country mansion, later a United States officers' wartime mess, then a prep school. There was an ornamental lake complete with moorhens, and pheasants inhabited the hedgerows. The design studio occupied what was once the chapel. Racing cars lined up in what had been the stables. It seemed a charming place – very English, a combination of Old World elegance and modern technology.

On the edge of the park was a former bomber base where, 35 years before, Flying Fortresses had taken off to bomb Hitler's Germany. Now the hangars were assembly plants for Lotus cars, part of the airfield a test track. It was here that Chapman, year after year, attempted a new design in Grand Prix cars while other designers seemed to have reached a plateau of performance.

It was here, also, that Chapman had his main business – although not his chief interest – of designing and building, with exacting precision, his high performance, high-priced sports cars. Once he had made more than 4,000 cars a year. Now he was down to less than 400, and he was spending heavily on the research and development of a new car, the Turbo Esprit. It would be easy enough to design two cars at once, use some of the same components, some of the same design team – build a car for DeLorean and for Lotus side by side.

Until DeLorean could strike a deal with Chapman, there wasn't even a place for Collins and his team to sit. Chapman put them in the chapel of Ketteringham Hall and at first they found it a delightful place. 'Anne Boleyn lived here,' a Lotus man told them. There was supposed to be the ghost of an airman in the rafters of one of the old hangars. But history and graciousness were no compensation for their growing frustration.

Collins had expected to explain his prototype to the Lotus people and help them through the next stages. He was, after all, the chief engineer. He was an experienced man with a good record at the biggest auto company in the world, making more cars in a single hour's production than Lotus did in its entire history. There were four years of his work in the car, and he had a good team with him – experienced American car men who knew the DMC-12 as well as he did. He never got a chance to.

In the early weeks of October, DeLorean's dealings with the Juhans in Geneva had moved to the point where there was now a draft contract. It laid down the amounts: $12.5 million to be paid by the Oppenheimer Limited Partnership scheme, which had officially come into being on September 22, its net $15.5 million after expenses and fees now deposited in the Chemical Bank in New York; another £2.5 million to be paid by DMCL in Belfast for the rights to the VARI plastic moulding process developed by Lotus since the mid-1960s, starting with its Europa model. (Even at this early stage, and still without serious negotiation with Chapman, DeLorean was prepared to surrender on ERM, now that he was talking about an actual production car.)

Mid-October and the pace was now increasing. DeLorean had to have someone to build that car, and he knew it had to be Chapman – no one else could do it in the time available, no one else had the same reputation in the type of engineering he wanted. And no one else was available.

On October 17 there was a tiny but highly significant signing ceremony in Panama: the three members of the Junta Directiva, or board of directors, of GPD Services Inc – Rodrigo

Arosemena, Eloy Benedetti and Cecilia Arosemena de Gonzalez Ruiz – gave power of attorney to Mrs. Denise Juhan Perrin, more often known as Denise Juhan. Control of GPD had now officially passed to Switzerland.

A day later, DeLorean turned up in Belfast with the draft version of the GPD contract. He convened a board meeting to seek approval for two major moves. The GPD contract was the second and lesser one. The first was the acquisition of a controlling shareholding in Lotus. For that, however, he needed NIDA approval – and NIDA was cautious, insisting that it was not its position to support a foreign-owned company in the acquisition of a British concern. That took DeLorean aback. He had relied on NIDA support. Would the Agency object if he raised the funds separately and made the acquisition? He got a grudging approval to do that. He also got from his board approval for the GPD deal.

There was one problem with Chapman, DeLorean is said to have admitted. Chapman was reluctant to do the work except on his own terms – and that meant through an intermediary in Switzerland. Everyone there understood his point. Chapman did not want to pay tax which at that stage under the Labour government in Britain ranged up to 83 percent. He would do it, hinted DeLorean, if the money could be paid in a 'tax efficient' way. 'It was absolutely clear in everybody's mind that it was being done this way because that was the only way that Lotus would play ball,' says one of the people present that day.

The board that day approved a payment to GPD for £2.5 million. Britain still had exchange controls, so it was not a simple matter transmitting funds. The Donegall Square West branch of Northern Bank Limited in Belfast handled it, filling in a form of 'application to purchase foreign currency'. Later that day John DeLorean and Myron Stylianides dropped by to sign it, each of them twice. The name and address of the beneficiary was clearly stated: GPD Services Inc., European Office, 120 Rue de Lausanne, 1202 Geneva, Switzerland. And the amount: $4.9 million. It was not yet a transfer of cash – but it was well on the way to it.

3,000 miles away another cheque was made out to GPD that day. On Broad Street at the Wall Street district branch of Chemical Bank, a clerk filled in the amount: $12.5 million. The net $15.5 million raised by the DeLorean Research Limited Partnership, which had finally come into being on September 22, had been deposited there. On that Wednesday the bank had received a telex from John DeLorean. Now one of the DeLorean financial staff turned up, signed the cheque on behalf of DMC which was the General Partner, and carried the cheque back across town.

It would spend most of the following fortnight in John DeLorean's wallet, carefully folded.

From Belfast DeLorean returned to London and then New York, where he spent the weekend, picked up the cheque and by the middle of the following week was back in London again. He had to do that deal with Chapman, and it had to be quickly. He had let the Collins operation in Coventry slide to the point where now it would be doubly difficult to revive it. Collins was in Norfolk with his team, and mentally DeLorean seemed already to be counting Lotus as part of his burgeoning empire. He would find a way of talking Chapman into seeing things his way.

He assembled some of his team from Belfast in London. Robin Bailie, now DMCL's lawyer in Belfast, came over to work with solicitors and merchant bankers in London on the details of buying control of Lotus. Shaun Harte from NIDA came too at DeLorean's request and it was DeLorean, Harte and Bailie who went to the Bank of England's Exchange Control division just across the road from St. Paul's Cathedral. The Bank had to vet all transactions which involved transfer of funds out of Britain. If there was a bona fide contract for a bona fide business, then it was just a formality. DeLorean had the draft GPD contract with him. Harte agreed that the Northern Irish authorities accepted the payment as above board. It had been passed properly by the board at DMCL. The Bank gave its blessing without fuss.

DeLorean had been joined by Tom Kimmerly. Bailie at the end of the week went back to Belfast. But DeLorean asked him to be in Geneva on Sunday night. He and Kimmerly went to Geneva that Sunday too. By their own airplane, Colin Chapman and Fred Bushell arrived also, booking in at the President Hotel, Geneva's best. The serious negotiations were about to begin.

The next few days were neither friendly nor easy. Neither Chapman nor DeLorean were men who normally stayed in one place for three days on end, going over minutiae. DeLorean had not done it for Puerto Rico, nor for the Irish Republic, nor even for Northern Ireland. No one had ever known him stay so long in one negotiation. Chapman, if anything, was even more impatient. 'He was a man who couldn't sit still even through a meal,' recalls a friend. 'I remember once at lunch there were no tomatoes. And Colin liked tomatoes. Instead of waiting for the girl to come back in, he went out to the kitchen and sliced them himself. He was the most active man I've ever met.' They were, to that extent, two of a sort.

There were four separate rooms used during the negotiations: at the President, at DeLorean's hotel, at the offices of the lawyers, and at the Juhans'. 'Most of the meetings were to disagree,' recalls Fred Bushell. He remembers who was there: 'A host of people. Chapman and me of course. The Juhans from time to time, both of them. There were American lawyers. Tom Kimmerly was there. There was a series of lawyers wheeled in and out and other people, and really it was a marathon type of thing that went on quite late in the afternoon. There would be recessions where they would go and talk to GPD and then somebody would come and talk to us over coffee, and we would say "Sod that, we've been here long enough." For Colin to be in one room for three or four days was a miracle. He was running the racing programme, back at the hotel. Phoning up, running the rest of the business. And then we would meet again for another couple of hours. And most of it was negative.'

Bushell recalls that Chapman was negative from the beginning almost to the end. It was Bushell, worried about the finances, who wanted the DeLorean contract. 'Colin, while he was far-thinking, would not let financial considerations enter into the argument at all. He would be concerned about the product work, whether it was good for the company image, whether it was good for Colin Chapman's image. But I wanted to see that we could get that kind of work. I must have saved the negotiations two or three times, because I would go out of the room and talk to Colin and bring him back in and we would lower the temperature and talk again.'

The argument was not over the money – the Juhans seemed

to have set the rate for the job, according to Bushell. Nor was it over GPD's position – 'We had accepted that they had set the job up,' says Bushell. It was about the car itself and the tight programme. DeLorean insisted the job had to be done in 18 months – he argued that it was really quite simple, mostly a matter of re-sourcing American components to European components for a car which was already fully designed and ready to go. 'What you've got there is no more than a stage in a mock-up,' Chapman told DeLorean at one stage. From the ground up, he argued, Lotus would take three to four years to build a car like that – and this would be a 'ground-up' job.

There were long arguments over the configuration of the car, in particular the way the engine was to be mounted. DeLorean wanted the engine in the back; Chapman produced mid-engine cars and held strong views. From the engine, Chapman turned his attention to another part of the DMC-12 that he did not like. 'These gull-wing doors. Nobody does those, they're vintage, they belong to Mercedes twenty years ago. What on earth makes you think they are either marketable or feasible?'

DeLorean's strategy, however, was to appeal to Chapman's competitive instinct, set him the challenge. 'Nobody else could do it maybe – but *you* could.' And gradually Chapman gave way, saying, 'Yes, anything can be done, provided you are prepared to spend the money on it.'

Even if they made the doors work, he insisted, 'in my opinion they will not be a marketing aid.' DeLorean, however, had him on weak ground there: Chapman that year was making fewer cars than DeLorean planned to build in a single month. Marketing was not Chapman's strong point, and he knew it. All of DeLorean's reputation in the auto industry on the other hand came from his marketing successes. So Chapman switched his attack on the door to technical ones. 'There will be problems with getting it to fit and close properly. And what happens when the car rolls over? There will be difficulties with federal certification. We could do you conventional doors, much cheaper, much better.' DeLorean, however, hung on to his gull-wing doors, reckoning that – without them and his stainless steel shell – his car would be undistinguished, just another car.

Chapman raised doubt after doubt about DeLorean's

dream. 'The package is wrong,' he said. 'The performance just isn't there. We know that engine well and it's an unexciting engine. What place does it have in the sports car market?'

It was Bushell who kept persuading Chapman into a semblance of diplomacy. Chapman feared failure. 'Unless you let me have a free hand, I don't want to do it,' he said again and again.

DeLorean gave way on point after point, saying 'I don't care how you do it, just so long as you leave the engine in the back, the gull-wing doors, the stainless steel body and enough room behind the passengers for a full set of golf clubs.' He then added a few more points until Chapman said: 'You're not leaving me enough room.'

'We had a mental picture,' says Fred Bushell, 'that if anything was going to go wrong with the project, we – Lotus and Colin Chapman's personal reputation – would be sullied, we would be the patsies in the middle. There was an occasion when we were sitting there on our own, thinking about the latest comment from John, and we said, "Well, we can get over that – the way it's being offered to us, we can probably avoid Lotus being in direct contractual obligation to DeLorean." We had to be careful to avoid John DeLorean being able to lean on Chapman. Chapman said "He's not going to be able to walk in here and tell me what to do. I've already said I'm not going to sell him the company. There is no way you're going to drag me into that situation." '

Chapman continued to be very concerned about product liability. In his chairman's statement, written only weeks before he died in December 1982, he said 'Our company was initially chary of the implications of this (DeLorean) proposition, involving an American operation and predominantly an American market, from the aspect of possible future problems and product liability. You may recall we were already having some problems of this nature at the time.'

One example was then uppermost in his mind. Says Mike Kimberley: 'An 11-year-old Europa, with a Renault engine, was sold in Britain and imported into Canada before regulations became the norm. It was then transferred across the border and sold in Detroit and sold on 11 times. It was eventually converted to a race-track car with a roll-cage on it, a different body on it and the head was taken off and skimmed; it had a different carburettor put on it, two fuel tanks, one on either side were added ... And then one night, a Christmas Eve, the young chap who owned it was out at a party with his girlfriend and driving home at about two o'clock in the morning on icy roads, over the brow of a hill, doing 75 in a 45 mph restricted zone, girlfriend crying in the passenger seat saying slow down, he lost it on the ice, spun off, hit a curb, demolished a telegraph pole, slid for 100 yards. The bloke crawled out, but the girl was injured and she sued him. And he hadn't got any insurance so he sued us. Or a lawyer did on a contingency basis for God knows how many millions of dollars. And *that* was the sort of law-suit we were suffering under the product liability American situation.'

To an American auto company that sort of law-suit is part of life. To a small British specialist car company, it is terrifying.

'Here was a car,' says Fred Bushell, 'that we weren't very impressed with. We were likely to be involved in its design engineering and we thought to ourselves "Jesus, the exposure on that for the next 20 years could just about wipe us out."' A clause was inserted into the contract which read: 'The Partnership and Limited agree to hold GPD and its nominated contractors harmless against any or all claims that may be made in the future by users of the finished product.' The Partnership would take out insurance for $5 million minimum to cover it. So that hurdle was eventually cleared. That was in Chapman's mind perhaps the most important. 'It was only the fact that in this case GPD Services Inc. was the principal contractor and was able to cover the financial and other risks involved, that encouraged us to accept the assignment,' he wrote later.*

On Tuesday, October 31, the Northern Bank in Donegall Square, Belfast, had another application to purchase foreign currency. This time the amount was a modest $250,000, to take the total to $5.15 million, or £2,500,000. This time the signatures were Myron Stylianides and 'Buck' Penrose for DeLorean, but instead of the beneficiary being neatly typed in, as it was before, it was written in, in a hand which uncannily resembles

---

* Chairman's statement, Group Lotus, December 1982.

John DeLorean's. Again the beneficiary was GPD. With the Bank of England having approved the overall arrangement, permission was now a formality. The Northern Bank now had $5.15 million ready to be wired to GPD in Geneva. John DeLorean had another, and now slightly grubby, $12.5 million cheque folded away in his wallet. All it needed was a signature on that document – or documents, for there were at least three.

The next day, November 1, was signing day at last. The contracts were finally agreed. The GPD contracts were signed simply *Juhan* for Madame Denise Juhan. John DeLorean signed on behalf of both DMCL in Belfast and the Partnership. Both initialled every page of the ten-page contracts. GPD had a separate contract with Lotus.

Now, for still unexplained reasons, there were at least three versions, typed on different typewriters and individually signed, of the contract between GPD and DeLorean. One was later found in the files of DMCL in Belfast, a second and cleaner version was filed with the SEC, and a third was given to the authors by a DeLorean executive who had not noted the differences. The rougher two are dated November 1, 1978. The cleaner version is marked on the front 'Effective November 1, 1978'.

But there also seems to have been a fourth (and earlier) version that Strycker, Brown, Collins or Dewey never recall seeing. But Harry DeWitt, Dewey's original assistant, does.

'The original contract was typed on two sheets of paper, by a very flimsy typewriter, not an electric, obviously a manual typewriter,' says DeWitt. 'With very bad legal language in it. I don't know who wrote it, but that's the original agreement that came back from Switzerland.'

De Witt also recalls that although the amounts of money in the original contract were the same, the signatures were not.

DeWitt no longer has a copy of that contract. 'I had one in my files at home and when I moved, I'm sure I moved those files. When the shit hit the fan, so to speak, I went back to find it and all my files were intact except that particular one.' His garage had been broken into and the only thing missing was the GPD file.

The earliest version gave a fictitious address for GPD – a public building in Geneva. It also required 'upfront' payments of $12.5 million from the Partnership, $5.15 (£2.5 million) from DMCL. That was later changed to an 'upfront' payment of $8.5 million from the Partnership, the other $4 million to be paid in four instalments through 1979. This actually meant that $4 million was returned by GPD to the Partnership, and then paid back again, possibly so that it would be tax deductible in 1979. There are differences, apparently minor, in wording between the contracts which would interest the investigators later but the main provisions and payment schedules in all of the public versions are the same.

The contract essentially stipulated that the Partnership, now the owner of the rights to the car itself, intended to develop a 'prototype sports coupe with 6-cylinder V engine to series production readiness', and that DeLorean Motor Cars Limited of Belfast intended to develop a VRIM (Vacuum Resin Injection Moulding) 'alternative to ERM plastic components'. Both the Partnership and DMCL desired 'to engage the services of GPD for design, test and calculation work for these purposes.'

ERM had only come up near the end of the discussions. Chapman was caustic about it. DeLorean's original idea with ERM was to make a monocoque shell, a one-piece moulding for the whole underbody. The technology of that, however, was beyond him, and he now wanted to do it in a number of parts. Chapman argued that his VARI process was proven and that he could produce a body in two halves that met all the American crash regulations. 'We already know we can do that, because we've done it.' DeLorean gave way, but only on a number of early cars – the first 2,000 cars would be built of VARI, ERM to be used after that. In the event ERM was never used except for a few minor parts.

The contract was signed before Robin Bailie, still kicking his heels, saw a copy. He now raised a serious point with his client John DeLorean. DMCL and the Partnership had a contract with GPD. They had no contract with Lotus, although Lotus was to do the work. How could the DeLorean company therefore be assured that Lotus would carry out all the research and development work that GPD had contracted to do? It had not occurred to anyone before. It was Bailie who suggested that Lotus should guarantee GPD's contract, and Chapman agreed.

This meant that a contractor was guaranteeing the work of an agent – a highly unusual procedure, and one that indicates that Chapman had by now become very anxious for that contract.

The result was a letter, written on Lotus headed notepaper, and addressed to DMCL and the Partnership. It read:

> Gentlemen,
>
> In consideration of DRLP and DMCL entering into an agreement with GPD Services Inc. of even date (a copy of which is attached) and Lotus Cars Ltd., being named a sub-contractor under agreement of even date, we hereby warrant and guarantee to you the timely and full performance of each and every obligation of GPD Services Inc. under your agreement with GPD.

It was signed by Colin Chapman and Fred Bushell.

GPD, whatever its status, undertook to complete a product/vehicle layout, with detailed drawings of all the parts that could be used for production purposes. The concern had to provide complete component lists, assembly manuals, tolerances, material specifications. It had to perform analytical calculations of design variants, economy, handling, brakes. It had to make the tools, do the testing – basically build a car 'based on existing initial styling work and prototype's technical documents'.

DeLorean, for his part, was to make available to GPD 'the services of employees . . . to assist GPD in the performance of the services to be rendered by GPD under this contract'.

In other words, although he didn't know it, Collins and his team were working for a Swiss post office box.

On page four of the ten-page contract, Chapman made his first appearance. There it says: 'GPD confirms it has retained the services of Lotus Cars Ltd. ('Lotus') of Norwich, England, including the services of Mr. A. C. B. Chapman to assist in this project. It is acknowledged that the personal involvement of Mr. Chapman is fundamental to these arrangements.'

The Oppenheimer Limited Partnership was the visible senior DeLorean party to the contract. It was funding all the engineering work and agreed to pay $12.5 million for research and development. Salaries for personnel involved, 'who are anticipated to number approximately 80', were to be paid in addition, most of them from Partnership funds.

The Belfast company, on the other hand, was paying only for work on the VRIM process that would replace ERM. For its research and development work on the plastic, GPD was to be paid $5.15 million from the Belfast company, plus travel and salary expenses.

The contract therefore involved a payment to GPD of some $17.65 million for research work plus salaries, travel expenses and other costs. In the event the Partnership was to pay a total of $12.65 million. DMCL paid $5.15 million, plus another £12 million over the next two years. We now know how much Lotus got – just under £12 million. None of those 'research' payments, including all the Partnership's $12.65 million and DMCL's $5.15 million ever got to Lotus. They are still missing.

On November 1 John DeLorean took that $12.5 million cheque and passed it to GPD. The following day Mr. B. H. Menown, an assistant manager at the Northern Bank in Donegall Square, wrote to DMCL's financial controller, D. Tanney. The sum of $5.15 million, then equivalent to £2,499,258.50, had been telex transferred to United Overseas Bank, Geneva 'for account GPD Services Inc. per instructions of Mr. R. Bailie'.

What happened to that money? Who got it? Did DeLorean and Chapman divide it between them, either equally or on some predetermined share? GPD was only a convenient and empty shelter company used for the purpose of bringing the two companies together. Could it possibly claim $17.87 million commission on such a deal? For introducing people who already knew each other? It's possible – but not credible. The Juhans are perfectly reputable Swiss business people and there is no suggestion that they kept it, although they presumably took a commission for their work. (That commission would be paid by Lotus though, not by DeLorean who was awarding the contract.)

There was an elaborate attempt by certain Lotus people to pretend that GPD was something more than it was, that its 'personnel travelled the world looking for contracts', although it had not even existed until September 1978. In our research on this book we have found that those close to Chapman believed DeLorean had it all; those close to DeLorean believed Chapman spirited it away. That one, or both of them, did so is almost beyond doubt.

At the time, Brown, Strycker and others wondered enough to ask DeLorean. 'Colin Chapman, we were told,' recalls Brown, 'wanted it done in Switzerland because it was beneficial for him from a tax standpoint and Chapman was supposed to have this GPD thing.'

Chapman did have a GPD thing, but it was a different GPD – it stood for Grand Prix Drivers and was a company Chapman set up in Geneva when he had nearly made a deal with Olympus Cameras to sponsor his Team Lotus Formula One cars. The deal fell through. The GPD we are dealing with stands for General Product Developments, according to the letterhead on a letter we received from Madame Juhan.

It is important to be clear about one factor relating to the Geneva meeting: it was probably the most secret John DeLorean ever held.

None of his directors, including Walter Strycker, even knew where he was. Strycker in fact had been expressly forbidden by DeLorean to accompany him. If there were American lawyers there, as Bushell thought he recalled, they were none of the usual DeLorean lawyers at the time: they knew nothing of GPD either. DeLorean had been open enough about doing the deal with Chapman, and had even showed the draft GPD contract around in advance. Afterwards, however, it became a hush-hush subject, deliberately deleted from documents, its name carefully not mentioned even in later SEC filings, although a copy of the contract was filed.

Even Robin Bailie, DMCL's solicitor who had formerly been counsel to both NIDA and the Department of Commerce but had moved over to DeLorean, apparently never attended a single meeting. He spent his time either sitting in his hotel room in Geneva or in one of the lawyer's offices. Dick Brown, still in Belfast at the time, remembers Bailie coming home. 'He was a little worried. I think because they could never get the meeting put together. They were waiting for this, that and the other thing.' That indeed may have been the way Bailie felt (he still feels bound by his professional relationship with DMCL so would provide no details, although he did confirm he was in

Geneva). Dick Brown himself was more than a little worried about it. It was a crucial contract to the whole future of the company yet none of the directors were in on it!*

This meeting was central to so much that followed – and perhaps to so much that had gone before too, although no one realized it. Those 125 investors whom Oppenheimer had found had invested their minimum $150,000 in the belief their money would be used for research on the car. It was through GPD that almost all of it was diverted, with the result that those individual partners today stand to lose their tax write-offs.

To Collins, the GPD deal and the decision to go ahead with the money from the Oppenheimer Partnership rather than from NIDA are clearly linked. 'Northern Ireland wanted us to go ahead without that Partnership. Why would John want to go ahead with it, anyway? Ostensibly it was because all those important people in the Partnership had already made the commitment and we couldn't back out on them. But then he couldn't have started GPD, could he?'

Later DeLorean was to give two different versions of how the contract with GPD came about – both to the *Sunday Telegraph*. He first said that in the summer of 1978, when he was looking for someone to build the car for him, he was approached out of the blue by GPD, which he'd never heard of, and offered a deal with Lotus on 'very good terms'. In another interview, however, he told a different story: it was Colin Chapman who insisted on the GPD connection.

Chapman's version was entirely different from both of DeLorean's versions. 'DeLorean wanted the deal done like that,' he told the *Sunday Telegraph* in November 1981.

If DeLorean and Chapman did siphon off that money – and there is plenty of evidence to suggest that DeLorean at least did – at what stage were they planning it? There is no doubt of Chapman's early reluctance to deal with DeLorean. The arguments in Geneva were long and at times heated and for the most part technical. But at least in the early stages both sides seemed to be working on the basis that the figures already in the

---

* The details revealed in this book relating to that meeting will be as new to John DeLorean's most senior executives as they are to the new reader.

draft GPD contract were firm figures for doing the work on the car, to cover everything except for a few minor items.

Let us for a moment look at it this way. Lotus got paid roughly half the total for doing all the research and development. Would Colin Chapman, knowing as he undoubtedly did how much was being paid to GPD, have settled for none of it? On the other hand would John DeLorean, his companies stretched for cash, willingly pay out all the Partnership's cash and another $5.15 million from his Belfast company for a contract which Lotus was willing to do for half the price (and did do for half the price)?

In November GPD did pay Lotus some money: a $4 million 'good faith' payment, which indicated that Chapman did not trust his new partner. It was not an advance. When it became clear that the British government, through DMCL in Belfast, was picking up all the costs incurred by Lotus, the money was paid back. By that stage, all the payments going to GPD were already coming from DMCL, although the Belfast company was only supposed to pay for the (less expensive) work on the VARI plastic process. The Partnership had used up its resources with that payment to GPD and some payments for work on ERM. From April on, after a curious five-month gap, the money was flooding into GPD from DMCL and being passed on. From April 4 the payments from DMCL to GPD match, to the figure and the date, those received by Lotus, except for a few minor ones. Yet it was August 22, 1979 before the Partnership's obligations were formally taken over by DMCL. A brief one-page contract drawn up by Robin Bailie agreed that from then on any further prototype vehicles would be the responsibility of DMCL.

Whatever the truth – and the last word has not been written – by November 1, 1978, John Z. DeLorean and Colin Chapman had a deal. DeLorean had some further agreements to sign and decided to travel up to Norwich and tell his engineering team about it at the same time.

It was an awkward journey. Normally DeLorean used a helicopter or Chapman sent a plane to pick him up in London. That day Norwich was covered in thick fog and DeLorean came by car. He stayed at an old brick hotel northeast of Norwich where Collins had settled in.

In the evening the group had dinner together in the dining room: John DeLorean, Bill Collins, Alan Cross, the other members of the team and their wives.

'John came in and we had some wine and celebrated the fact that Lotus was finally on board,' recalls Collins.

Money had now gone to GPD, and Bill Collins's status improved to the extent that Chapman moved him and his team out of the chapel to more permanent quarters – an old barracks on the Hethel air strip. But once there, they sat all day long, doing even less than before. Chapman still ignored them.

To Bill Collins, it was a complete mystery. Here he was at the heart of the most important project of his career – a new car and a new company. Since he joined, he had been working all hours to get it off the ground, trying with all he knew to come up with the revolutionary, ethical car that John DeLorean had asked him to build. Collins had been trying to do it in half the time Porsche might take. And he had, in his own view, made significant progress. He knew there was still a way to go, but at least he had a starting point. Surely Chapman, as a professional engineer himself, would welcome his input? And surely John DeLorean, as another professional engineer whose name was on the car, would insist on it?

He took the matter up with DeLorean.

'John, I can't understand it. You know I have a guy who has been in the chassis area working on the car. I have a guy in the safety emissions area. I have an electrical engineer. My chief draftsman is here. We've all worked varying lengths of time on this car. I myself have worked on it since 1974, and I know why some of the things are the way they are, and why we've not done some things. Why are we being ostracized?'

'Well,' replied DeLorean unconcernedly, 'take it up with Colin.'

Bill Collins could tell that John did not care. Chapman was busy on other projects, including his new Formula One car for the next season.

There was another, larger, problem brewing. Collins and his Detroit-bred team simply did not do business the way the Lotus engineers were used to designing a car. At Lotus, the entire design philosophy was geared to producing limited copies of high performance vehicles.

What this means is that the Lotus engineers did not bother themselves with the staggering mass of documentation, the myriad sketches, drawings and detailed instructions that are considered essential by any engineer schooled in GM-style mass production. Such detail was viewed as fussiness by the Lotus designers. To the Detroit-men there seemed to be a 'file it down until it fits' attitude that worked very well indeed in the hands of the highly skilled workmen in the Lotus assembly areas. In fact, such on-site fittings gave the car a considerable cachet with its owners; each Lotus could truthfully be said to be a hand-built, superbly engineered machine.

Collins, however, was horrified. Surely Chapman realized that such apparently individual engineering and designing would prove disastrous if it was tried out on a Dunmurry plant full of inexperienced factory hands? But Chapman was spending very little time on the DeLorean project. Although DeLorean represented the biggest contract Lotus had ever undertaken and one that was to contribute nearly half its total revenues for the next two years, Chapman refused to schedule a meeting with Collins at which Collins could explain his fears: the car he had worked on from its birth was being torn apart, both physically and metaphorically, by the Lotus engineers who were now building their own version.

ERM, in which the Limited Partnership had been asked to invest, was an early casualty. There was no longer any pretence that it would only be the first 2,000 cars which would be built of VARI. 'After we were given the job,' says Mike Kimberley, 'we assessed the ERM process and we also looked at the car. With our own VARI process, we could produce a body with its structure in two halves that would meet the American crash regulations. It was decided by John in the end that he would go the way of the Lotus process, by utilizing known technology that would assure him of doing the job far more quickly to meet this very critical time limit that was set. That was the fundamental reason for going to the VARI process rather than ERM. The ERM was not proved at that stage. And it was incapable of giving all the characteristics that you need, which is very much an integrated structure.'

When Kimberley had finished his evaluation, Chapman had walked DeLorean through his own clean, businesslike factory

John DeLorean (*front row, third from left*) plays the clarinet in the Lawrence Tech band

1968 – a chubby DeLorean poses with the new Pontiac Grand Prix, designed by his division. The car boasted 'the longest hood in the industry'

1973 – a new style DeLorean. His chin had been extended by cosmetic surgery and he had touched up his hair. In the background, the Chevrolet Vega

DeLorean now openly derided the General Motors code about conventional style in clothes. He cultivated the part of the laid-back maverick tycoon

With his second wife, Kelly Harmon. She was 25 years younger than he was

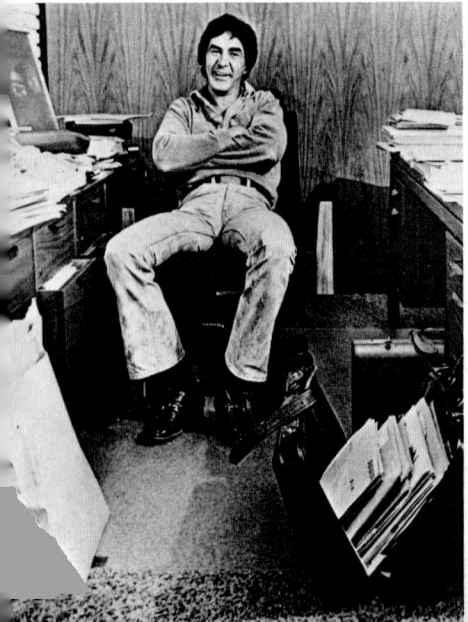

DeLorean's citrus ranch at Pauma Valley, near San Diego

With his third wife, Christina Ferrare, at their engagement party

'We aim to move from cow pasture to production within 18 months.' The DeLorean factory in Belfast, spacious modern buildings, models of their kind, brought jobs to thousands of unemployed

Colin Chapman, founder of Lotus cars, with two of his prize-winning racing car drivers, Gunnar Nilsson (*left*) and Mario Andretti

The competition: an early DM prototype (*second from left*) with Corvette, a Mercedes Benz and Porsch

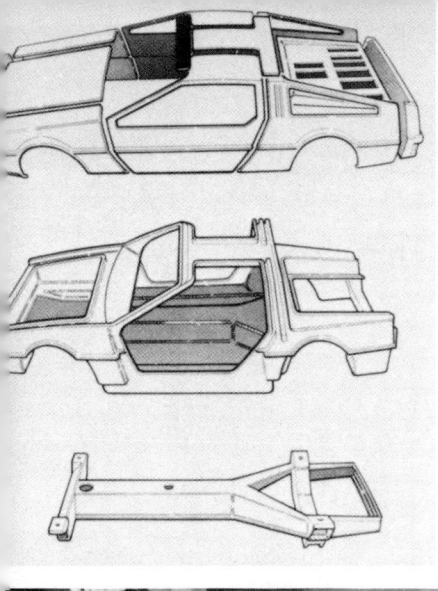

The original design, based on the revolutionary ERM plastic material, had no backbone. Chapman put one in

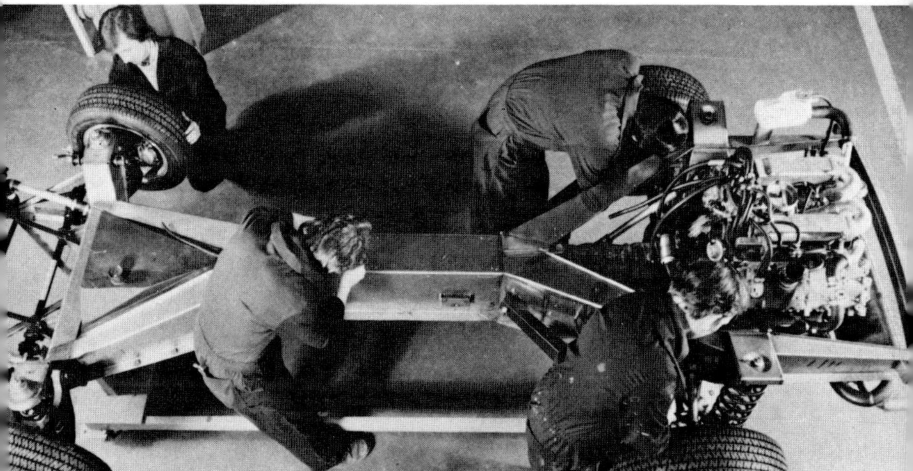

The interior: DeLorean laid down one requirement – there had to be enough room for a bag of golf clubs behind the seats

Chapman designed a chassis in the shape of a double-Y. The petrol tank went in the front notch, the engine at the back. Many of the parts were standard and conventional

The finished DMC-12. But the gull-wing doors gave problems on early models. And not everyone liked the stainless steel finish

DeLorean with Roy Mason and Don Concannon. They both remained fans until the end

At the height of his crisis, DeLorean took a turn on the stand at Earl's Court, greeting dignitaries such as Prince Michael of Kent

The team in Belfast: DeLorean and Gene Cafiero in the centre foreground. On the left is Shaun Harte and behind him Tony Hopkins of NIDA *Back row*: Hopkins, Alex Fetherston (NIDA representative on the DMCL board), Myron Stylianides, Joe Daly, David Adams (not a director), George Broomfield, Mike Loasby, Robert Donnell, Chuck Bennington and Brian Beharrell

The team in New York: *(above)* – Bill Haddad (public relations, 1979–81); *(below left)* – Bill Collins, the engineer who did the early design work; and – *(below right)* – Robert Dewey, the first chief financial officer

The loyal wife: Cristina (*left*) on one of DeLorean's rare visits to the Belfast factory; Cristina (*right*) with dramatic new hair-cut, outside the federal court

Unwanted cars pile up at the Belfast docks

Hands manacled behind his back, John DeLorean in Los Angeles on charges of distributing cocaine

floor, demonstrating again what VARI could do. DeLorean conceded that ERM would not be used on the DMC-12 model. He would, he told Chapman, probably save it for another model. John DeLorean neglected, however, to tell either his investors – or his own engineers. Collins was more bewildered than ever.

'You know,' Collins confided to a friend, 'there is Chapman who is a brilliant engineer. And there is DeLorean, who is a brilliant engineer. And there is lowly level engineer Collins down here, and there are too many engineers in the program with three of us.'

One of the reasons for the gap between Collins and Chapman was the Lotus man's open contempt for the prototype the Americans had delivered. There were now two DeLorean cars in existence, both of them made in the U.S. but by different model shops. One of them had a Citroen four-cylinder engine and, to the Lotus men, used to the fastest cars in the world, it was impossibly dull. They disliked almost everything about it.

'Look, it's got 19 welds in the exhaust system,' sneered a Lotus engineer.

'That's a prototype exhaust system,' argued Collins. 'That's the way you make them.'

'Well, it's not the way *we* make them at Lotus.'

Collins was to hear that refrain again and again. Lotus simply did not operate according to the strict mass-production codes and rules of Detroit.

'One of the first things you have to do in a new vehicle program,' he argued strenuously with Chapman, 'and I don't care whether it is a sports car or a passenger car or whatever – you start out after the styling is finished and you make a body draft and it is very accurate and it defines all the surface, all the exterior. And we have not gotten that done yet.'

Chapman just looked at him.

'That's not the way we do it here,' he eventually replied. 'We build a plastic underbody. We find out how much it shrinks and then we design the outside around it.'

Lotus, for all the brilliance of its engineers, of course, had never designed for any sort of volume. It was a problem that was to plague the production people in Dunmurry as they got the assembly lines going, and it meant that almost everyone involved in the project had to do considerable on-the-spot improvization before the cars began to roll.

Neither Collins nor Chapman was wrong. It was simply a matter, as both were realistic enough to admit, of a different philosophy of vehicle design. Chapman was designing the car in the way he always did – but in a way that was not necessarily ideal for a mass-produced car. Collins knew about designing mass-produced cars, but mass production to him meant a production line making hundreds of thousands of cars. The approaches of the two men were incompatible.

Early in 1979, still another engineer came on board. Mike Loasby was a slim, serious-looking, 42-year-old Midlander who had headed the engineering team at Aston Martin, producing some of the world's finest and most expensive luxury sports cars, machines in an engineering and price bracket way above the DeLorean.

He had been responsible for the V8 Vantage, the world's fastest accelerating production car, and the Aston Martin Lagonda, a machine that cost more than a Rolls Royce and was the last thing in sports car luxury – and whose technical problems nearly bust Aston. His final contribution to Aston was an amazing car called the Bulldog, which by coincidence also had gull-wing doors – something the DeLorean men, conscious that this was about the only unique feature about their car, were to resent. Only one Bulldog was ever made – and sold to an Arab for £120,000.

Like so many others, Loasby initially saw the DeLorean as an opportunity he could scarcely pass up. Here was a new project – a car being built by Colin Chapman at Lotus, a man absolutely at the top of his form. The project had all the government money it needed. It had a brand-new factory going up in Belfast. It had a dealership network. It had a man at the top who was still something of a legend to U.S. auto circles and to the American motoring public. How could it miss?

He landed right in the middle of Bill Collins's days of frustration and disappointment. The prototype that the Lotus people were now busily ripping apart was not Loasby's design, so he could watch it objectively at the beginning, although less so as time went by. Like Collins, Loasby soon wondered what he was doing there at all, since the Lotus people were so clearly doing all the engineering and there wasn't room for Collins, let alone him.

Soon the Lotus engineers were busily producing a car that Bill Collins would find virtually unrecognizable. One of the few similarities that remained was the distinctive Giugiaro design, and even that was altered later.

DeLorean had loftily stayed above the argument raging in the Norfolk countryside, refusing to support his own engineering team, almost never supporting Bill Collins's complaints. Collins now decided to try to shake him out of his aloofness.

'John, when you are at General Motors and you have a bum product like the Vega – and we both know that was a bum product – you can still rely on the Seville, the Pontiac, to carry you through,' he told him bluntly. 'But when you have only one product, you can't foul that one up because you have nothing to fall back on. You should be spending every minute with the thing and when those engineering changes are being made, you should be aware of every damn change!'

DeLorean was unmoved, uninterested. He went to Hethel once a month, his visits greeted by a flurry of activity by the Lotus people as they prepared the way for their biggest customer. Busy at any time, Lotus was particularly busy then.

Chapman, rarely seen by the DeLorean people, was always present if DeLorean appeared. The men who came over from Belfast were to notice the difference on visits when DeLorean accompanied them and when they were on their own.

The hangar would be cleared of Lotus cars, the Esprits that were taking shape alongside the DMC-12 moved out and the DMCs moved in. All the DeLorean cars would be sitting on ramps or in business-like positions.

Collins first, and later Loasby, pointed this out to DeLorean. But nothing changed, and DeLorean wasn't ever interested. It was Chapman's car and would be left to him.

'It's coming out as a stainless steel Lotus,' Collins grumpily told his colleagues. Later the engineers were to remark that if you added a stainless steel shell to the Esprit, the weight came out pound for pound the same as the DMC-12.

By early spring, Bill Collins had been ignored long enough. There was no place for him. The car being built had less and less of his own craftsmanship in it. It was time to leave. He saw

DeLorean one last time to say, as he put it himself, 'Adios John.'

DeLorean took it calmly and the meeting was amicable. DeLorean half-heartedly suggested that Collins stay on the board. But by March, he had gone to American Motors, and later teamed up with his old DeLorean mate Bob Dewey in starting their own company, Vixen Motor Co., in Detroit, making motor homes.

In their final meeting, Collins again brought up the mystery of GPD. He had been through the contract and he didn't understand it.

'John, this doesn't make sense to me,' he told him. 'You are paying Chapman this money, but then I think, in here, if I read it right, you also have to pay him time and materials.' To Collins it looked like a bad deal.

'Why should we pay him time and materials when we have already paid them?'

'Don't worry about it,' replied DeLorean. 'That's the way it is.'

CHAPTER EIGHT

The Dream Takes a Dark Shape

As 1979 opened, everything seemed to be in place for John DeLorean in Belfast. The bulldozers had worked through the winter, starting to convert the boggy fields of Dunmurry into what would become a custom-built, spacious factory, positively luxurious by the standards of the struggling British and European car industry.

Men who had never worked in their lives were enthusiastically seizing the opportunity they had thought would never come. From the Catholic estate of Twinbrook on one side to the Protestant enclave of Seymour Hill on the other, they watched as a small river was diverted and the steel framework began to appear.

350 miles away, in the Norfolk countryside, the car itself was being worked on by the man whose superb engineering skills were producing the fastest cars in the world's history.

In the United States, the dealer network was nearing completion, a body of wealthy men across the length and breadth of the nation, whose total assets mustered more than half a billion dollars. They had invested their money, had seen the prototype and liked it and were now impatiently waiting for the machine itself to arrive so they could begin selling it.

John DeLorean now had money, plenty of it. He had enough to build the factory, finish development of the car and get it onto the market. What's more, he had been able to construct the whole edifice without investing a nickel of his own. The British government had contributed far more generously than he could ever have imagined. The Oppenheimer Limited Partnership had come through – maybe not the full amount, but close. DeLorean was at last able to say he was really rich.

He was still working out of his room in the Chris-Craft office and there was no reason why he should be in New York at all.

But John DeLorean loved the New York scene, the feeling of being right at the centre of fast-changing fashions. Cristina thrived on it. They were making smart friends there, invited to the right sort of dinner parties, seen at the fashionable clubs and restaurants. DeLorean didn't belong naturally in that world: obsessed as he was with his health and figure, he had no interest in food and was happier with a bowl of zucchini at his desk than lunch at Le Pavillon. He barely drank – a single glass of white wine would be made to last through a long dinner party. Once, he had seen Hollywood as a great new world – faster, more modern, more progressive after the dull formal auto town of Detroit – but now even Hollywood had begun to wear off for him. New York was more exciting, more vibrant. His reputation there had gone ahead of him and, in a town of celebrities, John DeLorean stood out. But he needed an office to go with the new image.

By early 1979 he found what he was searching for: the penthouse suite on the 43rd floor of 280 Park Avenue, just across the street from the Waldorf Astoria. It was a smart building and an even smarter penthouse. The current occupant was the Xerox Corporation which had used it as its corporate headquarters. In a cost-cutting exercise Xerox had moved out, leaving behind a modest art collection and some fancy furnishings. It suited John perfectly. There was an express elevator to the 43rd floor; plenty of space. John had his own private bathroom, and his roomy office in the corner gave him panoramic views out over Manhattan. Ironically the General Motors building was visible, even on an unclear day. In one corner he placed a telescope, though no one ever saw him use it. His own desk was a standard burlwood veneer that Xerox had left. He covered the walls with photographs of Cristina, a framed copy of the formal agreement with Northern Ireland and some of the pictures he inherited.

At the same time he moved apartments, buying a Fifth Avenue duplex formerly owned by the wealthy widow Mabel Dodge, herself a Detroit matron. It was in Cristina's search for help in decorating this old-fashioned apartment that she first hired the services of an art-dealer and decorator named Maur Dubin who soon became a close friend of both of them. Later Cristina would write of Dubin in her diary on the day her husband was arrested: 'He does and does and does everything for you and never asks for anything in return.'

In addition to the new Fifth Avenue home, DeLorean showed Dubin the new Park Avenue office. For the decorator it was good material, and with a generous budget he went to work. The lobby area acquired two elegant life-sized dolls, in the style of George Segal, on either side of the reception desk. On the white marble floors he put rugs and red water buffalo hide chairs. Behind the reception desk he hung an enormous blown-up picture of the DMC-12 in full glorious colour. And, having acquired some paintings and sculptures, Maur Dubin began to kindle DeLorean's interest in building an art collection. Soon both of them were busily shopping in the art galleries.

In January 1979 the *Wall Street Journal* did a long piece on DeLorean with the headline: 'Taking on Detroit, John DeLorean says he'll show industry how to build cars!' A wry sub-heading read: 'Was he a pain in the neck?' referring to his GM fracas. The article concluded:

> Mr. DeLorean is moving faster than ever, spending half of each month away from his New York City home, jetting to and from such places as DeLorean Motor headquarters near Detroit, an auto test track in Phoenix and various spots in Europe – often with a stop in Belfast. His car collection has dwindled to a mere 25 vehicles, his two ranches in Idaho and his California avocado farm get scant attention, and he has sold his interest in the San Diego Chargers football team. He retains a small chunk of the New York Yankees – but his novel, dealing with the nuclear-arms race, remains unfinished and long-neglected.

That same article contained a quote from a Wall Street auto analyst, David Healey: 'When people ask my advice about investing in Mr. DeLorean's venture, I tell them to put the money into wine, women and song. They'll get the same return and have more fun.'

While DeLorean was concentrating on office furnishings, 3000 miles away there were swarms of engineers working over his dream car. Collins of course had gone, and with him much of the American flavour of the early prototype.

Collins never did work out why he had been ignored, and why the engineers at Lotus had treated him with such lofty contempt. In fact it had a great deal to do with the Geneva agreement, and the terms that Chapman then extracted for building the car. But it also had to do with another factor of which Bill Collins was ignorant, and which only now was becoming apparent: DeLorean had exaggerated greatly the work already done on the prototype. He had persuaded the Northern Irish authorities that the basic car was already built. Chapman too believed much more work had been done than was the case – otherwise he would have been even less convinced about hitting DeLorean's 18 month target.

It was Mike Kimberley, Lotus managing director and a favourite engineer of Chapman, who wrote the assessment that Collins referred to as 'War and Peace'. This document set the tone of the work on the car – and determined many of its features. 'War and Peace' was utterly damning of the prototype Doris 1. The body chassis structure was weak and needed a steel backbone; front and rear suspensions were unsatisfactory; almost every component fouled its neighbour; there were no sunvisors, ashtray, or space for a spare wheel. The door latches and water sealing were poor; the electrical system was incomplete; the rear lamps were only mock-ups. DeLorean had produced written results of tests on the air-conditioning – but the air-conditioning had not been connected on the car and would not even fit.

John DeLorean himself was at the meetings at which the basic parameters for the car that Lotus would build were laid down. The discussions were professional and long, seldom heated, although Chapman brusquely attacked some of the key points which DeLorean would not give way on, particularly the stainless steel shell and the gull-wing doors. 'It has to be designed from the skin inwards,' he told DeLorean at a meeting in Norwich in December 1978, 'which makes it very difficult. The most effective engineering process is to design from the structure outwards.' Several times he told DeLorean he wanted to start from scratch, and re-engineer the entire car. DeLorean, however, held on to the aspects of the car he regarded as crucial:

the stainless steel shell, the rear-mounted engine and the gull-wing doors. Chapman finally accepted these as 'important marketing features' but ran a back-up programme for standard doors just in case the gull-wings gave too much trouble. He took DeLorean around his paint-shop, showing him the gleaming colours they could paint the Lotus cars in, and the superb finish they could produce. 'As good as anything in the world,' he enthused, and DeLorean had to agree. But he wanted his stainless steel.

DeLorean also insisted on: Pirelli P7 tyres on 16-inch wheels; his own instrument package which had been expensively designed for his prototype; a rear three-quarter glass; air-conditioning for the American models; and of course the Giugiaro design. He wasn't worried about the spare wheel: Chapman could stick it on the rear of the car in 'continental touring' fashion if he preferred.

There was one other factor which DeLorean made much of and raised again and again until it became a great joke with the engineers: there had to be room behind the driver and passenger for a full set of golf clubs. 'This car is aimed at a particular section of the market,' he told the Lotus team as well as his own growing organization in Belfast. 'The horny bachelor who's made it!'

For the rest he increasingly accepted Chapman's recommendations. The cigar lighter, ashtray and door mirrors from the Lotus Esprit. A bigger engine – Chapman wanted to use something sprightlier than the 2.6 Renault engine DeLorean originally had in mind, and they compromised on the 2.85 litre Volvo P.I. engine which would not only give a bit more power but would also give 'read across' in the United States where it was used already, thus cutting down considerably on the tedious process of federal certification.

But now, as Lotus started transforming those specifications into a prototype, more and more DeLorean features dropped away. The tyres for example. The Pirelli tyres were 'too much shoe for too little performance', and also expensive – $200 each. Goodyears were cheaper, more readily available in the United States – and were adequate, although they did give a softer ride.

The man who took the decision on the tyres was DeLorean's new managing director in Belfast, the man who now became his most senior executive outside the United States. Charles 'Chuck' Bennington was another Chrysler man, picked out by Myron Stylianides. Tall and thin, in his early 50s, Bennington sported a wispy blond moustache and goatee beard. Although he still retained his American accent, much of his working life had been spent overseas, building plants and factories everywhere from Cape Town to Turkey. At first the Lotus people did not know what to make of him with his cowboy boots and his polo-necks. Soon, however, they came to regard him as their closest ally and the relationship was to outlast the DeLorean project.

Bennington soon established a reputation as a 'workaholic' – and insisted that others followed the same arduous work schedule, which meant at least six days a week and sometimes seven. DeLorean had made him a tempting offer, which included share options in DMC, and a big salary raise. He arrived in December, set up his office in Belfast but in those early months of 1979 spent two to three days a week at Lotus. He was the man to whom DeLorean had given responsibility for building the factory, building a team, and overseeing the work at Lotus. It was a tall order. But his team was growing rapidly: Barrie Wills to head up the purchasing side; Loasby on engineering; George Broomfield, another American, for actual production of the car; Joe Daly, an Irishman who had also been with Chrysler, for finance.

At Shoreham, on England's south coast, Bennington had the interior mocked up while Lotus were working on the rest of the engineering. He brought DeLorean down to see it in the spring. One key DeLorean requirement at least was there. 'We actually went out and borrowed a set of golf clubs and threw them in the back, more as a joke to show John they would fit than anything else.'

DeLorean during this period was turning up in Belfast and Norfolk around once a month. That suited both Bennington and the Lotus people who preferred to be allowed to get on with the job. DeLorean, once he had sorted out the arrangements with the Northern Ireland government, done his deal with Chapman and agreed the basic parameters of the car, showed less and less interest in the details of both the factory and the car. In fairness the factory could more or less look after itself:

there were competent people building it, and that part of the programme was nowhere near as tight as the car. The car, however, was a different matter – Bennington early on remembers telling DeLorean he wasn't going to hit his schedule on the car. 'I'm inclined to believe you,' DeLorean replied. 'But I don't think we want to go public on that at this stage until you get more detail on it.' In fact DeLorean never did 'go public' on it until he had already missed his programme. During this period he seemed far more interested in what was happening in New York than on the other side of the Atlantic.

In Belfast, however, he was a hero. His name was on the factory, and his visits were almost royal events. He had brought jobs and hope and given Northern Ireland its great chance to break into the car industry, something it had always wanted since the pre-war days when Chambers and Ferguson made cars there and a local veterinary surgeon named John Boyd Dunlop fitted his son's bicycle out with the first pneumatic tyres and started an entire new worldwide industry.

The centre of Belfast may have been a gloomy spot, with its security checks and constantly patrolling armoured cars. But Dick Brown soon came to believe that the IRA attacks were, on the whole, concentrated on the security forces. The factory was left alone. Factories usually were – it was not in the IRA's interests to damage jobs. The number of civilian killings in the Province were less than in most major American cities. Compared to Detroit, Northern Ireland was a relatively peaceful place. Its reputation for violence far exceeded the reality.

Soon, as the engineering and production teams at Dunmurry began to come together, they spilled over into a group of quonset huts set up on the perimeter of the 73-acre site. A large, stately home, Warren House, was taken over too, and work began on converting it into living quarters for visiting 'royalty' such as DeLorean, whom Dick Brown expected to live there more often than he would in New York. A proper kitchen staff was hired.

Myron Stylianides hired Mike Loasby from Aston Martin to head the engineering team, and Loasby, in turn, began hiring others, eventually creating a production engineering department totalling some 80 people, who would be working – or so they believed – with Lotus.

2

In the second week of February John DeLorean was in Las Vegas. It was to be a big time for him – the National Automobile Dealers Association convention was held there. He had one of the two prototypes set up on a stand and he invited his board and his backers. Johnny Carson came along to look personally at his investment and posed beside DeLorean, looking solemn. Behind them Cristina and a young Hollywood starlet looked bored. DeLorean and his team came to the convention, as Edward Lapham, financial editor of *Automotive News*, wrote, 'like plunder-laden legions returning to Rome'.

But, despite the Northern Ireland plunder, the team was hard at work on yet more fund-raising: with SEC approval DeLorean would soon begin signing dealer-shareholders for the project again. He had raised $5.16 million at $5 a share from his initial offering, but now, with the Northern Irish money behind him, he was in a much more attractive position. In Las Vegas that week he bubbled with confidence. The original offering was made at $5 a share, minimum subscription $25,000. Now he was asking for $10 a share, still demanding a minimum investment of $25,000. The S-2 report filed with the Securities and Exchange Commission showed that DeLorean's personal company JZDC owned 64.1 percent of DMC. After the offering, assuming a full subscription of 400 dealers, he would be diluted down to 58.9 percent. At $10 a share, that still made him worth $100 million. But it was a purely paper value – he could not turn any of it into cash.

He had not only invited Johnny Carson to Las Vegas but also his other backers from Northern Ireland. Ronnie Henderson and Shaun Harte turned up. Both men were enthusiasts. Harte's role was technical, while Henderson as the NIDA chief executive was the decision-maker. But Harte had been assigned as the NIDA man who would monitor the investment. The Irishmen stayed for three days in Vegas, watching Dick Brown's marketing team at work presenting the car and recruiting dealers. Brown had it down to an art and was genuinely good at it. Both NIDA men were extremely impressed by what they saw, as DeLorean intended them to be.

3

In the spring, the pioneering atmosphere was beginning to deteriorate in Belfast. There began a war between the engineers in Dunmurry and the engineers at Lotus which would continue through the whole project. Lotus understood that they had the contract to engineer, design and develop the car ready for production. Mike Loasby in Dunmurry felt that he and his growing engineering team should be involved in the conceptual stages too, rather than the more mundane job of translating Lotus's work from drawing board to quality produced car. Loasby's role had not been made fully clear to him – he had joined on the basis that he was the chief engineer, a successor to Bill Collins. Neither Bennington nor Lotus saw it that way.

The first skirmish was over the design that Lotus was working on in the spring of 1979. Collins's prototype was the laughing stock of Lotus who had a little trick of asking newcomers to the project to guess the weight of the front bonnet. It looked light – yet could only be lifted by a strong man. Collins had deliberately weighted it – it weighed nearly 500 pounds – to balance the car.

Loasby, who felt a certain sympathy for Collins, believed Collins's prototype was like any other prototype: it could have been developed as easily as the Lotus version and should have been used – because of the tightness of the timing.

The most experienced of the DeLorean engineers was Ted Chapman (no relation to Colin Chapman) who had been in the motor industry all his life. Now nearing retirement age, his great value was that he had been through several similar new ventures in his career, and the younger men on the team (Loasby was nearly twenty years his junior) looked to him to anticipate problems and find solutions.

In the spring of 1979, the engineers in Belfast designed body sections to incorporate everything they would need when it came to mass producing the body – all the little tricks that Ted Chapman, whose specialty was body engineering, had learned through the years. The designs allowed for metal adjustment, door sealing and other features that the engineers felt would be absolutely essential when it came to getting the gull-wing doors to fit properly on the production line.

In May, Ted Chapman took these designs along to Colin Spooner, the man at Lotus who was in overall charge of the DeLorean project. Spooner brushed them aside. The Lotus team had it all under control.

Not as far as he was concerned, retorted Chapman. It was his job to make sure that what Lotus designed would work on a production line, and he must be involved in the design now. Lotus, he challenged, was actually intending to do the design itself, then present the team in Belfast with a *fait accompli*.

The two became so angry that Spooner telephoned George Broomfield, the production manager, in Belfast. Ted Chapman, he told him, was making a nuisance of himself and could not get on with his engineers. Would they kindly keep him away from Lotus?

Reluctantly, Ted Chapman had to accept it, but he bluntly declared that this meant that, 'I cannot fulfill my obligations to DeLorean Motor Cars Ltd.'

There were a number of similar battles as the car took shape, but the decisions on the car were taken by Colin Chapman, Kimberley and Colin Spooner at Lotus; and agreed by Bennington in the short term and by DeLorean himself on his visits.

The car that was emerging under the Lotus engineers bore increasingly little resemblance to Collins's prototype, now gathering dust in a neglected corner of one of the hangars. ERM of course had gone before the project ever got under way, although dealers in the United States as well as the Oppenheimer investors were still under the illusion that it would be used. Chapman and his team now designed a car with a steel backbone welded to two sub-frames in the shape of a double-Y. The rear subframe would support the engine – Chapman had given up hope of persuading DeLorean to go for a mid-engined car. The petrol-tank went in the notch of the Y in the front where it was well protected, but small. Chapman redesigned the luggage space, although he remained unhappy about the tiny amount available. He managed to get the spare wheel under the front bonnet, still leaving space above it for another set of golf clubs ('in case the horny bachelor's girlfriend plays,' remarked one of the engineers cynically).

Colin Chapman used more and more standard parts, knowing there was no way special parts could be designed in time. Standard parts were easier to fit and work with – but increasingly made the DMC-12 an ordinary car. Chapman himself put none of his genius into it. He was involved in the major decisions, but the DeLorean job to him was a money-earner and no more than that. It would keep his company from dying under him for lack of funds. Colin Spooner, a competent engineer, did put everything he had got into it, working the same sort of hours that Bennington had set for himself. Spooner in 18 months, however, was not going to produce a Porsche or a Ferrari.

The airbags for the driver and passenger had long since disappeared after some horrendous tests with dummies, although DeLorean himself retained his belief in them. GM's testing programme had revealed that the bag had tended to squash passengers so that limbs or other parts of the body had been forced sideways through the doors, and could be sliced off as the doors had been forced shut again by the impact.

DeLorean's original plans had talked about a front-end structure solely devoted to 'energy management', jargon for absorbing the impact of a crash. Originally, too, he had talked of a foam-filled rear structure that would provide similar crash protection. The car that emerged had a number of useful safety features and was certainly in a 'crash-sense' safer than many cars on the road, but the features were nothing new or special.

The high sill that had been part of the original prototype was gone, no longer needed because of the backbone chassis. The dash and instrument cluster remained substantially unchanged, but more European parts were used, mainly because DeLorean had spent a large amount of money having it designed and tooled in the first place. The computer featured on some of the mock-up models was never used, nor was the Craig overhead system.

4

That spring Britain was heading towards an election. The previous October Labour's Jim Callaghan seemed to be sitting comfortably in Number Ten Downing Street, all set to be re-elected prime minister. He made the mistake of delaying the election, reckoning things might look better in the spring. Instead, it became Callaghan's 'winter of discontent'. Margaret Thatcher and the Conservative Party were making a comeback. On March 30, however, Mrs. Thatcher received a deep personal blow.

The Conservative politician with special responsibility for Northern Ireland was Airey Neave, Mrs. Thatcher's friend and confidant. He had persuaded her to run for leader in the first place, organized her campaign, tirelessly drummed up support for her, and in the end helped her defeat Edward Heath for the top position. Neave also acted as her eyes and ears in the parliamentary party; he was her political strategist and close adviser. He had taken a keen interest in the DeLorean project and was critical of it – early in March he told colleagues he was going to press the government for answers on a number of issues. He never got the chance. On March 30 as he was driving up the ramp from the underground car park in the Houses of Parliament, his car exploded and he died immediately. A bomb had been placed on the car outside his home that morning, and was triggered by a tilt-mechanism as he drove up the ramp. Both the Provisional IRA and the Irish National Liberation Army, the military wing of the Irish Republican Socialist Party of Northern Ireland, claimed responsibility.

His replacement was the gentler Humphrey Atkins, a tall, former Royal Navy man. He had been a competent enough whip. As a minister he was to prove no match for John DeLorean.

Callaghan finally set May 3 as polling day and lost heavily. The Conservatives were now in power and Margaret Thatcher took over in Number Ten with the avowed aim of 'rolling back the State frontiers', which meant cutting back sharply on government involvement everywhere. That did not bode well for a project dependent on government money.

John DeLorean turned up in England in election week with a new member of his team. Eugene Cafiero was another auto *wunderkind* who had got to the top of Chrysler. In November 1978 Cafiero, a slim, good-looking 52-year-old Italian-

American, quit his $310,000 a year job and began looking for something else. He found it with John DeLorean. 'I thought it would be fun to go with a small company where there was no history, no built-in constraints. I wanted to start with a clean piece of paper.' He became president and chief executive of DeLorean Motor Company which technically made him senior to DeLorean himself. DeLorean however quickly squelched any thought of that, 'Gene is the boss but he answers to me.'

DeLorean gave Cafiero a five-year contract at $375,000 a year plus cost-of-living adjustments, pension rights, a $164,000 interest free loan to compensate him for any loss of pension rights at Chrysler and a car. Soon Cafiero was installed in the office next to DeLorean's at 280 Park Avenue.

On that floor he joined another new recruit; in March, William F. Haddad had been recruited by DeLorean as his public relations adviser. Haddad had known John DeLorean since the mid-1960s when he contributed a ghosted chapter to Haddad's book on the development of black business enterprise. Haddad was a journalist with a long involvement with the Kennedy family. He was born in Charlotte, North Carolina in 1928 to an Egyptian-Jewish father and a Russian-Jewish mother, grew up in Florida, took a physics degree at New York's Columbia University and was soon involved in liberal politics, becoming an aide to Tennessee Senator Estes Kefauver who won the vice-presidential nomination from young Massachusetts Senator John F. Kennedy in 1956.

Haddad later worked for Kennedy and became deeply involved in the Peace Corps, the plans for which he would later say 'came out of my typewriter'. He married Kate Roosevelt, a granddaughter of Franklin D. Roosevelt and an adopted daughter of John Hay Whitney. Haddad went to work as a journalist with the *New York Herald-Tribune*, owned by his father-in-law, before going back to Washington to a Johnson Administration job in the ill-fated Office of Economic Opportunity. Later, John V. Lindsay put him on the New York City Board of Education, where the *New York Times* attacked him in an editorial as 'Haddad the Heater', accusing him of making 'grossly intemperate remarks'. He was a prize-winning investigative journalist, a skilled public relations man, and a person who knew his way around Washington and the Democratic

Party. More to the point, Haddad regarded himself as something of a DeLorean friend: he had been at DeLorean's second wedding, had helped set up the National Alliance of Businessmen office that DeLorean headed after he left GM, and DeLorean had consulted him about Puerto Rico where Haddad had some business interests.

It was June when Chapman and Spooner raised a query over one of DeLorean's cherished fixed instructions for the car: the Giugiaro design. To them it looked old-fashioned and would look even more out-of-date by the time it hit the market. It was a 1970s design, but the car would be on sale in the 1980s. On DeLorean's next visit they discussed it: it was up to him, nothing to do with Lotus. But Chapman suggested getting Giugiaro to 'freshen' or 'tweak' his design. DeLorean and Cafiero saw the point – and Chuck Bennington went down to Milan to have it done.

By August Giugiaro had sent back his changes. He had done it cleverly: half the car was the old design, half the new one. The differences, subtly softening the original shape, were small but quite startling. Mike Kimberley recalls: 'Gene Cafiero and I looked at Giugiaro's styling exercise, and there was no doubt about it. Although we were both concerned about what it would do for the timing programme and what it would do for the cost, Gene and I both decided it was a hell of an improvement. It took the car into the eighties.'

It also meant that – ten months into an 18 month programme – the whole exterior of the car had been redesigned. DeLorean was still not admitting it publicly, or even to NIDA in Belfast. But the programme was steadily slipping and a change of styling now would drop it back several months. Although to the casual observer the changes seemed slight, it meant that every body drawing had to be redone.

The pressure was now intense. A body stack, which is a wooden body actually carved by craftsmen to the engineer's design and from which mouldings of items which cannot be drawn (such as windows and body panels) can then be taken, had to be made. Visioneering in Detroit got the job and Chuck Bennington and Colin Spooner began commuting at the week ends to Detroit. Bennington's working week at this stage was more than seven days: on Friday night, after a tough week, he would catch a plane to Detroit and turn up at Visioneering first thing on Saturday, work all weekend, fly home Sunday night and start in Belfast early Monday morning. 'I was a bit whacked Monday night,' he reflects. By mid-week, however, he would be at Lotus, and on Friday he would repeat the cycle. Time was short.

Through July and August the gap between the Dunmurry engineers and Lotus widened, with Bennington enraging Loasby by continually appearing to take the Lotus side. On July 23 Loasby complained bitterly to Bennington that the engineering department had received 'about six assorted drawings, mostly out of date; but these represent . . . such a small proportion of the total available'. In Coventry Barrie Wills had more drawings than Loasby, and this was rapidly becoming a major bone of contention. Loasby and his engineers were now convinced the project was heading for major engineering problems. Lotus, they kept pointing out, had never engineered a mass production car. They were going about it the wrong way, starting with the doors and windows and working outwards to the corners. 'You have to start at the corners and work in,' Loasby insisted.

But it was when Loasby, on August 28, asked Colin Spooner if he was ready to incorporate the body sections suggested by Ted Chapman in mid-May, that the real explosion came. Spooner, a slight, intense, serious engineer, had his own ideas on the body. He respected Ted Chapman, whose comments were down-to-earth, practical and to the point. But there was a fundamental difference: Ted Chapman's expertise was in sheet metal and the DMC-12 underbody was to be fibre-glass. Lotus prided itself on having a greater expertise in fibre-glass bodies than any company in the world. And Ted Chapman, good as he was, was not a man to absorb easily the new ideas and concepts that Lotus specialized in. 'He was not prepared to consider anything that was in any way different to the way he had done it for the past 20 or 30 years,' said a Lotus engineer. This again was a major philosophical difference which so dogged the product: many of the engineers at Dunmurry were older men, steeped in conventional motor industry practice. Building a stainless steel body shell, and then designing a plastic underbody to fit inside and to work on from there to the chassis – from the outside in – was incomprehensible to them. Even Lotus objected to it, but DeLorean insisted on it being done that way. 'It was not a conventional car,' says Colin Spooner. 'Hell, it was a completely different concept to anything that had been done before.'

5

Back at Park Avenue DeLorean took an Olympian attitude about the Battle of the Engineers. He was moving on to other things. At the end of May he and Cafiero were 'too busy' even to make it to Detroit for the annual meeting of DeLorean Motor Company.

DeLorean was negotiating a new business venture: to become sole U.S. importer of Alfa-Romeo cars as well as Suzuki four-wheel-drive vehicles. He was also planning to become a bus manufacturer. In May he organized a 'task force'. In September, a prototype Transbus was shown at the American Public Transportation Association in New York.

But it was in Belfast that John DeLorean was making his most ambitious pitch yet. He now decided, with everything on the surface going so smoothly, that it was time to tap the British government for more money. He wanted to build another new car, a four gull-wing door sedan, to be called the DMC-24. And the contractor he wanted to build it for him? None other than GPD Services Inc. Early in July DeLorean instructed Chuck Bennington to ask NIDA for the money, having done what he could to clear the way first with the still enthusiastic Shaun Harte.

On July 10, Bennington wrote a formal letter to Harte at NIDA and to Frank McCann at the Department of Commerce. He started with a glowing paragraph about the sedan model. In Milan, Italian designer Giugiaro was already at work and the plan was to introduce the sedan into production 18 months after the sports car. But the engineering work would again have to be done outside Belfast. Coolly ignoring the experiences of his engineers, he then wrote:

> Approaches have been made to both Porsche and GPD Services Inc., to carry out the detailed engineering develop-

ment program. While cost estimates provided by these firms are comparable, it seems reasonable to contract the services of GPD and Lotus because our present relationship with respect to the development program for the DMC-12, has been totally satisfactory. This experience leads me to believe that the most effective route both technically and as regard cost effectiveness would be to develop our program based on their continued involvement. In addition, the personal brilliance of Colin Chapman's engineering is a vital additional ingredient.

This request is almost breathtaking in its audacity. GPD had already been paid approaching $20 million and had passed none of it on to Lotus. Every bill, every cost that Lotus incurred was paid for month by month from the Belfast company out of funds provided by the British taxpayer.

Now DeLorean, through Bennington, was going to ask for more. Bennington was an unwitting party to it all – almost certainly the letter was drafted by DeLorean who felt it might come better from the man on the spot.

GPD, went on Bennington, had already been approached and 'have indicated a willingness to undertake the development of the sedan series'. That was scarcely surprising in view of the money involved. But, he added – and here we get to the crunch – 'as they have been approached to design and develop a line of prestige products for one of Europe's leading automotive manufacturers, they are insisting on an early commitment on our part.' GPD had no design capacity and there was no big contract in the offing. DeLorean was simply putting the pressure on. Then Bennington got down to money. GPD, he said, proposed 'a similar arrangement to that entered into in respect of the DMC-12 with an initial prepayment of £10 million'. With a bit of negotiation the payments could probably be phased, he added helpfully. He then enclosed seven pages of detail on the sedan.

Harte recommended to NIDA that the Agency should give the company further guarantees of up to $22 million to build the sedan. NIDA, however, was beginning to worry about Mr. DeLorean and his odd accounting habits – it was not getting the information and progress reports that were part of the agreement. The board decided to let this one pass – NIDA could wait, even if the busy GPD, with its profitable workload, could not.

At Dunmurry that summer, the atmosphere among the engineers and production men continued to deteriorate. On August 29, Broomfield and Loasby wrote a joint memo to Bennington. They marked it 'personal and confidential' and put on record for the first time their serious doubts about the project. If the Northern Ireland authorities, who were supposed to be monitoring the project, had even caught a hint of it, they would soon have lost their composure.

The two men protested the decision, which they had only learned about from Colin Spooner at Lotus, to drop their work. They had learned that the sections in question had actually been completed nearly two weeks earlier and 'were hand-carried to Visioneering by Messrs. Peacock and Parker to be incorporated in the flanging details of the master model.' It was now obvious, they wrote to Bennington, 'that the design is a *fait accompli*'.

'Based on the Lotus proposals, the vehicle parameters cannot be achieved,' they concluded gloomily, recommending that 'a complete review be made of all body sections prior to finalization and inclusion in the master models.'

It was quite a blast, and Bennington was in no humour for it. He and Loasby were increasingly at odds. Loasby he felt was turning out to be too much of a perfectionist. The constant friction between Colin Spooner and Loasby was also annoying – and between Loasby and Barrie Wills, the purchasing man who had become Bennington's closest ally. Loasby kept accusing Wills of taking 'discussion only' drawings from Lotus and going off to component makers to have them tooled up. In November Loasby came back from a trip to Visioneering and accused Wills of having had the front and rear fascias and all the pieces of glass made from drawings instead of the proven system of taking models from a finished body stack, which effectively becomes the master model for moulding all the parts.

Loasby shot off an angry letter to Wills in Coventry: 'If the window glasses and fascias are manufactured in isolation from the body stack we cannot, in any way, ensure their proper alignment with the bodies in our assembly.'

It was a fundamental point and, as in so many cases involving the car, both men were right. But Wills argued, probably correctly, that unless he anticipated final designs, there would simply be no car. He had to take something rough along to component makers, get them to quote him a price, decide on who would make it, and then place the order. Many parts would have to be re-tooled with the design still not 'frozen'. That, Bennington decided, was the only way to keep the programme within sight of even the (privately) revised timetable.

6

Early in November John DeLorean was back in the news again. Late in the afternoon of Tuesday, November 6, a new book suddenly appeared all over Detroit. Within hours it was the talk of the auto world. It was published by a firm no one had ever heard of – Wright – which also was the name of the author, J. Patrick Wright. *On a Clear Day You Can See General Motors: John Z. DeLorean's Look Inside the Automotive Giant*, had finally hit the market after four years of vacillation. And Wright, a 38-year-old automotive journalist, had published it himself.

The story of the book is an extraordinary one. Wright sets it out this way. 'In February of 1974, John Z. DeLorean asked me to write a "no nonsense, no bullshit book" with him about his life and experiences at the General Motors Corporation. The work would "open up the board room from the inside," he said, adding, "I know you have to name names and talk about specific decisions." '

DeLorean, according to Wright, handed him a large 'stack of material which contained personal papers, memos from GM, business analyses he had prepared, rough drafts of several chapters, his hand-written notes about items and sections to be included in the manuscript and his correspondence with several literary agents and publishers. "Here," he said, "You're the doctor." '

Wright and DeLorean prepared a detailed proposal and received a $45,000 advance from Playboy Press. By Labor Day

1975, Wright had finished and presented the manuscript to the publisher who, he said, 'was ecstatic'.

John DeLorean was not. He refused to let the book be published. His objection as expressed to me was that the book we'd written would anger General Motors executives who he said would make it difficult, if not impossible, to build and market an 'ethical sports car' which he was developing. He admitted that this consideration was a latter-day influence on his plans for the book and was not a part of our original discussions or agreement on the project.

Despite his objection to publishing the book, he praised it on several occasions, including one time during a meeting in New York called by Bill Adler, executive editor of Playboy Press, to try to resolve the book crisis. It was February 6, 1976 and John said flatly to Adler, Philip Spitzer, our agent, and me: 'Pat has done a fantastic job . . . The book is what should be said about American business. The book is what should be published. It really is the only book.' But he also reiterated his fear of reprisals from GM if the book was printed. A month later he added, 'I've got to play with the system for another 18 months. Then I can say this stuff.'

Rather than flatly ban the book, DeLorean vacillated and stalled Wright for the next four years. 'At times he said he was eager to get the book published. At other times he was adamantly opposed to it. And at still other times he offered to help me do my own book about General Motors, provided I leave him out of it.'

Twice DeLorean told Wright he would repay the Playboy advance and cancel the contract. But he refused to sign a cancellation agreement when Playboy submitted it.

Before terminating the Playboy contract he first wanted me to sign an agreement with him not to publish the book on my own or write anything about him without his permission. He also wanted me to turn over to him all of the documents, notes and tapes used in writing the book. In return, he would give me $5,000 and 20% of the author's revenue of any 'DeLorean General Motors Book' that he might write. This proposal was unacceptable to me and thus the book remained tied up into 1979.

Wright finally decided to publish it himself at a cost said at the time to be $50,000. No publishers would take it. It proved to be fortunate for Wright for, by publishing it himself, he made close to $1 million. Despite his unhappy experiences, Wright remains a DeLorean fan. Referring to the book:

> It is not a dispassionate overview of an industrial giant. It is one man's heartfelt story about the business world about him as he worked his way toward the summit, and then found that the climb was not worth the reward. In this case, that man is one of the most successful and talented executives in the post-World War II automobile industry.

Soon the book was headed for the bestseller list. John DeLorean found himself a hero. He had revealed that the ill-fated Corvair's 'questionable safety' was well known and debated inside GM before its introduction; he told of management blunders where hundreds of millions of dollars were wasted; of how GM executives stifled initiative; of his own battles with them over his lifestyle. 'John DeLorean's story,' said the book jacket blurb, 'is more than an exposé.' It is 'a personal account of one modern executive's struggle with big business management.'

Wright chronicled John DeLorean's version of how he got to near the top at GM and then found that:

> Life at the top was a disappointment. DeLorean found his job on executive row to be boring. Moreover, he began to question GM's management system which he felt often promoted mediocrity, sometimes produced illegal and immoral business practices, and stressed personal loyalties to the detriment of the corporation. His efforts to push for change from within were fruitless. To these frustrations was added the startling revelation that resentments inside GM had been formed into a campaign to destroy him. So he quit.

In short, what Wright took down and wrote was certainly, as he said, John DeLorean's own story. Wright is a first-class journalist. His role originally was to be little more than a ghost writer, using his professional skills to turn DeLorean's writings and jottings into a readable book. The book is in the first person, and Wright's sole original injection into it is the foreword – about the only part that has not been questioned since. The book brought about some interesting reactions, but only very muted ones from the GM men whom DeLorean savaged. That was not the way things were done at GM.

DeLorean himself at first expressed surprise and disappointment when the book came out. But when the highly favourable reactions began to build, he changed tack and called it an accurate portrayal of the information he had given Wright. He said his objections had more to do with tone rather than content. 'I am not disavowing the book at all.'

But while *On a Clear Day* did much for DeLorean's image with the outside world, it also generated growls of dissent from within Detroit's automotive industry press corps, which knew him better than anyone else – with the exception of his former colleagues at GM.

The most telling critique came from veteran Detroit journalist Robert W. Irvin, who had 'leaked' DeLorean stories back in 1972. Irvin reviewed the book in his popular *Irvin at Large* column in the *Automotive News* on November 26.

> DeLorean spares no one but himself. He criticizes fellow executives for pettiness and playing office politics. He tells us about a conspiracy among some top executives to force him out of GM – even using the press to discredit him. Yet DeLorean did the same things in his career at GM – engaged in office politics to further himself or hurt others and tried to use the press to further his own ends.

Noting that the book was coming out in embarrassing coincidence with DeLorean's efforts to launch the DMC-12, Irvin made a dark prediction.

> ... GM, meanwhile, is preparing a second assembly plant in Bowling Green, Kentucky, to increase production of its

Chevrolet Corvette, America's only production sports car
... Then in late 1982, GM will bring out a redesigned
Corvette to be built in the new Bowling Green plant. Anyway
you look at it, this is going to be tough competition for
DeLorean from GM's Corvette. Some people, mindful of
DeLorean's book, will probably be working extra hard on the
new Corvette project.

Irvin never lived to see how true his prophecy would be. He died in 1980.

7

Earlier in 1979, even though he had promised in writing to NIDA to restrict his business efforts to the car company, DeLorean was determined to gain control of the Logan Manufacturing Corporation of Logan, Utah. The firm made the track vehicles that scrape and pack the snow for ski resorts and in the early months of 1979 Logan, then a division of Thiokol Corporation, had about 80 percent of the U.S. market despite competition from Canadian and West German snow-grooming equipment makers.

In its annual report to the Michigan corporation commission filed in November 1978, the assets of the DeLorean Manufacturing Corporation – DeLorean's privately held company – totalled just $650,000, obviously not nearly enough to cover the $15 million asking price Thiokol wanted for Logan. DeLorean began a much publicized sell-off of his private real estate holdings as a means to raise the money. First to go were three plots of ranch and farm land in southern California which netted him $4.6 million. Then DeLorean was contacted by a real estate investor named Kurt Kuennecke with an offer for his luxurious Pauma Valley estate. DeLorean wanted $2 million; Kuennecke offered $1.5 million in cash.

Kuennecke is a refugee from Hitler's Germany who emigrated to Calgary, Canada, and prospered as a real estate investor and speculator. He and his wife fled the Canadian winters in the early 1970s and settled near San Diego where he has continued his investments. When he first approached DeLorean, Kuennecke and his wife suddenly found themselves being included in the DeLoreans' glamorous social life. They spent a weekend as guests at Pauma Valley. The deal was agreed to verbally, as Kuennecke recalls:

'I offered Mr. DeLorean $1.5 million cash with delivery of clear title for the property because I didn't want to have a mortgage on the house. At first this was fine and dandy with him, then the deal was changed and he asked if he could – for tax reasons – take 29% down, a little less than $500,000. I agreed to do that and to deposit another $1 million in a certificate of deposit that would pay him $200,000 a year over the next five years.

'The next thing I know I get a telephone call from Mr. DeLorean's banker informing me that Mr. DeLorean had tried to borrow $1 million against my certificate of deposit and the bank wanted me to co-sign the note. I refused. I told them that Mr. DeLorean's security was the property and that I had offered payment in full.

'And then the banker said, "Well, John needs the money and he wants to borrow the million against the certificate – that way he can defer the taxes." And I said I had no intention of giving Mr. DeLorean a mortgage on the property for $1 million and then co-signing a $1 million promissory note to the bank – that's some sort of double indemnity because Mr. DeLorean can take the money and not pay off and leave me to pay twice.

'So that died out and after a couple of weeks I was called by Henry Bushkin, a lawyer in Los Angeles for Johnny Carson, and he had another similar deal going with Mr. DeLorean and wanted me to sign a note. I refused. But Mr. DeLorean still refused to deliver the property under our earlier agreement and so I sued him for delivery.'

The suit prompted a handwritten note to Bill Haddad about Kuennecke, '... have him checked out – he is suing me maliciously – a Canadian – is he an undesirable alien?'

By mid-June Haddad had a report back from a private investigation firm that DMC regularly used to check up on prospective employees. After listing Kuennecke's family and business ties to Calgary, the report concluded, 'There is no known derogatory information as concerns Mr. Kuennecke and he is not known to Canadian police authorities insofar as any criminal record is concerned.' However, DeLorean did not stop at a mere private eye search for possible 'S.O.S.' material to use as a lever against Kuennecke.

'I started hearing about a man named Nesseth, a friend of DeLorean's. There were never any direct threats, just friends of ours would relay warnings. And finally a friend brought to my attention what had happened in Puerto Rico – the double dealing there – so I just dropped my suit and bought some land in Valley Center,' Kuennecke says.

'It's all very sad. I'd never experienced anything like the shenanigans that DeLorean put us through; saying one thing and then contradicting himself in the next 15 minutes or sending a telegram that refuted what he had said. I told him at the time we called the deal off, "John, you are a man on the run. I don't know what you are running from." And he said, "Kurt, you don't know what you are talking about." '

With Kuennecke's money out of reach, DeLorean tried other ways to raise funds. And, suddenly, the deal with Thiokol went through, even though DeLorean was short of the purchase price by $4 million to $8 million. At the time, Walter Strycker remembers DeLorean bragging about 'a Swiss bank loan'.

The Logan company quickly began to lose market share not only to the equipment made by neighbouring Bombardier in Canada, but also to a West German producer, Kassbohrer Fahrzeugwerke GmbH. Again, in April 1980, DeLorean relied on his favourite tactic of harassment. A memo to Haddad ordered, 'Please check Kassbohrer – are any of them Nazi collaborators, guilty of war crimes, etc. See if your Washington contacts can come up with anything at all.'

Haddad responded six days later, 'Kassbohrer comes up clean. Intelligence files list no present or previous negative information.'

But DeLorean was not satisfied and in November 1980 filed an unfair trade practices complaint with the U.S. International Trade Commission, charging Kassbohrer and other competitors with unfairly pricing their products to beat out the DMC's snow groomer in the American market. After examination, the ITC's staff recommended no action be taken; they reported that the company's market share problems were due to management deficiencies, not unfair trade inflows.

DeLorean's business dealings were now being questioned by Edward Lapham of *Automotive News*, who took the DeLorean financing deals from the first corporation all the way through the NIDA contracts. The article dated February 5, 1979 was titled, 'Analyzing DeLorean's Project: Is it just a paper empire?'

In painstaking detail Lapham worked from the beginning. He disputed DeLorean's claim of having put $4 million of his own money into the project. The claims, he said, were 'fuzzy and undocumented'. At each step from the formation of DSCP through the DMC stock offerings to the new offering for the DRLP, the piece showed how DeLorean's stake and control over the project and its rising capital holdings grew without any real contribution from him. Interestingly, even at that early date Lapham had tracked the connection with GPD but had mistakenly confused the Swiss account with a legitimate design firm in Ferndale, Michigan of the same name.

Finally Lapham concluded, 'Some critics say the only weakness in the plan is the ERM process which hasn't proven itself enough for a production run. Others claim there is no market for such a vehicle and as the S-2 (SEC document) admits, "the success of the company depends to a large degree on the efforts of a few individuals" – DeLorean, C. R. Brown and William Collins (who was already leaving).

'And some critics still believe the entire DeLorean enterprise is an elaborate scheme to enrich a few individuals at the top.'

Years later, Lapham muses on just how close he came. 'I take a lot of pride in that article. It stands up pretty well over the years,' he says.

CHAPTER NINE

Crisis and Confusion

NIDA was starting to worry about DeLorean's finances and his money-spending habits. A special DeLorean monitoring committee had been set up in August 1979 with both NIDA and Department of Commerce people.

The committee held its first meeting on September 23. It included Shaun Harte and local businessman Alex Fetherston, the two NIDA nominees on the DMC board. From the Commerce Department, Frank McCann was appointed the senior Department officer responsible for the DeLorean project. The monitoring committee was chaired by Tony Hopkins, who had taken over as NIDA chief executive from Ronnie Henderson after the latter departed that summer, proving to be something short of a dazzling success.

By the time Hopkins took over, euphoria with John DeLorean was beginning to turn to disillusionment. Promised business plans were not turning up, despite repeated requests. Memos and letters were going unanswered. The extravagance of DeLorean's lifestyle was becoming apparent. But there was little they could do about it, except write their letters and send their telexes. The monitoring committee sounded impressive, but it was a watchdog with no teeth.

Part of the July agreement between DeLorean and NIDA specified that he would provide the agency with a detailed plan of operation that set out the timing and goals for production and, more important, employment. But it was October before the DMCL office presented the final plan, and NIDA officials found it anything but reassuring. Harte was the man who had to dig it out of the Dunmurry management and it gradually dawned on him, too, that the financial controls were poor to say the least. Government money was flowing without anyone worrying too much about how it was spent. It was going to

Lotus in far greater quantities than anyone ever expected, because of course, no one realized that none of the Oppenheimer Partnership money, which went to GPD's Swiss bank account, was getting through to Lotus at all.

Back in New York, the man theoretically responsible for financial controls was complaining about them, too. Walter Strycker was the chief financial officer, but he was an increasingly reluctant and rebellious chief financial officer. 'It really was like the difference between night and day, before we got funded and after we got funded,' says Strycker now. 'John was a whole different person. Looking back on it, he had to do a lot of things that were personally distasteful to him. He didn't want to be out talking to all the dealers and hustling them for money to become a part of his dealer program. He hated them and he didn't like talking to the investment bankers. He didn't like raising money. He didn't like working with Oppenheimer and the others. So the minute that was over, why he had to forget about it. After we got funded, he turned all his attention to promoting John and Cristina and he hired a PR firm that was paid $10,000 a month plus expenses.'

The more Strycker examined the way money was spent, the more uneasy he became. 'The use of the government money was all wrong. The salary levels and type of compensation paid out were not justified for the initial stage of a start-up company. DeLorean was paying himself $500,000 directly, and another $500,000 indirectly via people hired to do work for him that had nothing to do with the company.'

For example, Strycker found on the books a consultant in Detroit who was supposed to be doing systems work for the company. Strycker never met him, nor could he identify exactly what he was doing.

'He gets $3,000 a month,' Strycker complained to DeLorean. 'What's it for?'

'Just pay him,' replied DeLorean.

Strycker never learned what the man did.

Then there were two servants on the DMC payroll, a practice that Strycker objected to. Jonathan Mazzone was supposed to be a driver and 'supplemental supply clerk' for the New York office. Strycker calculated he spent less than 10 percent of his time working for the company. He acted as personal chauffeur for Cristina, kept Maur Dubin's books and took his orders from Cristina and Dubin, not from any executives at DMC. There was also Edward Chasty, a personal servant and driver for the DeLorean family, who received his entire salary from DMC.

Strycker kept straying upon items that he feared could involve the company and himself as chief financial officer in serious trouble with the SEC.

Maur Dubin was not only using company employees for his own private business with DeLorean's blessing, Strycker discovered, but he was also using company property. DMC kept a van in the underground garage and when Strycker went down one evening to use it, he found that an employee of Dubin's was driving it. Later he discovered that the van, driven by Dubin's man, had been involved in an accident on December 6, 1979.

There was also $75,000 a year paid to a man out on the West Coast who worked on DeLorean's private ranch and property. 'He acted as John's manager and the company paid for him,' Strycker says.

But it was DeLorean's own personality that disturbed Strycker as much as anything else. He was astounded when one day DeLorean told him quite casually of his great new idea: 'Walt, I'm going to take over Chrysler.'

Oppenheimer was to be asked to put together a $2 billion limited partnership. At that stage Chrysler was at its lowest ebb. It is interesting to speculate on what the British government would have thought about this particular fantasy – Chrysler's red-ink U.K. operations had cost them many millions already.

Chrysler escaped. But Strycker had had enough. Like Dewey before him, he decided to bail out.

In Belfast, at the insistence of a now agonized NIDA, the local DMCL finance director Joe Daly (the former finance director for Chrysler Europe who had been hired for the Belfast operation by Myron Stylianides) had been given responsibility for preparing and issuing a formal updated business plan – but he still had not seen the DMC business plan. The company was running increasingly out of control, and John DeLorean displayed the same contempt for administrative work in his own company as he had shown at Pontiac. In any case, that was the responsibility of Eugene Cafiero.

And what was Eugene Cafiero, president and chief executive doing at this time? He features briefly in the saga. For such an obviously able, tough professional, he remained obscure and distant in his nearly two years with DeLorean. He worked in the offices on Park Avenue, but did not seem to be part of the inner circle, which was essentially DeLorean and Kimmerly with Nesseth coming and going randomly.

But on September 27, Cafiero accompanied DeLorean to Belfast for a meeting with NIDA. Dennis Faulkner was there in his capacity as chairman, so was Tony Hopkins. The two Ulstermen wanted to sound off about their serious worries: the overall financial control was not satisfactory and NIDA needed a proper flow of information; and the role of chief financial officer in New York was not being properly filled. DeLorean and Cafiero promised they would correct both.

Faulkner and Hopkins were increasingly worried about Bennington. They had nothing against him personally, but they reckoned no man could work for long at the pace he set himself and, unless he had more support, the project was going to get further behindhand. DeLorean agreed. (It was a good excuse to get Gene Cafiero out of the New York office where he was irritating him.) Cafiero, he told NIDA, from now on would spend half his time in Belfast.

Faulkner and Hopkins brought up another couple of points: regular board meetings of DMC must be held, and the two NIDA men on the board, Harte and Fetherston, must be supplied with discussion papers in advance. They had been attending without first receiving an agenda.

Finally, Faulkner and Hopkins insisted that the DMC-12 project must be given priority over all other projects being run out of New York – they were horrified by the venture into the Transbus. DeLorean and Cafiero accepted that, although DeLorean would only slow his search for outside businesses when he began to run out of money the following year.

On October 19, Cafiero was in Belfast again. He undertook to put the whole financial control and information systems through a major shake-up.

Now there was another move which would later raise eyebrows and about which, even at the time, the NIDA board had mixed feelings. DeLorean offered Shaun Harte a job as director of planning, with responsibility for coordinating the production programme between Dunmurry and Lotus. Harte wanted to accept – it would mean a significant increase in salary for him, and he was still enthusiastic about the car project. DeLorean had gone out of his way to be charming to Harte, in the way he originally had with Strycker and Brown and any of the others he had wanted to join him.

At 41, Harte was a bright accountant whose greatest fault, perhaps, was his naivety. But it was not difficult to become enthusiastic about John DeLorean and his dream.

Hopkins was dubious, however; it would not look good if the NIDA man, who was essentially responsible for monitoring the Agency's biggest investment, were to join the recipient of that investment less than halfway through the programme.

On October 29 he raised the issue with DeLorean at a meeting. DeLorean said that he and his team were just interested in building the car, which was all that mattered. Everything else was administration and paper work. If NIDA wanted information, who better to provide it than their own man?

Hopkins put it to a NIDA board meeting on November 28. The trade union leader John Freeman objected. But the NIDA board finally agreed, primarily on the basis that Harte had been providing information from the outside until then, but could now provide it from the inside. They also hoped Harte could discover what exactly was happening at Lotus.

On December 1, Shaun Harte joined DeLorean Motor Cars Limited.*

At this stage NIDA genuinely believed it was getting somewhere in its efforts to control DeLorean. Two weeks before Christmas, Cafiero was again in Belfast – honouring DeLo-

---

* He would stay on until the bitter end. It was Harte who courteously and generously opened the gates and allowed the authors into the plant on the day of John DeLorean's arrest – and amiably chatted while the authors test-drove the last cars off the production line.

rean's promise that he would be there half the time. On December 13, Faulkner and Hopkins met him and again emphasized, as they were tiring of doing, their dismay at the meaningless quarterly revisions to the plan without reconciling the figures with the original budget.

They had to have budget figures in one column, actual expenditures beside them, they complained. Only then could they see clearly where the money was being spent – or misspent. And they needed it monthly.

Meanwhile, Hopkins had decided he could not ignore Strycker's impending departure. At a NIDA board meeting on December 19, Hopkins presented a long, detailed paper on DeLorean. He outlined his battles to persuade DeLorean and Cafiero of the need for financial controls in the group, and his optimism that things might now improve. But he also recommended that Faulkner, as chairman of NIDA, should write to DeLorean setting out the Agency's unhappiness and insisting on further improvement in the supply of information. It was to become something of a historic letter. Unfortunately, Faulkner took nearly a month to write it and it was eventually sent on January 17.

By then Walter Strycker had become the second chief financial officer to leave John DeLorean. The final straw was that Strycker was excluded from the auditing and record keeping on the snow-grooming company.

Strycker believed the auditors had been far too easily satisfied. 'You know, John can look you straight in the eye and tell you that black is white and I sat there while he gave Arthur Andersen a bunch of discrepancies, and they just believed him.'

The man at Andersen's to whom Strycker complained was Dick Measelle. He had been performing the DeLorean audits for several years. Strycker brought with him Harry DeWitt, the young accountant who was hired as Bob Dewey's assistant, and who was now feeling similarly nervous about the way the money was being spent. Together, they were the finance division of DMC.

'We had people working on the bus,' says Harry DeWitt. 'We had people working on a four-wheel drive recreational vehicle. We had people looking into replicars. We had lots of people not working on the car at all. We were concerned with corporate expenditures for travel and reimbursement. And we were concerned with the GPD contract.'

DeWitt could not see the point of the GPD contract. Like Collins, it remained a puzzle to him why DMC should pay a Swiss company to get Lotus to do the work. GPD had by now become a talking point among Brown, Strycker and Bill Haddad, but DeLorean gave them all the same answer: 'Chapman wanted it that way, it's a tax scam for him.'

'Two of the things that were on the list to be discussed with Arthur Andersen were automobiles that were in Los Angeles that were owned by the company', says Strycker. 'One of them was a $54,000 Mercedes and Dick Brown had delivered the car to the Golden Door* with a red ribbon around it. John had ordered it for Cristina to drive around in Los Angeles, and so Dick took it over there. The only people who ever saw the car were Cristina and Cristina's family. Nobody else in the company ever saw it.

'And then they had a Mazda that was delivered to Cristina's brother who drove to USC in it – it was his personal car. The auditors went and talked to Dick Brown and Dick told them Cristina got the car to go to work and the kid is driving the other car to USC. And so they came back and they had a list and they say, "John, what about this car in Los Angeles? Who is using it?" He said, "Oh, that's a test car. We are testing the sedan because we are manufacturing a luxury sedan and we are testing all the quality sedans that will be competing with it."

'And they said, "Okay, fine." Crossed that off. They said, "What about the Mazda? Cristina's brother is driving that." He said, "Well, he's taking that over to USC and letting some fraternity brothers drive it and fill in some questionnaires on the car so that we could get a feel for competing sports cars." They said, "Oh, okay," and crossed that one off.

'And I thought: "Oh, shit. I don't belong here."'

Finally, Strycker gave DeLorean notice that he was leaving at the end of the year and they hammered out an agreement whereby Strycker would remain as a consultant, but he would be in California, not New York. It was an arrangement that

---

* The posh California health spa frequented by celebrities.

lasted 30 days. On December 15, Strycker went on vacation. And DeLorean began his familiar process of 'SOS'.

Within weeks Strycker received two calls from people in New York. Both were friends and both said the same thing: they were sorry to hear that Strycker was having a problem.

'What problem?' asked the astonished Strycker.

'Well, we heard that you were being indicted for fraudulent activities in delivering coal to a Kentucky buyer in West Virginia.'

Strycker had never been indicted for any such thing. Nor was he even involved in a dispute. John DeLorean's imagination was hard at work.

2

Now, over a year into what was supposed to be an 18 month programme, six and seven day weeks at Lotus and Dunmurry were not preventing that programme from slipping. Even before they realized the full extent of what they had to do, Lotus's own critical path analysis showed two years. Bennington and Wills were desperately trying to cut months off that by taking the 'discussion only' drawings away to be tooled up; but for every month they gained, they lost two because of further changes to the car itself. Lotus had now decided it needed to build 15 prototypes instead of the original 12. The new interior and exterior decided on by DeLorean meant that 80 percent of the work done had to be done again; this put back other parts of the programme – the interior trim style for example – by up to 12 months. Now the original programme, seemingly impossible in 18 months, was having to be crunched into nine. Spooner reckoned the only way to come near it was extra manpower – which meant extra expense. Bennington agreed. It would have been even more expensive to let the timetable slip further. DeLorean went along with that too.

Lotus's role was expanding all the time as new jobs were given to it. Take the engine. Its fuel economy under EPA conditions turned out to be 18.6 mpg, which meant that DMC would have to pay a penalty, and also detracted from the attractions of John DeLorean's economical car. A penalty of $5 per 1/10th mpg would have to be paid on every car imported into the U.S. if it failed to achieve an average consumption of 22 mpg. Improving it should have been the job of the engineers in Belfast, but DeLorean asked Lotus to do it.

Then there was the steel backbone. Early in 1980 the stainless steel backbone had to be abandoned. It simply did not weld as well as mild steel and would have been weaker. No one had ever built a stainless steel backbone, but DeLorean insisted on it as essential for his long-lasting car. There was simply no time to make it work, but by the time it had disappeared from the programme it, too, had cost both time and money.

DeLorean kept putting in other additions. On one visit to Lotus he noticed the rear louvre designed for the new Lotus Esprit Turbo. It was eye-catching and modern. 'Let's have that on the DMC,' he told Chapman. Then there were electric mirrors, which had not been planned, electric door locks, the new instrument package, a wiper system and many others, either not on the prototype or added and changed later, usually by DeLorean. For the most part they improved the car – Lotus were impressed by DeLorean's observations and his eye for detail. But they meant further delays, only partly made up by the extra engineers who now occupied the sealed-off area allotted to DeLorean at the Lotus plant. (Chapman even had a small office there although he only used it infrequently.)

The immediate deadline to be hit was the NADA convention to be held in New Orleans in February. The dealers and auto press had not yet seen the 'tweaked' design and DeLorean wanted to make a big thing of it. Visioneering was working on the new show-car, but it was going to be hit or miss to get it ready on time. Bennington and Spooner took it in turns to commute at weekends to Detroit to oversee the work. Bennington was now beginning to show the effects of a punishing 15 months with barely a day off. DeLorean increased the pressure on him, insisting the showcar must be at New Orleans – and Bennington responded.

Hopes that Cafiero would relieve the pressure on the Dunmurry managing director were being only partly realized. His exact role remained a mystery to those in the company. 'I don't think Gene was ever allowed to contribute as much as he was capable of doing,' says Bennington. 'He and John were not getting along terribly well in New York. A lot of things that

Gene wanted to do, John didn't want to do and John was John and so he had his way.'

'Cafiero was supposed to be responsible for manufacturing,' says Walt Strycker. 'My feeling was that John hired him to be a buffer between him and the people in Northern Ireland – to be the presence that *he* said he would be. He was afraid somebody would shoot him, so he got someone else to stand there in his stead.'

Cafiero's standing in Belfast and Norfolk was not improved by statements he was quoted as making in New York. 'I'm not afraid to be the S.O.B. who has to go over there and tell them "No" after they've been working on something for months,' he was quoted as saying in *Auto Week* in February. The engineers hoped he might side with them in their dispute, but he never involved himself in it, for which Bennington was thankful.

In January 1980, Cafiero took a party of journalists to Dunmurry to show them the factory. It was still a muddy construction site, but the buildings were rising fast. The speed at which the project was running at Dunmurry was impressive by any standards. The 263,000 square foot assembly plant, the heart of the whole complex, had been finished by the end of the year. Work had begun on the 200,000 square foot body press plant, a 50,000 square foot marshalling building, a 50,000 square foot fabricating building and a boiler/pump house.

A half-mile proving track had also been finished, although the journalists were not to know that this, too, had been a project of some controversy, with the engineers designing the track they wanted only after a struggle.

There had been some lighter moments to break the tension. Dixon Hollinshead, the American building contractor, invaluable in the early days of putting the plant together, was fond of relating the incident of the 'fairy' tree in the middle of the boggy field.

The Northern Irish are no more superstitious than anyone else, but they are prone to attempts to convince the Americans that there are still some who believe in leprechauns. (Contrary to legend, it would be difficult to find anyone in the whole of Ireland who has ever truly believed in leprechauns. But many an Irishman has earned a drink with a good leprechaun story. At Dunmurry it was no different.)

Someone told Hollinshead that there was a local legend that if a tree in the middle of a field survives the elements, there is something special about it – it must be protected by leprechauns.

'Somehow, this one tree didn't get knocked down by the dozers,' Hollinshead related to Edward Lapham of *Automotive News*. 'So one cat operator decided to have some fun and said he couldn't knock it down because it was a fairy tree. Naturally, all the other operators joined in – no one would knock down this damn fairy tree.'

The tree was right in the middle of the assembly plant site, and it was getting to be beyond a joke.

'I thought about transplanting it or building an arboretum or something. But that just wouldn't have been the same. It got to the point where I started spreading the word that there was a $100 bill buried under the tree, but there were no takers. Finally one day a woman who works here said she knew someone who would cut the tree down. A few days later it was gone.'

There was some ribbing that Hollinshead had crept out at night and chopped it down himself, but he denied it stoutly.

'It just disappeared. I guess the little people decided to move it.'

The Catholic area of Twinbrook had a reputation as a housing area of 'last resort', since as much as ten percent of the population were estimated by the security forces to be either IRA members or sympathizers. It was not really the sort of place where there was much local folklore of any kind, but there was not much violence either. On the other side of the factory was the Protestant enclave of Lisburn and the small village of Deriaghy. The factory was giving the area a status it had never enjoyed before, with ministers and television crews coming in regularly.

'Mr. DeLorean has a great chance to do good by doing well,' said John Simpson, an economist at Queen's University, Belfast. Even as the factory was emerging from the field, there were clear signs it was beginning to bring the communities together. An air of hope hung over them, although Catholics and Protestants still had their separate entrances: the Catholics from the north side, the Protestants from the southeast.

There was not much levity on the penthouse floor of 280 Park Avenue, however. DeLorean was stepping up his 'SOS' job on Walter Strycker. The opportunity for the blast had been unwittingly provided by Dennis Faulkner who on January 17 had finally got around to writing his letter to DeLorean as directed by his board on December 19.

'I would like to express firstly that the Agency fully recognizes the scale and complexity of the project which you and your colleagues have undertaken,' wrote Faulkner politely. He also recorded the Agency's 'recognition of the very significant progress' that had so far been made. Then he got into the points he really wanted to raise.

> We have criticized the financial control within the group as a whole and with particular reference to the function of the Chief Financial Officer of the group where we felt that the task was not being adequately performed. You had indicated that you hoped to fill this position with an individual having sound financial experience in the automotive industry by 1 January 1980. I would be grateful to know when you expect to make this appointment.

Faulkner then went through the various control procedures and better information flows that he and Hopkins had taken up again and again with both DeLorean and Cafiero. Shaun Harte's transfer, Faulkner added, 'will enable more attention to be given to the critical aspect of the timing and coordination of the various activities necessary to enable the project to be implemented on schedule'.

None of that should have been too offensive to DeLorean. The next paragraph certainly was.

> We have also discussed the question of the group being involved in activities other than the DMC-12 project. I appreciate that these other activities may assist the Company in the United States environment in its relations with the U.S. Government and its image in the market place and

may therefore assist the DMC-12 project itself. I am sure you will agree, however, that between us we must ensure that the DMC-12 project has total managerial priority and that the financial resources are employed solely on the DMC-12. I know that you have indicated a willingness to drop other activities if NIDA should so insist. At this point, I would welcome an assurance from you that other projects will not be undertaken without prior discussion with us and that in no case will other projects be considered if they cannot clearly be shown to be entirely complementary to the DMC-12 project.

The 'Faulkner Letter' arrived on January 25. It caught DeLorean in a foul mood.

When something went wrong, DeLorean found someone else to blame. When his rich Saudi backer, Ojjeh, had backed out in 1977, it had been First Boston's Cookie Gibb he complained of (although never to). When the auto dealers were not rushing forward to subscribe for his shares, he blamed Brown.

Now John DeLorean's wrath turned on Strycker, although he must have known that Faulkner was not even referring to Strycker. After storming round the office, DeLorean pulled out his usual engineer's log paper and wrote a steaming memo, ostensibly to Eugene Cafiero and Tom Kimmerly, with a copy to Haddad.

The attached letter from Dennis Faulkner reiterates politely the very strong NIDA opinion that Walter Strycker was not competent to perform the Chief Financial Officer function in DMC.

Dennis and Tony Hopkins also told us privately that Strycker would spend all of his time in Dunmurry on the telephone handling personal business back in the States, much to the chagrin and disappointment of our staff there. In addition, Joe Daly and Bob Dewey have found that Harry DeWitt completely botched the accounting job in Detroit, in spite of his large staff.

I must also confess, I was deeply hurt by Dick Measelle's comments that he had not seen such disloyalty and insidious treachery in all of his years in Arthur Andersen; when

Strycker and DeWitt asked for a private audience with Arthur Andersen and then revealed a number of nonexistent breaches of propriety. Obviously, Strycker was building a case to show that his dismissal was on grounds other than his incompetence and NIDA's dissatisfaction with him. He was also trying to hide his own $40,000 misappropriation of funds by accusing all others.

3

February 1980, an important date: the first showing of the new prototype. Visioneering, Inc. of Fraser, Michigan built the car just in time for the National Auto Dealers Association convention in New Orleans.

Ostensibly it looked the same as the Bill Collins model, which the dealers had already seen. The styling was softer, but it was still a stainless steel, gull-wing, luxury sports car. Underneath, however, it had changed completely.

DeLorean had brought his board, plus their wives, and was regaining his momentum.

'We think Ireland is an excellent place to do business in,' he remarked for the record.

Off the record he was less formal.

'If Northern Ireland can build the *Titanic*, they can build this car.'

The second great oil crisis, ushered in by the revolution in Iran and the exit of the Shah, had already caused sales of luxury sports cars to peak and go into sharp retreat. The Corvette sold 42,247 cars in 1978; it sold 38,631 in 1979 and was doing even worse in 1980. The Porsche 924 was selling at $16,000 – $2,000 less than the price then planned for the DMC-12 – yet its sales had also fallen sharply, down 3,000 in 1979.

And the design for the DMC-12 was already beginning to look dated. Rear-mounted engines were going out, front-wheel drive was now the rage. But the car still had its admirers.

Said *Auto Week* of the DMC-12: 'It has the performance characteristics of the Porsche 911 and a Renault Alpine, a ride similar to the Mercedes-Benz 450 SL and the power train punch of an unfederalized BMW.'

Back in Belfast, the engineers did not know what the magazine was talking about. They were at the point where they could only see problems, and there were more than enough of them to obscure everything else.

On February 13, DeLorean wrote out another memo on the subject of Walt Strycker. This was 'To File' and was DeLorean's version of a conversation he had with Harvey Hament of Resources for Industry, a small venture capital operation in New York. According to this memo, Hament came into DeLorean's office, closed the door, and said he had been visited by Strycker. The former DeLorean executive, said Hament to DeLorean, told him not to raise any money for DeLorean, 'since we were not honest and honorable people. He said we were dishonest and were cheating our investors and employees.' There was more along the same lines. The final paragraph was the most damning, showing the true depths of what DeLorean saw to be Strycker's betrayal of him: 'Hament said that Strycker said he was going to tell the same thing to all of our investors, investment counselors, and bankers.'

He marked the memo, 'cc: Cafiero, Kimmerly and Haddad.'

The following day, DeLorean and Kimmerly met Alan Cohen of Paul Weiss, Rifkind, Wharton and Garrison. DeLorean showed Cohen his memo 'To file' on Strycker who had, as DeLorean put it, 'bad mouthed me and the company'.

He had by now worked himself into a state of loathing of his former financial officer. 'Strycker was a regular dinner guest in our home and I treated him as more of a friend than an employee, never once sensing that he was stabbing me in the back with a series of self-serving memos and accusations,' he told Cohen.

The memo 'To file' that he wrote the next day about this meeting concluded:

> Alan Cohen had the distinct impression in his last meeting with Strycker that Strycker had gone off the deep end. This would certainly seem the case. In order not to hurt Strycker's reputation we had contrived a consulting arrangement paying him $10,000 per month plus expenses for ten days work per month. We were prepared to say that Strycker preferred to live in San Francisco as a reason, rather than

surface the UK Government's demand that he be terminated on the grounds of incompetence and inattention.

This memo 'To file' was also marked for copies to go to Cafiero, Kimmerly and Haddad – but DeLorean never signed it.

A fortnight later, on February 28, a Western Union telegram arrived from Strycker from San Francisco. It read, 'RESIGNATION FROM DELOREAN MOTOR COMPANY BOARD OF DIRECTORS EFFECTIVE 31, DECEMBER, 1979.'

Kimmerly got it; he scribbled on the top right hand corner: 'Bill, what about DMCL? Tom' and shot it along to Haddad. Strycker seemed to have forgotten that he was not only a director of DMC but of the Belfast company as well. Kimmerly played around with a draft letter of resignation, suggesting that DeLorean and Strycker would agree 'not to cast the other's participation ... in an unfavorable light' and that Strycker would not solicit DMC investors for his own private interests. In full settlement, Strycker would get $24,000 for the January and February period that he had still been working for DMC.

Strycker refused the 'soliciting DMC investors' provision, but accepted the rest, although it was reworded to read that he would 'refrain from derogatory descriptions.' He honoured it for a few months only. DeLorean does not seem to have honoured it at all.

In February 1980, both DeLorean in New York (along with Cafiero) and Bennington in Belfast were insisting that production could begin by July and that the car would be on the U.S. market by the autumn.

'I'll build this car on schedule,' Bennington told *Automotive News* in November. 'I may miss it by 30 days, but by no more than that.'

By that stage, however, the public schedule and the private one were two different matters. DeLorean was keeping up the public image because he still needed to raise money, and Bennington was under instructions not to argue with it, at least not openly. That public schedule meant pilot production in May and Job One in July. It was not even remotely possible.

By May, not only was the car not in pilot production, but the target date continued to recede as new technical problems came up. Now it was the window.

Originally DeLorean had promised electric windows. But the shape and design of the gull-wing doors ruled out a decent-sized dropping window. Bill Collins had an early version of a sliding window that could be pushed back far enough to allow the driver to crawl out if the door jammed shut – he even had a photograph of himself hauling his lanky frame through just such a window on one of the early prototypes. His longer-term aim was to add an electric motor to it.

Ted Chapman came up with a similar solution. Loasby too was a 'sliding window' man – he had designed one at Aston Martin. Bennington and Spooner, however, produced a dropping window that really was just a small inset into the larger fixed-in-place window – an opening only large enough for an arm to reach out to pay toll-booth fees and car-park tickets. It was a solution about which no one was entirely happy, but Lotus reckoned the sliding glass would have put back the project by several months – and did not have the right image for an expensive automobile.

For all their self-assurance, the Lotus men (other than Chapman who bowed the knee to no man on earth) were over-awed by DeLorean and his reputation. They were a small car company, stuck in the back of nowhere, almost unconscious of their own world reputation, but very conscious of DeLorean's. 'He'd be saying to us, "I've got to go now because I'm having dinner with the Chancellor of the Exchequer," says Fred Bushell. 'OK, so we're all used to bullshit but you've got to be somewhat impressed. He would arrive here with his helicopter and his entourage. And then suddenly Cafiero turns up. Jesus, Cafiero is ex-president of Chrysler and even if Chrysler is in the doldrums a man who controlled Chrysler Motors is no slouch. And if he thinks he wants to throw in his lot with John DeLorean, who are little Lotus personnel to tell him what he should put in his car?'

Thus DeLorean would arrive roughly once a month, look at the work done, agree some, suggest changes in others, sometimes insisting on changes which caused considerable anguish since they would slow the programme further. He and Chapman grew less and less close and after a while seldom spoke about anything other than technical matters. But he could still side with Chapman against his own staff. Bennington recalls one incident. 'Chapman wanted to go for fixed alignment front end. I didn't want to. I was able to convince John we should stay with one that allowed some adjustment. Then one day he and Colin were on one of their walkabouts and this subject came up and John immediately agreed with Chapman, and at that point I lost the argument so we ended up with a fixed front.'

In May there was the most vicious argument yet between the two sets of engineers. Ken Bunker had just joined the Loasby team to work on the suspension, which was his specialty. He was an experienced, professional engineer, but in the three weeks he worked for DeLorean riled Lotus more than any other individual. Bunker turned up in Norfolk unannounced and spent the next fortnight studying what had been done so far, without Colin Spooner being aware of his presence. At one stage he was actually thrown out of an office for looking at confidential DMC material – the Lotus man thought he was a rep. On May 17, he wrote his valediction: 'When I joined DMC I realized the situation in respect of product engineering was not good but I had no idea that it would be as bad as it appears.' In his view the emphasis was entirely on producing a car that could be assembled by hand rather than mass produced. Bunker criticized just about every aspect of the car: it was 'considerably over the design weight' and now weighed more than 3,000 lb against DeLorean's original (and hopelessly optimistic) estimate of 2,200 lb; its steering was 'very close to being unacceptable'; the suspension was designed in such a way that all components would have to work 'harder than necessary' thus negating the DeLorean principle of a long-life car; there were no design parameters, no properly organized team, the drawing situation was 'disastrous'. The whole project he reckoned could only end in failure – and he was not going to stay around for that.

He himself, he concluded, had been employed by DMC

> 'as design and development manager and I can see no way of fulfilling that function. Lotus Cars are contracted to design

and develop the DMC-12 and my input at the best is advisory. Had I known this situation, I would not have exposed my family and myself to such a risk. I therefore wish to terminate immediately my contract with DeLorean Motor Cars Ltd.'

He signed his name, 'K. J. Bunker' and departed, leaving behind an engineering department even more worried than before.

Bunker's letter went to Loasby who passed it on to Bennington who in turn sent it to Mike Kimberley. At Lotus, Kimberley and Spooner were enraged. Who was this man Bunker? 'He was never even introduced to me,' stormed Spooner. Bennington was apologetic – it had been done stupidly, he acknowledged, Loasby should have brought him over personally. But what about the charges he made?

Kimberley wrote a four-page letter back, rebutting Bunker's comments paragraph by paragraph. 'You have had many individual and team experts into Lotus in the last 18 months studying, assessing, analysing etc, all of whom, to the best of our knowledge, assessed the situation diametrically opposed to the view of Mr. Bunker,' he concluded. The Bunker affair died there, but the taste lingered.

CHAPTER TEN

DeLorean's Pen

John DeLorean's dream was going to live or die on his chances of getting more money from the British government. And that would be determined, to a large extent, not by DeLorean himself, but by the pressure of outside events, notably the continued desire of the Conservative government to go to considerable lengths to keep a factory that would help reduce those horrendous unemployment figures. The big battle in Northern Ireland was against the men of violence.

When Roy Mason took over from Merlyn Rees as Secretary of State in 1976 he had pursued a two-pronged policy designed to end what was then an eight-year conflict in the Province. His strategy was to combine a tough security policy designed to wipe out the Provos, with a massive programme of overseas investment designed to provide jobs and wean the young away from violence. DeLorean might have been the answer to Roy Mason's prayer: in his effort to win more – and the right sort of – investment for the Province, Mason had launched a billion-pound plan to stimulate Northern Ireland's competitiveness and the DeLorean project, taken at face value, was a perfect fit. With that project in West Belfast, Mason was hoping to show the Catholic community that, if they continued the path of peace and spurned the IRA, he would deliver jobs and prosperity for all, or at least for some.

When DeLorean arrived, Mason was recording some visible successes. The use of undercover Special Air Services (SAS) teams, a generous allocation of resources to the Royal Ulster Constabulary and expansion of the police reserve were beginning to pay dividends in terms of the number of IRA men arrested or killed on 'active service' in the 1977-8 period. The number of bombings and shootings declined noticeably and there was a general lessening of tension, although in the summmer of 1980 the IRA was far from a spent or defeated force, as Britain still knows to her cost.

But in crude terms the IRA did not have to attack factories, even if it wanted to. For the world recession in 1980 was dealing the Province a far greater blow than any bombs of less than several megatons could have done. Factory after factory was still closing. Only John DeLorean's factory and a few others were going up.

Thus when DeLorean emerged in the spring of 1980 with a request for a major new injection of money, Mason's successor, Humphrey Atkins, had to take it very seriously indeed. The request was based on the clause in the Department of Commerce's formal letter to DeLorean offering additional money if the original amount proved insufficient because of currency fluctuation or inflation. That silly little clause was to cost the British government at least £14 million. The NIDA team may have been boiling with rage and frustration at the way DeLorean was spending money, but they were not in a strong position to complain to Atkins's ministers. They had recommended the investment, although they would probably have constructed a better deal if Roy Mason had not applied pressure, but it was their job to monitor and control the project after that and they were only too aware that they were not succeeding. Nobody in Belfast had ever encountered anyone like John DeLorean and reports from New York that DeLorean was boasting he had them 'over a barrel' only brought from them a grudging admission that he did. They had few weapons.

They did have one, however, and they were deploying it with a tentative but growing skill through the early summer. DeLorean wanted more money and if he did not get it, there would be no factory and some £54 million would be down the drain. But that argument could be turned against him, too. There would be no more money unless DeLorean reformed, cut his expenses, stopped flitting about on other projects, and put all his efforts and money into the car. To ensure that he did so, there could be a major renegotiation of the Master Agreement, giving NIDA a larger vote, untying the absurd clause in the agreement that gave DMC sole distribution rights (so that one DeLorean company in Belfast was required to sell all its products to another DeLorean company in New York) and generally tidying up the arrangements that NIDA was beginning to regret bitterly having left so untidy in the first place. Some good might come out of the crisis.

DeLorean, probably under Cafiero pressure, decided to be conciliatory to NIDA. His telexed reply to the Faulkner letter in January had been an angry, insulting effort and for two months NIDA and DeLorean had swopped nasty messages. It was March 20 before DeLorean formally answered Faulkner, and the letter was deemed so important that Cafiero carried it by hand and delivered it personally to Faulkner in Belfast. DeLorean may have seen it as an olive branch. But he could not avoid filling it with classic DeLorean braggadocio.

> Having high-caliber dedicated people is what is bringing this very challenging program near to fruition. Our very lean organization has made our response rapid, thoughtful and decisive in overcoming many difficulties which would have swamped a less experienced group of automobile people.

And there was much more of that: no financial officer yet but Daly and Dewey were coping; Shaun Harte was making a great contribution. Towards the end DeLorean allowed himself a little homily. Why didn't the large automobile companies... see the energy crunch? Do more about safety and pollution? He, John DeLorean, was not going to make that mistake – which was why he was exploring new ventures.

Faulkner and Hopkins were getting increasingly tough with DeLorean. They were chipping away. In June DeLorean sent Hopkins a telex, starting 'Dear Tony' which was unusually friendly. He had, DeLorean said, now got the accountants to quantify DMC's actual out of pocket non-reimbursable costs on non-DMC-12 projects. He listed them: $106,571 on the Transbus, $39,210 on the DMC-44 four-wheel drive vehicle, $14,016 on the Stirling engine project, $49,600 to prepare the study to take over Chrysler and $69,581 on a Replicar project. Total: $277,978. It was a very selective bit of accounting. But DeLorean, beginning to feel nervy about his claim for extra money, was still conciliatory.

But, in actual fact, he was still spending as hard as ever. He was expanding on the 35th floor, which he had taken in addition to the 43rd floor penthouse.

2

There were by now nearly 300 people working on the DeLorean project at Lotus, seven days a week. The pace and pressure had reached a peak, the engineering and design problems had come to a climax. Many of the Dunmurry engineers had moved over (including Mike Loasby) and the hotels and private houses within driving distance of the factory were filled with DeLorean men. Bennington, under pressure from Loasby and Broomfield, had taken on extra men, often semi-retired American auto draughtsmen, to help with the flow of drawings. Lotus didn't want to release drawings until the specifications were complete; Bennington and Wills decided not to wait. But the backlog was huge: every day counted.

From early morning on June 18, 1980, there had been a noticeable added edge to the atmosphere. Busy men already became even busier; Colin Chapman was very much in evidence, checking progress, sending men scurrying around to finish off jobs and others to tidy the drawing offices and factory floor. Some of the Esprit Turbos, built alongside the DMC-12, were rolled out; DMC prototypes were wheeled in. The big white chief himself was paying a visit to the Lotus works.

DeLorean had as usual come in to London overnight by Concorde. An early car had taken him to the Battersea Heliport, and shortly after ten he was touching down in front of Lotus' gleaming modern plant, before being driven in a Lotus to the older hangars which housed the DeLorean operation. Chapman brought him through every drawing office. Spooner and Kimberley did most of the talking and explaining. But it was Mike Loasby and some of his team who wanted to draw their worries to his attention.

Peter Allinson, the DeLorean engineer in charge of safety and emissions, was increasingly concerned that the car was not going to make it through its federal certification tests.

He had pulled together some Lotus figures, and drew Loasby's attention to the steady increase in weight of the prototypes. Lotus was now up to Doris 7, and each of the preceding six cars was heavier than the one before. Once it was fully fitted out, the D7 was going to have a weight, without passengers, fuel or luggage (in the jargon, this is 'dry curb weight') of 2,614 lb, which was considerably more than anticipated. As the weight crept up, fuel economy was creeping down. And if the weight got really high, then the car might be in a test weight category beyond the capacity of the rolling road at Lotus. (A rolling road is a set of rollers on which the car can simulate normal speeds while actually remaining stationary.) There would be problems with the Californian emission tests. The DeLorean sales literature was citing a weight of 2,400 lb, a weight the car never really was.

DeLorean could not avoid the weight problem, but he could fudge it, and he did.

At first, however, there were a few pleasantries at lunch in Ketteringham Hall, which he envied Colin Chapman. He was still trying to buy something similar. He asked Chapman how the Grand Prix team was doing. It was a sore point. Chapman's new car, with its revolutionary aerodynamics, was having problems. It had not won a Grand Prix, and the Lotus team had been out of the winning stakes since Peterson was killed.

In the afternoon, with both DeLorean and Chapman present, they went through a series of points. Weight was the first and major one. DeLorean, as usual, doodled, drawing artistic shapes on his pad but also noting the figures that Lotus had prepared for him. The dry weight was now 2,471 lb, and the vehicle needed to be less than that to make the 2,750 lb inertia weight class at which it would be certified.

They went through a series of items: leather trim and new upholstery cloths, the leather-covered steering wheel, and so on. Then they moved on to controls, the switches and knobs in the car. DeLorean produced his pen and held it up. It was black plastic, a very fine matte finish, expensive. 'I want them similar to the finish on this Lamy pen,' he said. The pen was reverently passed round the table. Later, it was to be placed on a cushion and borne round as if it were the crown jewels.

'That damn pen,' the engineers called it, as they tried to copy its finish for their switches. The finish was so fine that the switches scratched easily and, all too often, had to be rejected or replaced.

On his way back to New York from that meeting, DeLorean wrote out his version of it. He had it typed up and sent to Bennington in Belfast with a copy to Cafiero and to Mike Kimberley, managing director of Lotus. 'Summarizing my understanding of our meeting at Lotus today,' he began, before going on to 'emissions'.

DeLorean had been doing some thinking on the Concorde home. He started off with that dry weight figure of 2,471 lb. Under it, he wrote a list of eight items, originally planned as standard features of the car, that he now proposed to make theoretical options on 'at least the first few thousand cars'. He wrote a column headed 'Delete' and then started with air conditioning, tool kit (a modest three lb), spare tyre (40), louvre panel above the rear window (18), the stereo radio (22), sound package (43), rearview mirror (3) and the central locking system (8). It all came to 192 lb which, if taken off the original figure of 2,471, gave 2,279 lb. 'On this basis,' concluded DeLorean triumphantly, 'you could leave the louvre panel in and still be under 2,300 pounds.'

It was a cynical exercise. For five years DeLorean had been making the point that his great 'ethical' car would be fitted with these features. Without air conditioning, the car, with its tiny side windows, could be unbearable. The vehicle could not be marketed without a spare tyre; it would look absurd without that louvre panel, an essential part of its styling; the stereo radio and sound package were standard items on a luxury sports car.

DeLorean knew as well as everybody else did that a car sold without these items, most of them standard equipment on expensive cars, would be a disaster. Particularly at the price he was proposing to offer it. He was not seriously intending to sell it that way. He was just going to make these items '100% options' in order to get over the weight problems for emission control certification.

In his eagerness to fiddle with the figures, he missed one factor: the starting weight of 2,471 lb already allowed for the deduction of these items. In presenting him with the figures, the engineers had done the same calculation he was now doing, except that their 'net' figure was his 'gross' figure. They had deducted his 192 lb for the same items. DeLorean was double counting.

DeLorean went on remorselessly to recount 11 points of discussion at Lotus. Point 8 showed he was at least still conscious of some of his original concepts, although it also showed that he was trying to evade them.

'We will look quickly at a gull-wing door passenger belt system that will also serve as the gull-wing door pull down strap. I'd like to see a mock-up of this within the next few weeks. We are publicly committed to safety and air bags. This is an important but small pallative (sic).'

DeLorean raised other points. The seats, for example, which Kimberley in particular had found uncomfortable. 'I don't know the experts but we need the best. This could be a fatal flaw.' The Craig stereo system: 'Like everyone else, they must be competitive in both performance and price.' DeLorean had an ability to focus on detail as fine as the trim and the washer system and a dozen other points mentioned that day. Loasby and his engineers, however, felt he had ignored the most important problems, although Lotus themselves hoped that they were now over the hump and – unless DeLorean insisted on further major changes – that their part in the car would be completed by the end of the year.

In Belfast from June onwards there was a flood of memos from Loasby and his staff setting out problems. Bennington, Wills and Shaun Harte accused the engineers of being too fussy, of destructive criticism and simply of 'minding their own backs' and ignoring the project itself. Spooner at Lotus welcomed the Bennington/Wills approach, although still nervous about allowing unfinished drawings out. He too accused Loasby of not 'joining the team' but criticizing from the outside.

If DeLorean was aware of the ill-will, he remained aloof from it. Whenever he appeared he so dominated the normally blunt and outspoken professional engineers that they only spoke when spoken to. Bennington wasn't the sort of man to go running to DeLorean with his problems.

The pace Bennington had set for himself and the pressures of finding himself the buffer between DeLorean and the Irish officials and the Lotus engineers began to tell. It was around this time he had his accident. He was living in a converted apartment at Warren House, the stately home on the edge of the site which had been taken over and was being 'modernized' at considerable expense for future visiting VIPs. His marriage was breaking up under the lifestyle he had chosen and several times Mrs. Bennington had irritated John DeLorean by ringing up the Park Avenue office to complain about it. Bennington drove a Lotus but was no Mario Andretti.

Late one night, he was driving home along the winding Irish roads. As the story was related afterward, the road turned sharp right but Bennington didn't. He went straight on, cleared a low wall and ended up in the field beyond. He caught the DeLorean plane to Norfolk the next morning, in considerable pain. His ear had been almost severed and he had several cracked ribs – Colin Chapman built his cars of tough materials. Barrie Wills remembers flying home with him the next evening 'and he was in real distress with his ribs. But he still never missed a day.'

Yet, now in the summer of 1980, the launch date was slipping further and further away. There was no lack of activity. Most of those involved, including Bennington, were working six or even seven day weeks. Shaun Harte, in his capacity as project coordinator, was drawing up flow chart after flow chart, each one showing the dates gradually slipping back, although Harte himself stayed among the optimists. His 'Activity Chart', as he called it, dated April 19, 1980, which NIDA received for its meeting on April 25 and didn't believe, showed series production beginning in September. Even that was optimistic.

NIDA had retained the McKinsey group to provide a monthly independent analysis of how the DeLorean project was progressing. In its May report, McKinsey assumed that production 'would build up steadily from October onward, with sales of nearly 1,280 units by the end of December and almost 3,900 by the end of March'. Now at the end of July, as Humphrey Atkins was persuading the Cabinet to put in the additional money that DeLorean was requesting, McKinsey reported to NIDA, that 'present DMCL plans call for the buildup of volume production to be delayed until February 1981; and only 1,000 units will have been sold by the end of March 1981'.

The engineers knew that even that was still over-optimistic. There was hardly a part of the car that was not giving some problem, mostly to do with quality control. The engine was not meeting the EPA tests; the fibre glass in the body moulds was not setting properly; the gull-wing doors were not fitting; and almost no testing had been done.

Through July, DeLorean and his senior men were explaining away the delays to the dealers and other interested parties in the U.S. The latest delay was a 'stretch-out' of the final pre-production and training phases, said Eugene Cafiero in his capacity as DMC president. This 'stretch-out' would allow the company to commence pilot production in November (it had previously been May), after the vehicle finished its 50,000 mile EPA endurance testing.

Cafiero told *Automotive News* that the company had hoped to do just the 4,000 mile test and 'piggyback' on the Volvo 262 50,000 mile test because both cars used the same power plant. 'We made certain changes to the engine which greatly enhance mileage, and the EPA told us we would have to do the 50,000 mile test after all,' he said, adding that the mileage was now 22 mpg.

Then Cafiero went on to say that 'the emissions work was essentially done, with very comfortable margins,' and he gave figures which apparently showed the DeLorean vehicle well under the 1981 standards.

Soon afterwards, John DeLorean himself addressed the *Automotive News* World Conference, a prestigious event in the auto calendar. DeLorean intended to give the world the latest optimistic picture of the DMC project, but typically, went on to turn his address into a plan for concerted action to save the entire U.S. auto industry: tax code changes that would 'provide stimulus for capital formation' needed for the modernization of the industry; a revision of the regulatory process which would include 'simultaneous consideration' of the 'interaction' between health, safety, environmental considerations, fuel economy and other standards; 'incentivization' of research and development through an investment tax credit; a cohesive energy policy and much else, full of jargon like 'prioritize national goals'.

On the future of his own company, DeLorean got quite carried away. Capacity at the Dunmurry plant, he said, was '120,000 to 150,000 units a year' and more if the company used additional outside sourcing. That was pure cloud cuckoo-land. He might make them, but where would he sell them?

Any day now, the British government would be deciding whether to give him more money, so DeLorean put in a few kind words for Mrs. Thatcher. 'Mrs. Thatcher is a significant world leader. She has the potential to do for England what DeGaulle did for France.' The Dunmurry workforce, he went on, was 'superb' – there were now nearly 400 of them, and the absentee rate was 1.2 percent. 'Do not let anyone convince you that the labor in Belfast is torn by industrial or religious strife – it isn't.'

2

By the end of July the tension had really mounted. DeLorean had started by asking for £2 million, which soon became £5 million, then £12 million and now even more. It would not be new cash – the Commerce Department would provide a government guarantee that DeLorean could use to borrow from a commercial bank. But it would still qualify as Government spending and would need Cabinet approval. Humphrey Atkins was not sure if he would get it.

On July 18, 1980, McKinsey had produced yet another status report. The launch date of the car, it announced, had been postponed. It would now be February 1981. Furthermore, there was bad news. J. D. Powers, the market research analysts, had done a new survey. And it showed that, at the new planned sticker price of $24,000 a car, no more than 8-10,000 cars could be sold. With its overhead, the company could make nothing but losses at that level. But worse news still: 'DMCL will run out of funds during the third week of August and the cumulative funding gap will approach $25 million by February 1981.' Disaster was once again approaching. The New York operation would soon face an even bigger cash crisis, warned McKinsey.

It was now up to the government. Would Margaret Thatcher agree to more money for DeLorean? The House of Commons was under the impression that the amount of new assistance, if it were given, would be no more than £8 million, and even at that level many Members were already rearing in indignation.

On August 4 Atkins brought up the subject of DeLorean at a Cabinet meeting. It was a late one – ministers were overdue on their holiday break and the Cabinet normally never met in August at all. Telling only a select few the result, Atkins took his ministerial plane to Belfast that evening. DeLorean was waiting.

Hillsborough is a small linen town on the Dromore-Lisburn Road, five miles south of Dunmurry. At 9.15 on August 5 DeLorean's car rolled into the forecourt of the castle now used as the Northern Ireland Secretary's private residence, and DeLorean and Gene Cafiero stepped out. They still had no idea what to expect. Had they got the money?

There were three people in the room they were ushered into: the tall figure of Atkins; Giles Shaw, the Minister of State; and Atkins's senior civil servant. No NIDA people, no one from the Commerce Department. Atkins was doing this deal direct, cutting the Agency and officials right out of it. The meeting lasted half an hour. It was the first time Atkins had met DeLorean. The Cabinet committee had met the night before, he told DeLorean. They had considered his request for more money. They had been made aware of the McKinsey report. It was the government's policy to restrict public expenditure but at the same time there was an interest in creating and preserving as many jobs in Northern Ireland as possible. In the circumstances, therefore, he had obtained Cabinet approval for the Department of Commerce to guarantee bank loans of up to £14 million. This would cover the extra costs incurred because of the rapid rise in the British inflation rate, now running at 20 percent, and the rise in the pound as a result of the new oil crisis. But there would be conditions – a reorganization of the royalty arrangements on the car and, most important of all, an agreement that this would finally and fully discharge the government's commitment to DeLorean. There would be no more money after this. He was providing enough to see the project through and that would be that. Not a penny more, whatever happened.

So DeLorean had done it again – he had got his money. And what is more he had slipped out of the chains Tony Hopkins thought he was about to bind around him. The NIDA people were furious. They had lost their best chance yet to control DeLorean.

3

It was some months before the money would come through, and DeLorean was short. Just how short is emphasized by an incident just before he left for his meeting with Atkins. Dick Brown was sitting in his office in California talking to Bob Dewey on the telephone in the New York office. In Brown's secretary's office a paper was coming in over the telecopier – a resolution from DeLorean. Brown's secretary laid it on his desk and as he was talking to Dewey he idly started to read it. It was a board resolution sent to him for his signature. Brown's casual interest had become intense.

'Bob,' he said into the phone, 'I'm reading this resolution. Do you know anything about it?'

'No,' answered Dewey, who was not on the board. 'What is it?'

'It's a resolution to borrow $600,000 from John's personal company and assign all the assets of the company as collateral for the loan,' replied Brown. 'I'm not going to sign this. $600,000 will last us 30 days. What happens 30 days from now when the $600,000 is gone and John gets all the assets?'

Brown then called Gene Cafiero. 'Gene, did you sign this resolution?'

'I did,' replied Cafiero. 'But I wanted all the directors to sign it rather than just do it through the executive committee.'

'Well, Gene,' said Brown, 'I'm not going to sign it.'

And he explained why. There was a strangled cry at the other end of the phone. 'Oh, my God,' said Cafiero. The ex-Chrysler man clearly had not thought through the implications of the resolution.

'If you want, Gene,' proffered Brown, 'I'll get my attorney to verify what it says.' He wasn't entirely certain his quick interpretation was correct. But the idea appealed to Cafiero. 'I'll tell you what, Dick. If you get your attorney to look through it, I'll pay half the cost.'

According to Brown he then checked with his lawyer 'and he verified in spades what I suspected, and Gene never paid me half the costs!'

By that time Brown was in a long dialogue with Kimmerly and DeLorean on the phone. There were four or five other telephone conversations on this matter, which he carefully documented. Wendy, his secretary, took his side of the conversation in shorthand and after the conversation he filled in the other side.

'It was ugly. Messy. And I told John, "Why can't you be man enough or executive enough to live up to your responsibilities? You are the chairman of this company. You founded the company. You are the 84 percent stockholder. Do you mean to tell me you would not loan this company $600,000 without pledging all the assets? Is that all the confidence you have in this operation?" And then it got very ugly.' The conversation went on for hours. 'And I just told him I wasn't going to sign it, period. But Cafiero had signed it. Henry Bushkin had signed it. Edmund King had signed it. Then Bushkin found out my position and he called me and said, "Thank God somebody in the company was thinking," and he and Edmund King withdrew their signatures. Before I would sign I requested an opinion letter from Kimmerly saying we had authority to do this and that it conformed to all the applicable SEC regulations and other regulations governing corporate activities in the states of California and Michigan. When the opinion letter finally came forth, it said that they didn't have the authority to do it and they nixed the thing anyway and the loan fell apart.'

By then Humphrey Atkins had come through and the loan was no longer needed. But this incident was to have an extraordinary sequel.

Brown was the one man who could seriously challenge John DeLorean. Bill Collins, although he probably had more to complain about than anyone else, had avoided confrontation and left quietly. Bob Dewey's protest had been to leave, only to experience the humiliation of having to come back. Walt Strycker was more vocal and had gone to the auditors and the lawyers – but he too had lost as he knew he would. Brown, however, was not easily replaceable, because he had signed up the dealers and his job had yet to come – selling the car once it came off the production line, which was now scheduled for only six months ahead.

Brown was no sycophant or toadie, nor was he a weak

character whom DeLorean could easily brow-beat. He also had the advantage of being removed from the politicing going on in 280 Park Avenue – he had his own separate DeLorean operation in Irvine, California.

In the middle of August with the financial crisis past, Brown was summoned to New York for a staff meeting on Monday, followed by a full board meeting on the following Wednesday, for which the British directors, Bennington, Shaun Harte and Joe Daly, plus NIDA representatives Tony Hopkins and Alex Fetherston, were due in.

That day, Shaun Harte got a telex from Loasby stating simply: 'Re telex forwarded today, please ensure you have copy of second part sent to CKB.' 'CKB' was Bennington, but Harte knew it was not Bennington that Loasby was trying to get to. He wanted the whole board to see this.

The main telex was an attempt to go over Bennington's head and reach DeLorean himself. It was read out loud at the board meeting.

Loasby started, 'I am very concerned with the situation in the emission area of Lotus.' There then followed a detailed complaint that, although target figures for the normal performance of the engine had been established on July 3, 'we have had one set of results within the target figures and no repeat tests of the same specification.' To ensure certification by January 1, the 4,000 mile tests would have to start by September 1 – that was the very last date, 'and we have not yet defined a specification'.

Loasby was not pulling his punches. 'It cannot be over-emphasized that time is being apparently frittered away, for whatever reason, pursuing frivolous investigations at the expense of establishing a reliable base calibration which can be reasonably expected to give satisfactory results when tested by EPA at EPA.'

DeLorean had asked Lotus to re-engineer the standard engine to improve its fuel economy and escape from federal penalties. Loasby reckoned there was no time for that and with such a tight programme they should stick with what they had got. But the 'frivolous investigations' he was complaining about were actually John DeLorean policy decisions, on the whole supported by Lotus. Loasby was already desperately concerned at the lack of testing time. He wanted no more additions to the car.

DeLorean by this stage had decided to shove Bennington aside. The excuse was that he had done his job, created the factory and the team, got the car to the point where production was soon to begin. In effect, it was probably for other reasons. 'Chuck said "No" to John once too often,' says Barrie Wills.

On Thursday, the day after the meeting, Brown was sitting in an office in 280 Park Avenue when DeLorean sauntered in. He perched himself on the arm of a chair and looked across the desk at the short, solidly-built figure of Brown. 'Dick, we didn't think you were too comfortable on the board and we're making some changes, you know, bringing in some new people.' He had had a shareholders' meeting and 'We have reconstituted the board.'

DeLorean had brought on eight new people, including Cristina, who was now listed as 'business woman' in company documents. Off went Brown – he had been appointed, without knowing about it, vice president for North American operations. And off went Shaun Harte, also without knowing it. He didn't mind too much – he was really only on the board as the original nominee of NIDA and was now relieved to be out of the firing line in New York. Bennington was to be moved out to Coventry.

Brown, however, refused to let DeLorean off the hook too easily. 'I know what you've done here, and it doesn't bother me. The only reason I stay in this company is because of the people I've brought into it. I recruited the people. I built your company. I brought in a lot of investor money and built the Northern Ireland operation and now you pull something like this. But I'm going to stay, even though you may try to get me to leave. I'm going to stay here to protect their interest. I'm telling you, John, Nesseth and Kimmerly are going to be your nemesis in the final analysis.' DeLorean just looked at the floor before saying, 'There isn't going to be a final analysis.'

Finally, when both men had talked themselves out, DeLorean proffered peace. 'Let's you and I start over and forget all this.'

'So that was that,' says Brown. 'I continued. I wasn't on the board here in the United States, but I was on the board in Northern Ireland.' DeLorean had won again, but Brown had scored a few points.

4

Meanwhile, Loasby and two of his engineers, Peter Allinson and Joe Hillebrand, had held a meeting with Lotus chief engineer Tony Rudd, and it was Rudd himself who dictated the minute. It was a single sheet of paper, and the DeLorean engineers regarded it as a major breakthrough, although to an outsider it is meaningless. 'Below is the agreed job one specification for DMC-12,' it starts. Then there are three subheadings: automatic transmission, manual transmission and engine specification. The automatic, they agreed, would have middle of tolerance change speeds, the same Renault torque converter now on development car D3, and the same step gear ratios as standard Renault transmission. The manual would have the same unit now used on D8 and D10, and the engine would be the 1981 Californian Volvo base engine.

That was all. The document was dated August 21, 1980. Hillebrand, Allinson and Loasby signed it; but although he had agreed to it at the meeting and it was his document, Rudd would not. There was too much inter-company DMC politics in all this.

By now, the McKinsey consultants were gathering information for their reports for NIDA. They apparently saw everything and talked to everyone, but the engineers were under instructions to 'be positive', keep their doubts and friction to themselves and show them only problems that had been solved and the progress they were making. McKinsey knew nothing of the worries over emissions or of the batteries of telexes that flew between Bennington and the Lotus engineers.

The division between the engineers and the purchasing department had also widened. Over and over again, the engineers pointed out that unless parts were tooled up to final specification, they would not fit and would have to be tooled again; not only was that more costly but, in the end, it would also take longer. The purchasing people, under Barrie Wills, supported by Shaun Harte, felt there was no time for these niceties and that unless they did a bit of engineering ad-libbing here and there, there would be no car.

By now parts were arriving in Belfast, and Broomfield was trying to set up his production line. Although they had missed the 18 month schedule (which was never *their* schedule, but DeLorean's), Lotus were producing a car in under two years which was an extraordinary effort by any standards. There were still plenty of problems to solve, and there were still considerable tensions, but Lotus were beginning to allow themselves a feeling of modest pride. The Lotus worry now was not their own standard of work – but the quality of the work that would be done at Dunmurry. The emphasis was beginning to switch from Norwich back to Belfast, where the development work of Lotus now had to be translated into a workable production line.

NIDA was beginning to hear more encouraging news about the progress on the car, in contrast to DeLorean's continual money problems. In July McKinsey listed nine problems with the vehicle, but missed out the weight and emissions problems which were giving Loasby sleepless nights.

By the autumn, as dealers in the U.S. were told they could not expect delivery until the spring, there was further agitation over another factor: the price of the car.

Don Lucas, a dealer in California, for instance, was quoted in *The Economist* as saying he spent $100,000 buying four DeLorean franchises and invested another $25,000 of his own money. He was told, but not guaranteed, by DeLorean that the car would sell at $18,000. Now, the car was going to sell at $25,000 and that, he believed, would scare off half his customers. The Corvette was only $17,500, and the Porsche between $17,000 and $20,000. Another Californian, a San Francisco dealer, was also quoted in the same article, saying that he would need to sell the car at $30,000 to compensate for the delay and to get back his promotional costs.

In its July report, McKinsey had included an estimate of sales at different prices, prepared once again by market research analysts J. D. Powers. This showed that at $16,000-$18,000, the company would hope to sell around 20,000 cars a year, which was the planned production level. At $21,000 the forecast sales dropped sharply to 13,000-16,000 in the first year, and at $24,000, which by then was the planned sticker price, an estimated 8,000-10,000 vehicles would be sold. Powers also included an estimate for a $28,000 price tag and got 4,000-5,000 cars in the first year, which in the light of events was astonishingly accurate.

Nonetheless, McKinsey was content to warn that planning should be done on the basis of no more than 15,000 vehicles a year, although, 'the prices for components were originally negotiated on the basis of sales volume of 30,000 units a year'.

Now road tests in the autumn were throwing up new and unexpected difficulties: the manual car was only doing 7,000-8,000 miles on a set of tyres against the originally estimated 30,000; and on a frontal crash test, the bonnet crumpled into the windscreen.

On the other hand, the standard engine had passed EPA requirements on its 4,000 mile test and, although it would have to be retested by the EPA itself to see that it passed the 22 mpg requirement for 1981, that had cheered people up. Unfortunately, it could not repeat those figures and failed the next tests, plunging everyone back into gloom.

CHAPTER ELEVEN

A Day in the Life

'I can hate the sin and still love the sinner, can't I?' asks Arvid Jouppi. 'Well, that's the way I feel about John DeLorean. I may not approve of all the things he's done in his life, but I have to stick by him now because he is one of the few genuine geniuses our industry has ever produced. And what he accomplished – nearly – was monumental.'

Arvid Jouppi is a combination of authority, expertise, integrity and good humour, rare among corporate securities analysts. He is *the* financial and marketing authority on the American automobile industry and he can chide it with the love that only comes from devoting a lifetime to watching its companies stumble and falter. Jouppi consults for leading brokerage houses as well as advising scores of the industry's top executives. When Arvid Jouppi talks about cars, the impact is felt from Detroit to Wall Street.

Jouppi admits to having been a long-time admirer of John DeLorean's drive, even when he disagreed with some of the end results.

'You can't understand how exciting it was to watch John shaking things up around here 20 years ago. Sure, things were said about him, about his personal life. Some of them were pretty weird. But even if they were all true, the fact remains that John tried to do something that had not been attempted in nearly 50 years. Not since Billy Durant has anyone tried to start a major competitive large production car company in this country,' he says.

Jouppi is a rumpled senior cherub. Presiding at a luncheon table at the Recess Club atop the Fisher Building in Detroit, he keeps a running account of the top industry executives as they enter this private sanctuary; there are none he cannot call by name, and few fail to stop by his table to greet him. The contrast between this gentle, generous man and John DeLorean is difficult to understand.

'I didn't say I *liked* John. We were never social friends, if that's what you mean. But the lack of competition, the trend to consolidation was killing the industry long before the oil crisis. And John DeLorean was trying to do something that would have reversed that trend. He came up with a good concept, he raised the money, he put together a good dealer network and he built the car. Every step of the way people were waiting for him to fail. Well, now he has failed and you have to ask yourself whether we are any better off for his having failed. I think not.'

Jouppi was not alone in his admiration for DeLorean's adventure, even as late as the autumn of 1980 and the spring of 1981. During this period, John DeLorean could argue with some effect that he was doing what he said he would.

In fact, with the capital injection from the British government, he had done even more. He had not only raised more than $200 million in capital for his venture in the previous five years, but he had also welded together a dealers' network, which, along with the money, gave him a potential economic clout equal to the fourth largest car producer in the United States – American Motors Company, with its working capital at that time of $236 million.*

And John DeLorean was viewed by many people as a political symbol, proof that the failures of American big business and big American government were not inevitable. Life could be changed for the better here in these United States if someone could, as DeLorean was always saying, just cut through the bullshit and get on with the job.

Inside the DMC executive offices in New York, the feeling of us-against-them steadily intensified as DeLorean's setbacks mounted. A high level of personal commitment extended well down into the staff, where that commitment was embodied solely in the person of John DeLorean.

'I'm a real flower child idealist of the Seventies, an anti-draft counsellor when I was in college during Vietnam, all that. And I had plenty of job opportunities at the time but I chose to work

---

* Moody's Handbook of Common Stocks, 1983.

for DMC because I wanted to work for John DeLorean. I wanted to be a part of what he was doing.'

The speaker is another who shares Arvid Jouppi's persistent admiration for John DeLorean's dream. Beginning as a low-level clerical employee, this loyalist stayed on through the final days of the DMC and at the end became a close personal aide to DeLorean himself.

'No one worked harder than John DeLorean. He was all business. This nonsense about a jet-set lifestyle was just media hype. I'm pretty bitter about the news media generally, and the car enthusiast magazines, in particular. They made John. They made an image to suit themselves and then hoped he couldn't live up to it. David Davis and people like him never gave John a chance; all we ever heard once the car began to come off the assembly line was that it had this fault or that, or that it would not be as cheap as a Corvette. They never wrote that the new edition of the Corvette was kept off the production line for a full year because GM was having so much trouble with it,' the aide says.

'And this crap about John being a swinger. I can truthfully say I never saw John DeLorean take a drink in my life. He was too much of a health freak to involve himself in booze or drugs. If I wanted to set him off, all I had to do was leave a candy bar on my desk – I'm a choco-holic of sorts – and he was good for a 15-minute lecture on what I was doing to myself,' the aide adds.

'I wasn't part of the inner social circle, but I don't think he or Cristina were big on parties. They both watched their diets and from what I could see, their idea of a good time was a small dinner party at home with close friends. I was at their Christmas party at the Bedford Springs farm in December 1982 after John was released from jail. They had neighbors and their children in and the punch bowl was just fruit juice.

'As for his personal life, it was really inseparable from the company in those days. We got in together at about the same time, around 8.30 in the morning, and often I wouldn't leave until 7 at night and he would still be there. He rarely ate lunch out of the office – invariably it was a tuna fish sandwich and a diet soft drink – and the rest of the time it was phone calls, memo writing and reading, reading, reading.'

The portrait is apparently an accurate one. Other DeLorean

employees, former secretary Marian Gibson included, confirm DeLorean's almost legendary capacity for working long hours without complaint. A normal working day begins at 6.30 a.m. with DeLorean, by all accounts, slipping out of bed in the couple's Fifth Avenue apartment and going to a separate room, that he and Cristina had fitted out with exercise equipment, for a minimum half hour rigorous work-out.

The DeLorean mania for a youthful appearance remains unchecked. Although he no longer dyes his hair an unnatural black and has stopped posing for magazines lifting weights and flexing, shirtless, for posters, John DeLorean is more concerned than ever about appearances. His leanness appeared almost skeletal in the days after his arrest, when his face was so thin that the outlines of the plastic chin-extender implanted by a plastic surgeon 15 years earlier stood out in sharp relief in the news photographs.

After taking his shower and dressing for work, DeLorean sits in on breakfast with Cristina, young Zachary and their still toddling daughter Kathryn. DeLorean eats little, often experimenting with vitamin, malt and fruit juice concoctions done up in a blender.

It is an important family time and one that the couple apparently keep as part of the regular routine whenever their two schedules permit. No one has ever disputed DeLorean's affection for his children, or for Cristina for that matter. The marriage of John and Cristina DeLorean has survived a decade of tumult and pressures that would have wrecked many another couple, standing in stark contrast to his previous record of failed relationships and bizarre sexual wanderings.

DeLorean keeps his life in almost hermetically-sealed separate compartments. He keeps his family in one – a very calm island where the pleasures are simple and low-key. Then there is the public image of the glamorous still-swinging corporate executive and his famous ex-model wife and their Studio 54 coterie of friends. In truth, this part of their life is the greatest sham. And of course there was DMC itself, but even there his career was fragmented between the car company's problems and his growing desire to break free into other business ventures that would create the DeLorean empire he dreamed of – only then would he be truly free.

That DeLorean was able to walk from compartment to compartment without losing his way is further proof of the driving forces inside him. Indeed, he could *not* have been much of a swinger and have survived as long as he did. During this period from 1979 right up until the end, every minute of his life was spoken for.

After breakfast, DeLorean's personal routine rarely varies. The maid and houseboy have by now arrived and are bustling about their appointed chores; the live-in nanny has taken Kathryn in charge and seen Zachary off to school. Cristina is planning her day of calls to photography studios, fashion houses and magazine offices. DeLorean himself finishes with the morning newspapers and then selects one of the dark, modest print neckties that are as much a part of his unchanging wardrobe as his dark, French-cut three-piece suits and blue shirts with the elongated collar points. Even here, the myths about DeLorean's $700-custom-made suits are an exaggeration; to be sure, he has his suits custom-tailored because of his height and slender frame. But $400 was the most he would pay for a suit, and he often marvelled at the reports that they cost more. In a rare personal joke, he wondered aloud whether people thought the suits looked *so* good on him that they must have cost $700.

On most mornings DeLorean walks to the office. The route never varies; down Fifth Avenue to 51st Street and into St. Patrick's Cathedral. Although he had been baptized a Catholic, his father had never been active in the Church and his mother had experimented with several Protestant church affiliations throughout her life. DeLorean freely concedes that he is not an actively religious person and certainly not denominational. Yet, every now and then he seeks the sanctuary of a church both in New York and in London.

After leaving St. Patrick's, DeLorean walks briskly over to Park Avenue and then further south to 280 Park Avenue, where a special elevator stands apart from the bank of elevators for other tenants; an express that stops once at the 42nd floor at a private club called The Boardroom before going on to his offices on the 43rd floor. The sun shines through large glass windows looking out over Park Avenue from the DMC suite which occupied half the floor.

DeLorean steps briskly through the foyer dominated by a huge glass table and four water buffalo-hide chairs on either side of the room. Pictures of the DMC-12 in various poses dominate the corridors through which he sweeps every morning on the way to his office. If a receptionist or secretary is in, at that early hour, there is no greeting, not even an acknowledgement.

'All the girls complained that he walked straight past them,' recalls his English secretary Marian Gibson. 'He was so tall and imposing but he never said a thing. Once in the early days, I was in the elevator with him and I was carrying a basket of flowers for my birthday and he didn't say a word for 43 floors.'

Another secretary recalls an office legend. 'It was Christmas Eve in Detroit one year. He put his coat on and walked out. And everyone said, "Well, that's nice. Isn't he even going to wish us a Merry Christmas?" His secretary then was named Colleen O'Neill, and she had worked day and night to help get this thing on the road. So she called him later in New York and said she was very embarrassed for him because he hadn't wished anyone a Merry Christmas. He made some excuse, but he was really indifferent to it and never improved. That's not really nice when you've got a small crew of about eight people working for you, but he was just indifferent.'

The loyal aide agrees. 'You had to get used to it. That was his style. No small talk at all.'

DeLorean's spacious office is on a level with – and directly opposite – the twin towers of the Waldorf Astoria and their green copper rocket-like heads. There is a framed photograph of Cristina on the desk, perched between two telephones, and there is an even larger picture of her on the wall. He sits in a high-backed chair to begin the day.

Marian Gibson brings in the morning mail. It is voluminous. DeLorean has installed a General Motors-type system of communication, which means that everything is written, even within the office. 'I felt sorry for him,' Gibson says. 'Without exaggeration it was two feet thick. And it wasn't just like insurance fineprint, it was worse. It was emission standards and newsletters from Detroit and Washington and material on the cars and he read through it all and dropped it on the floor.'

The morning's pile also included magazines like *Country Life*, advertising fine country houses either in England or New Jersey. DeLorean still had the house-hunting bug. 'He was bidding for everything,' says Marian Gibson. 'You know, Sutton Place, Paul Getty's old place, came onto the market and we sent away for the material on that. It went for millions of pounds! He was looking for estates in Ireland too and I think he was trying to emulate Colin Chapman with that boys' school of his. Our back-up secretary Barbara Bates would write off and follow up with the correspondence on the houses.'

There was seldom any material in the morning mail related to Belfast – in fact almost nothing on it. 'Everything transmitted between the New York and Belfast offices must have been verbal because I saw only a few letters,' says Marian Gibson.

Having worked his way through the mail, DeLorean then begins his interminable memo writing. Many of the memos go to Tom Kimmerly who is only ten yards down the corridor. DeLorean pulls out a pad of high-gloss engineering graph paper and starts writing in his large, angled scrawl (often he would sign documents at a 45 degree angle). These memos are then dropped on Marian Gibson's desk. She types them, and walks them down to Kimmerly's office. From her office outside his, Gibson can keep her eye on DeLorean by her own private method – she catches the reflection of his grey hair in the grey tinted spandrel glass that lines the halls outside. If she can see the grey hair, she knows his head is down, he is writing – as he always seems to be.

Then there are phone calls. DeLorean has a habit of not taking the calls as they come in; Marian Gibson intercepts them, promises her boss will call back, and a few minutes later he does. He is efficient at returning calls, even unwelcome ones. And there is a steady stream of people coming in to see him now – Haddad, Kimmerly, perhaps visitors from outside the office. He works hard all morning, setting a pace that the office has to strain to match. The DMC-12 and the factory in Northern Ireland, however, scarcely figure in the daily routine, which is mostly work on outside ventures – the snow-grooming company, an idea for Bausch and Lomb sunglasses to go with the car, or an expensive suede DeLorean jacket that Maur Dubin has designed.

Often DeLorean stays at his desk through lunch. He doesn't

eat much – perhaps Marian Gibson will send down to the Cowboy Restaurant in the building for a bowl of chili and a soda. No alcohol. At other times, he will walk back along Fifth Avenue for lunch with Cristina and the children, but most days he is too busy to go home. The afternoon is spent much the same way, except there is usually a lawyers' meeting. DeLorean is thinking about floating a new company, although he hasn't yet told anyone other than Kimmerly, who is designing the structure. Kimmerly is the only one he allows close to him, trusting him as much as he has ever trusted anyone. The slight, bespectacled Michigan lawyer repays his trust with a dog-like devotion.

Some of the memos that DeLorean exchanges with Kimmerly are bizarre, grandiose. Marian Gibson recalls one: 'Will you find out how I can buy the Harrods name? I want to use it to distribute in the U.S.' At this time he is also trying to set up a test track in New Jersey that would cost millions of dollars.

At 5.30 DeLorean leaves his office for the day. He has made no decisions whatsoever that affect the DMC-12 sports car and the factory in Northern Ireland, although he has talked to Dick Brown out on the West Coast, now working at full blast for the expected arrival of the cars in the spring. DeLorean takes the elevator to the ground floor and walks home. Sometimes he and Cristina go out to dinner parties, but with increasing rarity.

DeLorean now arrives back at his Fifth Avenue home. Does he plunge into a frenetic evening at Studio 54? A wild party organized by Maur Dubin and his friends, where he'll meet Frank Sinatra or Raquel Welch? A film premiere? Surely at least a smart dinner party given by his friend Sheldon Tannen, one of the owners of the '21' club, or Don S. Hewitt, executive producer of *Sixty Minutes*? Or a cocktail party at the apartment of independent film producer David Brown and his wife, Helen Gurley Brown, editor of *Cosmopolitan*, with dinner afterwards at Le Cote Basque?

No, he does not. John DeLorean once undertook such glamorous engagements but, after an initial flurry on the fringes of New York society, he has given way to his own better instincts and stays at home whenever he can. He is never fully at ease in the circles he has aspired to. The DeLoreans will have a Halloween party later this month and Cristina will amuse everyone by clowning as a witch, which she does with style and humour. And they will throw a party for Herb Siegel's birthday. For this party Cristina will call in her mother from California to help her prepare dinner for 50 of the Chris-Craft chairman's friends. 'There was pasta, salad, a fancy dessert and gobs of caviar,' a guest will later relate. 'She did a fish covered with carrot chips to look like scales. But John was abstemious. He ate very sparingly. I don't think he cares much for food.'

DeLorean has more than enough time away from home already. At this stage he is travelling to London for torrid meetings with the Northern Ireland office, or to Belfast for more meetings there. He is jetting to the West Coast for meetings with possible investors in his project. He goes to Utah to see his Logan snow-grooming company; he gives speeches and lectures from time to time out of New York, requiring an overnight stop. Although the DeLoreans are spending large sums of money making further improvements to the beautiful house in Pauma Valley near San Diego (they have installed an eight-person hot-tub and over the next year they will extensively remodel and redecorate the house), they are spending very little time there either. Cristina likes to have a good time, but she too is happy to stay at home. Friends will say they think of her as being 'in jeans, a woman of simple tastes'.

So this evening they are both happy to stay home. John makes some phone calls, mostly to California. He is negotiating for an injection of new capital – he is always negotiating for that. And he spends hours on the phone persuading the would-be investor what a splendid opportunity he is passing up. The unfortunate fact is that although plenty of people express an interest, no one will give him money. And increasingly he needs money – again.

On that note we send him to bed. He does not read a book – he cannot concentrate or sit still that long. He watches TV for a while, perhaps his friend Johnny Carson. But he has no interest in that either. His mind is active, leaping about all the time. Perhaps this is why he sleeps so little. But we eventually lower him into a restless and slightly troubled sleep.

CHAPTER TWELVE

Delays and Indecision

By the autumn of 1980, only months after Humphrey Atkins had agreed to the extra £14 million loan, DeLorean was running out of money again.

In August he had accepted Atkins's money on the promise that this would be all, the very last drop of British taxpayers' money. In September NIDA in Belfast received yet another nasty shock: McKinsey delivered a bombshell. 'Despite the commitment of £14 million by HMG . . . the funds gap by April 1981 is likely to be in the range of £2 million to £14 million, with a "most likely" level of some £9 million.' The report noted that the cost of supporting the New York and United States operations was running at $900,000 a month 'and is planned to rise to $1.5 million in February – although thereafter expenditures will be reduced by revenue from car and parts sales'. NIDA had known, even as Humphrey Atkins was excluding Hopkins from the Hillsborough meeting with DeLorean, that there would still be a funding gap. But not as large as this.

McKinsey wasn't altogether gloomy. The gap, it reported, was bridgeable. For John DeLorean had a plan: New Court Securities, part of the New York office of the Rothschild company, had prepared a proposal that could raise $20 million in two portions, the first $10 million by November, the second by early 1981. The first part therefore could come in time for a key accounting date at the Belfast subsidiary: for DMCL had lent DMC in New York about £4 million to finance the lavish lifestyle and salaries of the American operation. £3 million of it was due to be repaid by the end of November, which was the DMCL year-end. If the loans were not repaid, the British Inland Revenue had intimated it would consider the loans as a paid-out dividend, and DMCL would be required by British tax law to pay £1.7 million of Advance Corporation Tax on them. That little item was already setting teeth on edge at NIDA – not only was it having to support John DeLorean in New York but it was having to pay tax for the privilege. Of course it was all government money, and would involve simply taking it out of one pocket and putting it into the other. But it still came off the Northern Ireland budget.

McKinsey had high hopes for New Court Securities' $20 million, and John DeLorean continually raised these hopes. Rothschild in New York, however, never saw the proposal as more than an outside possibility and was astonished to learn eventually how centrally it featured in the finance plans. It was yet another example of wishful thinking, or exaggeration, by DeLorean. But he kept the prospect of this Rothschild money at the forefront of his talks with the Northern Ireland authorities for months to come. By now Tony Hopkins was not easily misled, however. At the end of September he reported to his board that while McKinsey felt the funding gap was manageable, he himself was 'sceptical of this evaluation' even if New Court did come up with the money.

On September 23, DeLorean flew in to Belfast for a board meeting, full of optimism. Lotus, reported Chuck Bennington, had virtually completed the transfer of the production drawings on the car. There was good news on the 50,000 mile certification test: it was no longer required, at least not for the 1981 model. The performance of the Volvo engine had now improved measurably and was averaging 23 miles per gallon, manual and automatic taken together, compared to the 1981 official requirement of 22 mpg. The Volvo engine, widely used in the U.S. on other cars, would get the benefit of a 'carry-across' and would not have to undergo rigorous testing.

DeLorean himself reported on the good news on financing: Rothschild was working on its $20 million special loan 'which will have conversion rights and will be secured by way of a warranty fund' – a complex plan involving the creation of a $1,650 mandatory warranty payment which would be added to the price of each car. To those sitting at the boardroom table, the car seemed expensive enough without burdening it with another cost. DeLorean brushed that aside. Oppenheimer's Limited Partnership, went on DeLorean cheerfully as if this were even better news, was being revived to find more money for the sedan version.

DeLorean was in such a confident mood that he even raised the Transbus again. He wanted, he announced, to seek the board's view (in fact of course he meant NIDA's view – Hopkins was glowering at him from down the table) on whether the Transbus could be completed within the legal framework of DMC – or 'should we hive it off to another company?' Everyone looked to Hopkins for the reply. And, controlling his anger, he gave it. NIDA, he reminded DeLorean, had a formal agreement which had been agreed by both the DMC and the DMCL boards which stipulated that '*all* activities not directly relevant to the launch of the DMC-12 car' had been stopped. If the project had nothing to do with the development of the car, and therefore with employment in Northern Ireland, NIDA would take an extremely dim view of it. Hopkins was firm, barely polite.

Day by day the men at NIDA were approaching nearer and nearer to despair, Hopkins bearing the brunt of it, although Faulkner and Freeman fully supported him. They were now reaping the bitter harvest of the badly negotiated master agreement and Humphrey Atkins's move back in August to give DeLorean money. Atkins genuinely believed he had an agreement that DeLorean would not ask for any more than the £14 million he had given him. The men at NIDA knew differently. What they could not know yet was how DeLorean intended to get that money.

If they had seen the papers which DeLorean carried with him in his slim briefcase, they would have been even more dismayed. This and subsequent meetings were only part of DeLorean's softening up process. He was preparing his major offensive for the new year and had set it all out in New York only two days before in one of his interminable memos to Tom Kimmerly. This one was also marked: cc: E. A. Cafiero, W. F. Haddad.

There is nothing subtle about it. Rather, it is a sledgehammer approach, with some rough blackmail as part of the deal. Dated September 21, 1981, the memo stated:

In developing our strategy for collecting the balance of the money due us from the UK government, I think we should do these things:

1) Get statements from all involved in Master Agreement Meetings confirming the £8 million obligation in relation to royalty NIDA is getting. This has partially been accomplished.

2) Develop, from outside counsel, a legal opinion citing the responsibility and obligation each of the officers and directors incurred as a result of telling our investors we were getting the inflation adjustment in the identical manner to original funding (50% grants, 25% equity, balance, loans, more or less) and that NIDA would give us the £8 million when and if we needed it since we were paying them the royalty for providing this money.

    This opinion should include the statement that to minimize personal and corporate liability, the company and its officers and directors are obliged to take all necessary legal remedies, including litigation, to enforce this agreement. Otherwise dealers and investors can demand their money back and money damages – potentially devastating to DMC.

3) We should have our UK counsel prepare but not file our case demanding the specific performance from NIDA, DOC and the UK government. We will then front it to the government with the legal opinion in paragraph 2). This presentation will be on the basis of a mutual problem – we don't want to sue – it would destroy the credibility of NIDA – but our lawyers tell us we must.

This memo is breathtaking in its boldness: he is actually proposing to sue the British government, which has already given him nearly £70 million!

DeLorean's 'ideal outcome' was this:

> ... the government has cited their royalty income many times as the factor that makes DMC a good deal for them, they never once mentioned their equity ownership publicly.

When we get through rattling the sabre we would hope they would return their stock to us to fulfill their obligations.

In other words, DeLorean was now trying to persuade the British government to surrender its modest equity interest in the venture, as well as some more money.

'Obviously,' he concluded, 'this is an idealized scenario fraught with potential pitfalls and problems, but one we must pursue aggressively. We should be ready to spring this in January 1981, about the time they are ready to take the bows for the success of the project.

'This proposal requires careful planning from a government relations and public relations standpoint.'

This last was Bill Haddad's job. The money involved meant very little to Haddad at the time – he was not particularly good at figures. What he was good at was presenting a case, and that he understood full well. He was still in the honeymoon period, and had not yet begun to have serious doubts. It was perfectly logical that if you needed more money, and genuinely believed the British government owed it to you, the time to ask for it was when they were feeling most favourably inclined towards you, and when they were in no position to say 'no'. To Haddad and DeLorean that pointed to January, when the car would be in production. No one would dare pull the plug at that point.

2

In November DeLorean acquired his third chief financial officer, nearly a year after he first promised to replace Walter Strycker. James G. Stark was 52, a Canadian who had spent some years with Northern Telecom where he had been chief financial officer for five years from 1974 to 1979. DeLorean was increasingly in the mood to pay out lavish salaries, despite the growing financial plight of the company: he paid Stark $300,000 a year, although Strycker had been making only $100,000. Stark moved onto the 43rd floor, but took some time to get used to the set-up. NIDA hoped he might tighten up the financial strings a little, but Hopkins was not optimistic. By now he knew all too well who ran the company.

Later that month, however, there was an appointment that

did make a noticeable difference. NIDA had indicated earlier in the year it thought the pressure on Chuck Bennington was too much, and DeLorean admitted freely that Bennington was no longer up to the job now required. The pressures on him were too intense. At the same time his wife was starting divorce proceedings. 'Chuck was very much of a loner by inclination,' says Shaun Harte. 'He would be happiest in the Sahara desert with a bunch of natives, building an Early Warning System. Without doubt not a man to build a management team, but he *is* a man to put bricks and mortar together.' Bennington, like Collins, had served DeLorean's purpose and had worn himself out.

Now DeLorean moved him to Coventry and brought in Don Lander who had been managing director of Chrysler U.K. from 1974-76 and far from creating emnity among British government officials, as DeLorean was doing, still had considerable respect in those circles. He was yet another of what came to be known as the 'Chrysler mafia' – which included Cafiero, Bennington, Joe Daly, Myron Stylianides.

Lander hit his stride instantly. He settled into the Conway Hotel (later he moved to the caretaker's flat in Warren House) and began to pull the programme together. Gene Cafiero was supposed to spend half his time in Belfast but he never did. And with Lander's arrival Cafiero was seen there less and less often. 'Lander was a super guy,' says one of the Belfast executives. 'He really made things begin to happen.'

3

The tension in the months of November and December 1980 would have been too much for most men. DeLorean deliberately sought more. While his men in Belfast were now literally working round the clock seven days a week in a desperate effort to get the bugs out of the car and the production line, John DeLorean turned again to his Transbus. He refused NIDA's instructions to abandon it, and Hopkins could only grin and bear it. DeLorean had learned a useful lesson from playing off Northern Ireland against Puerto Rico and now applied the same formula to his Transbus. He went to riot-torn Liberty City, a Miami suburb, and offered to become a large-scale local employer. He was offering almost exactly the same package to the South Bronx in New York. His executives in Park Avenue were spending hours working out the details, putting together the packages. Yet the only source of income in that office was the management fee of $290,000 a month paid by the Belfast company, plus large loans flowing from Belfast to New York that were never repaid.

On December 3 the first DMC-12 came off the production line and the men gathered round it in the forecourt for a ritual picture. It was hardly a smooth production process. Parts were being filed, bent, forced together, even bolted where they did not fit. But Don Lander had brought a sense of order and purpose to the production line, and the men were learning fast as they went. There were some horrendous mistakes made in those early days, but this is understandable in any new car venture. Even at GM changes were always being made at the last moment.

And the miracle had happened – there was a car. By the spring there would be enough for a shipful. John DeLorean's dream was a reality.

The dreamer himself wasn't thinking very much about his car. It was raising money that preoccupied him. He was working on plans for yet another public issue of shares. A larger one this time, which would make him personally much wealthier, and at the same time free the company from tiresome cash restraints. It would be timed for the launch of the car so as to get maximum publicity.

4

Belfast, December 17. There were a few brave attempts to hang Christmas decorations around the city and in the NIDA office where John DeLorean arrived to begin one of his most important meetings in Northern Ireland. He brought Jim Stark with him, giving the Belfast officials and his own team their first look at the new finance director. He also brought Bill Haddad, who would be needed for that tricky public relations job, one which Haddad himself was beginning to resent. How do you persuade a government it is in their interests to deprive them of their equity in a venture which has been kept alive by them?

DeLorean was not going to wait for January. Two to three cars a week were coming off the production line, and although not even DeLorean with all his flair for hyperbole could claim they were fit to go into dealers' showrooms, they gave him an extra bargaining edge. The time to 'spring it' was now, and he did. It had a devastating effect.

The NIDA people knew by now he was going to ask for more money, and that the financial position of the DeLorean companies was more serious than ever. But nothing had quite prepared them for DeLorean's extravagant demands that day. He wanted that $25 million loan converted into a non-repayable grant – it was the company's clear contractual understanding that the money given for inflation should have been a grant and not a loan. This was the case with all NIDA-sponsored firms and should be the case with DeLorean. He was, he pointed out humbly, only doing his duty. 'We don't wish to appear to be biting the hand that feeds us nor, I expect, would NIDA wish to appear as failing to honor contractual obligations.'

He then went on to the $20 million that NIDA was to advance in place of the Oppenheimer money, but never had to because Oppenheimer came back in. Now, he told the NIDA board, he wanted that money – he was due it and NIDA must either advance it or cancel its royalty agreement.

He appreciated that NIDA might have 'cash constraints' just now, so he had a proposal. If the $25 million could be converted into a grant, that would make it easier for him to raise new money through the offering of new shares in his company. Then DMC would redeem NIDA's shares (for nothing) – in effect this shareholding would be cancelled. NIDA didn't want it anyway, he pointed out. They only had it because of those silly SEC rules which had required a conversion of the original deferred shares into proper equity.

Then he went on to point out how easy it would be politically for this package to be presented inside the United Kingdom. No one in Britain even knew this NIDA shareholding existed. The Master Agreement was still a secret document; the terms of NIDA's support for DeLorean had never been disclosed. The redemption of NIDA's shares wouldn't even be noticed – it was a 'painless solution for NIDA'.

Hopkins and the NIDA board were stunned. But worse was to follow. DeLorean now turned from cajolery to threat. The alternative was to go to arbitration – he would sue NIDA, which he was entitled to do under the Master Agreement. His London solicitors had assured him he would win and the entire $25 million would be awarded to him as grant, whereas now he might even settle for half grant/half loan. It all must be settled quickly, otherwise he wouldn't be able to raise money in New York with his new offering. It was up to NIDA, their responsibility. Then he threw in his bombshell. Until the situation was resolved, he had no option but to withhold royalty payments to NIDA (£185 on each of the first 90,000 cars produced and £45 a car after that). How could he do that? asked a shaken Hopkins. 'We simply won't pay it,' said DeLorean.

While the NIDA men reeled from that one, DeLorean quickly followed up. This would all have to be disclosed under SEC rules in the United States. Think, he warned, what the press was going to make of the story: 'DeLorean withholds NIDA royalty payments.' That would make NIDA look a bit foolish.

It was the stormiest meeting yet. DeLorean was unruffled. For him, it had gone more or less as planned, except that he had expected Hopkins to cave in more easily. But the man probably more appalled than anyone else was a member of DeLorean's own team: Bill Haddad, his public relations expert. Haddad was a newcomer to corporate PR, but he was a specialized lobbyist, and there really was very little difference between lobbying a United States government department and lobbying a British government agency. It was very clear to Haddad that DeLorean's way of doing things was not going to win friends and influence people.

Haddad had other reasons for becoming disillusioned. While in Belfast he talked to the engineers and heard his first doubts about the engineering of the car. None of these had percolated back to New York at his vice presidential level, and they had been glossed over on his previous Belfast visits, when he had been with DeLorean.

One of the people he talked to at length was Mike Loasby. 'I liked him very much,' says Haddad. 'I thought that he was a straight arrow. He opened up to me once he realized that I was not John's eyes and ears. And he opened up to me about a problem. Loasby was disgusted at the way they were cutting corners.' Haddad had brought it up with DeLorean, not mentioning Loasby's name, and been brushed aside. Now after a week in Belfast he returned to New York without DeLorean, to brood on events. He and DeLorean were barely on speaking terms, and Haddad did not go into the office in those days before Christmas.

He even missed the Christmas party in the penthouse. DeLorean, back from Belfast, suddenly decided there should be an office party and deputed Marian Gibson to organize it. But he had left it too late, and Marian could not find a place that was not already booked. 'Let's have it here,' said DeLorean, gesturing at the broad, elegant spaces of the 43rd floor.

Christmas was on a Thursday that year and the office was closed for a long weekend. On Boxing Day, Haddad sat for a long time over his typewriter before starting the memo that would become variously known as the 'Boxing Day Memo' or more commonly the 'Gold Facet Memo'. He wanted to put down for John DeLorean's attention a summary of all the doubts and questions that had come up in the traumatic last month.

> I continue to be concerned about our efforts to set up a scenario under which the British relinquish their share of equity in the program. I just don't think it will work. And, if it does work, it will only follow a storm of public protest which will reach from London to Detroit to Washington.
>
> Perhaps I don't understand the reason for the push at this time. I don't see how it can help our cash flow problem. So I assume the action is taken in conjunction with our plans for a public offering. If that is the case, while it may enhance the DMC equity position and, consequently, what people are willing to pay for the stock, the public outcry may reduce the attractiveness of the offering and even require the postponement of the offering.

This was a good point and very true. Wall Street investors would be far more influenced by the political stink involving the company than by the figures in its balance sheet. DeLorean should have been thinking about that. But even if he wasn't, Haddad was doing his job as official company PR man in pointing it out.

This was only part of Haddad's concern. He wasn't in the company at the time of the 1978 agreement with Northern Ireland and wasn't in the best position to judge the legal argument now raging. But he had seen enough to know that DeLorean's case was far from being airtight. 'For the purpose of this memo,' he wrote, 'let's assume our position is legally correct.' Even then, there would be problems. Haddad went on:

> I know you believe the power of the logic and the facts presented to the British in a closed room, will create the conditions for them to relinquish their equity position. However, I don't believe that any action of this magnitude can be decided below the ministerial level, the Whitehall level, and that, of necessity, given the British system, will produce, I am convinced, a violent Parliamentary outcry and a mandatory Parliamentary inquiry. Given the Fleet Street nature of the British media (sic), and the cynical attitude towards private enterprise (and DeLorean in particular) exhibited by the BBC, I think you and the company will be painted in the blackest of terms.

Until this point the British press and TV had been remarkably kind to John DeLorean, with one or two notable exceptions. But as Haddad would often say, 'You have to exaggerate to get John's attention.'

While he had that attention (he hoped), Haddad was going to bring up all the matters on his mind:

> I am also worried about what a Parliamentary inquiry will uncover about our expenditures on both sides of the ocean. There are the 'official' complaints which can be sensationalized even though Arthur Andersen, SEC, et al, will give a clean bill of health. The Strycker picture is a highly personal one of John Z. DeLorean milking the company for his private profit. Some of the discredited Strycker charges can be

succulent journalistic morsels for the Fleet Street crowd never overly concerned about separating accusation from fact.

Until this point Haddad had not taken sides over Walter Strycker; he had arrived too late to be involved. But now all the doubts raised by the Strycker incident were fitting into a different context. His eyes had been opened to a new John DeLorean, although even now he was not wholly ready to admit it. Haddad went on to list some of the other little matters that might be revealed.

> As you know, I am also troubled by some of the Bennington actions regarding the house and some of the expenditures which appear to have been 'fuzzed' (like a 10,000 pound expenditure at Harrod's for gold faucets,* etc.). I recently learned, for example, that we may have hidden some of the capital expenses of the house in expenses for the project. In short, the books were altered. Silly, because the house can be justified.

The house he referred to was Warren House, beside the factory in Belfast. Chuck Bennington had, in the view of a number of people in Belfast, gone overboard in doing it up, apparently with the idea of housing visiting dignitaries. Again Haddad was exaggerating: the renovation of the house had certainly been absurdly expensive, but there were no 'gold facets' – there were some gold-*coloured* taps, and they were not from Harrods. But he was right: expenditure on the house had been mixed in with expenditure on the factory.

In recent weeks Haddad had strayed upon something of much greater importance, although he did not yet know what it all meant: GPD. He knew none of the details but there were whispers that disturbed him. 'GPD was not a word in the company. Nobody ever heard of GPD, nobody ever saw GPD. We always dealt with Lotus. John told me that GPD was a Colin Chapman idea and that's why they used that device,' Haddad said later. As with the other items, his concern was essentially in how the press might play it.

---

* His secretary would mistype this as 'facets'.

'The Lotus situation troubles me too,' he wrote. 'I know everyone approved it, but, no matter the hero status of Colin Chapman, hidden Swiss accounts to avoid British taxes may be viewed differently in the media than in the courts or in the higher circles of sophisticated government bent on getting something done quickly and efficiently.'

Haddad's point was that, even if it was a perfectly legitimate tax avoidance scheme, it would still look bad for British taxpayers' money to be used in that way. He was more deeply troubled than that about GPD, but in this memo he confined himself to the publicity risks.

There is also the problem of moving so quickly. I understand from my University contacts that it is fairly well known that the architects made a small fortune on us (so did Lotus!). They may have deserved it, but what are the small items which made up this fortune? Did we monitor closely enough? Why wasn't JZD there to oversee everything? Was he, as Strycker charges, pursuing other interests?

If we were in production, and the British could taste the recovery of their money, the contrast between these items and the general state of their economy would not be so dramatic. After all, any of the higher expenses will cost us as well as them, and we, in the end, are not only repaying their investment, but with a dividend in people off the dole and 2,000 new jobs in one of the most unpopular areas of the world (their goal in providing us the money). Perhaps, due to the offering, we were legally *required* to take this unpleasant action. I know the counter-arguments.

The story which could emerge, however, is that DeLorean (it is your name on the door), who got £60,000,000* of British taxpayers' money is so greedy that he wants to take more and deprive the British of their rightful equity.

No matter your legal briefs, the accurate comments of those present at the time, that is the story which *could* emerge: The 1980 American robber baron image, enhanced by Fleet

---

* Haddad was underestimating: it was already £68 million, and DeLorean was trying to get another £20 million.

Street's love of the spectacular. And the British are on record, as you know from the recent Belfast interviews, as stating they owe us no more money.

Until now Haddad's comments had been reasoned, professional. But he wholly misunderstood the nature of the politics of Northern Ireland and of the IRA in particular. He now went on to set out what he told DeLorean were the areas that worried him 'deep down'.

We are *not* now a target of the IRA because we have 'good will' on our side. On my last trip to England I met with one of the producers of the [TV] show where you were surprised with questions which they had promised not to ask. The producer said he tried to halt this line of questioning during the show, but the presenter kept pushing. However, he did say that *never* in his experience did any show produce such a negative response from the audience. He was literally flooded with angry letters complaining that the presenter was harassing a man who only wanted to do good for Ulster. You are a hero in Ulster, untouchable by the IRA or any of the more loosely organized terrorist groups.

If that attitude changes, and they paint you black, and it sticks for even a short period of time, and evokes a local response, the IRA could put us on the list. They won't go for the factory, they will go for you. In Belfast or, just as easily, and more dramatically, here in New York.

Those are the stakes. That is what worries me.

The IRA had no interest in John DeLorean. His quarrel with the British government was of no concern to them. Although investment in his factory in West Belfast was perceived by Roy Mason as part of the anti-IRA campaign, the IRA never seemed to concern itself with this aspect of foreign investment in Northern Ireland. Whether John DeLorean thrived or failed, employed 2,500 or none, hired more Protestants than Catholics or *vice versa*, built a world-beating car or something that was not even roadworthy, mattered not at all in their calculations. The IRA campaign at this time was just moving into a new gear, aimed at winning the hearts and minds of Irish Americans and of world opinion. Nothing could have been more disastrous for the IRA than for John DeLorean to be blown up or gunned down in Belfast, unless it was his slaughter in New York. Haddad may have been trying to jolt DeLorean – he knew already his phobia about Belfast and the IRA – but he possibly detracted from the more pertinent message in the rest of his memo. After that bit of drama he finished lamely:

> I just want these views factored into any decision you make.
> As I said, I don't know the rationale or the urgency, but I do worry about the potential consequences if we continue down this road.
> And don't shoot the messenger, just review, carefully, the message.

Haddad finished typing at last – four and a half pages of memo. Then he called a special messenger and had it run into Manhattan where his secretary was ready to retype it. Later there would be controversy over whether it was ever delivered to John DeLorean's office; Bill Haddad claims he has written proof in the shape of a signed affidavit.

DeLorean was not in New York over that weekend. He and Cristina had taken the children and entourage to the house in Pauma Valley and stayed there over the New Year. The renovation was not yet complete, but it now had six marble baths, a skylighted family room with an aviary wall by the fireplace, and a large sunny breakfast area. La Cuesta de Camellia occupied a knolltop overlooking John DeLorean's 45-acre estate including 17 acres of citrus groves. The DeLorean estate included two guest houses, each with its own private garden, plus the main house – a nine-room adobe building with 7,000 square feet. On the valley side there was a terrace onto which glass sliding doors opened from all the main rooms; it ended in a screen of thick flowering shrubs and the main new feature of the ranch, an eight-person hot tub. There was also a 41-foot swimming pool and a five-room house for the ranch manager. By any standards it was a magnificent place.

Bill Haddad was almost certainly not at the front of the DeLorean mind that week in California – the battle with NIDA was. Before Christmas he put his proposal in writing, as Hopkins insisted. But he pulled back, as Hopkins must have thought he would, from the categoric statement that he would not pay any royalties at all. He stated instead: 'In the meantime we are forced to withhold our royalty payments to NIDA until this matter is cleared up.'

NIDA was proving unexpectedly stubborn. And at Dunmurry, after the first few cars, the problems had proved too much for the production line and it was almost at a standstill. There were only half a dozen cars produced so far. From his idyllic spot near Escondido, DeLorean would soon have to return to the firing line in Belfast. It could not have been a prospect he relished.

The opening days of 1981 were gloomy. At his board meeting at Dunmurry on December 17, DeLorean had approved a budget for the new financial year which showed a cash flow shortage of £766,000 by April. That was absurdly optimistic. On January 5 it jumped to £5.7 million and a week later was over £8 million.

The options were running out. Yet again, there was only one source of funds: the British taxpayer.

Tony Hopkins and NIDA had little choice. Without more money, there would be no project – that much was now all too clear. Her Majesty's Government was the only source, and NIDA could not really refuse DeLorean, not at the point where the car was finally coming off the production line and would soon be in dealers' showrooms. But Hopkins would not give in to DeLorean's blackmail: NIDA would keep its shareholders' rights, and its royalty rights.

5

January 21, Dunmurry. John DeLorean folded his long body into a DMC-12 at the end of the production line, reached up an arm to grasp the leather strap on the gull-wing door, pulled down the door, and drove the car out into the forecourt of the Dunmurry factory. He was in Belfast personally to deliver a formal request for 'short term working capital', the face-saving formula Hopkins had worked out. But he did get a bit of publicity for the car at the same time. 'We aim to get about 700 cars into the States by the end of April for a coast-to-coast market launch early in May,' he announced to the journalists outside. Yes, he admitted, there had been delays. But as always DeLorean was turning them to his advantage. 'It is fortunate there have been a few delays because the United States market has been dull but is reviving again. We will hit it at just the right time.'

Production of the car was speeding up – three a day were now coming off the line – still a desperate crawl. By now there were 865 people working at Dunmurry, the number having doubled in a month as production got underway. Recruits were being taken on 40 to 50 at a time and given basic training. The workforce was quick to learn. There is a long industrial tradition in Northern Ireland and although many of the new men had never had jobs, some had been motor mechanics, garage workers, or had worked in the Grundig factory nearby, at the shipyard or in one or other of the factories now closed. Commenting on the numbers employed, DeLorean made the statement: 'By the end of this year we will have 1,500 working here, and 2,000 by the middle of next year.'

On this same day he made his formal request to the Department of Commerce: he needed £10 million urgently, which could not wait for the legal battle over his other demands to be resolved. It would just be a short-term loan. He had banks standing by willing to lend the money, if the Department would provide a government guarantee. The ministers in Westminster would be able to present it as 'short-term assistance', although it was still another £10 million of government money. But Hopkins was determined he was going to impose his conditions on DeLorean, who was gradually giving way, surprised by the opposition to demands that by now he had persuaded himself were entirely reasonable.

Back in New York a few days later, DeLorean exploded in anger over breakfast in the Fifth Avenue duplex. He was reading the *Wall Street Journal* when an item caught his eye: *DeLorean Motor Cars asks Britain to Provide $24 million More in Aid*. It was a short, five-paragraph story, but for DeLorean it was more than enough. Later in the day he discovered the *Financial Times* in London had run a similar story, and the *Detroit News* had picked it up. He sent a telex to Frank McCann, the man dealing with DeLorean at the Commerce Department.

The telex read:

AN INVESTMENT BANKING FIRM WHO HAD TENTATIVELY COMMITTED TO HANDLING A PUBLIC OFFERING FOR US HAD THEIR INVESTMENT BANKING COMMITTEE MEETING TODAY. THEY DECLINED TO RAISE FUNDS FOR US BECAUSE OF THE ARTICLES IN THE WALL STREET JOURNAL AND ONE IN THE DETROIT NEWS SAYING WE COULD NOT MAKE PAYROLL AND WERE BACK TO THE GOVERNMENT. DOC AND NIDA MUST UNDERSTAND THAT THIS 'LEAK' OF THEIRS HAS CLEARLY COST US OUR PUBLIC FINANCING. IT IS UNCONSCIONABLE THAT SUCH CONFIDENTIAL INFORMATION BE LEAKED TO THE PRESS. IN ADDITION THIS LEAK HAS SERIOUSLY INJURED OUR DEALER CREDIBILITY AND PERHAPS OUR BANK LINES.
REGARDS,
JOHN Z. DELOREAN

He sent copies to Gene Cafiero, Tom Kimmerly and Jim Stark in his own office, and Bill Haddad, Frank McCann and Tony Hopkins in Belfast. It was several days before the puzzled but outraged McCann sent back his reply.

I WAS DISMAYED BY YOUR TELEX OF JANUARY 29. YOU MAY BE ABLE TO SUBSTANTIATE YOUR STATEMENT ABOUT THE WITHDRAWAL OF A TENTATIVE COMMITMENT AND ITS CLEAR EFFECT OF YOUR PUBLIC FINANCING BUT THE FACTS ON THIS SIDE OF THE ATLANTIC ARE THAT THE MINISTER OF STATE IN ANSWER TO A SPECIFIC QUESTION IN THE HOUSE OF COMMONS CONFIRMED THAT DELOREAN MOTOR CARS LIMITED HAD APPLIED FOR THE ASSISTANCE OF THE DEPARTMENT IN RESOLVING A SHORT TERM WORKING CAPITAL REQUIRE-

MENT. NO ADDITIONAL INFORMATION WAS GIVEN IN THE HOUSE OR TO THE PRESS. THE DEPARTMENT MADE NO FURTHER COMMENT AND WAS NOT RESPONSIBLE IN ANY WAY FOR THE PRESS SPECULATION WHICH OCCURRED. ENDS

By early February the story of John DeLorean's fresh demands and his written statement that he would withhold royalties had leaked. The *Belfast Telegraph* picked up the story first, and again DeLorean hit the roof. In New York he denied the story, and then ordered Bill Haddad to serve a writ for libel on the *Belfast Telegraph* whose story was based on British government documents. It was, as Haddad advised him, the worst possible move. The *Belfast Telegraph* is a powerful voice in the local community and in the early days had been as enthusiastic about the DeLorean project as anybody. In recent months, however, reporters Alan Watson and John Kane had learned about the battle with NIDA and in the first week of February carried three long and informed stories, soon picked up by other papers. They had the effect of reversing the pressure back on to DeLorean, although Hopkins was angry enough to initiate a witch-hunt to find the leak. After another few days of heated telexes flying across the Atlantic, DeLorean reluctantly retreated. He was rapidly running out of money, and needed that £10 million 'short-term assistance'. With ill-grace he assented to Hopkins' terms. On February 11 he wrote to Northern Ireland's Minister of State Adam Butler formally saying so, personally handing the letter to Butler that day in Belfast. It was another terse meeting, with DeLorean going back over all the old arguments, and Butler holding the Hopkins' ground – no more money unless he accepted the conditions. He would be making a statement to the House of Commons the next day. They had to agree now.

6

Thursday, February 12, the House of Commons. Humphrey Atkins finished his stint at the despatch box, and as he sat down Adam Butler, his number two, stood up to field a battery of questions on DeLorean. The two men he feared most were in the House: the left-wing Labour MP, Bob Cryer, and Jock Bruce-Gardyne. Jock Bruce-Gardyne belonged to the same party as Butler; he had developed a grave suspicion and dislike of the DeLorean project, attacking it both in the House and in his *Sunday Telegraph* column. His first question asked why, in view of Humphrey Atkins's statement in August 1980 that the government's obligation to consider further finance to DeLorean had been discharged, he was now considering a further application?

Butler could cope with that one. The application was for a government guarantee for a commercial loan 'to help the company resolve a short-term cash problem and take the DMC-12 car through to market launch'. He had, he announced, agreed to a time-limited guarantee of up to £10 million, subject to DeLorean accepting that neither NIDA nor the Department of Commerce had 'any financial obligations towards the company and which confirm that royalties remain payable as agreed'. He made no mention of DeLorean's other demands, knowing all too well what Bruce-Gardyne's reaction would have been. But the back-bench Tory MP already had enough for a fair-sized broadside which he now delivered at Butler.

> Does not my honourable friend realize that those undertakings were given to the House six months ago? Is there not a danger that my right honourable friend in his dealings with Mr. DeLorean, will come to resemble the young lady from Riga who went for a ride on a tiger? Is my honourable friend aware that Mr. DeLorean apparently has a T-shirt on which is emblazoned the slogan, 'I am a con-man?' Would he consider sending him a character reference? Can he seriously give the House the assurance that it needs that we shall have the opportunity to debate the matter and vote on it before any further money is given to that con man?

Adam Butler's indignant reply was misleading. 'My honourable friend does not help his cause,' he told Bruce-Gardyne. '... In fact, no more money is being provided but purely a government guarantee behind commercial loans to help the company to launch a car that it believes has good market prospects. The obligations were removed in the agreements last summer but, because of certain press statements about the beliefs of one or two parties to the arrangement, I felt it necessary to come to a firm written understanding with Mr. DeLorean that no such obligations now exist.'

In view of all that went before, this was not quite the whole truth. Butler was adopting the old adage of 'if there's no one else, blame the press'. In the rest of the debate he repeated that there would be no 'more selective assistance' for the DMC-12 project, that he was perfectly happy with the information the company was providing, and he and his opposite number Don Concannon ended up with a little burst of mutual self-congratulation on their joint determination to support the project. It is cruel to subject Butler's performance to the test of hindsight, but even then his remarks sounded fatuous and out of touch.

7

DeLorean's tally of British government money by this date stood at £78 million, £24 million of it from a Conservative government that was supposed to be cutting all State spending savagely. When he got his original £54 million from Labour's Roy Mason, he did so on the basis that he would ask for no more. When he got the extra £14 million from Humphrey Atkins, he agreed there was no further obligation and would ask for no more. Now he had another £10 million, and was promising he would ask for no more. He had yet to sell a single car, or repay the British government its first penny, except insofar as his growing band of workers in Belfast paid taxes.

By sheer hard work, plus a great deal of inventiveness and innovation, the men at Dunmurry were producing cars off the production line. And on February 20 the first cars began leaving the factory to wait on Belfast docks for shipping across the Atlantic. John DeLorean's dream was heading for the market at last. But not, alas, without problems. The engineering difficulties had not simply gone away, though Mike Loasby and his team, plus the Lotus people and anyone else who knew anything about engineering, had been trying desperately to make good the defects.

On February 17 a memo from Peter Allinson, one of the more experienced engineers, painted a worried and gloomy picture of various aspects of the car. When he got to its certification in the United States, however, he voiced his real concern. Because of the 'shortcomings' he believed the car 'currently being certified will not be acceptable . . . There is now a serious question with regard to vehicle weight which has not yet been fully recognized,' said Allinson. 'Cars are being built to a different specification from the one they are being certified at.'

Allinson's fear was that the cars now being loaded at Belfast docks were not actually certified for use on the American roads, that the certification had been done for a different weight car, with different emission specifications, and that the engine was not performing up to the standards the EPA had been led to believe. If his fears were confirmed, the project was even now heading for disaster – there was no time for recertification.

Certification had become a major bone of contention between the men at Dunmurry and Lotus. The Lotus engineers argued that they were going through the certification process on their own cars all the time and knew how to do it. Two cars had been prepared for the certification tests in July but the programme had been aborted when it was discovered that the cars, worked on in Belfast, had many 'quality/production' problems such as leaky exhausts, inoperative catalysts and bad mixture distribution. At that point there had been another battle between Lotus and the DeLorean people, with Lotus arguing that a new programme should be designed and the Belfast men saying that when it came to actual production, the component makers would have sorted out those problems, and since the engine had worked on the Volvo, it would perform on the DMC.

By the autumn the problem was still a major one. DeLorean in September reversed the original decision that Lotus should present the car for certification, and instead of doing the tests in approved American laboratories decided to do them at home. In October the automatic passed the EPA tests, but the manual failed. A week later the manual was re-presented – and this time it passed but the fuel economy was poor – the average was 22 mpg for the two cars.

Finally DeLorean passed the job back to Lotus and early in February the two cars were tested by the EPA in Michigan – and approved, the automatic on 21 mpg and the manual on 23 mpg, giving a CAFE rating of 22.5 mpg. Allinson, however, was concerned that there had been so many changes to the car, even on the production line, that the certification might not cover what was now being produced. His discussions with friends in the EPA increased his doubts. 'Lotus have said that Fuel Economy Label is approved. EPA have advised that it is not.' He and Loasby were by now reading something more sinister into it all. Chapman's cash flow problems had become so apparent at Lotus that they believed he was deliberately spinning out the DeLorean programme to keep the money coming in – the DMC project at this stage accounted for nearly half Lotus's revenues and, although the mid-summer peak of 300 engineers and draughtsmen on the project had now passed, there were still 180.

DeLorean had just telexed to ask about his gull-wing sedan, the DMC-24, on which Bennington in Coventry and Giugiaro in Milan were now working – how about some money for it to keep the team together? Not from NIDA, replied Hopkins. The DeLorean men reckoned therefore Lotus was not going to do the final few bits on the project until the last possible minute, although Lotus itself insisted it was still breaking its back for its biggest ever customer. 'Lotus are presenting data to EPA in a manner that will prolong their activities in the certification programme,' wrote Allinson, 'and are not in the best interests of DMC.'

In the final section of his letter, headed 'Politics,' Allinson spelled it out bluntly:

The current political situation between Lotus and D.M.C. is delaying completion of the programme.

1. I believe Lotus are deliberately withholding information that would prevent us from completing our programme. I have requested information on the specification details on at least six occasions, without obtaining the information. I have

been told that the fuel economy label info is in the post . . . it has not arrived.

2. I believe that we will not see a certificate of conformity if the political situation is not resolved. It is a too-powerful bargaining tool.

As Allinson wrote this to Don Lander the cars were winding their way out of the factory gates, through the streets of Belfast, to the docks. It would be some weeks yet before there were enough for a shipful. And there is no evidence that Lotus did anything other than its considerable best to speed events. But the doubts and controversies still hanging over the car as it was loaded on the ship were not the most auspicious of send-offs. Now it would be up to Dick Brown at the other end.

CHAPTER THIRTEEN

Bobby Sands

On April 20 the first batch of almost 400 DeLorean cars set sail for Long Beach, California, well behind schedule. Adam Butler sent a message of congratulation, but pointed out too that the company's task now was to demonstrate to both taxpayers and private investors that 'their faith in the project has been justified'. Gene Cafiero in Belfast made a little speech to the effect that 'the effort of the workforce has been outstanding'. There were now over 1,000 men in the Dunmurry factory and, under Don Lander's experienced hand, the production line was beginning to settle into some sort of rhythm. But everyone, management and workers, Catholic and Protestant, was increasingly listening for news coming out of the prison room where Bobby Sands, now in the eighth week of his hunger strike, lay on a waterbed covered in sheepskins, life-saving equipment standing by should either he or his family request it.

Bobby Sands had already become a hero to the Catholic population. Soon he would be what the IRA needed badly: a martyr. His fame was spreading into the circles the IRA wanted. Senator Edward Kennedy called on Britain to make 'new and urgent efforts' to halt the hunger strike. Former U.S. Attorney General Ramsey Clark arrived at the Maze prison but was refused permission to see Sands. The Pope sent his personal secretary, Monsignor John Magee, who saw Sands twice. Prince Charles, on a trip to Venezuela, was handed a petition by 11 U.S. Congressmen asking him to use his 'good offices as heir apparent to the throne to intercede'. Soon, however, nobody could help Sands – he went into a coma and in the early hours of May 5 he died.

It was just after 1.30 on that Tuesday morning when the news reached Twinbrook. At first there was only the banging of a single dustbin lid. Within seconds it was a crescendo of noise and blazing lights as the entire Catholic population of the housing project on the edge of the DeLorean factory poured out onto the streets. The noise of clanging lids spread on towards central Belfast, through Andersontown and the Falls Road until the whole of the capital was awake. Around the Province the same scene was taking place in Londonderry, Strabane, Newry. Protestants bolted their doors and stayed inside.

No one in the whole of Northern Ireland that night needed to be told what the noise meant: Bobby Sands, 27-year-old IRA man and Member of Parliament for Fermanagh and South Tyrone, had died after 65 days on hunger strike in the Maze prison. For the British security forces, it was one of the worst setbacks they had suffered in a decade of fighting the IRA, bringing as it did a new wave of bombings, shootings and civil unrest; for the IRA it was a major propaganda victory, demonstrating to the world what the IRA had failed to do until that moment, that its members believed in their cause sufficiently to die for it. For John DeLorean it was an irresistible opportunity to ask for more money.

The death of Sands was of special importance for the workforce at the DeLorean factory. If the IRA man had a home at all other than the Maze and the streets of Belfast, it was Twinbrook. His mother lived there, within sight of the car factory. Sands himself had spent some of his teenage years there. He had friends, relatives, supporters, many of them on the DeLorean payroll, living in Twinbrook.

That night, the DeLorean factory was locked and silent, the security guards keeping out of sight so as to provide no provocation. For weeks the management had been taking what precautions they could. 'We knew that the centre of the demonstration was going to be fairly close to us,' says Shaun Harte. 'But we felt, and I'm sure retrospectively we were right, that the target of the fury wasn't going to be the DeLorean factory, but rather the situation in which this had happened in Twinbrook. And the first thing that comes up in their sights that isn't theirs is good for a target.' Less than an hour after Sands died the factory did come into the rioters' sights. Already the violence had taken root. The sounds of spontaneous riots in the Falls Road, New Lodge and Antrim Road areas of Belfast could be heard (and seen) above the tumult in Twinbrook. By 2 a.m., 43 minutes after the final flicker of life had passed from Sands' emaciated body, swathed in bandages to prevent his bones from piercing the skin, the whole of Belfast seemed to be caught up in the worst blaze of violence it had seen for years.

The main gate of the DeLorean factory was formidable enough to turn back the first halfhearted onslaught. The security men were out of sight and reach, and there was nothing inside within petrol-bomb-throwing distance that would burn. The gate on the Twinbrook side, however, was a flimsier affair. A bunch of the more hot-headed rioters broke away from Twinbrook, grabbed an old car and drove at high speed at the gate. The lock gave and the mob was inside the DeLorean compound. Not very far inside, however. The factory had been well designed: it had two fences – the rioters were now inside the outer one. The inner gate, made of sturdier stuff, held. But just inside it was a row of temporary wooden huts, occupying the approximate area of two tennis courts. A few weeks later, when the main buildings were complete, these huts would have been gone, their occupants and contents housed in the comfort of properly built buildings. That night they made an irresistible target for the youths. Within seconds petrol bombs, mixed with paint to make the blazing mass adhere better to the target, were being lobbed over the fence to land on the flat roofs of the huts. 'They burned like fun,' says a DeLorean executive. No one in the factory had a hope of putting the fires out. The fire brigade was called but by the time it arrived, they had taken hold and the wooden buildings were burning well. The violence of Northern Ireland had entered the world of John DeLorean for the first time.

The press soon descended. For the next few days, as the death of the first IRA hunger striker dominated world news, the riots of Belfast were echoed by demonstrations from Irish-Americans all over the United States. The focus of it all was Twinbrook.

When DeLorean heard the news just before midnight at home, he at first appeared shaken, his almost pathological fear of the IRA confirmed. He was in the office early the next morning to read the first reports of the damage. It was some hours before his old trick of turning every disadvantage to an advantage came to his rescue.

At 8.30 that morning, Shaun Harte walked into the Park Avenue office to learn of the fire damage to the factory. He was in New York on business unrelated to Bobby Sands but DeLorean quickly summoned him to a conference. All the engineering drawings had apparently been lost, said DeLorean, who had just heard from an unruffled Don Lander. How serious was that for the car project? he asked Harte who was the coordinator of the whole programme. Not serious, said Harte instantly. 'There is a set at Lotus and I know where they are – we can get them. In any case we took the precaution from the beginning of keeping a spare set filed away off-site. That's no real problem.' What else was kept in the pre-fabricated huts? DeLorean asked. Harte tried to recall. There were personnel records – that would be a nuisance because they were busy interviewing new recruits as the factory rapidly expanded, and all the forms and records would almost certainly be in the burned huts. There was a computer terminal, too, he remembered, but not the computer itself. More seriously there were purchasing records and much of the systems work – that could all be reconstructed but it would be an irritant.

DeLorean's mind turned to the cost of the thing – was the factory insured? Could they claim for damages from the British government? During that day, his plans became steadily more ambitious.

By the following morning the full extent of the damage had been analysed and it was much less than first feared. For DeLorean it was enough. He watched the groundswell of anti-British feeling build up around him in New York, dominating the news broadcasts. The British, he decided, were in their weakest ever position. No one was going to argue with him now. Bobby Sands was just being buried when he laid out his plan to his team of Cafiero, Stark, Kimmerly, Lander and Haddad, followed up in a May 7 memo to Haddad:

> Today DMC is faced with the greatest opportunity of your corporate lifetime. With the troubles in Twinbrook/Belfast for the first time in our tenure there, *no single person in UK begrudges us the $160,000,000 we got from the government!* Most today think we've earned it!

For DeLorean there was no tragedy – only an opportunity to press his claim for more money.

> The government who dealt with us in bad faith, and in effect made us borrow $50,000,000 that they owed us, is in a position where they must become responsive to our needs.

A few months before, Hopkins had forced him to retreat. Now it was DeLorean's turn.

> We should become the industrial heroes of the UK – bringing jobs and prestige to an area all Britains (sic) now agree is uninhabitable. The government should throw money at us to expand and continue. Our failure today would doom Northern Ireland industrially forever and cost the government another billion or two dollars. We have a chance to become competent, professional benefactors in the eyes of our customers throughout the world. An image worth more than an infinity of advertising. In short, this is the single, great opportunity to give our company the ultimate shining image and provide all of the finances we will ever need – but 60 days from now it will be too late.

On the day of the Bobby Sands' funeral he despatched Haddad to Belfast.

> Upon due consideration you should plan on moving to Belfast for at least the next six months. Take your wife and child with you. Plan to stay there and help get this job done.

Bill Haddad had been in and out of Belfast since the hunger strikes had started and he had developed his contacts in Queen's University in Belfast and in the city's political world. He had some understanding of the political tension the Sands death had created. But this was something more than a strategic decision. It was punishment. DeLorean himself hated and feared Belfast and would have done a great deal to avoid the fate he was now ordaining for his public relations man.

The reasons for his annoyance with Haddad were similar to his reasons for falling out with Strycker: Haddad was making a nuisance of himself by querying and objecting to his new master plan. Most of the other directors were objecting to his new master plan, too. But Haddad was the most outspoken – in fact he seemed to have become the spokesman for the others.

DeLorean himself was very pleased with the plan. He had decided he would not issue more shares in DMC after all. He was still annoyed with the fact that NIDA had shares in it, for one thing. So he decided he would float an entirely new company, a holding company, which would be the new parent for DMC. Haddad had 100,000 options in DMC – they would now become worthless, since the shares would never be issued. Gene Cafiero had 500,000 options worth a potential $5 million that would also become worthless. Stark had options in DMC as did Lander and Bob Dewey and most of the others. It had been DeLorean's method of tempting them in: big salaries but also options on shares in the business. Now he was proposing to take them all away.

He had finally found an investment bank that would handle the issue for him: Bache, Halsey, Stuart Shields, one of the biggest houses on Wall Street. The new company would be called DeLorean Motor Holdings and it would buy out the Oppenheimer Limited Partners, issuing them shares in the new company. And it would give John DeLorean himself well over half the shares. Bache was already estimating $12 to $14 a share, which would make DeLorean personally worth $120 to $140 million. Oppenheimer would get another fee of $2.4 million (on top of the $2 million they already had) for organizing the buying out of the Partners. The dealers, on whom the whole project would soon depend as the cars arrived in the U.S., would be left in DMC. And so would the British government.

Haddad was the man with the easiest access to DeLorean when he was in New York, and he was less awed by him than the others, less bound by the Detroit tradition that you don't argue with the boss. His initial protests were met with technical explanations. He switched his attack to the position of the auto dealers who had bought shares in DMC and would not be brought up into the holding company.

'They are going to open up the paper,' he told DeLorean, 'and see that DeLorean is going public, and then they are going to realize that they have been motored, just at the time when the car is coming over and we need their excitement. John, we need their anticipation and their excitement. The dealers really like you, there is no two ways about that. But this is a bad idea.'

DeLorean was hearing the same from others and eventually he acquiesced, deciding to offer the dealers shares in the new DeLorean Motor Holding Company in exchange for their shares in DeLorean Motor Company. Haddad, however, still pursued the issue of the senior executives who would be left out in the cold with their worthless options.

'That really created a furor in Belfast,' says Haddad. 'The auto industry is very much like the Japanese – you only work for one company. A lot of these guys gave up a lot to come and work for him and they were very talented people and they were very upset. Everybody was. In New York too. These guys were ruining good careers and giving up pension plans. They took a risk with John and now he was depriving them of their equity.'

It was only days before Bobby Sands died that Haddad had a major confrontation with DeLorean. He had already sent him a memo, and DeLorean had not bothered to reply. Now they had it out face to face. 'First of all,' DeLorean told him, 'what we are doing is legally necessary. We've been through all that before. Secondly, you are misrepresenting the attitude of everyone. You say they are all upset. Well, they are not upset. You know, Bill, you are full of shit. It's you who are upset. You're the only one who's upset.' Haddad held his ground. 'Guys worked like hell over there,' he told DeLorean. 'And they really are very upset. I've talked to them. You've destroyed their morale.'

In the aftermath of Sands' death, DeLorean decided to kill two birds with one stone. Sending Haddad to Belfast would keep him out of harm's way in New York and it might get him out of the company altogether. No one, he believed, would stay in Belfast for long – and certainly not Bill Haddad, accustomed as he was to the high life in New York and Washington. At the same time Haddad could be used to follow up the advantage the IRA man's death gave him.

The scenes of the funeral on TV convinced DeLorean the British government would put up no serious opposition to a request for more money.

In Belfast between 50,000 and 70,000 mourners turned up by

train, bus or car to honour the dead Republican. The funeral service itself was held at St. Luke's in Twinbrook, only 200 yards from the small, whitewashed, terrace house where the Sands family lived, and not much further from the DeLorean factory. A third of the DeLorean workforce did not report that day.

Outside the church nearly every house in Twinbrook flew a black flag, most of them clearly visible from the DeLorean factory. It was another miserable day of driving rain and wind. A masked bugler and two pipers marched in front of the coffin as it wended its slow way to the cemetery of Milltown, a two mile procession following behind the hearse. The IRA provided the guard of honour, seven sinister men in battledress, hoods and black berets. Sands' own black beret and gloves rested on top of the coffin which was draped in the Irish tricolor.

In the climate of Northern Ireland and particularly of West Belfast, the threatened closure of the DeLorean factory would have been unthinkable. 'We lost 60% of our offices, our vital engineering records, our MOS data, our N.P. purchasing records and our employment records,' said DeLorean. 'Enough to put any business on its knees. We lost the equivalent of two or three weeks productions, with more losses to come, as a result of the violence and unrest.' It was nonsense – his excuse for the claim. Within a fortnight he had his money – £7 million more, bringing the total to £85 million.

Again it was Adam Butler who announced it. Again he faced the anger of Jock Bruce-Gardyne from his own benches and of Bob Cryer from the Labour benches across the other side of the House. But the Sands episode had thus accomplished for DeLorean what months of steady attrition had failed to do. Once again NIDA felt undermined by the ministers who took the decision over their heads. Hopkins complained bitterly that Atkins and Butler had not even asked for NIDA's view before agreeing to give DeLorean the money, and made no attempt to extract further conditions from DeLorean himself.

In the days following the Sands death, the more dedicated troublemakers became better organized. On the day of the funeral, for example, Northern Ireland's own patented catapults came into their own. Late that evening a group of youths gathered on an empty knoll on the edge of the plant. They hammered two stakes into the ground and slung a pair of women's tights between them. Then bottles full of a petrol-paint mixture were fitted in the crotch, pulled back, and sent whizzing off into the night, high over the wire fence of the factory. The plant was pretty safe from this form of attack, the bombs falling harmlessly on the metal test-track or smashing off the concrete walls or asbestos roofs. As the days lengthened – and in Belfast in mid-summer it is still bright past eleven o'clock – the attacks slackened. The army stayed clear for the most part preferring to avoid provocation, and the security guards and management also stayed out of sight. 'Once when the bombers got a bit obnoxious, the army came in,' recalls Shaun Harte. 'But mostly what they did was to lob their bombs onto the test track where they had a good flame-up for a while and then the whole thing died down. If we brushed the glass off before we tested the cars the next day, there wasn't much problem.' There were a few shots in the air during this period too, but no evidence that anyone was ever singled out to be shot at. Says Harte, 'It was pretty edgy around Belfast particularly at night, for the next three weeks. And after that it went away altogether.'

It was John DeLorean's only real encounter with violence in Northern Ireland. By the time it had run its desultory course he had his money.

2

While DeLorean was successfully negotiating the new cash injection from the British government, the first shipload of cars arrived in California.

Brown had set up two Quality Assurance Centres – in Bridgewater, New Jersey and Santa Ana, California. He organized the operation well: the cars were delivered either to Wilmington, Delaware (cost $370 per car) or sailed through the Panama Canal to arrive in Long Beach ($470 per car). They were subject to import duties but only modestly: less than 3 percent. Just outside Wilmington, on a 30-acre site, Brown organized a third 40,000 square foot facility. The cars were brought to these centres, thoroughly checked over, and then shipped by truck to the dealers. The idea was to give them not just a pre-delivery check, but to road test them, safety check them, and give the stainless steel shells a good polish.

Brown was apprehensive before the first cars arrived, anticipating that the unpractised workforce in Belfast, working against the clock, might not have produced the quality a $25,000 car was expected to have. Nothing, however, prepared him for the reality.

'If you were a dealer and you had seen the cars as they came in initially,' he said later, 'you would have – you know, if you didn't have faith in this guy, you would have just walked out the door and said, "Hey! We can't sell this shit!"

'And that's exactly what it was. Shit. I'll tell you what it looked like. It looked like somebody put a hand grenade in the front seat and the back seat and then set them off. All the guts were out. You couldn't ride in them. You looked in the window and all the components were just stuffed in. They weren't built in, they were stuffed in. Doors wouldn't function. Electronics wouldn't function. We had to redesign and retool some parts here just to make the car saleable.'

Brown hired teams to rebuild the car more or less from scratch, though as the workforce in Belfast gained experience, the cars were better made.

The cost of the operation was enormous. Nearly $700,000 was spent in June – $2,178 per car. In July it was $2,914 a car, another $746,000. In August it dropped just below $2,000 a car for another $1 million. In those three months alone, the company had spent $2.5 million just for quality control on cars that should already have been up to standard.

When the cars did get to the auto journals for testing, they did not have a smooth ride either, although in retrospect the DMC-12 got off surprisingly easily. Don Sherman, technical director of *Car and Driver*, wondered whether 'the firm will exist a year from now' because of the quality control problems, although he praised the car's handling and the 'boldness' of John DeLorean's whole project. Sherman, one of the United States' most respected auto journalists, complained that he felt 'entombed' when he first sat in a DeLorean car. He had tested the car in Belfast earlier in the year and thought those early models were 'abysmally short of any commercial standard of acceptability'. He went on: 'Switches popped loose, parts fell off, the rattles had squeaks, doors jammed shut, doors refused to latch, and windows fell out of their tracks. What's worse, there wasn't a single car, either in our entourage or up and down the long assembly line, that you could point to and say, 'This is a perfect (or even acceptable) door-to-body fit.'

Sherman was fairly sympathetic. He pointed out, in DeLorean's defence, that the first 500 cars had been pressed out on prototype tooling – the production tooling had not yet arrived. If the car's problems were solved, Sherman told an *Irish Times* reporter, the DeLorean firm had a bright future. But if the car was deficient in a U.S. market where high quality was vitally important 'it runs the risk of being cast into oblivion within a short time.' In Park Avenue Mike Knepper in the public relations department was busily countering the Sherman article, insisting that there had been 'considerable refinement to the car' since Sherman tested an early model.

Sherman's doubts, and those of other auto critics, did not affect the sales of the car in those early days, at least not badly. There had been so much publicity, and so much talk about it over the years, that buyers could not wait for it. By early in July, when Brown reluctantly allowed the first cars out of his Quality Assurance centres and sent them to the showrooms, some dealers were reporting waiting lists of from two months up to a year or more. One dealer reported more than 200 names on his waiting list, although he would only receive 20 cars by December. Brown was trying to get cars to all the 345 dealers as soon as possible, but he knew he could not release any without doing substantial work on them first. By the first week in July the 1,000th car had rolled off the line in Belfast. Dealers all around the country were reporting the cars were actually commanding a premium – in many cases up to $5,000 and sometimes even more.

It was a euphoric beginning to the sales, brushing aside for a while the gloom that had so haunted the engineers and production men in Belfast and causing even Brown, still desperately worried about quality, to relax a bit. In its August 13 issue, *Automotive News* surveyed the sales scene, talking to dealers round the country. The picture seemed to be the same everywhere – supply could not keep up with demand. The car was a roaring success. 'Our list is so long that, even with a good deposit, the wait will be two to three months,' said George Attelt, general manager of Jerry Goodwin Dodge, Fullerton, California. 'We're only expecting about 20 more cars through the end of this year, after which the supply will be better.' *Auto News* quoted Wayne Jones, sales manager for Melrose Ford, Oakland, California, saying that his dealership had more than 50 DeLorean customers on its waiting list, each of whom had put $5,000 down on a car even though some of them faced a 10-month wait. 'Before McInnis Petersone Chevrolet in Baton Rouge' said *Auto News*, 'had advertised the DeLorean, it had a list of 10 customers who each deposited $3,000.' On the West Coast, where most of the early cars had been delivered, new DeLoreans were reportedly fetching $30,000, with actual prices at individual dealerships ranging from $25,950 to $31,000. The DeLorean sales team was worried by the premiums. 'There's nothing we can legally do to hold down the prices,' said Jack Fearer, one of Brown's team. 'We set the manufacturer's suggested retail price at $25,000, and that's about it.' Fearer reported some customers using the long waiting period for personal gain by selling their places on dealers' waiting lists.

In that same issue *Auto News* carried a little boxed item that epitomized this brief period of euphoric sales. The first second hand DeLorean turned up on the used car lot of Ellis Motor Company of Maplewood, a suburb of St. Louis. Its price: $33,900. It is the highest recorded price asked for a DMC-12.

NIDA even got a royalty cheque – a modest £205,000, representing £185 a car on the first 1,100 cars sold to dealers. Cars were now coming off the line at 175 a week, the factory in Belfast employed 1,600 people and in the United States dealers were reporting that just having a DeLorean in their showroom meant that their 'floor traffic was fantastic'.

While Bobby Sands was starving himself to death and other IRA hunger strikers were joining him in this new form of protest in the Maze, DeLorean was busily shopping for yet another new home for himself, Cristina and the children. He was moving up again, intent on getting into the best social set. For over a year he scoured his favourite magazines for a suitable house, bid for several and went to see others. In the late spring of 1981 he found it: 430 acres in Bedminster, New Jersey, with a three-storey, 25-room mansion. It was a beautiful place and DeLorean paid big money for it: $3.5 million. But he wanted changes and a landscape architect named John Smith was contracted to produce a 'grand design' complete with swimming pools, a tennis court, fountains, gazebos and a stone boathouse.

Cristina later claimed the house was principally bought with her money. It wasn't. It was bought by an offshore corporation called 'TK International'. The initials stood for Tom Kimmerly, and Kimmerly later admitted that TK International was a 'personal corporation' which purchased the Bedminster estate so that DeLorean could make a tax-free exchange of other property. What property? And why did he need to avoid taxes so much at that stage since his only source of income was his salary from DeLorean Motor Company? Where did he suddenly get another $3.5 million?

TK International assumes an extra degree of significance for this reason: at the end of 1980 Bill Haddad claims to have strayed upon evidence indicating that roughly $9 million of the money that went to GPD was funnelled back again into TK. Haddad certainly believed that the purchase of the New Jersey house was made with GPD money. Kimmerly, however, denied it, insisting no GPD assets were involved.

At any rate, the DeLoreans had a new home, although not without a haunting echo of other days. In a lawsuit, the architect, John Smith, charged that DeLorean did not pay him for his landscaping. DeLorean claimed that Smith had gone over budget. 'My original impression was that he was a gentleman with great ideas and expectations,' said Smith later. 'I liked him. At first.'

The new house was only a sideline, a minor pleasantry in the serious business of getting the new DeLorean Motor Holdings launched despite the obvious and growing antipathy from his own executives, voiced openly by Haddad, but more keenly by Gene Cafiero who would lose options valued at $5 million in the deal. Now Tom Kimmerly, already close to DeLorean, came into his own.

It was Kimmerly, the small-time Detroit lawyer whose three

man firm Kimmerly, Gans and Shaler was still based in Bloomfield Hills, who took charge of the massive job of preparing the legal documents and SEC prospectuses. The fees on this project were high by any standards – except it seems, Kimmerly's. During this period they were running at $1.5 million a year.

Even at the time of peak sales for the DMC-12, John DeLorean was spending more on lawyers' fees than he was on advertising. In this period the car may have been selling at a premium, but once Dick Brown's Quality Assurance costs, plus extra interest charges and other costs directly related to the delay in getting the car onto the market, had been added on there was still only a large trading loss. But DeLorean was going for his biggest deal yet, his eyes now intent on the flotation that would show his paper worth of $120 million.

The issue taking shape under Kimmerly's organization was a complex one. The new DeLorean Motor Holdings would be an umbrella parent corporation, but at the same time it was floated, the DeLorean Research Limited Partnership put together by Oppenheimer would be bought out and so, now, would all other holders of DeLorean Motor Company stock – the dealers, NIDA, Wood Gundy and of course Johnny Carson. All would exchange their stock in DMC for new stock in the new company. Options on stock in DMC, which is what had tempted Cafiero, Haddad, Lander, Stark and others into the company in the first place, would be worthless.

DeLorean would also be freed from royalty payment obligations to the original Sports Car Partnership investors, and the Oppenheimer Partnership's right to 23.4 percent of profits would end, albeit at a high price. The figures show just how expensive this money had become: the 125 partners found by Oppenheimer put in $18.7 million. This became a net $15.5 million after Oppenheimer's $2 million fee, Javits and Javits legal costs and DeLorean's own charges. Of this, some $1.3 million went, according to the Holdings prospectus, to 'ERM process work'. The rest went to GPD. Less than three years after that money, which was not needed anyway since the Northern Ireland government had offered to fill the gap with a cheap loan, was put up, DeLorean was now proposing to buy out the partners and offering them a total (assuming a price of

$12 a share) of nearly $50 million. On top of that, Oppenheimer would get another fee of $2.4 million if it could persuade all 125 partners to accept. If the original Oppenheimer money had actually gone into the car project, which it never did, DeLorean would still have raised $15.5 million and repaid it three years later at a cost of over $52 million. Yet even now there were very few who suspected John DeLorean might have had a different motive for raising that Oppenheimer money. It never entered the mind of Mike Hayes or the sophisticated market-hardened men at Oppenheimer to question that motive.

A formidable battery of New York's well known lawyers, led by Paul, Weiss, Rifkind, worked on the prospectus through that summer. Kimmerly recalled later: 'There would invariably be thirty to forty people in the conference room for these sessions, most of them lawyers.'

The team met regularly in the conference room at 280 Park Avenue. Kimmerly was always present. Despite Darrell's continual probings, there was a mood of something more than ordinary optimism. The car and John DeLorean were big news. It would be a big issue.

There were, of course, some intrusions to jar the air of euphoria. Bill Haddad, more and more opposed to the issue, got his own legal opinion suggesting that the draft prospectus he had managed to get hold of violated Rule 10-b-5, the SEC regulation requiring disclosure of all material information. He sent a copy of his memo to Paul, Weiss, and to Bache. Norris Darrell acknowledged he had seen a copy.

There is evidence that the Haddad memo was certainly discussed by the lawyers as they worked on the prospectus. Their principal concern appeared to be safety. Haddad had found an ally in Mike Loasby, or perhaps it was the other way around – Loasby thought he could get some of his concern across through Haddad since he had failed in every other way. But the prospectus eventually only included a meaningless criticism of the car to the effect that 'commentary to date . . . has included criticism in respect of certain aspects of the DeLorean, such as the driver's field of view and the acceleration rate'.

The early draft prospectus showed a simple corporate structure with the new Holdings company at the top, DMC directly underneath as a wholly owned subsidiary, and then two arms from DMC off to the Belfast company and to Composite Technology. Some of the lawyers became concerned by the GPD allegations, and by the fact that the principal shareholder in the new company would not be John DeLorean personally, but the DeLorean Manufacturing Company, which in turn was wholly owned by a Nevada registered company called Cristina. DeLorean owned 100 percent of Cristina. Those ramifications appeared in later drafts.

There was another, more serious and in the end fatal obstruction to the successful flotation of the Holding company. It came from a direction DeLorean had almost dismissed: NIDA. At the end of May DeLorean summoned Hopkins to New York to tell him and the other directors about the issue. Hopkins immediately raised an objection, or more accurately he set six conditions for going along with it – and without NIDA agreement the issue could not take place. Hopkins wanted NIDA's shares to be in the top company, DeLorean must agree that there would be no more arguments about converting loans into grants, there would be no further requests for money and he must supply proper forecasts and figures for monitoring. All of these DeLorean accepted after an argument over the next month. One condition, actually the fourth in Hopkins' list, he baulked at.

This stated that DeLorean would agree not to sell his own shares in the new company for an agreed period, probably two years. It seemed a simple enough clause: if the company was so great, why would he want to sell them? DeLorean exploded.

> YOUR REQUIREMENT IS A CLEAR VIOLATION OF THE MASTER AGREEMENT AND AN ATTEMPT BY NIDA/DOC TO USE THE PUBLIC OFFERING AS ANOTHER OPPORTUNITY TO RENEGOTIATE THE MASTER AGREEMENT

he stormed in a telex on June 9. If NIDA had insisted on such a restriction back in 1978 'it is unlikely I'd be in Northern Ireland now'. If Hopkins insisted on it, he threatened, 'we'll terminate the offer.' He had done everything he promised, yet here they were imposing new conditions on him.

DESPITE THE BURNING OUT OF OUR EXECUTIVE OFFICES AND THE DESTRUCTION OF OUR MAJOR RECORDS BY TERRORISTS, DESPITE THE CONSTANT HORROR OF SNIPER FIRE OUR EXECUTIVES ARE SUBJECTED TO, AND DESPITE THE HURLING OF OVER 150 FIREBOMBS ON TO OUR FACTORY SITE AND THE THREAT OF MANY WORK-STOPPING SCARES, WE HAVE INVITED AN UNDERWRITER TO PROCEED WITH THE PUBLIC OFFERING SO OFTEN REQUESTED BY NIDA/DOC.

Over the next weeks he sent telexes threatening dire consequences 'if we lose the offer as a result' of NIDA's intransigence. DeLorean by now was getting worried – the 'window' for the offer was slipping away. He brought in the lawyer Alan Cohen, formerly of Paul, Weiss, Rifkind to advise him personally and wired Hopkins: 'Al Cohen says NIDA/DOC are both morally and legally wrong in this matter.' His fury mounted day by day.

I AM INCENSED THAT NIDA/DOC SHOULD ATTEMPT TO GET BY BLACKMAIL WHAT IT COULD NOT BY NEGOTIATION. I HAVE A PERFECT RIGHT TO SELL MY SHARES TODAY AND AM FAR ALONG IN NEGOTIATION TO DO JUST THAT

He wasn't of course, but he was using every pressure he could think of to move Hopkins. In the NIDA office the more DeLorean protested, the more determined they became not to give in. If he was making such a fuss, then clearly he did want to sell his shares. And if he wanted to sell his shares after the issue, then something must be wrong. On June 23 DeLorean broke off negotiations altogether, saying he was going to go ahead regardless of NIDA.

It was a letter from Ken Bloomfield, the cool, and able permanent secretary in the DOC, who brought him back to his senses somewhat. 'I'm sorry you've broken off negotiations,' Bloomfield wrote at the end of June. 'In these circumstances it will be difficult for the Department to pay over the £3.5 million still outstanding.' DeLorean had still only had half the extra £7 million agreed after the Sands death. The other half was due any day. Hastily he resumed negotiation but it was too late. He had missed the summer 'window' and would now have to wait until the autumn for his issue to go ahead. And he had raised alarm bells in Belfast – the issue, not large enough to finance the company, would still have set a market value on DeLorean's shares. NIDA now believed he had some other purpose in mind – and they had a feeling they might not like it.

NIDA never did get DeLorean to agree not to sell his shares, even for a short fixed period.

While all this was going on, John DeLorean was making life harder and harder for Bill Haddad. Haddad went to Belfast just after the death of Bobby Sands and stayed there most of the summer. He was ill with stomach trouble but DeLorean did not let up. 'John kept the pressure up,' recalls a DeLorean official. 'He sent him a memo saying "You came back Concorde although you shouldn't have. We will charge you!" '

DeLorean would later say that one of the reasons he fired Haddad was because he wouldn't go to Belfast. 'I practically lived in Belfast,' says Haddad. He initially resisted going, since his job was obviously in New York. But DeLorean insisted, 'and in the end I said "Yes, I will go to Belfast" and took the family. That shook him up. I decided to call his bluff. But he had us all over a barrel.'

In Belfast that summer, the calm professional hand of Don Lander was having its effect. Workers were learning their skills actually on the production line with only a few weeks training, but Lander, Broomfield and the others had installed checking systems and higher standards of quality control. Everyone was still working six or even seven days a week and, as the workforce increased, production was steadily stepped up, and the quality of the car got better. It was still a long way from ideal, but Lander felt that given a bit of time it would shake itself down. The factory was first-class; the production processes, particularly in the body shop, were worked out more or less as the car passed along them, but in a way that made them better rather than worse. The working conditions were ideal, and the workforce enthusiastic.

From Belfast, Haddad kept up a steady flow of memos to

DeLorean. He had few replies and was often not sure DeLorean even read them. He proposed a new DeLorean scholarship for Catholics which he told DeLorean would 'solve that problem'. The British security forces must have wished it was as simple as that. DeLorean scrawled an OK on the memo and sent it back. Haddad had raised his objections to the new company and lost. Now he concentrated on the safety aspects. But he also, unwittingly perhaps, fed DeLorean's neurosis about Northern Ireland.

'John, I have been here when an angry mob (confronted by police firing plastic bullets into a crowd of teenagers) has tried to rip our gate down, and seen them hurl fire and acid bombs within feet of our executives. I have seen our executives retreat to the manufacturing building to keep things going. I have watched them leave in their unprotected individual cars, passing alongside the unpredictable areas. (And we know that steel tipped sniper bullets have ripped into this place.) I have watched them work away under these conditions to try to maintain schedules and meet C.R.'s [Brown's] parts orders, even when the security has repeatedly advised them to evacuate a building.'

This was pure fiction of course. Haddad was not even there on the night of Sands' death, which was the only time the gates were really threatened. And no executives were anywhere near them.

In between the rhetoric about the IRA, Haddad did make some good points. He was hearing more and more from the engineers regarding their worries about quality. And he was the only executive to raise the issue seriously with DeLorean. Because he was not an engineer, nor even an industrialist, he was actually the least qualified person to do so, but he did at least listen to the professionals doing the job.

DeLorean was not interested in quality at that time. Now that the car was coming off the line, he was impatient with the small numbers. After all at Chevrolet he had made over three million cars a year; in his last year at GM he was in nominal control of seven million vehicles a year. Against those numbers, what was 20,000 a year? Sometime during this summer, he decided that he must go for something more ambitious. At full speed and with enough skilled men working around the clock seven days a week, the production line at Dunmurry could produce far more cars than 400 a week.

Cafiero was opposed to the idea, feeling that the company should not run before it could walk. But he seldom crossed DeLorean openly, preferring to urge others to do it, watching quietly at board meetings while his own questions were raised by Bill Haddad or one of the others. Don Lander was violently opposed and that was more serious. He was the man who would have to make the cars.

By July, however, DeLorean's plans had taken root. He would double the workforce immediately – there were plenty of people available, so there was no problem finding workers, although they would be wholly untrained because all the skilled men had already been hired. The plan had two advantages. First, it would look very impressive in the new stock prospectus – an indication that the prospects were so healthy that the workforce, planned at 2,500 after four years, would hit that figure a year after production started. The second advantage also had to do with money – if DeLorean employed 2,500 people in West Belfast and possibly the same number indirectly making components in the rest of Britain, he could exert immense pressure on the British government. When he needed more money for his sedan and for his expansion, he would get it. How could they refuse?

It still took some persuasion to get Lander to go along. In fact, he probably never was fully persuaded. From California Dick Brown was reporting that he could sell all the cars he could get. In Belfast, the executives felt they were licking the quality control problems, and were bitter about the money Brown was spending re-doing the cars. 'He's taking every wheel off just to check if the nuts have been put on,' one manager remarked. 'All he has to do is kick the wheel.'

Later Lander remarked: 'I've said my piece. DeLorean has control of this company and I can now either resign or do what he wants.' Lander was not a poor man and with his reputation he could have easily found another job. But like so many other men in this story, he too gave in.

Lander accepted the plan almost to double the workforce; he also swallowed his annoyance over the flotation of the new Holding company, although he too would lose his options.

Gene Cafiero was deciding during this period that he had better get clear; so was Jim Stark who, like previous chief financial officers, was beginning to realize what sort of man he worked for. Cafiero's position remained a mystery, and still does, since he has not cared to explain it. Stark's role was less central, but perhaps even more obscure. DeLorean hired him on the basis that Stark would be reporting directly to him. When he arrived he found he was reporting to Cafiero. His health was poor too (he had a spinal injury) and that summer he wore a neckbrace much of the time. In Belfast the NIDA officials saw only a little of Stark and were not overly impressed by him. It was nothing personal; they simply realized he was not going to make a stand against DeLorean and help them in their battle. Like Cafiero, he became irrelevant.

Then early in August the whole internal turmoil began to come out into the open. The catalyst was the revelation in the *Sunday Telegraph* of the proposed flotation of DeLorean Motor Holdings – plus the details contained in the prospectus which opened the way for the first examination of the relationship with Lotus, of GPD and of so many other aspects that had been secret.

The paper was already regarded by John DeLorean and his team in New York and Belfast as their strongest critic. By this stage there were many angry DeLorean executives, cheated of their options in the unmarketable DMC shares, and damaging documents began to leak out. The medium chosen was the *Sunday Telegraph*. On Sunday, August 9, the *Sunday Telegraph* disclosed John DeLorean's plans for selling 2.25 million shares to the American public at between $12 and $14 each; he himself would have 9,950,000 shares, 50 percent of the company. The amount of money to be raised was really very small: by the time Oppenheimer had received its new fee, Bache Halsey had taken its slice and the lawyers' hefty fees had been covered, there would be no more than $10-$15 million. This money was supposed to finance the sedan, but that would have cost $80-$100 million. So DeLorean would still have to ask NIDA and the Department of Commerce for more money – much more. And the prospectus indicated as much.

The story was picked up round the world and there was a

mass of publicity the following week, much to DeLorean's discomfort. The *Sunday Telegraph* began probing the relationship with Lotus, which was staying as far out of sight as it could. 'We are not allowed to divulge confidential details of contracts with clients,' said finance director (later chairman) Fred Bushell. The paper also picked up the annoyance and anger among the executives – on August 16 it warned 'there may be a mass departure of key executives'.

In the penthouse on the 43rd floor of 280 Park Avenue, everyone seemed to be waiting for someone else to make the first move. Who would go first: Cafiero, Stark or Haddad? Who would bring out into the open the doubts and accusations they were all making privately? By September Stella Shamoon of the *Sunday Telegraph* had discovered GPD and stories on it began to appear, causing panic at Park Avenue and heightening tension even more. Soon someone would break.

It was not any of the men whose options on DMC stock would be made valueless by the new issue. The real danger to DeLorean came from an entirely unexpected source. It was not even a senior executive. In fact, it was not a man at all.

CHAPTER FOURTEEN

Marian Gibson

Marian Gibson was speeding north. It was Tuesday, September 22, 1981, and she had caught an early train from Euston Station to Macclesfield.

Marian, personal secretary and office manager for John DeLorean, was determined that her former boss must be stopped. Her instrument was to be Nicholas Winterton, the Macclesfield MP.

Gibson had come to hate DeLorean. When she landed the job as his administrative assistant at $30,000 a year in September 1979, she was delighted. She knew little about the man, but had vaguely heard his name. She was too experienced to be attracted solely by the glamour, but the job, DeLorean told her in her interview, would be considerably more than just personal secretary. She would be working for the president of a new company and operating out of plush offices.

Marian Gibson was 41, single, blonde, attractive, a bit inclined to plumpness. She still spoke with the distinctive English accent that is an asset for secretaries in Manhattan. Her accent was more London cockney than Oxbridge, but no one seemed to notice.

She was born in Paddington, London and worked for a few years in the garment industry in Oxford Street. When she was 21, she came to New York for a six-month stay and never went back. She worked in the cut-throat garment industry on Seventh Avenue and then went on to the more fashionable Fifth Avenue trade. At one point in her career, she was a buyer at Gimbels, the large department store.

In the late summer of 1979, John DeLorean was looking for a private secretary for the new offices he had taken over from Xerox. Gibson had heard about the job from a friend who knew someone at DeLorean, and she applied. She suited DeLorean perfectly in manner, ability and experience – and he picked her out in a final selection from two.

Marian was aware that DeLorean chose her because of her English accent. His deal with the British government was less than a year old. Officials from Northern Ireland occasionally appeared in DeLorean's office, staring with astonishment at the expensive furnishings and art collection, and beginning to make what seemed to DeLorean unnecessarily carping comments about the money lavished on salaries and offices in New York when funds were so badly needed for the car factory in Belfast. An English secretary, thought DeLorean, might help to soothe them.

For a year after she joined the company, John DeLorean shared with Marian almost every business secret – perhaps not consciously, but through his habit of communicating even to his closest staff in memo form. Marian typed memos to general counsel Tom Kimmerly whose office was just across the hall, memos 'setting up' Walter Strycker, letters to NIDA and the Northern Irish officials.

It was a six-day-a-week job for her, sometimes seven. Bill Haddad called her 'the door' – unless you got through her, you didn't get to DeLorean. She made out his cheques, and he signed them. She kept his diary. She organized the office Christmas party.

Marian had other secretaries to help with the typing and filing while she concentrated on installing efficient systems. DeLorean brought with him from Detroit the full General Motors system and installed it in his own tiny operation: note paper styling, filing systems, the habit of writing everything out even when it was quicker and easier to walk across the corridor – the full modern and efficient procedure of a major corporation. Marian was an essential cog in it. And for the first year she was intensely loyal. Yet DeLorean never allowed her to become close in a personal sense – no one, not even Tom Kimmerly, was truly close to him.

Marian Gibson had been in New York for more than twenty years and DeLorean, for all his cosmopolitan lifestyle, was still a Detroit boy at heart. He was surprisingly gauche in the circles to which he now aspired. Marian knew people he did not and she was only too pleased to share them. She took DeLorean to visit various Arab friends and former employers, especially when DeLorean was seeking money, as he constantly was. There was one group for whom she had worked, coincidentally, in the General Motors building. DeLorean wanted to meet them and Marian arranged it. Ironically, DeLorean would have to see them in their offices on the 14th floor.

'Can't they come over here, Marian? You know, I'd kinda like them to see the spread here.' DeLorean was very proud of the penthouse office at 280 Park Avenue.

'Well, perhaps they'd like you to see the spread there,' replied Marian.

Later when DeLorean returned, he announced, 'You know, I'm just bowled over by that office.' But he wasn't pleased that someone – anyone – had a grander office than his.

In October 1980 Marian's position at DeLorean changed. She later claimed it was a promotion, but DeLorean claimed it was just the opposite. Her new title was Deputy Administrator for DMC, which really meant office manager.

She could still walk into DeLorean's office to have, as she put it, 'a nose around his desk'. He didn't mind, and never seemed to notice. For all his tangled business deals, DeLorean was curiously open about letters and files. One day he walked in as she was leaning over his desk and he just remarked casually, 'Hi, Marian, how're you doin'?'

Marian was still protective of him, breaking in a new secretary, doing her best to make things work more smoothly. She would pass back to him the mood she detected in the office.

'You know,' she said one day, 'you have a lot of enemies.' DeLorean was unimpressed. 'Is that right?' he asked.

But increasingly, like so many of the others who were to leave, Marian Gibson came to see John DeLorean in a different light. The doubts originally implanted by some of the memos she read or typed began to crystallize. Walt Strycker's departure had left a sour taste; so had the objections of Brown and more recently of Bill Haddad.

She started to contrast the casual attitude in the Park Avenue office towards spending company money, with what she knew was happening in Northern Ireland. She began to follow the battle the NIDA men were having with DeLorean, and her latent patriotism began to stir.

It was enough for John DeLorean to sense that she was no longer wholly on his side. In June 1981 he moved her again, this time a definite demotion. She was sent to the public relations department with the clear implication that it was only a temporary stopping place. DeLorean wanted her out, just as he also wanted her new boss Bill Haddad to go. Marian suspected that the new man in the department, Mike Knepper, was under orders to make things as unpleasant as possible for her.

She decided she was not going to go quietly. Her friend and lawyer Clarence Jones proposed the course of action that many other women had taken in such circumstances: a civil rights suit for women. Jones, a tall, elegant, articulate black man in his fifties, had been one of Martin Luther King's advisers and knew all about civil rights suits. She began collecting her material in preparation for such a case.

In that curious way he had of ignoring minor matters that no longer concerned him, DeLorean sought her help as if nothing had changed. By July 1981 DeLorean was once again running out of money. The officials at NIDA were grinding their teeth in frustration as they tried to restrain the outflow of money from the Northern Ireland company to New York. For more than a year they had winced at the extravagance of that Park Avenue office, insisting it was far too lavish for a company that still made no profits and had such huge debts.

The officials believed they were getting nowhere with John DeLorean, but in truth, they were. One day Marian had a call from the 43rd floor penthouse. 'Are you alone?' asked DeLorean. She was, but pretended not to be – making a show of saying goodbye and closing the office door. Finally she told DeLorean she was ready.

'Do you know a rich Arab who might be interested in taking the 43rd floor?' he asked her. Marian quickly concocted a scheme.

She had an Arab friend, a Saudi, whom she thought would be interested. She would ask him. 'These redwood doors and marble floors should go down well,' Marian suggested to DeLorean. 'Meanwhile I'll put out the story that we'll be moving to a joint showroom and office on Park Avenue, similar to the one Mercedes has. I'll be sufficiently vague about it so that people won't be able to ask the exact spot – I'll say we can't say exactly where yet.'

Marian went ahead and put the story out, with the intention of saying the deal on the showroom had fallen through once they all moved down to the 35th floor. But DeLorean didn't move for another nine months – when the company was already in receivership.

During the summer of 1981, Marian's resentment turned to hatred. In the public relations department, Mike Knepper assigned her a job he thought she would despise – going through the Hansard reports of proceedings in the House of Commons and picking out all the references to DeLorean. There was a huge bundle of the reports piled on the floor.

Two streams in Marian's discontent were now coming together. Jones was still advising her on the preparation of her civil rights case, and her anger at everything she saw going on around her – heightened now by a very discontented and worn-down Bill Haddad whose health was visibly suffering – was being fed by what she read in those Hansards.

Marian became familiar with the names of the MPs who persistently questioned the project. The loudest and most frequent critic was the left-wing Labour member for Keighley, Bob Cryer. During the entire DeLorean episode, he was to ask by far the most informed, perceptive and penetrating questions that were to receive blind and naive answers from equally uninformed Labour and Tory governments. Britain had a history of sending her worst politicians and civil servants to Ireland. In the late 1970s, little had changed.

There were other critics of course: the Tory Michael McNair-Wilson and, from May 1979 onwards, the doughty Jock Bruce-Gardyne, who used a double-barrelled weapon – his oratorical prowess in Parliament and his literary skills in his weekly column in the *Sunday Telegraph*. All that year, Bruce-Gardyne and Cryer, from opposite ends of the political spectrum, had increasingly pressed the hapless Northern Ireland Minister of State, Adam Butler, with question after question. The thrust of the inquiries was immediately apparent to Marian.

She could see that Cryer knew a great deal; he had asked

about GPD within months of the signing and had pressed on the deal with Lotus. He questioned the role of the DeLorean Research Limited Partnership put together by Oppenheimer. He knew about ERM.

One cannot read through the Hansard reports without catching other significant items. References to DeLorean were usually included in Northern Ireland debates that often consisted of ministers reading long lists of casualties in the battle against the IRA; of the horrendous unemployment the Province was experiencing; of companies going out of business for lack of funds.

In 1980, there had been less violence in Northern Ireland than in any year since 1971. There were fewer murders, fewer injuries caused by terrorist violence, fewer explosions and fewer shooting incidents. And 1981 had started just as promisingly. But then came the hunger strike and the Province had exploded again. Marian was now rediscovering it all through the debates recorded in Hansard.

In her emotional state the figures became real for her, something more than dry statistics. Bob Cryer was alleging that the money that went to DeLorean had only become available because of cutbacks in spending on education and housing. Bruce-Gardyne was insisting that the new Tory government should think again before 'we lay on any extra saunas, sun-parlours or anything else for this extraordinary affair'.

Meanwhile, Bill Haddad had arranged a meeting with Clarence Jones and had turned over a copy of his 'gold facets' memo. He also had copies of other memos that had come his way, and many he had written to DeLorean. He had outlined his own doubts about Lotus and the GPD deal.

Jones, who was advising Marian on her suit, eventually took the decision to hand her a copy of Haddad's 'gold facets' memo. It was the final bit of fuel she needed.

That evening, in her Manhattan apartment, Marian began organizing her notes. What to do with them? Her first instinct was to go to Jock Bruce-Gardyne – she felt she knew him best, both from his *Sunday Telegraph* articles and his speeches in the House.

The next day was Saturday, but she was accustomed to working on Saturdays. She had slipped into the habit of lunching at The Cowboy Restaurant with Tom Kimmerly and Kimmerly's assistant Jackie Feddock. Sometimes DeLorean came, too.

At lunchtime Marian took the elevator to the 43rd floor and sought out Jackie. She noticed that DeLorean's office door, which was invariably open, was closed.

'Is Tom coming to lunch?' she asked Jackie.

Jackie gestured at the closed door. 'They're in there.'

At that moment, the door opened and Kimmerly walked out. As the three rode the elevator down to the ground floor on their way to The Cowboy, Kimmerly suddenly blurted out in an uncharacteristic burst of candour, 'We're going to sue the British government!'

It provided yet another bit of impetus to Marian's plan of action.

After lunch she slipped across Park Avenue to the Waldorf Astoria. In the foyer she turned right and then left as she walked through the plush carpeted corridors with their boutiques and bars. On the left was a row of pay phones that had the advantage of being in booths with doors. She entered one and dialled the Park Lane Hotel. Her friend Eddie Koopman was staying there.

The Dutch-born antiques dealer from Cheshire, whom Marian had met eight years before in New York, was a regular visitor to the Sotheby-Parke Bernet art sales and was attending one now. He had no interest in DeLorean and had heard more than enough from Marian already. 'What do you think, they're so stupid over there?' he shouted. 'You think they just give away their money and then forget it? You think they don't even check where it's gone?' Marian explained that she and Clarence Jones had some papers she wanted Koopman to see. Would he meet them?

'I don't want to see a thing,' exclaimed Koopman. 'I don't want to be involved in any of it!'

'Eddie, I have a problem,' insisted Marian. 'I've got to get past the mole DeLorean has in the Northern Ireland office. It's really important. I really would like you to come along and meet Clarence and me.'

Koopman, drawn reluctantly into a matter that had nothing to do with him, agreed. They met in one of the cafés in the United Nations building – neutral territory for all – and well out of the way of DeLorean moles.

'Eddie, I'm going to Bruce-Gardyne. He's the most vocal on this issue,' Marian began.

'No, you don't want to do that,' said Koopman. 'I've got a better man, very reliable. He's in Macclesfield and he's a friend. We could meet at my house. If you're going to go through with this I'll make an appointment with Nick Winterton.'

It meant going to England: the cost of the airfare, the inconvenience and trouble. But Marian had now made up her mind. Clarence Jones approved the plan and agreed to follow her to England to support her. That Saturday evening she rang Bill Haddad at home. 'Bill, I'm taking a vacation.' Haddad did not object. He was only too aware that the skids were under both Marian and himself – he had not been paid since July.

She took a shopping bag and went into the office. From the shelf where they had sat for a year, she took down two binders, each about four inches thick. They contained copies of almost all the letters and memos she typed for John DeLorean in the thirteen months she was his executive secretary; she had filed them with no purpose other than the instincts of a trained, efficient secretary. But when DeLorean had moved her out of his own immediate area to Bill Haddad's department eight floors down, she had taken them with her and parked them on a shelf for all to see.

The deeply ingrained philosophy of Detroit men such as Bill Collins, Bob Dewey or even of Cafiero was that you might object, but you did so privately, you never washed your dirty linen in public. Dick Brown and Walt Strycker, to a lesser extent, shared the same fear of making a public fuss. Marian Gibson proved to have fewer inhibitions.

The black binders also contained copies of memos and letters she had seen on Bill Haddad's desk. When she finally decided to make the jump, she gathered together all the papers from her own desk, put the two big binders in a bag, scooped up everything else she thought might help make her case, and left.

She slipped into Bill Haddad's office and made copies of some of his files. She was aware that what she was doing was illegal, but she needed the documents as a trigger.

By Tuesday she was back on her native English soil and by Saturday was journeying north to Macclesfield for an initial and exploratory talk with Winterton. She had not brought her files to the meeting – she would not entrust them to him until she had got to know him.

It was a fine September day. Winterton was at Koopman's home with his wife Ann. He was a blond, fresh-faced cheerful man with a little Union Jack (his trademark) on his casual sweater. They strolled on Koopman's grounds for half an hour, but Marian had not come all this way, as she said to Koopman, for 'a social occasion'. Koopman led the way to the dining-room and they sat down across the table.

However emotional, Marian still had the ability to marshal her facts. She described DeLorean's lifestyle and the way it was supported by money that should have gone into Northern Ireland.

Ann Winterton and the Koopmans chatted in the drawing-room while, for an hour and a half, Winterton went over Marian's story. He was puzzled by her reasons for blowing the whistle – was she a spurned mistress of DeLorean? He soon rejected that idea, but at the same time, he was convinced that she had once been trusted by DeLorean and should therefore know what she was talking about.

He asked for a meeting to see her documents. Marian wanted to set it up for early the next week. She was already resentful that she had been in England for five days and only now had seen Winterton for the first time.

Winterton suggested the same time and place the following week. Marian was horrified – it would be too late, the Bache issue would have gone through, and there would be no stopping DeLorean. Even her own civil rights suit would have been better than this. It might have held up the issue while the prospectus was redrafted to include mention of it. Marian had no understanding of the busy schedule even a backbench MP must keep, although Parliament was then in recess, and Winterton did not appreciate her feeling of urgency.

The following Saturday it would have to be, with Marian hoping to have the support of Clarence Jones by then. The following Tuesday she phoned Jones in New York. When was he coming over? Unfortunately, he told her, he couldn't. Something else had cropped up and he couldn't make it.

Marian was feeling increasingly vulnerable and alone.

Her flight home to New York was booked out of Heathrow for the following Sunday, September 20. Her appointment with Winterton was set up for the day before that. Now she decided she would board that plane without seeing the Tory MP again. It was all too slow and too late.

She phoned Koopman, told him of her decision: she was going home, taking her binders with her. She told him repeatedly, 'I'm just disillusioned.' Why couldn't Winterton make it sooner, if he were really interested? 'What blasted whist drive is he at today?'

Koopman laughed but Marian was nearer tears than laughter.

'Eddie, Winterton doesn't understand this thing. Bruce-Gardyne understands it. I wish I'd gone to him.' During the week that Marian arrived, however, Bruce-Gardyne had been drafted for higher things by Mrs. Thatcher. He was now watching the nation's purse strings – including spending on DeLorean – from his office in the vast Treasury building in Great George Street. Marian had read about the appointment two days after she arrived.

She cancelled the Sunday flight and rang Haddad in New York.

'Bill, I'm going to be late in getting back. I won't be back until Wednesday.' She felt curiously guilty about that. She was at the point of delivering what could possibly be a fatal blow to her employer, removing from him the $120 million fortune that was within his grasp – yet she was worried about being a couple of days late for work. The habits of a lifetime die hard.

She now arranged to see Winterton on Tuesday – this time with her files. On Tuesday morning she journeyed into London and across town to Euston Station, clutching her carrying bag with the precious papers in it. She was apprehensive and afraid. On the train, she went over the documentation she had collected. On top she placed three pages of her own notes, written late at night in her apartment as she tried to make sense of the information and material she had compiled in the two years she worked for DeLorean. She had copies of the memos Bill Haddad gave her lawyer, Clarence Jones, including the 'gold facet' memo. There were copies of cheques, both corporate and personal – DeLorean was not fussy about the distinction – for everything from art work bought from Christies or Sotheby Parke Bernet to expensive jewelry from the shops along Madison Avenue. There was even John DeLorean's private address book, listing the telephone numbers of his family, and friends, his favourite restaurants, hotels and clubs both in New York and London – all in a neat little book designed to slip into the pocket of a well-tailored suit without disturbing the lines of it.

Marian's own notes contained some half-formed yet pointed allegations that she hoped the memos and other materials in the binders would support. She charged that instead of the $4 million that DeLorean often said he had put into the car project, he had actually only invested $750,000, and that was Cristina's money. She claimed that the money DeLorean received for the petrol-bomb damage to the Belfast factory after the Bobby Sands hunger strike was excessive: only a few shacks were damaged. She also linked this payment to the purchase by DeLorean of his estate in Bedminster, New Jersey – the timing of the two coincided and she claimed they were connected. She suspected that the money approved by Humphrey Atkins and paid by the government through the Department of Commerce had not been sanctioned by NIDA – she had seen letters from Tony Hopkins and knew of his continuing attempts to put pressure on John for tighter controls.

And there was more. Her notes laid out how she thought but could not prove that DeLorean had diverted British government money into other private ventures of his own: the Stirling engine project, the Transbus and others. Dick Brown could list 18; Marian knew of only half a dozen but even that was enough. She had also strayed upon the well-kept and tightly guarded secret of GPD, mostly from conversations with Haddad. She did not know what it meant, but to her, no legitimate deal was done through a Swiss-based, Panama-registered company that was deliberately excluded from public documents by both parties.

At Macclesfield Station, Winterton met her on the platform, took her to his car, and drove to Eddie Koopman's home.

Koopman himself was away that day, but his wife Kit, whom Marian knew well because she often accompanied her husband to the New York art sales, was there. Kit prepared lunch for them. Marian was still nervous, but there was something reassuring and very familiarly British about Winterton.

She had never voted in her life, having left London when she was only 20. But if she had, she would not have voted Conservative. She was no left-winger either – politics simply did not concern her much. But Winterton's very Britishness was now important to her. She had come to perceive the situation in terms of the British taxpayer being cheated and she believed that the more obviously British the person, the more easily he would see that.

The two spent three hours in the Koopman dining-room that afternoon, sitting opposite each other at a large mahogany table on which Marian had spread out her papers. Winterton went through them with mounting interest: here were details of John DeLorean's travel itineraries worked out in extraordinary detail – down to telephone numbers of everyone he might conceivably want to telephone or see on his trip. Each travel itinerary was pages long, even when the trip might only be a few days. There were accounts relating to purchases from the sales rooms and, of course, the memos. From the detail of the items, Winterton could instantly assess the close working relationship that Marian once had with DeLorean. She was not likely to be exaggerating.

Winterton was less sure of his ability properly to assess the material itself. He was keenly aware that his neighbouring MP, Jock Bruce-Gardyne, was something of an expert on DeLorean. Whom should he give these papers to? The office involved was the Northern Ireland office, but Marian convinced Winterton that DeLorean might have a 'mole' there. She told him about Nesseth, too.

This was a matter too big to bring to a mere department; it touched the whole government. Winterton finally decided to take it right to the top. 'It would be best,' Winterton told Marian, 'if we went straight to Margaret Thatcher with this.'

Marian caught the train back to London and then took a taxi

to her cousin's home near Heathrow Airport. Winterton took the spare copies of some of the more pertinent documents, including Bill Haddad's 'gold facets' memo, and returned the original material to Koopman.

The next day, September 23, he wrote a letter to Ian Gow, the Prime Minister's Parliamentary Private Secretary and a fellow Tory MP. He did not mention DeLorean.

'I am afraid at this stage I cannot be specific,' he wrote cautiously, 'but information has come to me which leads me to believe that the British government is being misled and deceived, and the taxpayers' money misused in a substantial project with which the British government has been involved for some little while.' He had the necessary papers, he added, to substantiate that view. 'The problem is that I cannot refer this matter to the Secretary of State concerned because, of course, it would be handled by his officials, and inquiries would be made, and I say with some regret that there are moles within government departments and the perpetrators of the fraud and deception would inevitably be advised that inquiries were in hand.' He asked Gow to arrange a meeting with the Prime Minister 'some time in the not too distant future' so he could discuss the matter with her personally.

On the same day he wrote that letter, Marian flew back to New York. But even while Winterton's secretary was typing out the message and Marian was aloft, back in New York John DeLorean was in the process of firing Bill Haddad. Of course, neither DeLorean nor Haddad knew what Marian was doing, although Haddad knew she was in England. The two events were not connected, although John DeLorean later refused to believe there was no conspiracy between his head of public relations and his own former executive secretary. Haddad later said he could not fully understand why Marian had done it.

Marian Gibson herself found it difficult to explain later – or at least to make people understand.

Her betrayal of her boss was the turning point in DeLorean's career. Doubtless, events would still have caught up with him. But without Marian's move, the Bache, Halsey issue of stock in the new DeLorean holding company would have gone ahead. The alarm bells might not have rung until much later. And the British government might have gone on putting money into a factory that was already producing cars at twice the rate they were selling. The crash would have been all the more severe when it came.

CHAPTER FIFTEEN

Scoop

Winterton's letter to Ian Gow arrived at the Prime Minister's office on Friday, September 25. It was opened by Gow's secretary, Tess Jardine Patterson. Gow himself was out of the country on a trip to the Middle East and Australia and would not return to Number Ten Downing Street until October 9. He was accompanying the Prime Minister to the Commonwealth Prime Ministers' meeting in Australia, the whole party visiting various points in the Middle East en route. Jardine Paterson wrote a polite letter back to Winterton, pointing this out, and adding that 'the Party Conference begins the following week, so it may not be possible to arrange a meeting with the Prime Minister or Mr. Gow until after the Conference.'

Once back in New York, Marian relaxed slightly since she believed, erroneously, that events were going to move faster now.

It required all Marian's nerve to return to her office at DeLorean Motor Company. She was not reassured by Haddad's greeting.

'You know, our phones are tapped – yours and mine,' he warned her. 'It's only a matter of time.'

From across the street she called Koopman. Where were the files? Koopman said he had wrapped them up tight and had them under lock and key.

That was not what Marian wanted to hear. Why hadn't the Prime Minister received them? What was going on? Marian had mentally worked out a likely timetable on her flight back to New York, and had calculated that the effective date, four weeks from the date the Securities and Exchange Commission gave its go-ahead for the issue of the new company stock, had already passed.

She was too late.

Now, as she put down the phone after talking to Koopman, she suddenly noticed a stack of cartons in the office. 'What are those?' she asked Denis Patouhas, one of DeLorean's more recent recruits in the accounting department.

'They are the old prospectuses,' he replied gloomily. 'They all had to be reprinted. There were errors in them. Cost us $46,000.'

There was still a chance! She phoned Koopman again. 'Where are those binders?' They were still in his cupboard. No one had asked for them yet, nothing was in motion.

Marian felt she was walking a tightrope, just waiting to fall off. For the rest of the week she sat in her office, waiting. By Friday evening nothing had happened – DeLorean seemed to be going about his business undisturbed. The prospectus was ready to go. DeLorean was visibly taking pleasure in the $120 million fortune it would provide him. He was going to get away with it.

Saturday, still nothing.

On Sunday at about five in the afternoon, Marian received a call from London. It was not one she expected nor even wanted, and it sent her into such a nervous state that she called the phone company the next day to have her phone service cut off. It was to make things very awkward in the following days, but she wanted no more calls of that kind.

The caller was a freelance journalist named John Lisners, an Australian who had gravitated to Fleet Street several years before and who now made a living writing stories for the 'pops', the less restrained, mass circulation papers – mostly tabloids. Lisners knew Koopman: his child and a Koopman grandchild had been born in the same hospital at the same time.

Lisners had just arrived from Australia. From Koopman he learned that John DeLorean's former secretary had a story to tell, and if she couldn't get a police investigation going quickly, she might be prepared to start moving another way, such as through a newspaper story.

It was ten o'clock in the evening London time when Lisners phoned Marian in New York. Would she tell him the story? Very definitely not, was Marian's reply.

Monday morning brought Marian back to 280 Park Avenue.

Still no news from London, still no sign that DeLorean or anyone else in the office knew what was building up.

By Wednesday, Marian could stand the tension no longer and called Koopman. What was happening? She didn't dare use the office phone so, during the day, she used the booths in the Waldorf Astoria and, in the evening, the public phone on the corner of Sutton Place and East 55th Street, round the corner from her apartment. When she ran out of coins, she used Bill Haddad's credit card number.

Koopman tried to calm her. 'Don't worry Marian, they'll handle it. They can't do anything because Margaret Thatcher is in Australia.'

'Eddie, are those papers still in your cupboard?' They were.

Thursday morning before dawn, Marian went down to the corner phone and called Lisners. It was ten in the morning in London.

Marian was terse, unfriendly – but willing to talk.

Lisners caught the first plane out of Heathrow, grabbed a taxi at Kennedy, and by eleven that evening was at Marian's apartment.

No time for jet-lag, no time for sleep. Lisners didn't even check into a hotel. The two worked through the night, showered and changed early in the morning, and before anyone was around, went down to 280 Park Avenue.

With some trepidation, Marian pressed the button for the express elevator that took them straight to the penthouse on the 43rd floor. She took Lisners in, showed him the layout, the two life-sized dolls standing at each side of the spacious marble-floored foyer, the giant pictures of the DMC-12 behind the reception desk, the red buffalo-hide chairs. She pointed out the art work, some pieces inherited from Xerox, others bought by Maur Dubin in his capacity as keeper of the DeLorean art collection.

Right turn at Kimmerly's office, along the corridor lined in grey smoked-glass. Another left turn, past the office where Cafiero once whiled away his day, and in front was the door to the office occupied first by Walt Strycker, then later Bill Haddad and now Denis Patouhas. On the left was John's private bathroom, used only by him, with its shower and red-tiled walls. On the right, the door open as usual, John

DeLorean's own office with its panoramic views of Manhattan. The telescope stood in one corner; there were pictures of Cristina, the car, the Northern Ireland agreement framed and mounted.

No one else had come into the office, and they went down to the comparative haven of the 35th floor and Marian's own office. Soon Bill Haddad came in and Marian briefly introduced Lisners without directly identifying him as a journalist. 'He does what Ellen's boyfriend does,' she said obliquely. Ellen was Haddad's secretary and her boyfriend was a journalist. But either Haddad didn't get it, or didn't want to.

At eleven, Lisners met Clarence Jones in the Brasserie restaurant in the Seagrams building and they talked for an hour. Marian joined them for lunch. Jones needed to get away – he had personal problems of his own – but one look at Marian's face and he knew he couldn't leave her. She was now finding the tension nearly unbearable. But she made it back to the office after lunch; it was the last afternoon she would work for DeLorean. They had decided over lunch that at five she would leave and not go back.

By Sunday Lisners' story would be breaking in London, complete with pictures of Marian and quotes from her. The offices at 280 Park Avenue would be no place for her after that.

She decided she would not even stay in New York, but would ride out the storm in the more friendly surroundings of her native London. Lisners had already sold the story to the *News of the World*, whose circulation numbered some four million. The newspaper was owned by Rupert Murdoch and was Murdoch's leap from the relative obscurity of Australian newspapers into the bigger time. Income from the paper helped finance his later purchase of the *Sun*, *The Times* and the *Sunday Times*.

The *News of the World*'s editor, Barrie Askew, who prided himself on his crusading journalism, had been hired by Murdoch from the *Lancashire Evening Post* after a series of stories involving corruption and brutality in a mental hospital, the exposure of malpractice in the police, and a story that led to the investigation by Scotland Yard into alleged corruption among public officials in Lancashire.

Askew's long hair and cocky manner, in the brief interval since Murdoch put him in charge of his big British money-maker, had become something of a legend, with constant references to the cot he had moved into his office for purposes other than sleeping.

Murdoch, according to Askew, had decided on a change of format for the *News of the World*. He wanted to move away somewhat from the traditional fare of the broadsheet into more serious fields in an attempt to arrest and reverse the decline in circulation of over two million in a decade. The story that Lisners offered from New York fitted the new formula perfectly, Askew decided.

On Friday afternoon Lisners went off to the Associated Press office to file his story and send photographs through – at lunchtime he had photographed Marian and Clarence Jones together.

It would be the lead story, with a follow-up feature inside, Askew told him.

Marian quietly packed her things, knowing she would leave in just a few hours, never to return. Eight floors above, DeLorean himself was still blissfully ignorant of what was happening. In London, Askew briefed a few select journalists on the story, including his assistant editor Bob Satchwell, who was now handling the story in London.

There would be quite a few points to firm up before going to press, but they would have to wait until Saturday morning. Premature enquiries would trigger interest by other papers and the story might be out before the *News of the World* hit the streets.

The main point to be established was the Prime Minister's reaction: at that stage Lisners was writing the story on the basis of the documents having been sent to Number Ten, which made it a 'Mrs. Thatcher gets secret file of DeLorean papers' story, listing the allegations made in those papers. A 'Mrs. Thatcher orders police investigation of DeLorean' story would be better still. They did not yet know there *was* an investigation, still believing that Mrs Thatcher in Australia was as ignorant of the file of documents in Eddie Koopman's locked cupboard as John DeLorean was.

Clarence Jones called Bill Haddad in the middle of the afternoon. 'You know, Bill, Marian has been speaking to a journalist.'

Haddad was at the height of his own personal battle with DeLorean. But now he could not even get in to see him, his original automatic access blocked off. DeLorean did not even want to talk to him, although as far as both men were concerned by that stage the only thing left to talk about was Haddad's severance packet. He knew DeLorean would never believe Marian had done it all on her own; he would believe Haddad had put her up to it. Haddad's anger and frustration had been public knowledge around the office for nine months now. He made no secret of it, and he knew what DeLorean's reaction would be.

'You know, I'll get the blame for this.'

What no one in the Park Avenue offices or the *News of the World* realized was that events *were* finally moving in the vast Whitehall machine, too. The Winterton-inspired investigation was at last clanking into gear.

Clarence Jones had phoned Winterton to tell him that he believed that the *News of the World* would carry a story the next weekend, on Sunday, October 4.

It was fair warning and Winterton had been appreciative. He phoned Number Ten and asked for the Prime Minister's private office. She was still away, would not be back until Monday. But he reached a private secretary, Michael Pattison, one of five bright, ambitious Civil Servants culled from other departments around Whitehall and detailed for a spell to Number Ten. The DeLorean business, Winterton explained, was about to break and the government could be made to look silly if the *News of the World* were to break it first. Pattison instantly saw what Winterton meant and went into action.

He knew he must brief the Prime Minister herself. That night the telex machines buzzed between Downing Street and the British Embassy in Canberra. By Friday morning, even before Marian and Lisners had visited the DeLorean office, Mrs. Thatcher sent back her decision: order the Attorney General's office to begin a police enquiry into the allegations.

The Attorney General, the Cabinet minister with responsibility for the country's legal affairs, was Sir Michael Havers; he passed the order on to his deputy, the Solicitor General Sir Ian Percival, and Percival phoned Winterton at home. Nicholas was out, his wife took the message: could the MP call him as soon as he got in?

Winterton phoned at 6 p.m., while Marian, Jones and Lisners were still at lunch in New York. He briefed the Solicitor General in detail on everything that Marian had told him, laying out the allegations as clearly as he could.

First, Winterton said, instead of the $4 million that DeLorean had often boasted he put into the company in Belfast, the real amount was only $750,000. He continued: the contract with GPD for the building of the car and the placing of sums of government money in a Swiss bank account needed some investigation, and money was being spent on projects that had nothing to do with the car. Winterton listed some of them: the bus, the gasahol engine, and DeLorean's idea, related to him by Marian, of turning the company into what she called a 'boutique' with DeLorean sunglasses, made by Bausch and Lomb, DeLorean jackets, DeLorean scarves and all the rest of it. Winterton reminded Sir Ian about the pending flotation of DeLorean Motor Holdings that, he said, would enrich John DeLorean at the expense of British taxpayers.

Percival told him there was indeed going to be a police investigation, that the Prime Minister had ordered it personally, and that the Director of Public Prosecutions, Sir Thomas Hetherington, would be contacting him.

After talking to Percival, Winterton called the DPP. Hetherington had asked Scotland Yard's Serious Crimes Squad to carry out the investigations, he told Winterton. The man in charge would be Detective Chief Superintendent John George. George had been asked to see Winterton as soon as possible, which would probably be the next morning when he and his assistant could get themselves up to Cheshire where the papers were located. Could Winterton meet them, give them the documents and tell them all he knew? It wasn't so much a request as an order. The full weight of the law was grinding into action.

At five o'clock in New York, Marian Gibson left her office for the last time, without a word to anyone except Bill Haddad.

Emotionally, Marian was in turmoil. She had arranged to meet Clarence Jones and Lisners on the ground floor of 277

Park Avenue, an office building across the street. Jones was there, but Lisners was late – stuck in traffic.

Marian expected that at any moment DeLorean or Kimmerly or even Nesseth would appear; she was jumpy and very upset. Jones, normally calm and collected, wasn't in much better shape.

Eventually Lisners appeared, his grin of triumph contrasting with Marian's and Clarence's misery. His story was on the wire, Bob Satchell was highly pleased with what he had got. In the morning, the *News of the World* reporters would begin their follow-up phone calls – to Downing Street, to Winterton, to Bruce-Gardyne and Bob Cryer, to Haddad and perhaps to DeLorean himself. It was going to be a beauty.

The trio went across the street to Harry's Bar in the Waldorf Astoria and each had a glass of red wine. They went on to El Parador, a Spanish restaurant. Jones had had enough by now; he couldn't eat, drank three margueritas, and suddenly left – but not before he passed on the news from London.

He had talked to Winterton: the Prime Minister had asked the police to investigate.

For Marian it was both good news and bad. She was relieved that it was all happening at last. But now that the police investigation was going ahead, she no longer wanted Lisners' story splashed across the *News of the World*. Lisners' copy had to be cleared by Jones in his capacity as Marian's lawyer. That had been one of her conditions.

Lisners played the situation carefully. His story was gone, was already on the editor's desk waiting for his arrival in the morning – the front page and page three were laid out, reporters briefed and photographs prepared. He knew – or thought he knew – that nothing could stop it now. They went back to Marian's apartment where Lisners' suitcases were still parked. He had been working on her typewriter and she left him to it, went to her bedroom and lay down, still sleepless. She had not slept properly for weeks and neither of them had been to sleep the previous night.

She could hear the sound of Lisners working on her typewriter in the living room. Every so often he would go out of the door and let himself in a little while later. Since there was no phone in the apartment Lisners was using either Marian's well-established communications centre – the public telephone on the corner of East 55th Street – or else one at the back of the apartment building near the porter's quarters. He had given the *News of the World* the porter's number and it rang so often that the man was now answering it with a facetious, 'Miss Gibson's secretary speaking.'

Finally suspicious, Marian followed the journalist downstairs and heard him dictating more copy into the phone to Bob Satchell.

Furious, Marian snatched the instrument from Lisners, shouting into the phone, 'There's no story, do you hear? No story! You better hang up now because there's no story!'

Back in her apartment, she and Lisners had a blazing fight. 'Clarence has not cleared it,' she shouted at him.

'Sometimes you can't stop these things,' he replied.

She called Koopman, reversing the charges. It was two o'clock in the morning in New York and five hours later in London.

'Eddie, what the hell are you doing sending me this cheap hack? You never told me he was Australian! I'd never have agreed if I knew he was Australian! I have enough problems already trying to make the British see the American problems and the Americans see the British. Now I've got an Australian hack!'

Under the circumstances, Koopman showed remarkable patience. He was not a young man, wanted no part in the events that were raging about him, and had done what he could out of friendship for three people: Marian, Winterton and Lisners.

But he knew Marian had been through the wringer. He calmed her down and she returned to her apartment where she and Lisners now forged an uneasy truce. Later in the night, however, she heard him tapping away again on her electric typewriter.

'I don't know why you're bothering. I told you, there's no story.'

Lisners turned from the typewriter. 'Look, Marian, it is very difficult to stop a story like this,' he repeated.

That sent Marian into a fresh paroxysm of fury, and again she dashed for the telephone on the corner to call Koopman.

Then she tried to phone Winterton reversing the charges, only to hear his wife on the other end decline to accept the call.

It was 5.30 in the morning and Marian felt friendless and even more alone. In desperation, she ran to Clarence Jones's apartment – all the way to 68th and Second Avenue – running in the middle of the street since New York at that hour was no place for a woman to be out alone.

'Clarence, he's called the story in,' she gasped when she arrived.

Jones had regained his characteristic composure. 'Don't worry Marian,' he tried to reassure her. 'Maybe we can still control it.'

Later that morning, he took Marian back to her apartment. Jones stood a head taller than Lisners and without threats or raising his voice, settled down to get Lisners to produce an approved version.

Jones knew almost as much about the DeLorean situation as did Marian. In preparing her suit, he had talked to a number of disaffected former employees, as well as to others such as Bill Haddad. He had talked half a dozen times to Winterton and been a major factor in the MP's determination to press ahead with his demand for an inquiry.

'He was very articulate, very delightful over the phone,' Winterton recalled later. Now Jones was able to reach the compromise he wanted for Marian quite quickly.

While they were talking, Bill Haddad called. The *News of the World* team in London had been unleashed: first stop, DeLorean; second stop, Haddad.

'They've been in touch with DeLorean and they've been in touch with me,' reported Haddad. 'I've said I'm not firing the bullets. But it's getting pretty hot.'

At that moment, Marian's doorbell rang and her maid, Alnora Sharrie, came in to say it was DeLorean's interior decorator and confidant, Maur Dubin. DeLorean had sent him. Marian would not see him, so he sent up a note written on gold letterhead. 'John is not angry or bitter,' the note read. 'He just wants to know why you are doing this, Marian. He just wants to talk to you.'

But Marian did not want to talk to DeLorean.

Later there was another caller: George Hayward, who worked with Kimmerly. Marian was fond of Hayward, but she wouldn't see him either that morning.

'Tell her John DeLorean is not angry,' Hayward told Alnora. 'He just wants to talk to her. Please will she talk to him?'

Marian would not.

But Lisners did. The *News of the World* was chasing DeLorean, leaving messages for him to call back. But the switchboard in the office was unmanned because it was Saturday. DeLorean was in the office. Haddad talked to him there that morning.

Lisners knew the layout from his surreptitious visit the day before. Clutching his tape recorder, he took a taxi to 280 Park Avenue, caught the express elevator to the 43rd floor, and walked into the office.

There was an electric eye at the door that instantly alerted those inside of a new arrival. But Lisners hurried past the empty reception desk, past the empty offices of Stark and Kimmerly and walked straight in on John DeLorean. For twenty minutes or so, he asked questions and DeLorean answered them, with Lisners all the while expecting to be leaped upon by heavies. But DeLorean, despite the abrupt intrusion into his private office, was surprisingly polite, at least at first. Finally, he asked Lisners to go.

The journalist gleefully played back the tape in the taxi he shared with Marian on the way to the airport until she made him switch it off – she could not bear to hear the voice of her former boss.

Once at Kennedy Airport, Marian took the journalist to dinner. But three days without sleep finally caught up with him and Lisners slumped over and fell asleep in the middle of it. His elation had given way to dejection by then, because he'd discovered he was no longer going to be on the front page. A final phone call to check with the news desk had brought the bad news.

'Sorry, John, they've killed your story.'

Events in London that day had moved as briskly as they had in New York. Chief Superintendent John George and Detective Inspector John Hefford set out early in the morning for the long drive up to Macclesfield and Winterton's house. In the meantime, Downing Street was getting its first phone calls from the *News of the World* and calls were going out to other parties who might shed some light on the DeLorean situation.

By mid-morning Askew had his confirmation: the Prime Minister had indeed ordered the police to investigate. It was now a 'Prime Minister Orders Police Probe' story – and the *News of the World* still had it all to itself.

Winterton was out on constituency business and Ann, who answered the phone call from the reporter, made no comment. Winterton later drove over to Koopman's house and collected the folders of Marian's papers, tightly wrapped and sealed by Koopman.

Just after noon, Rupert Murdoch called his editor. That was his invariable habit, no matter what part of the world he was in. Whether it be from Australia or New York, every Saturday he phoned Askew to discuss the main stories with him in considerable detail.

Murdoch was in Oxford that Saturday morning, lunching with Lord Goodman, Master of University College, Oxford.

Goodman was one of the best known figures in British life, not just because of his extraordinarily memorable features – his huge eyebrows, enormous forehead and generous girth – but because of his unequalled range of contacts and friends. In the past twenty years, Arnold Goodman – made a life peer by Harold Wilson – seemed to have been at the centre of every major dispute, every problem, every big legal battle. He was not involved as the cause, but as the man who produced the solution or compromise. Lord Goodman had served as chairman of the Arts Council, chairman of the Newspaper Publishers Association (all the Fleet Street newspaper owners), senior partner of the law firm Goodman Derrick, and friend and conscience to a polyglot of politicians, artists, real estate tycoons and newspaper barons. Murdoch, naturally, belonged to the last category.

When Murdoch's call came through, Askew was excited about the DeLorean story as he briefed his proprietor on it.

'That's one hell of a story,' Murdoch told the editor. 'I hope you have proof of it.'

Murdoch, by an odd coincidence, knew DeLorean. Not well, by any means. But his New York apartment happened to be in the same apartment building on Fifth Avenue as the DeLorean duplex. It was impossible not to run into each other occasionally. 'I have never been in Mr. DeLorean's company more than five minutes at a time,' Murdoch later recalled, 'and I cannot claim to know him even slightly, let alone his wife, whom I have only met in an elevator.' Cristina was a noticeable figure around the building, and John could scarcely be missed, either. Later, the coincidence was to be misinterpreted in Fleet Street bars as word spread that the *News of the World*'s DeLorean scoop had been killed by Murdoch.

At lunchtime that Saturday, October 3, Rupert Murdoch was hearing about the DeLorean story for the first time and his editor, at least, was convinced that he liked the sound of it. Askew explained the enquiries they were making in New York, London and Australia where he had a reporter out for a direct quote from Mrs. Thatcher.

Sunday newspapers have an early deadline. The Fleet Street presses, the largest in the world, start to roll at six o'clock, which means last copy must be in by four. They can replate for later editions, of course, but that usually happens only when a late story breaks. This was not a late story and it was all running smoothly. Lisners was constantly calling from New York with updates; Downing Street had made the necessary confirmations. They had not reached Winterton yet, but there was still time.

Winterton was greeting the two detectives, George and Hefford, who arrived on his doorstep early in the afternoon. He went through the papers with the men from Scotland Yard in his drawing-room.

George asked him to outline the allegations that were made to him and that he had passed on to Downing Street. Winterton also relayed his conversations with Clarence Jones as further support. The detectives stayed about an hour, then left with the files, heading for the nearby police station.

Just after they left, the phone rang again. It was Director of Public Prosecutions Sir Thomas Hetherington who wanted to speak to the two policemen.

'They've gone down to Congleton Police Station,' explained Winterton. 'If you hold on a moment, I'll get you the number.'

He put the phone down and looked up the number, but when he came back it was dead – the DPP had hung up.

Soon afterwards, the *News of the World* reporter caught him. 'We understand you've sent a telegram to the Prime Minister on the question of DeLorean,' said the reporter. The MP confirmed he had contacted Downing Street and that he had seen the police.

By now the *Sunday Telegraph* picked up the story, too. They knew nothing of Marian Gibson, but learned that Winterton had made certain allegations and that the Prime Minister had ordered an investigation. But the *Telegraph* had not seen the documents. They were now at the Congleton Police Station, being puzzled over by a bemused pair of detectives who, until the day before, had barely heard of DeLorean and who, lacking Marian's guidance, could make little of most of the items in the file. They immediately seized on Haddad's 'gold facet' memo, although the names mentioned meant nothing to them.

By mid-afternoon the *News of the World* had laid out its two DeLorean pages and they were being set in type. Murdoch arrived from Oxford and parked himself at what Fleet Street papers call the 'back-bench', the area in a newsroom where the senior editors and sub-editors sit and where the basic shape of the paper, evaluation of stories, pictures and policy are handled.

The Australian proprietor began examining the DeLorean material meticulously. The paper's legal manager Henry Russell Douglas was not on duty that Saturday, but his deputy John Hinchcliffe was there. Hinchcliffe had a few doubts. So did Murdoch himself.

There seemed more than an outside chance the paper would get involved in a costly writ for defamation of character. Murdoch was also worried about the main sources: newspaper editors have an inherent and well-founded distrust of stories presented by dissatisfied employees.

Haddad, although not a direct source, figured centrally in the story because of the memos that Lisners was quoting. Murdoch knew Haddad, too – he had worked for him at the *New York Post* for several months and had parted, according to both Haddad and Murdoch, 'on friendly terms'. Askew recalls

Murdoch instantly drawing back at the sight of Haddad's name and saying, 'He's a left-wing trouble-maker.' Murdoch, however denies that. 'I may have referred to Bill's love of "conspiracy theories" or even called him an "unguided missile".'

It was time to seek higher legal opinion. Charles Gray, an eminent counsel and the *News of the World*'s top legal advisor, was summoned to the office and arrived 15 minutes later. He supported both Hinchcliffe and Murdoch: the story was not safe enough. 'The story, as shown to me, contained no evidence or proof of any of the allegations,' says Murdoch.

Askew argued for rescuing parts of it – the fact that the Prime Minister had ordered a police investigation seemed safe enough. But now they were running against the clock. If DeLorean wasn't going to be the lead story, they had better find something else quick. Murdoch, Askew and the lawyers debated what other bits of the Lisners story could be resurrected to support the bald statement of a police enquiry. There were not enough to make sense.

Askew surrendered; he pulled the story out. Fortunately for him, there was a news story breaking that was not too bad a lead. 'IRA HUNGER STRIKERS SURRENDER' was what *News of the World* readers got for breakfast the next morning instead of DeLorean. On page three, the follow-up feature was replaced by a story of a little girl who prayed every day for Idi Amin's right-hand man as he went on trial in Uganda – he was her father.

Askew had lost an important battle with his proprietor. He had only been editor for six months and did not stay much longer.

When Lisners and Marian landed in London on Sunday morning, October 4, Lisners quickly grabbed the newspapers. There was no mention of DeLorean or Winterton, other than a single paragraph in the *Observer*. Soon, however, the story began to come out, first on the radio but soon afterwards in newspapers. By the next day, every paper carried the story on the front page.

CHAPTER SIXTEEN

The Storm

Whitehall Farm is no longer a farm, but a house built some forty years ago in rural Cheshire, ten miles north of Stoke-on-Trent, by a local farmer for his sons. It had been added to twice by successive owners and was marginally enlarged again by the Conservative Member of Parliament Nicholas Winterton and his wife Ann when they bought it in 1973. It is an isolated house, standing in six acres of ground, on the corner of a lane going up to Mow Cop. For the next few days this quiet country spot was to become the centre for the world's media following the DeLorean story.

Nick Winterton was out on Sunday, taking Ann to visit their children at school. The phone had been ringing all day but there was no one at home to answer it. The Wintertons returned to Whitehall Farm at 8.30 and half-an-hour later opened the door to a journalist from the *Daily Mail*. From then on the phone never stopped ringing, with Winterton doing his best to restrain himself to a cautious: 'Yes, allegations have been made to me and I have passed them on to the Prime Minister's office.'

Downing Street a few hours before had released a statement to the effect that Mrs. Thatcher had asked the Attorney General to look into 'allegations of financial irregularities' – careful language, which had not stopped the press jumping on it, however. Winterton had been quickly identified as the MP who had passed on the allegations, although the press still did not have Marian's name. Winterton was not renowned as a shy Member of the House – indeed on various issues he had positively courted publicity. But he had not intended to get embroiled in the centre of the DeLorean affair – it was not his subject and he had until this moment seen his rôle as a conduit for passing on the information which had come through him for no other reason than he happened to be the MP of the one man in England John DeLorean's former secretary felt she could trust. Now he had no choice. Late that evening he finally buried the telephone under a pile of cushions in his drawing-room, switched off the bedroom extension and settled down for a few hours sleep with Ann. He awoke to a nightmare.

The front door bell was ringing. The back door bell was ringing. There were journalists, photographers, TV cameras and radio interviewers all round the house. The phone was desperately trying to make itself heard under its cushion-mountain. Winterton was under siege. The national papers and TV networks had sent their men down from Manchester. Others had driven up from London, along the M1 and then M6 motorways. In the early morning local farmworkers and shop-keepers had found themselves giving Fleet Street's hordes directions to the home of the local Member of Parliament. Once they got into Mow Lane all they had to do was join the traffic queue – the lane outside was jammed with cars. There was no mistaking their destination. The TV, radio and press interviews that Nicholas Winterton, MP, gave that morning in his home in the Cheshire countryside were flashing round the world within hours. As America awoke, it was the major news item. John DeLorean too woke up to a nightmare.

2

Until now there had been a possibility, perhaps even quite a good one, that John DeLorean might have pulled it off. His hero status had scarcely been dented. He was able to answer his most vocal opponents with the argument that in Northern Ireland he had done everything he said he'd do – built a factory in a cow pasture and a car to be produced in it. He was employing not just the 1,500 people he had promised by this stage of development but over 1,000 more than that – and possibly another 2,000 to 3,000 indirectly in firms round Britain making components for his car. Against that, the anger of the NIDA officials was no more than the bleating of a few under-paid civil servants. The ministers responsible for Northern Ireland were not overly critical – in fact some were quite friendly. There was a new man in charge of Northern Ireland whom he had not yet met: Jim Prior, the leading 'wet' in Mrs.

Thatcher's Cabinet, had been moved from Secretary of State for employment (or 'unemployment' as the wags had it) only a few weeks before. But Prior's number two, Adam Butler, had been in the job all year and DeLorean got on well with him. Butler, a tall, elegant, bespectacled old Etonian, was the son of the famous 'RAB' Butler, the man dubbed 'the best Prime Minister Britain never had' who had served in the War-time Cabinet of Winston Churchill and every Conservative Cabinet after that until he retired as Foreign Secretary in 1964. Adam Butler was DeLorean's point of contact with the British government. The previous Northern Ireland Secretary, Humphrey Atkins, had been dropped from the Cabinet by Mrs. Thatcher in her September reshuffle. Some of the other ministers were openly hostile, notably Bruce-Gardyne, brought into the Treasury in the same reshuffle. Mrs. Thatcher herself was rumoured to regard DeLorean as a 'con' man and there was a general feeling about that the British taxpayer was being taken for a ride. But everyone, from the prime minister down, put Northern Ireland in a special category, fearful of the political consequences of the closure of the Dunmurry factory.

Most of the allegations that Marian was making were no more than pinpricks which he could easily argue his way out of. But when the storm broke that Monday morning in England, soon to be picked up in the U.S., DeLorean still did not know *what* Marian had taken. Lisners, when he had burst into his office the previous Saturday morning, had given him some idea through the line of his questioning. Overseas bank accounts? 'That was done with the Bank of England,' replied DeLorean. 'They approved the payment. Every single check we have ever paid has been with the approval of our auditors, the government auditors and the Inland Revenue.' Had he really paid $4 million for his stake in the company? 'Of course I paid it. We're just little poor guys. We're struggling our way through the world. We now have 2,500 people who are counting on us. Half of them have never had a job in their life. This is the most important thing that has ever happened to them. They want this company to succeed more than I do, and Goddamit, we're not going to let them down.' His deal with the British government? 'They're adults. This wasn't entered into by a bunch of morons on a Sunday afternoon when they were all blind drunk.'

But what else had she taken? And suppose the police enquired properly into the areas already identified? GPD would not stand much investigation, although she could know very little about that. Only he and Kimmerly in the company knew the details of GPD. The most worrying aspect immediately was on the Bache issue of DeLorean Motor Holdings: DeLorean needed that issue very badly. It had already been delayed several times and he was in no doubt of the opposition and resentment of most of his senior managers to it.

That weekend he took stock. Assuming he could get that issue off the ground, he was still a wealthy man, worth $120 million. The factory in Belfast was working shifts around the clock, turning out 80 cars a day, and although quality, never good at the best of times, had suffered considerably, there would be a period of grace before the investors on Wall Street, on whose goodwill he was dependent, became aware of that. He had a good man in Belfast in Don Lander. In California Dick Brown, the one member of his team who had seriously challenged him, was locked in by the fact that it was Brown who had signed up most of the dealers, Brown who had hired many of the key staff, Brown who had negotiated on his own personal reputation a loan from Bank of America of $25 million. If DeLorean could raise some money from the stock market issue of the new Holdings company, that would go some way to placating the British government. In his worst corporate crisis so far, John DeLorean kept his head.

He started with a press conference that Monday. Until now the press in Britain and the United States was not aware of Marian's identity. Winterton had described her as an 'executive' and referred to her as 'he'. But Lisners, foiled by the *News of the World*, was offering his story elsewhere and soon settled on the *Daily Mirror*. Lisners was offering the only exclusive interviews with her – plus her picture. DeLorean now rapidly demoted her: she was, he said, never anything more than a 'minor secretary' who had been reduced to 'clerk' and then further reduced to 'typist in the PR department'.

What about these charges that he was 'short-changing' the government? he was asked. 'That's a completely stupid and asinine question,' he snapped. ('Stupid' and 'asinine' were favourite words of his – another was 'moron'.) He didn't even know what the allegations were, he went on. 'But no company in the world has been subject to more scrutiny than this one. We are constantly monitored by Revenue, auditors, independent consultants, and there are two directors from the Northern Ireland Department of Commerce on the board.' This was to become a major theme over the next week. His contract with the British government was 'a matter of public record' (in fact it wasn't, but that was the fault of the government rather than DeLorean) and the company had 'more than fulfilled that contract' by employing 2,500 people in Belfast. What was more the company in Northern Ireland was making a profit: it had made net profits of £400,000 in August, £1.08 million in September and would be profitable again in October. Nobody hearing the figures that day could refute him – although the accountants in Belfast must have blanched. It would have taken some very fancy accounting indeed to justify those figures – four months later the company was bankrupt and it never did make a profit, not even in a single week, and no matter what accountancy sleight of hand was used. But only the day before DeLorean had ordered the Belfast company to send a dividend cheque to the British government for royalties on the cars. The sum was tiny: £395,000, bringing to £599,770 the amount so far paid to the government. But it was enough for DeLorean to claim that day that the government had already received royalties and 'should recover its initial investment and receive a profit'.

He then swung into his most powerful counter-blast. 'We are the most successful thing that has ever happened to Northern Ireland. But if I were a banker and somebody made these kind of charges, I'd cut my credit line off tomorrow. If our banks and financial institutions elect to do that, we're going to close the plant tomorrow because we have no choice.' That threat gave government ministers pause for thought in the crucial days that followed, although in fact it was wholly empty: there were no institutions or bankers, other than the Bank of America which was only financing the finished cars. Every other loan was guaranteed by the British government. But DeLorean played the card beautifully and to considerable effect. From that moment on government ministers in Britain were back-pedalling.

The newspapers the next day carried the headlines he wanted in London: ' "Allegations stupid", DeLorean says' (*The Times*); 'DeLorean angry over allegations of irregularity' (*Financial Times*); 'DeLorean denies cash accusations "made by typist" ' (*Daily Telegraph*). The exception was the *Daily Mirror:* it carried a picture of Marian on the front page and her quotes. 'I was concerned that with the small amount of money he had put into the company compared with the British investment of £80 million, he would come out on top and the British would lose control. It concerned me as a patriotic subject.' Lisners had finally got his story into print.

But DeLorean had to make another decision that day, one that was a real setback. He postponed the flotation of the new holding company – it could not go ahead until all the publicity had died away and the investigation was finished. Marian had accomplished what she set out to do.

Now he needed a London lawyer, someone who would stop the Fleet Street press from nailing him to the cross. It was Rupert Murdoch who arranged it for him – and it was no less a person than Lord Goodman himself, from the suite in the Savoy Hotel where he was living at the time, who agreed to act for him. That was a major coup – there wasn't a paper on Fleet Street which did not tread more carefully when it knew Goodman was about.

The next step was to get the government to tone down the attack, and that was easily enough done. DeLorean talked to Adam Butler several times during the week and there was much activity behind the scenes. On Sunday night Downing Street had put out the announcement of the police investigation on behalf of the Attorney General's office which did not have a weekend press staff of its own. In the new mood already prevailing by Tuesday, as DeLorean made his threats and applied his pressure, the Solicitor General felt the need for some elaboration on the original statement. The Prime Minister had not actually ordered an investigation into the affairs of any DeLorean companies or into DeLorean himself. She had asked the police to look into the *allegations*, which was a different matter. If the police found something in those allegations, then a full-scale investigation would get under way. The Solicitor General, Sir Ian Percival, went to some pains to spell this out. 'I think it is very important that a few facts be corrected and that the truth of the matter receive the widest possible consideration,' he said in the formal language which Solicitor Generals in their rare public statements tend to use. All that was happening was that he had authorized 'the sort of routine steps which are taken over and over again, indeed must be taken when allegations of the type now being bandied about are made.' The government was by now very anxious to avoid any accusation that it was acting simply out of spite in a way that would endanger the jobs of the DeLorean workers in Belfast.

Winterton was by now on the defensive, instantly worried by the threats of libel action, as DeLorean intended he should be. 'Nobody said the company was being investigated,' he protested. 'At no time have *I* said there is a full-scale inquiry into the activities of Mr. DeLorean. I find it interesting that Mr. DeLorean is to take libel action, I presume against Miss Gibson. If she is not that important the best thing would have been to let the matter drop as soon as possible.'

It was of course both Winterton and Marian that DeLorean had in his sights.

But already things were not looking so good for Winterton. Solicitor Generals do not use dismissive phrases such as 'bandied about' if they are taking charges seriously. Sir Ian Percival was indicating that he at least did not think very much of the evidence seen so far. The Attorney General, Sir Michael Havers, was not on Nicholas's side either. Two days after the investigation had been started, the country's leading law officers were already finding DeLorean innocent – and the two policemen, well out of their depth already in this political whirlpool, picked up the mood.

Detective Chief Superintendent John George and Detective Inspector John Hefford had spent the weekend going through Marian Gibson's files. They seemed a hotchpotch: bills, memos, copies of cheques, invoices, all contained in the two binders. The names did not mean anything to them. Who was Kimmerly? Or Strycker? Or even Bill Haddad who featured prominently? To complete their investigation – indeed to start it at all – they needed to go to New York to see some of these people. But first they wanted to see Marian. DeLorean's former secretary had gone to ground, her whereabouts known only to Clarence Jones. She wanted nothing more to do with Lisners, or with any press people. The publicity was enormous and every paper in Britain and the United States was mentioning her by name. Reporters were desperately trying to track her down, believing she was still in New York. In fact she was not far from Heathrow Airport, very concerned that DeLorean would send Nesseth.

On Monday night the two policemen drove down to Slough and picked Marian up, drove around a bit talking to her, then took her for a meal. Marian couldn't eat but the detectives were ravenous. Then they took her to the local police station and settled down to take her statement. Hefford wrote, George asked the questions, painstakingly trying to make sense of a story they could not seem to get to grips with: the complications, the names, the different companies and countries involved – it was all too much to grasp in just a few hours. They kept at it until one in the morning, all three of them exhausted, and Marian by now visibly wilting under the strain she had been under for weeks. Formally and for the record Hefford wrote it out: full name, Marian Frances Gibson; age of witness: 42 years, born 30.11.1938. Occupation? Hefford finally wrote 'assistant public relations officer'. George then took her through her full story. DeLorean had not invested the $4 million he claimed, but only $750,000 and that had been put up by Cristina. But could she prove it? Hefford carefully wrote down: 'Rumour had it that the original investment . . .' DeLorean had extricated a large slab of money for the firebombing in Dunmurry during the hunger strike. Hefford noted that she said the claim was 'extremely excessive'. DeLorean had used the money to buy the Bedminster estate in New Jersey. Hefford noted: 'Rumour was caused by the fact that the timing coincided with John DeLorean's purchase of the Bedminster New Jersey estate'.

They came to Bill Haddad's 'gold facet' memo, the policemen, like Winterton, seizing on it as the most immediately interesting document in the pile. This now became Exhibit Marian Frances Gibson 1. Her own four pages of typed notes setting out her thoughts on DeLorean plus her own personal particulars, jobs and even references, plus two sheets outlining her job description became MFG/2 – and Marian demanded them back, insisting they had inadvertently been included in the papers handed to Winterton and were her personal property. There were, as Hefford dutifully noted, also 'one black binder containing copies of inter office memorandum and letters marked Exhibit MFG/3 and one black binder containing copies of inter office memorandum and letters marked Exhibit MFG/4'. Again Marian tried to explain those binders: DeLorean, she said, would buy various art works, $22,000 ear-rings, this and that. She would write a cheque and Maur Dubin would take it off. DeLorean and Dubin were dealing with a number of galleries. DeLorean was constantly investing. Each time she wrote a cheque she would write a letter to the gallery and she would photo-copy it and in the corner she would put a copy of the cheque, so that she would know whether it was for DeLorean Manufacturing, which later became Cristina Holdings, but was John's private company, whether it was DMC or John's own personal account. The idea was that at the end of the year John would then re-imburse the company (she never alleged that he didn't). There were paintings and jewellery always coming in, or going to the DeLorean apartment or the house. There were cheques to Sotheby Parke Bernet and Christies. The policemen could make nothing of them.

To the policemen the one interesting bit of evidence was the 'gold facet' memo, implying wild waste of government money and secret 'hush-hush' Swiss accounts. They also suspected – wrongly – that Haddad in that memo was implying a pay-off to the IRA.

They finally dropped her back at her cousin's house at one in the morning, although by that stage she did not want to go – she wanted protection from whoever DeLorean might send after her, and would have stayed in the police station if they had let her.

The next day they prepared to fly to New York, an adventure for both of them – neither had ever been to the United States before. But they were aware of the political pressures heightening all the time: it is not often two detectives know they are carrying out an investigation ordered by the Prime Minister in person, with the Solicitor General wanting briefings on their findings so far, and the Director of Public Prosecutions watching their every move, and the story developing day by day in the press. Everyone was demanding a quick conclusion from them, and there was a strong bias to go for the DeLorean version, take his word against that of a tired, distressed former secretary.

Back in New York DeLorean had decided Marian could not be acting alone. She had to have had help. He sensed a conspiracy and equally he sensed that Bill Haddad must be behind it. Haddad had been Marian's last boss, DeLorean distrusted his liberal conscience which was always being thrust down his throat, and Haddad had been fired at the same time as Marian was spilling the beans.

Haddad, in avoiding the press, had also avoided the two British policemen. In the end they reached him through the one man Haddad did not want to be reached through: DeLorean himself. Haddad was aghast when DeLorean confronted him that week with evidence of his treachery: the police had a copy of that December 26 'gold facets' memo and would obviously question Haddad closely on what he meant by it.

On Wednesday Superintendent George and Inspector Hefford arrived in New York and booked into a Manhattan hotel. They were like fish out of water: they had no authority in New York and could not force anyone to see them if they didn't want to – including Haddad. They now found an additional hurdle – the following day, Thursday, was Yom Kippur. Haddad had engaged a new lawyer, Ira Lee Sorkin, of the firm Squadron, Ellenoff, Plesent & Lehrer. But Sorkin had not even seen Haddad's papers yet, had not been fully briefed on his position, and Haddad did not want to talk to the police without him being present. Haddad knew he would probably end up suing DeLorean over his options, and over loss of salary for termination of his contract. He was also very disturbed at the inside track DeLorean seemed to have on the line of questioning the police were going to take. Sorkin was a strict Jew and had no intention of being in his New York office that weekend.

Meanwhile, for DeLorean it was time to move onto the next stage of his counter-offensive. All things considered, it was not going at all badly. On Wednesday evening he wheeled on his secret weapon: Cristina. His wife always wanted to be an actress more than a model and there had even been a story, which the cynics said had been put out by Cristina herself, that she would play Elizabeth Taylor in the film of the star's life. Now was her big moment. That day the cameras were allowed into the DeLorean apartment on Fifth Avenue and focused on Cristina who had never looked more beautiful or more poignant, her eyes welling with tears, at times so overcome with what 'they' were doing to her husband she could barely choke the words out. 'It's so unfair. There are one or two people in Parliament who are against this project. He's put ten years of his life and four million dollars of his own into this project. He goes into this strife-torn area and creates 2,000 jobs and I worry one day he'll be brought home in a box. He hasn't seen a penny of personal profit yet. But he will, he will. And why shouldn't he?'

She pictured John as a softie, a pushover for the likes of Marian Gibson who were out to damage him for their own spiteful ends. It was 'nonsense' that Marian was now in fear of her life. 'He never locks anything. It would have been so easy to get into his files. He's been audited three times by Parliament and always comes out clean. As for Miss Gibson being in danger, he wouldn't hurt a fly.' Paying for the house in Bedminster was easily explained, too. 'John sold a ranch to pay for that. I work hard. I make a lot of money. I helped buy that house.'

The interview was effective, winning DeLorean support not just in the United States but in Britain. That too was to be important in the days ahead.

The next day DeLorean, Haddad and Knepper flew to Florida. Haddad had planned a chat with DeLorean, hoping that they could agree his golden handshake. He and DeLorean sat beside each other on the way down. Haddad raised GPD and Lotus. DeLorean produced his former bland defence.

The atmosphere on the way down was cold but polite. On the way back it was hostile. During the day DeLorean had had a call from Tom Kimmerly. That morning's *Daily Mirror* had yet another Lisners story. It had printed Haddad's memo, complete with 'gold facets'. Everybody else was following it up.

There was no more talk about amicable settlements. DeLorean now determined to do to Haddad what he had done to Dewey, Strycker, Marian and anyone else whom he felt had betrayed him. He would 'put some shit on his shoes.'

Friday October 9. The day's Concorde from New York to London carried the by now familiar figure of John DeLorean who stepped off the plane wearing dark glasses, a polo neck, blazer and flannels, an overnight bag slung over his shoulder. Waiting for him was half of Fleet Street, and he chose the moment to give an impromptu press conference. The Haddad memo, he said, was a 'forgery', he had never seen it before. 'We now think Miss Gibson's whole concept was to create a story to be sold for money. Without a doubt money was her motive. She asked for $200,000 for the story.' He himself had just flown in to 'get everything sorted out. I am confident everything will be cleared up, because it is so silly. The Attorney General has retreated and I would say the government will soon make an announcement which will clear up the whole thing.' During the week his conversations with Adam Butler had left him with optimistic signals.

Back in New York, the two Scotland Yard detectives had arrived at 551 Fifth Avenue, the office of Bill Haddad's lawyer Ira Lee Sorkin. Sorkin had been reluctant to come in at all because of Yom Kippur but the police had stressed the urgency of it all, the need to see Haddad before the weekend. The pressure on them for an early decision was mounting all the time and so far the only interview they had had was with Clarence Jones, whom they saw as very much a biased party in view of his connection with Marian.

The interview with Haddad did little to enlighten the detectives. Sorkin pointed out that he could not advise his client to give them material which would go straight back to DeLorean with whom he might be in litigation. Haddad then joined in to say that DeLorean had advised him before they had even arrived in New York of the questions they were going to ask him. Furthermore, went on Sorkin, he had only been brought into the matter that very day and he needed to go through the documents his client had given him before he could decide how to reply. But there was one important point Haddad was prepared to make: he had, he assured the policemen, written that memo; it was written on the date indicated – December 26, 1980 – and it had definitely been delivered. John DeLorean had seen that memo. Why had he written it on Boxing Day? Haddad explained he had written it at home after a visit to Belfast and in preparation for a meeting with John a few days later. In America, he tried to explain, 'Boxing Day' was a working day like any other. Sorkin advised Haddad not to say any more about the memo, but Haddad wanted to make two points. The first related to the 'gold facets' which were not in one of DeLorean's houses in the United States but in Northern Ireland. The second related to the IRA – to the best of his knowledge, the DeLorean Motor Company had not paid tribute to the IRA, he said. Sorkin would not let Haddad go further, much to the frustration of the policemen. Sorkin agreed to look at the Haddad documents over the weekend and maybe they could meet early the next week. Monday then, insisted George, worried by his time pressure. Sorkin consulted his diary and found he had a case out of town on Monday. It would have to be Tuesday. Reluctantly the police agreed.

A number of reporters had gathered outside Sorkin's office waiting for Haddad to emerge. But he slipped out the back way and went home. As he approached his doorway, however, two reporters emerged from the bushes: they were from the *Daily Mail*. Had Haddad written that memo, or was it a forgery? Haddad, a former journalist himself, had by now been convinced by his lawyer of the need for caution. He referred them to Sorkin, who formally made the statement: 'I am authorized to confirm that Mr. Haddad is indeed the author of the memo.' The *Daily Mail* the next day led on the story. The DeLorean affair was still the biggest running item of the week, the focus of attention getting stronger and stronger as everyone waited for the result of the police enquiries.

The police enquiries meanwhile were not getting very far. George and Hefford were not investigating DeLorean's company – they were investigating Winterton's allegations. That was all they had been instructed to do. By now they had begun to wonder about GPD and the Lotus deal, but they had no facilities for looking into them. They had been discouraged from tackling the DeLorean staff.

After seeing Haddad, they decided later that evening that they should make contact with his successor, Mike Knepper, who was being widely quoted in the newspapers. But how to get hold of him? They could not find him in the New York telephone book. So they rang Haddad at home. He was out, and they left a message on his answering service. It was Saturday morning before Haddad rang them back. By that stage the detectives had got hold of Knepper, but Knepper never knew very much; he was never close to John, and his job was to burnish the image, not to destroy it, a role he fulfilled nearly to the end. Haddad had been brooding overnight. If his lawyer agreed, he told them, he would give them all the proof they needed that the memo was prepared, typed and delivered to DeLorean's office. He went through with them the various ways the memo might reach the office of the president, and said it would be easy enough to discover which way it had been delivered.* By Tuesday he would have proof, he repeated.

Back in London, however, there were clearer and clearer signs that the authorities were not going to wait for that proof. The investigation so far had been a non-event – the reporters working on the DeLorean story had been at it far longer, had seen far more people and read far more documents, than the police ever did. Over the weekend several London papers picked up the result from their sources close to the Attorney General's office: a statement, now set for Monday, would indicate there was nothing to investigate, the allegations unfounded. Winterton, hearing the same from his own sources, was quick off the mark with the view that it looked as if it was going to be a 'whitewash', and promised to pursue the matter under the privilege of Parliament.

On Sunday the two policemen had a phone-call from London. It was from the Director of Public Prosecutions. From their sketchy reports so far it was clear they had found nothing

---

* Later he claimed he had done so but at the time this book was prepared was still reserving it for his suit against DeLorean.

to substantiate the allegations. There would be a conference in his office the next morning and he wanted them there. George protested that he had set up appointments for the following week. Cancel them and come home, he was told. Disgruntledly he rang Haddad and Sorkin to say he was having to change his schedule and was needed back in London. He would not be able to keep that appointment on Tuesday. The two detectives caught a plane out of Kennedy that night. It was the end of their investigation – the next day they would be back on other duties, never to take their enquiries deeper, although they continued to have considerable doubts about it all. They had not even scratched the surface.

DeLorean meanwhile was holed up in the Connaught Hotel. Reporters were everywhere that weekend, trying to interview him. He worked on the statement he would make the next day in Belfast. On Sunday evening he went for a walk in the West End on his way to dinner at one of the smarter clubs (he had joined Les Ambassadeurs and Harry's Bar and also used Annabelle's occasionally). His route took him past a church and, as he sometimes did when passing St. Patrick's Cathedral in New York on his way to the office, he popped in. He was later to recall the next few minutes thus:

'I am sitting in church praying, and I turn around and here is some guy behind me holding a tape recorder. And it's a guy from the *Daily Mail*. I said "I can't believe this. Is nothing sacred to you people?" The *Daily Mail* had a different version. According to its editor, Sir David English, the reporter approached DeLorean on the pavement outside the church and did not try to interrupt his prayers.

On Monday morning the two detectives arrived back from New York and went straight to a conference of the country's leading law officers: the Attorney General, the Solicitor General and the Director of Public Prosecutions. They had already made up their minds, long before the Scotland Yard pair got there. It was Sir Thomas Hetherington, the DPP, who later made the formal announcement. No evidence had emerged, he said, 'to support any of the allegations of criminal conduct against Mr.

John DeLorean or the company which bore his name.' The police enquiry, he said, had ended, although 'should any evidence of a criminal offence' subsequently come to the attention of the Director he would certainly give it his attention. It was to be another 13 months before any more evidence did come to his attention and new enquiries started, although the evidence had all been there at the time, had there been any informed attempt to search for it.

DeLorean did not even wait for the announcement. He did not have to.

In triumph, he caught a plane to Belfast, where he had a press conference further to refute the allegations against him, and throw a little mud himself with an accusation that shook everyone present, including his own executives.

'I have a strong feeling that the widespread publicity given to the allegations is part of a wider conspiracy.' He paused for effect. 'It appears to be an organized attempt to destroy this company. Wiser heads than mine will have to seek out the motives of those who would destroy us. The allegations could have been made for political or economic reasons. A foreign country may have been involved in the plot to destroy Ulster's proudest achievement.'

There were gasps. What foreign country? What was he talking about? 'I dare not name the country I have in mind,' DeLorean went on. 'It is unlikely that a group of minor people of limited ability could have created the problem alone. Why did it all happen suddenly when we started looking like we were going to make the grade? It is a distinct possibility that a competitor within the car industry was responsible.'

He ended with a threat: 'I will be issuing writs against the people who were the most serious perpetrators of terrible crimes against this company. Miss Gibson and Mr. Winterton have formed a combination of people with limited ability who caused all this trouble.'

What was the country, he was immediately asked? Were other people in the car industry responsible for the conspiracy against him? 'I do not know. It is a distinct possibility. It may even be a country,' he repeated. But what country? DeLorean was using one of his favourite techniques: plant his idea and let it grow in the other's mind. He would go no further, not even to his own executives who had never heard of any of this before, nor would they again.

All that remained for DeLorean to do now was to carry out his threat. He flew back to London that night and the next day Lord Goodman went into action on his behalf. Nicholas Winterton, at the Conservative Party conference in Blackpool, learned that he personally was being sued for sums he could not possibly hope to pay. DeLorean spread the libel net wide: Marian Gibson and Haddad, the *Daily Mirror*, the freelance journalist John Lisners, the BBC and Independent Television News were all included with the MP. DeLorean had settled on a nice round figure: $250 million was about right.

As he boarded the Concorde to fly back to New York on Tuesday morning, he allowed himself some further elaboration. 'We feel we have been damaged to the extent of $250 million and we are now at the stage of figuring out who is going to pay,' he told reporters. 'Some of the media have claimed I have taken too much money from the company. My hope is that when these writs are served and we've won the libel action, I won't be taking any more from the company because various members of the media will support me for the rest of my life.'

CHAPTER SEVENTEEN

The Money Runs Out

It was to be a brief triumph. Events that had conspired in DeLorean's favour now moved against him.

He was running out of money and it was going to be harder and harder to find more – even to persuade his existing lenders to continue funding the shipment of his cars. At the Dunmurry factory, the large courtyard was chock full of cars. The docks in Belfast could take no more. They were piling up in the warehouses in California and in the showrooms all over the United States. The production lines were now churning them out at a rate of 80 a day, but sales were running at just half that.

DeLorean had gambled heavily the previous summer when he had taken on 900 extra workers. 2,400 jobs – conveniently rounded up to 2,500 by DeLorean – sounded so much more impressive than 1,500. It indicated to the naive government officials and the outside world that demand was so great he could sell every car he could produce – and more. Against 2,500 jobs, what did a few 'gold facets' matter? But that decision, made to impress potential investors, did more to destroy the DeLorean empire than anything else. Components, wages and overhead were two to three times higher than they should have been for the volume of sales.

In the autumn, the United States auto market fell still deeper into recession than anyone anticipated. DeLorean advertised heavily, but the car itself had not lived up to its promise. At first Dick Brown had certainly been optimistic. He even vetoed an advertisement programme on the grounds that it would be wasted money – the car did not need it.

DeLorean, as usual, was in no mood for caution. It was win or bust. His bloated payroll was rapidly eating up the slender cash reserves, so were sky-high stocks of unsold cars and the cost of financing them. Overheads in Belfast and in New York were huge compared to the size of the company – DeLorean was paying General Motors-size salaries and even more in severance pay. He had built an exceedingly top-heavy organization. He had been able to keep juggling with all the balls in the air while the car remained only a prospect. But it was a reality now, and it was beginning to show badly in the marketplace.

2

Mr. Cryer asked the Secretary of State for Northern Ireland whether any further application for financial assistance had been received from DeLorean Cars Ltd.; and if he will make a statement.

Mr. Adam Butler: No application for selective assistance additional to that already notified to the House has been made by DeLorean Motor Cars Limited. The company has lodged a number of grant claims under the Industrial Investment (General Assistance) (Northern Ireland) Act 1966 (as amended) under which standard grants are payable in respect of eligible capital expenditure. These are under consideration.

Hansard, Written Answers.
October 23, 1981

Just one week after DeLorean had boarded the Concorde to return in triumph to New York, the McKinsey Company delivered its latest Status Report. In stark terms it warned NIDA chief executive Tony Hopkins that 'the relationship between DMC, DMCL and H.M. Government is once again entering a particularly sensitive phase. There is a strong likelihood that the Company will approach NIDA, and through it the Department of Commerce, for further assistance.'

The political difficulties that would ensue, the Status Report cautioned – as if Hopkins were not already aware – 'are clearly considerable – as are the economic risks for the Province if a satisfactory outcome cannot be negotiated.'

That report was dated October 21. Two days later, Butler was fending off Cryer's question and once more refusing his request to file either the British government's agreement with DeLorean (although most of it had already been revealed in

U.S. Securities and Exchange Commission documents related to the planned issue of DeLorean Motor Holdings) or DeLorean's contract with Lotus, in the House of Commons library.

John DeLorean was still desperately anxious to get his stock issue off the ground and that week he insisted to the Northern Irish officials and ministers that he needed all their help. DeLorean asserted that the major point of it was to fund the DMC-24, the four-door sedan that could be launched in 1983-4.

But he also talked openly about the 'tremendous damage done' to his company by two weeks of 'scurrilous allegations' that had led to the delay of that issue. He was still astonishingly optimistic. He continued to exaggerate, tossing about unrealistic figures. For example, he planned to raise production of the car in the following year by 50 percent, he said, which would mean 3,500 to 4,000 jobs at Dunmurry.

The last questions from the SEC on the prospectus would be replied to that week, DeLorean told the officials, and the issue could go ahead quickly. But it had to take place within 90 days, before the need for money for the sedan became urgent.

Once again this was a typically misleading DeLorean statement. The sedan would cost at least $80 million to develop. Bache was already saying that, because of the slump in the car market and the troubles DeLorean was having, they would not now get the $28 million they once hoped for; it would be less than $20 million. Of that, $3.1 million would go to the Limited Partners in DeLorean Research Limited Partnership and another $2.4 million to Oppenheimer in fees. Then there was Bache's fee – DeLorean never mentioned how much he thought that would be, but it wasn't going to be less than Oppenheimer's total. So even if he took in $20 million gross from the stock issue, the company itself would get only between $6 million and $8 million towards its already critical finances. There would be nothing for the sedan, but John's own shares in the company would still have a value of nearly $100 million.

A week after the DPP cleared DeLorean of Marian Gibson's allegations, he was still smarting.

'At the end of the day, it's like being given a certificate to say you're sane. You're still the only one with that certificate,' he said wryly.

DeLorean arrived in London the following Monday, only a week after he had left, and on Tuesday turned up at Earl's Court for the annual Motor Show. The DMC-12 was on display and, with all the controversy of the past weeks, it was getting star attention. For a few hours he stayed on the stand alongside the sales team, then hurried off for talks about the pressing matter of new money.

British government guarantees on £17 million in bank loans from Barclays and Citibank would run out at the end of the year and if DeLorean could not extend those guarantees, then his company would be bankrupt.

Bob Cryer was once again on the prowl, probing the Northern Irish Minister of State, who must have suspected by now that Cryer had a 'deep throat' either in NIDA or the Department of Commerce in Belfast.

Adam Butler could have done without Cryer's insider questions that week. He could also have done without an incident, amusing in retrospect but infuriating at the time, at the Dunmurry plant: the teabreak dispute.

It happened on the Thursday night shift when the workers in the body shop went off for their tea break. There was a problem: no water. The supply to the factory had been interrupted and, without water, there could be no tea.

Disgustedly the night shift workers eventually strolled back into the body shop to find that the foremen had refused to wait for them and had started up some of the machines. The foremen were anxious to catch up with their production targets – there were at that moment no fibreglass body shells in stock.

A shouting match followed as the men strongly objected to supervisors trying to take over their work. When the day shift came on, the shop stewards announced they would mount a token work stoppage. Management reacted by suspending all 250 of the men.

It was one of the few strikes at Dunmurry; the plant had been remarkably calm by British motor industry standards. The striking workers belonged to the Transport and General Workers, whose leader in Northern Ireland was John Freeman, by now deeply worried for the future of the plant. Freeman had a sense of humour: he described the incident as a 'storm in a teacup'. He was right: the workers were all back on the job on Monday, although over the weekend some 700 workers had become involved.

3

At 280 Park Avenue, the storm was in something larger than a teacup. John DeLorean was about to lose another of his senior executives, this time his president and chief executive Eugene Cafiero. In reality, Cafiero had been on the way out since the end of September, just before Marian blew the whistle.

Cafiero had negotiated himself a handsome contract when he joined John DeLorean. Now that he was leaving, he intended to get the full benefit of it. He began work in May 1979 with a five-year contract at $375,000 a year plus options of five million shares (then loosely valued at $10 each). To replace the benefits at Chrysler that he abandoned, DeLorean made him an interest-free loan of $168,000, repayment to be made only if he received benefits from Chrysler. In total, Cafiero got $3,200 from Chrysler – and the remaining $164,800 was now 'forgiven' by DeLorean and treated as compensation.

As the tea break strike was being settled in Northern Ireland, Cafiero's attorneys were drafting a letter for him and DeLorean to sign jointly. It started:

Dear John,
This will confirm my acceptance of the severance offer which you made to me, during the week of September 28th.

It then went on to list the particulars: Cafiero would receive his full $375,000 a year, payable monthly, plus cost of living increases, until May 15, 1984. In turn he would be available as a consultant (in the unlikely event that John would want to consult with him), but would not be required to travel or attend meetings if he did not want to. If DeLorean wished, Cafiero would stay on as president until December 15, 1981. He would also have the use of a DeLorean automobile 'to be delivered not later than November 15' and replaced each year on October 1, while he remained a director – through 1983.

It was remarkable that a company trembling on the brink of bankruptcy and begging the British government for more money would agree to pay its former president some $1.2 million (and more, including pensions and other benefits) in compensation.

Since he had formed the company, DeLorean had lost his senior executives in a steady stream. Bill Haddad had been retrospectively terminated on September 23. That same day, DeLorean's third chief financial officer James G. Stark, after long discussion with Roy Nesseth, had gone on 'medical leave' and never returned, except for fleeting visits. Nesseth was not directly responsible, although Stark was certainly afraid of him.

Bob Dewey resigned again, for the third time. 'The chief financial officer in this company is like a mushroom,' Dewey would remark. 'He's kept in the dark and fed manure.' Dewey negotiated a severance pay for himself of $100,000, but never received it. And DeLorean's false claim that Dewey had suffered a nervous breakdown stayed with him and made his life very difficult. He ended up on the five (later six) man committee of DMC creditors appointed in November 1982.

Bill Collins served John as loyally as he knew how, and was forced out by the deal with Lotus.

Walter Strycker forged the deal with Northern Ireland, but left a year after that; DeLorean did his best to destroy Strycker's reputation, too.

Dick Brown still remained, but only by virtue of the fact that he ran his own operation in California, away from the mainstream. Even he had been removed from the main board of directors. Without Brown the company would not have survived. It was he who had the relationships with the dealers and it was only his efforts at the quality control centres that made the early cars marketable.

Haddad had been fired for objecting too loudly to the formation of the new Holding Company.

Marian Gibson was forced out in the classic DeLorean method of demoting and demoralizing.

In Belfast, Chuck Bennington was sent to Coventry (literally) and was no longer an executive officer of either the Belfast company or DMC. And there were many others, including Terry Werrell and the Collins team.

Who was left on DeLorean's board?

Many of its members had significant financial and professional interests in the company, including DeLorean's closest confidant Tom Kimmerly. The general counsel and his Detroit law firm had a five-year contract for $180,000 a year. In the previous four years, the DeLorean Motor Company had paid his firm $1,077,087 in fees – and Kimmerly, Gans and Shaler, P.C., would be a creditor for the amount of $208,228.51, when the company went bankrupt.

Robert W. Benjamin was a 36-year-old New York lawyer who was also chairman of the audit committee. Benjamin was senior partner of Van Ginkel Benjamin, which in the previous four years had received $221,585 in legal fees and would also be a creditor for $36,631.

There was another lawyer on the board – 39-year-old Henry 'Bombastic' Bushkin, the designee of Johnny Carson. Bushkin's firm had been paid $108,306 in fees since 1978 and he went onto the creditor list for another $4,626.

Between December 1977 and November 1981, DeLorean Motor Company paid out $1.65 million in legal fees to firms in which its own directors were partners – including the New York law firm Javits and Javits, which had first introduced John DeLorean to Oppenheimer, and whose partner Eric Javits was a director until May 1981.

There was another director on the board whose firm benefited from its DeLorean connection. Robert S. Gay was the owner of the insurance agency Robert S. Gay Associates founded in Detroit in 1950. In 1980 alone DeLorean Motor Company paid that firm $857,640 in insurance premiums plus another $58,757 to Swanson Insurance Company, a company controlled by another DeLorean director Richard Swanson. These payments were not improper or even very unusual, just so long as they were declared to the SEC – which they were. It is, however, another illustration of the close business ties of board members to John DeLorean.

Edmund King, 48-year-old head of Wood Gundy, one of the early investors in DeLorean, was also on the board. King arranged the introduction to the Northern Ireland authorities, for which his firm earned a fee.

Alex Fetherston and James Sim were the two directors on the board who represented the British government. They were both Belfast businessmen of some seniority and respect in their own communities. They were paid the modest amount of £5,000 a year for their DeLorean duties (plus $600 a day for every day they spent on audit work that December). The two men were to display their naive assessment of the situation that December by proposing and seconding a motion – approved by the board of DMC in New York and DMCL in Belfast – granting bonuses of $760,000 to the most highly paid men on the team as a reward for their 'excellent' work over the past year. DeLorean, who already had been paid more than $400,000, would get another $101,000. Kimmerly would receive $76,000.

There was another member of the board from whom John DeLorean could also hope for support: Cristina Ferrare DeLorean. She was elected in the boardroom reshuffle the previous year.

The so-called 'Audit Committee', which was supposed to monitor the company's spending and, in particular, the British government's money, consisted of Benjamin as chairman, John DeLorean, Fetherston and Sim, plus Gay and Swanson.

Among the executive directors who remained were Jim Season, a 37-year-old financial man who was overawed by both DeLorean and Kimmerly. There was Buck Penrose, who joined DeLorean from Booz Allen & Hamilton at the height of the Northern Ireland negotiations and who was accused by the others of spending most of his time on DeLorean's outside activities. And there was Edward L. Smith, 56, who ran the plastics company (CTC) and who kept his head down.

That was the composition of the top-heavy, expensive board that John DeLorean had built round himself by October 1981. He was in the thick of his financial crisis.

Despite pressure from NIDA, he still occupied his luxurious offices on Park Avenue.

He was still building his empire with his outside projects: the hot-air engine; the 'boutique' of DeLorean sunglasses, suede jackets, cosmetics, etc.; the Transbus; the snow grooming company.

The DeLorean art collection, in which he had only ever expressed a spasmodic interest, was now piled up in a neglected corner of the 35th floor. NIDA had viewed it with disquiet, expressing the view that if DeLorean had money to buy art for his office, he had money to put into the factory. DeLorean hated that sort of comment. 'I don't need all this,' he once shouted at Tony Hopkins. 'I don't need this car operation at all. It's just a pain in the arse to me. I'm worth maybe fifteen million bucks, and I earn a couple of million a year that has nothing to do with you. I'm not doing this for money, I've got enough already.' Hopkins had quietly stood his ground: 'If you're so rich John, why don't you invest some of it in the car, instead of always asking us for more?' This brought a fresh tirade from DeLorean. But he stopped buying art, probably because he had lost interest. Later he bought the collection back from the company for what one of the creditors' committee called 'a pittance'.

He was still running an office and lifestyle worthy of an organization the size of General Motors. He used the Concorde on his frequent trips to London, stayed at the Connaught – one of the most expensive hotels in the world – and used London's best clubs, charging expenses to the company.

He paid huge salaries to men like Cafiero and Stark when they were barely coming into the office any longer. John DeLorean thought it was nothing less than he deserved, and he resented the continual carping of Tony Hopkins. The prospectus published by Bache showed that in 1980 salaries had doubled to more than $5 million. Travel, entertainment and promotion had risen from $540,000 to $1.1 million. Legal fees that year were $776,000. (Legal fees connected with the Bache issue in 1981 were to be nearly $2,000,000.)

4

Wednesday, October 28, 1981: The Board of the Northern Ireland Development Agency assembled for its monthly meeting at its usual time of 10 a.m. in its Maryfield offices. Dennis Faulkner chaired the meeting. Tony Hopkins, his chief executive, was present to report on DeLorean. NIDA had met twice during the height of the Gibson affair, but this was its first full board meeting since it had all blown up.

NIDA had set up a special Monitoring Committee for its largest investment, but that did not seem to be helping the situation. Hopkins had the latest McKinsey Report as well as his own report on the proceedings of the past month. Both were equally disturbing, but particularly McKinsey's assessment that DeLorean was running into another major cash shortage and would be coming back to them for at least £10 million – probably more. With DeLorean, it always seemed to be more.

But Hopkins brought up another point that morning. The DeLorean company in the United States was no longer holding board meetings. The two Northern Ireland directors did not know what was going on. The Audit Committee was 'not functioning'. The board of NIDA was aghast, knowing full well that they would take the blame for the venture gone wrong.

Hopkins could no longer get information. DeLorean wanted to deal only with the ministers.

But it was still a NIDA responsibility. After all, NIDA had the equity investment and was responsible for monitoring the government money. The meeting was a long one as the board discussed in some despair the possible lines of access to the U.S. company. Trade union leader John Freeman was particularly vocal. But everyone realized how powerless they really were. In New York, DeLorean had boasted openly how he had the British government 'over a barrel'.

No more money would mean that DeLorean would be bankrupt – and £85 million already spent would go down the drain with 2,400 thrown out of work at the factory.

NIDA itself, at this point, was undergoing yet another reorganization. It was to be merged and beefed up with a new board and executive as the Northern Ireland Industrial Development Board.

The feeling that things were going badly had now permeated the factory as well. The *Irish Times* sent a reporter to talk to the workers on the assembly line.

'No way would I buy one of these cars,' said one worker. 'I've seen what I put in, and no way would I pay for it.'

They had complained about the components and been ignored, the men claimed.

'Everybody more or less thinks it's not going to last. Everybody's attitude is "What's the point of complaining? We'll not be here in a few months." If they had anywhere else to go they wouldn't be here.'

They complained that their foremen had been appointed without training and 'haven't got a clue'. One of the stewards was more explicit.

'I didn't think things were all that good. I knew that something was amiss but I didn't think it was misappropriation of funds. I thought that the systems on the floor had no rhyme or reason. They just push the cars out of the door and I thought the cost was astronomical. When you get the heads of departments coming out and physically working on the floor, there is something wrong.'

Someone else said they felt sorry for the finance department. 'There are people working here seven days a week and getting a £12 cheque. It's human error but when there are 300 or 400 human errors a week, there is something wrong.'

The car itself had come in for some poor publicity. Mike Knepper later wrote in *Motor Trend* in July 1982: 'Although the problem with the doors continued, the electrical system soon took over the No 1 spot on the list. It was, as Brown called it, a mess. At the heart of the problem was an alternator that was drastically understrength. Its maximum output was 75 amps, but with all systems running the car could easily draw 80 or 90 amps. Batteries were down and DeLoreans were lying dead all across the country.'

Johnny Carson, his DMC-12 personally delivered by Dick Brown in honour of his $500,000 investment, fell victim to the alternator problem on the very first night he had his car. According to Knepper, who had to do some fast footwork the next day as the press rang him, Carson was stranded 'in plain sight of many adoring fans. His car was replaced by a later production number, and he has apparently since learned to love it.'

The doors on the early models quickly became something more than a joke. An inquisitive DeLorean fan climbed into a DMC-12 at a special display in a Cleveland museum and closed the gull-wing door. He soon regretted this – he couldn't open it again. Nor could anyone else and he was forced to stay there for hours while officials and mechanics worked frantically to extricate him.

'Other recurring problems that seriously damaged the car's early reputation included power windows that fell out of their tracks; fuel gauges that would never register full (sending units and gauges were incompatible); leaking cooling systems; side bolsters that were scuffed and eventually ruined by the doors.

'Not all early customers had lengthy tales of woe, but there were problems with almost every car sold. Some were so bad the company gave the customer a newer model, and actually bought the cars back from two, maybe three, irate owners.'

Early in the autumn, the front suspension on two cars collapsed onto the wheel assembly after a nut gave way. There were then 350 cars on the road; from Park Avenue, John DeLorean sent out 18 people to recall the cars and remedy this problem. He managed it then without having the secret leak out.

But in mid-November, DeLorean had to make a public recall. The nuts holding together parts of the front suspension began to unscrew themselves after just a few thousand miles. There were by then 2,200 cars on the road; there was no way a recall could be done quietly.

The engineers hastily substituted a 'castle' nut with a hole drilled through for a locking pin. Unfortunately, it was soon discovered that the drilling had caused hairline fractures in about 10 percent of the castle nuts that were sent from Belfast to the United States. The whole batch had to be sent back.

Some of the engineers who were concerned about the problems with the front suspension suggested that the car should go back to the drawing board and the suspension redesigned. There was no time for that, insisted DeLorean. But he did consult Porsche in the hope that they might come up with a solution. DeLorean engineers also discovered that some of the anti-roll struts that should have held the suspension rigid were made with the wrong size threads on the end, making them insecure. It was potentially disastrous. If either a nut or an anti-roll strut failed at high speed, the driver would find it difficult to retain control.

At one point, Dick Brown was spending 140 hours fixing up each car. The time involvement then diminished to 68 hours, but $600 per car was still a hefty expense on top of all the other costs the car had to bear.

Brown in California and Lander in Belfast were ensuring that the cars were saleable once they arrived in dealers' showrooms. But they could not easily cure the built-in engineering problems, which Lotus could have solved, given time, and which indeed were mostly solved on later models. Almost all of them were a function of that desperate rush to get the car to market at all costs, even if it meant cutting down testing time and quality control to an unacceptable minimum.

In December the weather turned cold, bringing the worst winter the U.S. had experienced in a century. It was not the time to sell cars, and certainly not sports cars. Sales plummeted.

The frigid weather coincided with the start of a $500,000 DeLorean print advertising campaign designed by the agency of Averett, Free and Fischer. It was the familiar 'Live the Dream' theme.

'Your eyes skim the sleek, sensuous stainless steel body, and all your nerves tell you "I've got to have it".'

Two-page, four-colour ads soon began appearing in the 'high demographic' periodicals: *Business Week, Newsweek, New Yorker, Forbes, Fortune* and the *Wall Street Journal*.

'The DeLorean, surely one of the most wanted automobiles in automotive history,' the ads proclaimed.

Only it was no longer true. In Dunmurry the cars still came off the production lines at 400 a week, but they were beginning to pile up.

5

Wednesday, December 3: John Banham of McKinsey, the members of NIDA and the Commerce officials met to prepare the way for the big show-down meeting with DeLorean scheduled for December 16. It would be only two weeks away from the deadline on the bank guarantees, so they would have DeLorean against the wall.

How to handle him? DeLorean was now asking urgently for an extra £5 million and his guarantees to be extended for another year. For once there was agreement. They must all be 'tough'. No more money. But they would propose extending the guarantees.

McKinsey's November report cheered everyone up. John Banham was suddenly so optimistic that he enclosed a covering note to Tony Hopkins. 'You'll see from the enclosed report that things are looking up,' he wrote, adding that it was 'not beyond the bounds of possibility' that the company could make $40/45 million next year (1982). If Hopkins believed him, he gave no sign to his colleagues. Banham, normally a cool-headed objective expert on both Northern Ireland and the car industry, was allowing his hopes to cloud his otherwise shrewd judgement. The project was an exciting one. Like many others involved, he was willing it to succeed against the rising odds.

The first week in December was a very good one at the factory in Dunmurry. The target of 400 cars was exceeded by three. But in the United States, sales totalled 123 during the first ten days of the month. Production during November had run at roughly twice the level of retail sales. McKinsey was now reporting accurate sales and production figures, although a little late, but not nearly as tardy as the minister Adam Butler, who continued to present the best face for John DeLorean.

The House of Commons, December 3, 3.15 p.m. The Prime Minister had just entered the Chamber for her bi-weekly session of prime minister's Question Time. The previous day, her Chancellor of the Exchequer, Sir Geoffrey Howe, presented a mini-budget that projected price increases of some one to one-and-a-half percent, a disappointing blow for a prime minister pledged to conquer inflation.

As Mrs. Thatcher slid into a seat on the government front bench, her attention was caught by the word 'DeLorean'. At the Dispatch Box was the tall, elegant figure of Adam Butler. From the back benches, Bob Cryer was at it again.

Butler was telling Cryer that the factory in Dunmurry was making 80 DMC-12 cars a day.

Cryer came back with a long and cleverly worded retort.

'Does the minister accept,' he stated in the time-honoured House of Commons fashion, where statements at Question Time must end in a query, 'that it is very much to be hoped that sales [of DeLorean cars] will catch up with output and lead to longer term, stable jobs in the Province?

'As regards public accountability,' Cryer continued, 'given that £80 million of taxpayers' money is involved, will the minister explain why he had failed to tell the House that three members of the Audit Committee have financial interests in the company, according to the minister's own paper, the *Sunday Telegraph*?

'In addition, will he explain why $18 million of taxpayers' money has been spirited abroad to a Panamanian company to pay Lotus Cars, which is in Norwich?'

The *Sunday Telegraph* was *not* Adam Butler's paper, but the wily Cryer knew that Conservative ministers were always more vulnerable to criticism from newspapers they regarded as being on their side.

Butler's reply could scarcely have been worse: 'The honourable gentleman's information about sales and production is erroneous, because sales are running ahead of production. The same comment might well apply to the honourable gentleman's other allegations. I ask him and others who attempt to detract from this exercise not to do so, because they will damage employment prospects in Northern Ireland.'

He sat down and Mrs. Thatcher rose as the Speaker called out the first questioner, the Conservative Tim Brinton, for prime minister's Question Time.

It is not suggested here that Adam Butler was trying to mislead the House. Clearly, he believed what he said.

Butler was to retain his confidence to the very end. Only a few hours before DeLorean was arrested for drug smuggling, the minister was interviewed in his Belfast office. He still insisted that DeLorean essentially was not dishonest. DeLorean, in Butler's view, was a marketing man; some of his more optimistic statements could be ascribed to that. In negotiations he was a bully and tough, but that was understandable.

In New York DeLorean was preparing for his big meeting with NIDA and with the Northern Ireland Secretary of State, Jim Prior himself. On Monday, December 14, he would fly to London. But now he assembled his board and senior staff, including Brown from California, for a major meeting. He produced a document listing the demands he was going to make of the British.

DeLorean could be foul-mouthed and savage about people who got in his way. 'He stood up and went through a long dissertation,' recalls Dick Brown, 'and he called the Northern Irish and British all sorts of derogatory names – ugly, dirty, filthy names. Things you would hear on 42nd Street. Just really bad names. And his theme was that they were going to do it his way.'

According to Brown, DeLorean told those at the meeting, 'We are going to do this thing the way we want to do it. We are going to keep the New York office, and keep California and keep all our operations. And if they don't like it, we'll close the plant.'

He was still going to ask the British for $60 million to build the sedan, DeLorean announced. Brown described him as almost childlike that day, a quality he had noticed before about him.

'He has fits of anger just like a child. But the thing is that we had no parent disciplining him, so as long as he got away with it, he continued to test the water even more.

'John was a great trial balloon guy. He would say these crazy things. But if nobody challenged him, he would go even further. As if he was a child. Who knows what a child would be like if he had no discipline whatever? It was destruct, destroy, call names, fight, scream, holler. If nobody ever stops him, what does he become?'

The new Northern Ireland Secretary Jim Prior had not yet met John DeLorean, although he was well briefed by his own officials and colleagues. From his residence at Hillsborough it was a brief drive to Dunmurry, and he arrived for his visit right on time at ten the following Monday morning. Don Lander greeted him – but DeLorean was late, just as he had been for that very first meeting in Northern Ireland back in 1978. A wiser man would have flown in the night before and stayed overnight. DeLorean never did that. He caught his usual shuttle from London but it was delayed. By the time he got to Dunmurry, Prior had finished his tour of the factory.

Lander and his team had the place in shining order. The full workforce, except for the night shift, was on display, the cars coming smoothly enough off the production lines. Prior, however, had been round many a factory in his day, both in Britain and abroad; he had visited some of the best Japanese factories, and American ones, too. And he saw instantly that there were too many people here. 'What the hell are they all doing?' he wondered aloud to an aide. He voiced the same question to Lander more formally, adding 'with all these people, you either have to step up production or cut back'. 'We're going to step up production,' said Lander, repeating the plan DeLorean had persuaded him to accept.

In the couple of hours before DeLorean arrived, Prior was increasingly impressed, despite his misgivings. There was an enthusiasm about the workers, not just put on for a Tory Minister for whom Catholics had no love. Lander explained why the early cars had been poor, why Brown had had to set up those quality assurance centres.

Prior had made no secret of the fact that he had been prejudiced against DeLorean before he even met the man. It was noon by the time DeLorean got there and for the next hour, before Prior left, the two treated each other cordially but formally. There was no bargaining; Prior simply reiterated what DeLorean had heard indirectly from him already – there was no more money for the existing project. DeLorean mentioned that he had other projects including the sedan car in which he was interested. Prior did not reject them out of hand. 'I think the government will want to be doubly certain that there is a future for anything else you propose but it is up to you to put forward proposals.'

Prior had seen the latest McKinsey report and was impressed by that too. DeLorean managed to get in a few highly optimistic comments of his own.

'In the first six months of sales,' he told the minister, 'more than 3,000 cars were sold to retail customers. It took Mercedes five years to reach this sales level in America, BMW 11 years, Porsche 13 years and your own Jaguar 17 years.' He had some $70 million of cars on the ground, with dealers clamouring for them. He just had no liquidity, he told Prior. 'Things look great – we are oversold. We have orders of 5,000 against a production capacity next quarter of only 3,800 units.'

A few days later DeLorean was again on the agenda at a Cabinet committee meeting in Whitehall. Prior proposed that the government should renew the guarantee. At present HMG was guaranteeing £17 million of bank borrowings which would run out at the end of the year, but DeLorean was only actually utilizing £8.5 million of the guarantees. 'I propose we renew for ten,' said Prior. Reluctantly his colleagues agreed.

DeLorean had won at his first meeting with his third Northern Ireland Secretary of State. Prior, unsympathetic before they met, had actually argued his case for him. But it was to be a costly victory for DeLorean. It was not many weeks before Prior discovered he had been misled, and that he in turn had unwittingly misled the Cabinet committee.

CHAPTER EIGHTEEN

Receivership

John DeLorean had been defeated by Tony Hopkins over the issue of being able to sell his own shares during the summer. That had been his only real setback in his dealings in Northern Ireland so far. True, it had become steadily tougher each time he came back and asked for more money. But by pleading, threatening, or blackmail – or a combination of all three – he had usually triumphed. He had not got any more money off Jim Prior – but he had persuaded the minister to support him, and that was no mean achievement. Prior, however, had yet to be tested in real battle – and a full-scale Waterloo was now looming. Back in New York, DeLorean began to stake out the high ground. He started with a statement that unless he got the $26 million of export financing 'to which we're entitled', he would take a 'strong look at curtailing our operations by cutting production and jobs dramatically'. Once again he was presenting a setback as something else, something it was not.

'All the politicians are scared to deal with us now,' he said.

By then, he must have known what was happening to sales, had to know that he could not indefinitely go on churning out cars that no one would buy. He would have to cut back production within days rather than months, even if he got all the money in the Bank of England.

There was a lull in the factory during Christmas week. But during the following week, DeLorean insisted that the Dunmurry factory go back to full blast. In the week ending January 4, it produced 315 cars. But then came crisis after crisis.

Bache Halsey could not get the public stock issue off the ground and, on January 6, asked for a postponement. It was the end of the issue – and with it went John DeLorean's paper fortune of $120 million. If the stock offering had been less ambitious and more saleable DeLorean might have been able to hold onto something. Now he owned half of nothing. DeLorean Motor Holdings, which had cost nearly $2 million in fees and countless hours of executive time – the SEC documents alone were more than 12 inches thick – died.

John DeLorean began to look for a partner, some 'good, solid organization that would provide us with some of the facilities that we as a company lack'. The Northern Irish were horrified. His agreement stipulated he could not sell any of his shares.

Only now did it become apparent how important Marian Gibson's intervention had been. The Bache issue had missed the window.

'We had to do it last July or August,' admitted DeLorean. That had been the original intention – but it was Tony Hopkins's stubbornness over DeLorean's rights to be able to sell his shares which had caused the issue to miss the window.

Would it have helped DeLorean if the issue had gone ahead?

The net amount the automobile company would have received was probably no more than $10 million, and that was supposed to go toward the sedan version of the car. In mid-January, DeLorean was short of $50 to $60 million and it was getting worse day by day as inventories overflowed and cars were not sold.

Now came a series of hard blows. The most serious was dealt by the Bank of America, which through Dick Brown's good offices had provided a $33 million line of credit. In December, DeLorean asked the bank to increase it and announced that the Bank of America had agreed to go up to $47 million. This was all export credit – the Bank of America was financing the cars themselves, lending money against the collateral of actual cars once they were shipped out of Belfast.

There was a safety clause that tied the amount of money it lent DeLorean to the sales volume generated by the dealers. For weeks, as the cars piled up in the showrooms, the bank had not exercised that safety clause. But in early January, it took that option. Instead of its hoped-for $47 million of credit, the company suddenly had only $24 million. The cash crisis deepened dramatically.

It also meant that a shipment of cars already at sea and valued in Belfast at nine million pounds had not been paid for – although the master agreement signed in 1978 stipulated very clearly that no cars must leave Belfast without being paid for, a safeguard designed to ensure that DMC bore the cost of unsold cars in America and that the Belfast company got its revenues on time.

Another shipment of six million pounds worth of cars was ready to go. It was cancelled. The flow of cars across the Atlantic had now stopped, but the production lines were still running and the stocks of cars began to build up in Belfast.

John DeLorean boasted of how 6,500 cars worth £85 million were shipped from Belfast. Indeed, they had been, but 4,000 of them were in inventories and 1,655 of them were with dealers.

The company was now running at an annual cash shortfall of some $50 million. Even at twice the rate of sales achieved during the months the car was on the market, there would still have been a loss. And sales, far from improving, were getting worse.

Belfast, January 11, 1982. When they arrived at work in Dunmurry, the men got the news they had been dreading: the factory was going on short-time. That week they would work only three days. DeLorean had found a convenient excuse to explain it to the outside world: there was a strike on the Sealink Ferry from mainland Britain that carried some vital components. But no one really believed it – certainly no one at the factory.

The panic that had set in with the first reports of Marian Gibson's revelations now began to spread. Across the United States the weather worsened. And during the first week of January, 100 DMC-12's sold. This was better than the 25 sold the previous week, but it was still hopelessly low. In Dunmurry, working on their part-time basis, the men made 60 cars.

But shipments had stopped. The factory now had no revenue. Unless DeLorean could arrange that export financing, not a single car could move from Belfast to its market in the United States.

The unions in Northern Ireland were getting restive and supported the government's attempts to force a showdown. It was an unusual alliance: trade unions alongside a Tory government.

DeLorean was tough: his body armour was impervious to the

criticisms of the officials at NIDA, whom he regarded with vague contempt. His remarkable capacity for self-delusion and his ability to convince himself that he was always right, that he had been let down by others or betrayed or deflected by incompetence, remained with him to the end of the project. John DeLorean had believed that only he at General Motors had glimpsed the truth, only to him had Divine Providence shown where the American auto industry was going wrong. His attitude now, as he moved toward his worst crisis, had not changed.

There was no hope of raising money from any banks. Bank of America had pulled the plug, and no one would touch him now. There was no chance of a private issue, no hope of a big investor. It would take too long to develop, and the money would be too late. But he still worked on it, as he always had.

He believed his one real hope lay with the British Export Credit Guarantee Department (ECGD), and he had been bombarding ministers, officials and everyone he thought could be useful with letters and telex messages about how much he deserved and needed the credit. It was a 'completely secured loan so far as the British government is concerned – secured by the cars themselves', he claimed.

The British government was less convinced. Export credit money was still government money, and there would be no more of it for DeLorean. In the Treasury, ministers including Jock Bruce-Gardyne were arguing that the time to cut a bad investment 'is always now'.

On Monday, January 18, Don Lander and Joe Daly travelled to London from Belfast to persuade the ECGD to lend the needed $70 million. Lander was an impressive representative, far more so than DeLorean himself under the circumstances. The Canadian was well known in London after his years running the British Chrysler operation, which had actually received far more money from the British taxpayer than DeLorean ever did.

Lander was out of the Strycker/Brown/Collins mould – a straight, successful, professional auto-man who was not particularly interested in building a vast private empire for himself. His reputation was strong enough to withstand his involvement with DeLorean. His big failing was his inability to stand up to

DeLorean, notably over the doubling of the workforce the previous summer which he must have known would damage the company. The Lotus people too found him weak, continuing to prefer Bennington (this relationship outlasted the DeLorean venture), regarding him as more of a politician than a real car-man. Prior, Cork and his own team, however, liked him.

Daly was the financial man, out of his depth and hating the limelight and publicity. He never quite knew what his responsibilities were. DeLorean kept promoting him to acting chief financial officer of the New York company, even though he was in Belfast, and then demoting him again when a new financial officer was hired.

John DeLorean caught the Concorde flight on Tuesday and arrived in London that evening. Before he left, he received another shock. Bill Haddad had lodged a $19 million suit against him, alleging slander, libel, fraud and 'malicious termination of employment for reasons contrary to public policy'. If it came to court, there would be a lot of nasty revelations that would do DeLorean no good.

When he arrived in London, there was not much to cheer him up. Even the luxury of the Connaught Hotel did little to keep out the February chill. As he was arriving, the morning papers had picked up the 'performance bonuses' voted to DeLorean, Kimmerly and other senior executives in December. That did nothing for the atmosphere, either.

DeLorean had ordered the factory back onto a five-day work week, in hopes of reviving some of the flagging confidence. But on that Tuesday, Adam Butler announced that the government was arranging 'major reviews' of the relationship with DeLorean. The government was furious about the bonuses, desperately embarrassed that they had actually been recommended by its own representatives on the DeLorean Board.

The *Financial Times* published a strong editorial that concluded, 'Further financial backing would be a disservice not only to the taxpayer but also to the company's employees; there is no security in jobs which depend on permanent government subsidy.'

John DeLorean himself was in Belfast, harping on his familiar theme of how unfairly the government was treating him.

'We're a political football,' he claimed. His main complaint was that inflation clause in the master agreement. DeLorean had been given £14 million under its terms; but it was a loan, not a grant. He figured he deserved it as grant money.

DeLorean talked to Tony Hopkins and his team at NIDA and to the Department of Commerce. He talked to the unions, indicating he was 'not optimistic'. On Wednesday, he was back in London to meet Jim Prior, Hopkins and Ken Bloomfield, the Permanent Secretary at the Department of Commerce.

Meanwhile, Prior was at Number Ten Downing Street for a Cabinet meeting where he brought up the entire issue of DeLorean with the Treasury ministers. He was irritated. He had argued DeLorean's case in December on the basis of the more cheerful figures. Now there were no cheerful figures, only gloom. DeLorean, he told his colleagues ruefully, had misled him, and he unwittingly had in turn misled them. He had been placed in a position of falseness with his Cabinet colleagues – and in Cabinet politics, where the stakes are especially high, that was bad news for Prior's already delicate standing. He did have the saving grace that by reducing the guarantees from £17 million to £10 million he had saved the Government a bit of money – and he tried to concentrate on that. But it was an uncomfortable meeting for him. DeLorean was going to pay for it.

Late that Wednesday evening DeLorean went to the Northern Ireland Office in London, an unmarked building at the back of the Treasury, overlooking St. James's Park. Prior was grim-faced, unfriendly – and uncompromising. The situation, he told DeLorean sternly, was 'difficult and disappointing'. It had come as a 'considerable shock' to him after the optimistic reports he had received just before Christmas. What on earth had changed so much in a month? DeLorean could not expect any help from him if he misled him in this way.

Prior is no gentle Humphrey Atkins, or naive Roy Mason. In his own way he is one of the most formidable politicians in Britain, so formidable indeed that Margaret Thatcher, despite her intense dislike for him, could not directly sack him from the Cabinet. He is not a man lightly to be crossed and, under the full force of his anger, most men would have quailed. John

DeLorean was not 'most men', however. He not only ignored Prior's recriminations, but came back with some of his own. He had now finally asked Prior for more money – £47 million of it in fact. In return he was still refusing to give an inch to NIDA's demands: no renegotiation of the Master Agreement, no reorganization of royalties, no concessions. Prior ripped into that. It was a long, angry, and heated exchange, with DeLorean continually playing the only card he now had left – closure of the factory. 'Closure does not change the situation,' said Prior. There would be no more money.

It was late in the meeting when Prior revealed his counter-proposal. He had been saving it to see how DeLorean would react. Now he unveiled it.

'You say your wish is to ensure the project's success,' he said finally. 'Well, it's mine too. I propose therefore that the DeLorean company in Belfast should invite an eminent accountant and solvency expert, who would be assisted by his own large firm, to look at the business. We would give him say, two weeks, to report on whether the company, in its present form, or indeed in any restructured form, could continue with any hope of commercial success. I have in mind Sir Kenneth Cork, who I have already approached – and he is standing by for your invitation. If you accept, you would also have to give an undertaking that until the end of the investigation, any transactions would have to be for cash only at the company.'

DeLorean barely knew who Sir Kenneth Cork was. But it did not take him long to work out the implications. 'That is tantamount to receivership,' he told Prior. 'It would completely destroy the business. How could we ever raise the money we need with a receiver in the factory?' After some more shouting, Prior had to go to the House for a vote, and DeLorean took the opportunity to talk to his colleagues. Lander filled him in on Cork – and what he heard only filled DeLorean with even greater dread.

That evening Sir Kenneth had a telephone call from a Northern Ireland Office official. DeLorean, he was told, had to catch the Concorde flight back to New York early the following morning. Could Sir Kenneth see him for breakfast? Eight o'clock at the Connaught? 'Well,' replied Sir Kenneth, 'in these circumstances it's more usual for people to come and see me.' But there was protest from the other end. Cork relented, although with poor grace. He lived in Great Missenden, and never ate breakfast anyway. It meant leaving home exceptionally early to get into town by eight in the London traffic. And Cork was doing the job more as a favour to Prior than for any other reason.

Prior and DeLorean met again half an hour later. DeLorean still protested that the minister had not given enough consideration to his requests and to the other points he had raised. But he would call a board meeting for both companies in New York the following Monday. It was late when they finally broke up.

For many years, Sir Kenneth Cork had been 'Mr. Receiver' in London industrial and financial circles. His firm, Cork Gully, had moved from ordinary audit and accounting work to specialize in receivership and had blossomed in the early 1970s when Britain suffered a banking and real estate plunge comparable to Wall Street's 1929 crash.

At 67, Cork was a tall, owl-like man whose lugubrious expression could change in a flash when a grin spread across his features. He had been Lord Mayor of London, a year-long position achieved only by the most established figures in the very establishment City of London. Cork had been involved with the precursor of NIDA, the Northern Ireland Finance Corporation, and had a connection with the Province.

Quite a number of companies had been salvaged through the process of receivership. Rolls Royce had been through the process. Receivership is a curious British institution. It is a limbo, halfway between viability and liquidation. A company in receivership is suspended, in a sense; the creditors are unable to foreclose and seize the assets while the receiver tries to realize as much as he can for them. The principle is that the components of a company are often worth more on a going-concern basis than on a forced liquidation.

Unlike a liquidator, a receiver has the power to carry on 'business as usual'. In fact, he has almost unlimited power in a company to which he is appointed. He is president, chairman, chief executive and financial officer – all rolled into one. No money goes out or comes in, except through him.

Shareholders – in this case, John DeLorean – have no power whatsoever over the receiver. He must answer in the long run to the creditors, but in the short run, while the receiver sorts out plans and proposals, he is in full charge.

Cork, the next morning, was at the Connaught by the appointed time and ordered a cup of coffee. No sign of DeLorean. 8.15 arrived and still no DeLorean. Cork fumed. Finally, at 8.20, the American swept in with his entourage, including Tom Kimmerly and Don Lander. Brief introductions were made and as he sat down, DeLorean looked across the table at Cork.

'Sir Kenneth, I want to ask your advice.'

'Yes, Mr. DeLorean, what is it?'

'I want to sue your government for £50 million for war damages and criminal damages and breach of contract and other things. And what I want to know is, do I do that before or after you write your report?'

Afterwards, Cork said he wished he had thought of a brilliant reply; but, considering his surprise, he did not do badly.

'Well, it depends, Mr. DeLorean, on how much money you've got.'

'What's it got to do with how much money I've got?'

'Well, Mr. DeLorean, you're going to lose it. So if you sue after my report, you may keep it in your pocket a little longer.'

There were no more facetious remarks after that. But Cork found John DeLorean unpleasantly arrogant.

Cork pointed out that DeLorean's claims for the damages he was talking about – bombings of his factory and disruption – were arbitrated in the courts. To get the money, one had to go through the entire legal process. Few genuine claims were rejected, he said. In fact, it was quite the opposite, since the British government fought to keep industry alive in Ulster.

After half an hour, DeLorean had to leave for his flight.

Don Lander, watching the performance, was appalled. He knew the weight Cork carried in government and City circles, even if DeLorean did not. As they walked out of the hotel, Lander followed Cork and apologized for DeLorean's rudeness.

In Belfast the unions, watching the toing and froing with growing unease, were now taking a hand – a helpful one.

'We told DeLorean he'd have to be realistic,' said George Clark, a union official. 'We told him to keep his feet on the ground. But he's overshot the mark with too much production.'

Suppliers in Northern Ireland were now laying off workers, too. CP Trim, a firm set up to support DeLorean Motors, halved its workforce and would soon close, with 220 left unemployed. Renault announced from Paris that it was tightening up its credit to DeLorean; without Renault credit for its engines, there was an even worse squeeze.

McKinsey was hastily asked by a desperately worried Tony Hopkins to report on three points: why had the expected cash shortfall doubled from £10 million to £20 million in January, when did DeLorean know about the sales drop in the States – was he hiding it from them, what were the prospects now?

John DeLorean flew home on Thursday. Prior had given him seven days to accept the appointment of Sir Kenneth Cork – or find a backer. DeLorean was furious. But, during that weekend, both sides faced up to the serious prospect of bankruptcy.

John DeLorean prepared yet again for the Concorde flight to London, but first he summoned his board from Belfast for a final meeting before the great confrontation – a move that did nothing to mollify opinion in Northern Ireland. James Kilfedder, a witty, boisterous Northern Irish MP, pinned down the unfortunate Butler shortly afterward in the House of Commons.

> Is it not remarkable and scandalous that the DeLorean company, which is in such financial jeopardy that it is seeking more taxpayers' money, should have provided Mr. DeLorean with first-class travel by Concorde to New York and back for one meeting and first-class travel for seven directors from Belfast to New York for one meeting, at a total cost of £15,000? Will that matter be investigated?

The British government was in an unenviable position. By its critics on the right, it was being blamed for supporting DeLorean at all. The government knew it would be accused by the left of pulling out too early when another £10 or £20 million might have made the previous £85 million investment all worthwhile. DeLorean was touting the latter point for all he was worth, but he was constantly undermined by events – the cars were now being offered at discounts all over the United States. Belfast officials were getting dealer reports that prices of the DMC-12 were being cut sharply. An advertisement appeared in the *Arkansas Gazette* offering $1,500 off. The Dallas *Morning News* featured an ad urging prospective buyers to enquire about special discounts on an 'excellent selection' of the gull-wing sports car.

In the event DeLorean's board meetings did not take place the following Monday. It was Tuesday, January 26, when they finally met: 22 of them, every single director of both companies except for Henry Bushkin and Cristina (who never attended board meetings). From Belfast he summoned Lander (a director of both companies), Jim Sim and Alex Fetherston (representing NIDA on the DMC board), and Myron Stylianides, Shaun Harte and Joe Daly, all directors of the Belfast company. Gene Cafiero turned up for this crucial meeting; and so did Jim Stark – both were still directors although they had played no part since September. There was Tom Kimmerly, of course, who as secretary kept the minutes; Edmund King of Wood Gundy flew in from Toronto; Robert Gay and Richard Swanson came from Detroit and Dick Brown from California (a director still of DMCL but not of the parent). There was the young lawyer Robert Benjamin; and Edward Smith who ran Composite Technology in Detroit; and Jim Season, a young financial man at DMC. There were also two non-directors: the Belfast lawyer Robin Bailie – and Roy Nesseth.

It was in short a full gathering of the clans. There were too many for the boardroom in Park Avenue, although DeLorean could have used (as he often did) the Boardroom Club one floor down. He hired a room at the Waldorf Astoria and at ten o'clock opened the meeting with what one director later described as 'a vicious attack on the British government and those who worked for it'. The minutes of the meeting, carefully kept by Kimmerly, show it as ordered and sensible. Jim Sim, however, reported back differently to Jim Prior the next day: 'It was a circus, a shambles and orchestrated.' DeLorean, according to Sim, said he had been 'badly received' by Prior the previous week and had been insulted. DeLorean himself, according to the minutes, seemed to worry more about the government 'leaking' stories.* He stated, say the minutes, 'that everything we tell to the government gets into publication, a sentiment in which many other directors concurred. Mr. DeLorean said that this has convinced him that the failure of all government controlled businesses is a self-fulfilling prophecy.'

There must have been an extraordinary air of unreality in that room in the Waldorf Astoria that day. Here was the company on the verge of collapse, the whole edifice about to crumble. Yet there was DeLorean going over and over the same stony ground. 'Mr. DeLorean stated that if we had been paid what is due us we would not have a problem,' wrote Kimmerly in the minutes. He also recorded a surprising sympathy with Prior's stance. 'The Secretary thinks that we lied to him in order to get the recent £10 million loan guarantees. Mr. DeLorean stated that in retrospect, he might think the same way.'

Joe Daly produced some wholly unrealistic cash forecasts, showing the company surprisingly solvent and Stark spoke up a few times, although for some reason in keeping the minutes Kimmerly kept mixing Stark up with the Ulsterman Jim Sim. Stark – or was it Sim? – had a nephew who worked for Cork and he could tell the meeting that the man was a liquidator whose appointment would create 'a seriously harmful impression'. However, despite some sweeping statements (according to the minutes) to the effect that it would be better to shut down than turn the business over to Sir Kenneth Cork, it was finally agreed he should be provided with information at least – although nothing more. 'Members of the board were as usual compliant,' reported Sim to Prior, 'and didn't raise a voice against him.' He did, however, report that 'There were some signs that the board was becoming more realistic than it had been in the past.' It does not say a great deal for previous board meetings.

---

* This does have a circus-like ring about it. Several of the main 'leakers', to our certain knowledge, were actually in the room with him, presumably nodding their concurrence at that very moment. The government itself was remarkably tight on DeLorean, reckoning, as GM discovered back in 1973, that the leaker in many cases was John DeLorean himself.

It was late in the evening when DeLorean arrived at Whitehall the following day after yet another Concorde flight. He went straight in to see Prior. It was one o'clock in the morning when he emerged. It had been a tough experience for both men. There had been various breaks in the meeting while both sides considered one proposal or another. The press release issued in the early hours set out the results of five hours of talks: Sir Kenneth Cork had agreed to prepare a report within fourteen days. If he concluded that the project could be restructured in a way that would make it still viable – almost certainly at a lower production level – then the government might support that. No promises, of course.

DeLorean would have to co-operate and make considerable concessions. Cut down his lifestyle that attracted so much adverse publicity. Move out of his ridiculously pretentious office. And above all, find some money from one of those mythical buyers he always had in the background. In the meantime, the factory would have to cut back sharply, preferably the following day.

DeLorean did not give in without a fight. He had bluffed Humphrey Atkins by threatening to take the government to court and got an extra £14 million. Now he tried it again, insisting he was owed £10 million for criminal damages to his factory. There was war damage and the adjustment for inflation, he argued, and credit guarantees that should have been automatic and that were always promised to him. He had had his lawyers prepare a case and would take the government to the European courts, he threatened. Prior was not impressed. DeLorean could sue if he liked, but in the meantime, Sir Kenneth was going to prepare his report.

The next morning, a bizarre incident occurred – a moment of high comedy in a time of corporate tragedy. It was ten in the morning in London and Belfast, but two o'clock in Los Angeles where Dick Brown was sleeping when the phone rang. It was a call from Belfast. Brown, still anxious about the quality of the car, had sent over a seven-man team to oversee the production line, headed by Doug Paterson. It was Paterson, in some distress, who was calling him now.

He had just ended an early morning meeting with Don

Lander and the other staff at Dunmurry, Paterson said, and there had been an uproar. John DeLorean had called up to tell Lander to pull Brown's quality control people off the line and let the cars go through 'regardless of quality'.

Paterson had been there just a month and was making a fight, but he wanted Brown's support. As he talked, Brown suddenly heard another conversation coming in on top of them. It sounded like a crossed line, and he recognized the voice – it was John DeLorean!

'Hold on a minute,' he said to Paterson as he heard his own name mentioned. 'Doug, just a minute – I'm overhearing another conversation. Hold on, I'll be back to you – don't hang up.'

Brown listened in for half an hour with Paterson hanging on at the other end, unable to hear anything. Brown came back to Paterson every so often to insist he stay there and not break the connection. What he was overhearing was an extraordinary conversation. Brown knew DeLorean was at the Connaught in London. He was speaking to Roy Nesseth in Huntingdon Beach, California, only ten miles from Brown's home.

All Brown's recent suspicions that his phone might have been tapped revived dramatically. His wife had been complaining for weeks that there was something strange about it.

The words that had caught his attention were John DeLorean's: 'Don't tell Brown, don't tell Brown.'

A shaken Dick Brown heard DeLorean order Nesseth to make arrangements to get ships over to Northern Ireland and clean out the plant, take parts, machinery, cars, everything and ship it, 'but don't tell Brown'. It seemed that DeLorean had decided that once the receiver went in he would lose control over those assets, but if he could get them to the United States, he could still sell them and would leave the receiver nothing more than an empty factory.

Brown never discovered if his phone really was tapped. But it seemed an incredibly strange coincidence that he should cross-connect with DeLorean and Nesseth.

When DeLorean went home, Cork went to Belfast, feeling jaundiced against the whole operation.

What he saw there, however, caused him to think again. The

factory was first class. Lander and his team, despite everything, were hard working and dedicated. Cork began to feel they might make a go of it, if they could get the financial structure right.

In his years as a receiver, Cork had seen many similar situations – a perfectly good operation that could be viable with half the employees, a quarter of the overhead and without the enormous burden of interest charges on borrowings.

Clearly there was not a market for 20,000 cars a year, but there might be for 8,000 or so. Keep the best men, make it a lean, tight operation and maybe it could go on, although it would still need an injection of cash from outside. Prior had made it very clear to Cork from the beginning that any proposal he put forward must start on the premise that there was no more government money.

In Belfast that weekend, 1,100 of the 2,400 employed had been laid off. In New York, DeLorean gave a press conference at which he said he had a 'serious offer' from an American company that would solve his difficulties.

'We do have a short-term liquidity problem,' he admitted. 'But rest assured, DeLorean is here to stay.'

And then he endeared himself even less to those in Belfast who were desperately trying to save him.

'Looking back,' he said nonchalantly, 'I probably made a mistake in going to Belfast.'

In February, as Cork worked on his report with a team of accountants who looked at every angle, the factory went onto a one-day work week.

On February 5 Sir Freddie Laker went bust. Meanwhile *The Times* was being threatened with closure by its new owner, Rupert Murdoch. DeLorean should have been off the front pages.

DeLorean suddenly made public his claim for £10 million in damage to the plant as a result of terrorist incidents. He had been 'told to stay away from windows when at the facility' and that 'bullets had landed in the area'. He went on to say that there had been a total of 140 firebombings at the factory and that executives had been the targets of sniper attacks.

140 incidents? No one could believe it. DeLorean himself wouldn't even stay overnight in the place, insisting to his staff that the 'Brits want me out of here by nightfall – I'm a target.'

In fact, he never was a target. And there was only one serious incident – at the height of the Bobby Sands hunger strike. For the damage done then, DeLorean had got £425,000.

An investigation showed there were scattered incidents when petrol bombs, no more than milk bottles half-full of petrol, had been thrown in over the perimeter fence. There had been no sniper incidents – not a single one. It was pure make-believe!

Tuesday, February 9. Sir Kenneth finished his report. It was not unhelpful to John DeLorean – in fact, it was astonishingly supportive under the circumstances. But Cork showed the true financial picture. In 1981, instead of the profit about which DeLorean still boasted, losses amounted to £23.1 million and the share capital had been wiped out. There had been a huge outflow of money from Belfast to New York with virtually all operations there paid for by British money.

DeLorean had a report of his own prepared at the same time by the accounting firm of Peat Marwick Mitchell & Company, and was now busily passing that document round. It showed that if operations were cut back and an injection of £20 million made, the business would become profitable. This was the basis for John DeLorean's search for new money that week. He kept repeating to Cork – who went to see him in New York and was astonished by the grandeur of the offices – and to everyone else, that he had buyers lined up to help.

That evening, in an office under the shadow of St. Paul's Cathedral in the City of London, Sir Freddie Laker was in conference with the man whom he hoped would bail him out. Tiny Rowland was the Chief Executive of Lonrho, a British conglomerate with mines, ranching and trading interests all over Africa. Lonrho also owned the Sunday newspaper the *Observer* plus 30 percent of the retail group House of Fraser which owned Harrods.

Rowland was a remarkable businessman. His interests ranged from gold mines in South Africa and the *Observer* newspaper in London to the Princess Acapulco, bought from his close friend, Daniel K. Ludwig, the 'world's richest man'.

Rowland had a penchant for lame ducks and, by coincidence, had met DeLorean ten years before. One of the companies Rowland bought for his Lonrho Group was Wankel, the rotary engine group. At one point he had gone to Detroit to see Ed Cole, who brought DeLorean into the talks with him when General Motors was planning a major push on Wankel engines. Unfortunately for Rowland, the oil crisis intervened and the Wankel was not particularly fuel efficient. But DeLorean told him afterwards that if it were not for the huge increase in the price of oil, 'Lonrho would be as big as GM.' Now, DeLorean turned again to Rowland.

Rowland was lecturing Sir Freddie on why things had gone wrong for him. 'Your problem is that you've been selling ten dollar bills for nine dollars and sooner or later that catches up with you.'

The phone rang.

'Hi,' said John DeLorean. 'This is Margaret Thatcher's biggest headache. I've got a deal for you – the biggest you've ever made.'

Rowland laughed appreciatively.

DeLorean went to the Cheapside office and spent two hours in the boardroom with Rowland while colleagues worked down the hallway on a plan to rescue Laker. Rowland set Laker up again in a new business. But he refused DeLorean.

Cork's scheme was very generous to DeLorean. DeLorean Motor Company could lease all the production facilities and tooling in Belfast simply by assuming two long term notes: a Department of Commerce loan (with no interest for two years) of £14 million, and £7.72 million of 14-year mortgage, also with a possible interest freeze. It came to roughly £20 million. The finished and unfinished cars, worth $30 million, would be paid for as they were shipped.

All it required was for DeLorean to come up with that famous investor of his to put up working capital.

Jim Prior studied Sir Kenneth Cork's report over the weekend of February 13-14 and then telexed DeLorean to come in and see him as soon as possible. He wanted DeLorean in London on Monday. DeLorean stalled, insisting he needed more time. He could not be there until Wednesday, he replied, when he would have his buyer and the money.

Prior was furious, but he had other things on his hands that week. He was persuading his Cabinet colleagues to adopt a daring plan for Northern Ireland involving an elected assembly, a sort of rolling devolvement from direct rule by Westminster for the Province. He achieved it, and later was to regret it bitterly. Ironically, the elections would take place on the very day that John DeLorean was arrested in California.

On Tuesday, DeLorean sent over Robert Benjamin, head of the audit committee. Benjamin took a DeLorean team consisting of the Belfast lawyer Robin Bailie and Don Lander along with him to see Cork. DeLorean himself arrived on Wednesday, too late for a scheduled meeting with Prior, which had to be cancelled. This time he checked in at Claridges; one of his 'prospects', whom he hoped might come up with the money, was staying at the hotel.

Cork met DeLorean that night. Time had run out, Cork told him. The choice was a bald one: either DeLorean could now accept his offer of a voluntary receivership, or the British government would appoint a receiver anyway.

Cork explained the details of the scheme he had worked out in New York the previous week. It was an ingenious arrangement. A new company would be set up. It would either lease the factory and equipment or take over the outstanding debts; revenues from the sales of the completed cars would go to the old company. Perhaps most important of all, DMC in New York would pay for those cars that had left Northern Ireland without payment; they would be paid for as and when they were sold. But to make it work, Cork had decided that DMC in New York would need a cash injection, and it would not come from outside. John DeLorean must put at least $5 million of his own personal money into DMC. Reluctantly, DeLorean agreed. But he continued to protest strongly against the appointment of a receiver. He had a backer, 'the head of an Arab state' who would put up $30 million over the next few days, perhaps even the very next day.

By now Cork was getting used to DeLorean's wiles. In his long career, he had seen all sorts of people and could be forgiven a certain cynicism.

'What state?' Cork asked.

An Arab state, replied DeLorean. His man did not want to be identified.

There was also a potential backer on the West Coast whose representative he wanted Cork to meet the next morning. The money was there, he insisted; just hold off on the receivership.

For once, Cork was at somewhat of a loss. He was a man who dealt in crisis or – more often – the aftermath of crisis. Too often in his career, he had had to close down entire companies and pick over the bones for the bits that could be resurrected in another life. He had lived with corporate death and was inured to the tragedy and human drama of it. He had turned receivership into a fine art, employing his skills to save companies that, under a different system, would have disappeared. Cork was a master.

The scheme he discussed again with DeLorean that night was what he called his 'Rolls Royce' plan. When Rolls Royce failed in 1971, its receiver created a new company, Rolls Royce 1971. The assets of the aero-engine side, whose contract to build the RB-211 engine for the Lockheed Tri-star had proven too costly, had been transferred into the new company. The car side was spun off with its own separate stock market quotation (it has since merged with Vickers). In that case, creditors got their money back and shareholders received a substantial repayment, too. The company is still running, although with government assistance.

Now Cork was proposing to create 'DeLorean Motor Cars Limited 1982'. To succeed, it would still need John DeLorean's active participation. He would have to sell the cars – he owned the distribution rights – although Cork was proposing to renegotiate that provision, too. The licence to the car was owned by the DeLorean Research Limited Partnership, so the company could not make the cars without permission from that group. DMC was the only general partner.

That evening the two men conducted a tough bargaining session. At 9.30 the next morning, they met again at Claridges. DeLorean's prospect was not willing to deal; he wanted more time and his interest was only exploratory.

But at the same time, Cork had met some of the prospects with whom DeLorean was negotiating and they were often highly reputable people. DeLorean had talked to General Motors and Chrysler, for instance, and Oppenheimer, too. Thus Sir Kenneth could not easily dismiss the potential investors that DeLorean always seemed about to produce.

Noon, Thursday: Cork and DeLorean went together to the Northern Ireland office in Whitehall. Jim Prior was not in a receptive mood. His two predecessors, Roy Mason and Humphrey Atkins, had been damaged politically by John DeLorean, and Prior had enough problems of his own – both in the Cabinet where he had now been manoeuvred away from one of the key economic posts into the turbulent waters of Northern Ireland, and in the Province itself. Prior wanted a solution *now* to DeLorean, and he had decided that meant receivership.

But Prior was not prepared for the news that John DeLorean gave him. If it had not been tragedy it would have been high comedy. Prior could barely keep his face straight as DeLorean announced he had not one but three people lined up to save the group. Who were they? There was Alan Blair from California who had put together a consortium and who Prior and Cork knew all about. Then there was an Arab head of state – 'I give that one a 60 percent chance,' he told Jim Prior. And the third one? 'A major British company,' said DeLorean confidently. 'I don't know the name of it myself yet because it wants to remain anonymous at this stage. But I guess it is your General Electric Company.'

Prior could not restrain himself. He laughed aloud. In 15 years GEC had come from relative obscurity to the number one spot, due to some aggressive takeovers and some even more aggressive management. It sat on a cash mountain of over $2 billion – which its tough, legendarily tightfisted chief executive would never have spent on DeLorean in a thousand years. DeLorean could not have picked a more unlikely man – and Prior instantly spotted it.

'I happen to know Lord Weinstock well,' he told DeLorean, still chuckling. 'And I also happen to know he's the last person in the world you'll get a penny out of.'

Within 12 hours, promised DeLorean, all three possibles would be certainties – one way or the other. He just needed more time. He was willing to invest $5 million at his own expense in DMC. The money from his criminal damage claim would soon be paid, he claimed. He just needed the rest of that day. But the press releases were all ready to go out. Prior was planning a statement to the House of Commons within a few hours.

Prior glanced at Cork, incredulously. Cork, however, indicated it just might be worth waiting for, there was a chance. Abruptly Prior made his decision. He would postpone his statement, delay the press release. DeLorean had until midnight New York time to have the money transmitted.

After just thirty minutes, Prior ended the meeting. John DeLorean returned to Claridges to spend the rest of the day on the telephone. He almost certainly believed he could persuade *someone* to come up with the money that day. He seemed incapable of facing defeat – intent on hanging on until the final seconds, unwilling to surrender an inch of ground. That night, as hope ran out, he could not even tell Sir Kenneth Cork the news himself.

It was midnight when Cork's phone rang at his home in Great Missenden. Robin Bailie, DeLorean's Belfast solicitor, was on the line. The Arab had not come through with the money. DeLorean needed more time. There was no other prospect who could come through in the time allotted. DeLorean would agree to the voluntary receivership. It was all over.

By six the next morning, the press release had gone out. Cork issued his own reassuring statement to the workforce at 9.30. At 11.00 Jim Prior rose to address the House of Commons. He had appointed Sir Kenneth Cork and his partner Paul Shewell as joint receivers, he announced, although he warned this did not 'guarantee a way ahead' for the company.

'It is clearly a matter of concern to the government that this position should have been reached.'

It would be wrong, he emphasized, to be too optimistic about the company's survival – as if anyone still were optimistic. But 'there is more goodwill to try to reach some successful position than one might have thought possible over the past few weeks'.

DeLorean was already twisting the story to his own advantage. From Claridges that morning, he issued a brief press statement. He was 'delighted' with the outcome, he said, and emphasized that the receivership was voluntary, rather than enforced by creditors. Then he went to Heathrow for his Concorde flight home. Curiously, he was not booked under his own name for that flight. He chose to travel, for whatever reasons, under the name of 'Nesseth', although his whereabouts were certainly no secret.

On the four-and-a-quarter-hour flight, DeLorean had enough time to prepare yet another counter-offensive. Cork's mention of Rolls Royce had struck a chord. By the time he arrived at Kennedy Airport, DeLorean had a statement ready. It never once mentioned receivership. Instead, it announced he had just completed an 'extremely advantageous reorganization plan' that was comparable to the 'similar restructuring of Rolls Royce in 1973' (actually it was 1971).

'By this action, the government has removed $130 million of primarily government debt from the balance sheet. Using this turning point agreement as a springboard, the many DeLorean customers who have hesitated to conclude the purchase of their automobile may now do so with complete confidence.'

John DeLorean ended his statement with thanks 'to Her Majesty's government for this powerful support.'

That afternoon, DeLorean defiantly faced the world. He chose to do it on the 35th floor of 280 Park Avenue where it would be crowded, rather than the more plush 43rd floor that would not fit so well with the new image.

He was beginning to show the strain, but he was still full of vigour. He had travelled to London on Wednesday, stayed up most of the two nights there and then travelled back only that day. For weeks he had been under intense pressure.

'Are you a con man?' asked an American reporter. 'Is your conscience clear?'

'My conscience is very, very clear,' replied DeLorean.

He had one final trick up his sleeve for that press conference. When Freddie Laker went down, his travelling public had bombarded him with cheques and cash to get him flying again. Now John DeLorean displayed some cheques of his own: one for $10, the other for $20. It was not much, he admitted, but it was proof of affection.

'We won't go out of business,' he said. 'Whatever it takes in the world, we will do it to keep in business.' No one guessed the lengths he would, in the event, go to.

CHAPTER NINETEEN

'You Have The Right To Remain Silent . . . '

Late in January 1982 an old acquaintance of John DeLorean, James Timothy Hoffman, was in a 'safe house' kept by the U.S. government's drug strike force near San Diego.

He had successfully infiltrated a cocaine smuggling ring run by a United Airlines pilot and a real estate developer from Manhattan Beach, California. Hoffman had worked his way into the ring, had worked with the smugglers and had even gone to Colombia to help with the buy. He had gathered enough evidence: the agents had caught the ring red-handed with $14 million worth of coke.

Hoffman was what the Feds call a 'confidential informant', or a 'cooperating individual', or simply a 'CI', a drug smuggler who had been caught and, rather than face imprisonment, had agreed to take the agents where they themselves could not easily go – down into the underworld of drug dealers. In February 1981, he had been indicted by a Federal grand jury on charges that he had been part of a cocaine smuggling ring from 1975 to 1977. Hoffman's special task had been to arrange transport, to buy or rent the aircraft to bring the drugs into California from Ecuador. In working out the logistics of each trip, Hoffman often recruited innocent friends and even family members, some of them children, to give his frequent visits to Latin America an aura of respectability. Innocent or not, the Feds used the hold over Hoffman's family as effectively as their hold on him.

So, while he protested, Hoffman knew he had no choice but to work on the three new probes Special Agent John Valestra had for him. But he was not prepared when Valestra handed him the list of prime suspects to be investigated – one of the names was that of William Morgan Hetrick.

Morgan Hetrick was a man who had spent much of his life

around the rich at play and he had had a burning desire to be one of them. He loved money as much as he loved flying. After World War II, Hetrick acquired some war surplus B-25s and embarked on the raffish career of a freelance cargo pilot, hauling exotic and occasionally illegal cargoes from South America and Africa. In the process he gained a reputation as one of the best pilots in the business. In the late 1950s Hetrick's flair won him a job as test pilot and personal pilot for William Lear, designer of the Lear Jet. The stint with Lear involved transporting his friends from show business, including such stars as Glenn Campbell. And this led Hetrick to another job as pilot with Fletcher Jones.

By the middle 1960s, Fletcher Jones was many times a millionaire. The Computer Sciences Corporation he helped found in 1959 with $100 was bringing in $50 million a year in sales. Preferring to take it easy, Jones created Westerly Stud Farms, a 3,600-acre ranch, in the Santa Ynez Valley near San Diego. He spent his time working on the 22,000 square foot villa and the miles of flowerbeds, white fencing and modern barns for his livestock. Jones also favoured the company of beautiful women and part of Hetrick's job was to fly them from Los Angeles to San Diego for long party weekends at Westerly. Cristina Ferrare soon became a favourite of Jones and a friend of Morgan Hetrick and his wife; it was to them that she confided Jones had asked her to marry him and that she was about to say yes.

But on a bright May morning in 1972 Jones was piloting his single engine plane for a landing at the Santa Ynez airport when he crashed eight miles short of the runway and was killed on impact. Exactly one year later, Cristina Ferrare married one of Jones's friends, John DeLorean.

After Jones's death Hetrick had drifted north again into a series of unhappy partnerships. He was a good mechanic. One of the enterprises centred on an anti-skid airplane braking device Hetrick invented and he hired Hoffman, a Pauma Valley neighbour and young playboy, as a salesman. In 1975, the business unravelled in a complicated court battle between the partners. One of the highlights of the case was Hoffman's appearance as a witness to testify that Hetrick had taken a $100,000 kickback from him on the sale of a plane. He also accused Hetrick of demanding a kickback of one-third on all commissions on braking systems sales.

So, Hoffman and Hetrick had gone their separate ways. Both men apparently developed ties with the burgeoning drug trade in the region. Hoffman, according to federal agents familiar with his case, was not very successful as a smuggler. But since 1975, Hetrick had been doing very well indeed. According to federal authorities, Hetrick used his extensive contacts among the network of private pilots to build up his own drug transporting business between Colombia and the United States via a refuelling stop at a field outside Biloxi, Mississippi. By the end of 1981, U.S. authorities considered him one of the major drug importers in the region. They also knew he would be hard to catch.

Part of the problem in any drug prosecution is to provide adequate proof of the flow of currency needed to pay for the drugs, to prove that money was handed over at the sale and to show what happened to that money after the sale. The federal agents believed that Hetrick was doing so well that the simple logistics of handling such huge sums of cash were beginning to cause problems. Hetrick's own aviation repair and maintenance business was not very successful, yet in early 1981 he established Morgan Aviation Company in a hangar at the end of the Mojave Airport at Mojave, California, 90 miles north of Los Angeles on the edge of the vast desert. Morgan Aviation quickly became the talk of the little community of pilots and mechanics based there. The hangar was air-conditioned and a computer-controlled lathe was installed to handle sophisticated machining jobs. Hetrick moved into a nice home and began to drive a Cadillac. His fleet of planes, half a dozen at a time, were parked around the hangars along with an equal number of vans and cars owned by the firm.

The only things missing were the customers. Hetrick was frequently absent, leaving a son in charge. Yet he appeared to prosper and was a genial free-spender who always reached for the restaurant bill. He also freely invited guests to fly with him to Fort Lauderdale, Florida for parties on his 46-foot Kita trawler, the *Highland Fling*.

Mojave Airport General Manager Dan Sabovich was proud of the addition to his community airport. 'I used to take friends there just to show it off.' Visitors were especially impressed by the aviation machine shop and computer which were better than the facilities at most larger airports. Everything about it was first class, and expensive. 'I thought he must have an angel – a financial backer,' says Sabovich. 'The business he was doing didn't warrant the operation he had here.'

But the government agents knew that Hetrick was his own angel by then, and that his planes were logging thousands of hours of flight time to Colombia and back to Mojave where the hangar was put to more profitable uses. The agents even knew that Hetrick boasted about his bank account in the Cayman Islands.

But knowing and suspecting is a long way from catching and proving. That is where Hoffman came in.

Ronald Reagan had campaigned the year before on a strongly worded pledge to launch a war on organized crime and in particular against the drug trade. The word moved out quickly through the myriad U.S. government law enforcement agencies that the President had declared an end to the long running inter-tribal war between the various forces. He appointed department heads who were determined to make his war on crime a success; there was to be a new government strike force that pooled the resources and information of all the agencies in a co-operative venture and it would work – or else.

Other powerful voices were being raised against the scandal of uncontrolled drug trafficking in California. Even Hollywood studio chiefs had begun to fret at the public scandal and the production problems caused by talented casualties of drug abuse.

James Timothy Hoffman was a valuable link with this new underworld. At least he knew who they were. At least he knew Morgan Hetrick.

2

Back in New York City, the shock of the bankruptcy of the company had generated such a siege atmosphere at the Park Avenue offices that some of the employees referred to the place as 'The Bunker'. DeLorean now devoted himself to a single-minded effort to revive his empire. To the traumatized personal staff waiting for him, he radiated quiet confidence.

Economies were hastily introduced. First to go were the penthouse offices. DeLorean fought for two years to keep the suite, against the constant complaints of Tony Hopkins and NIDA. Now he had no choice. So he, Kimmerly and the rest of the now shrinking staff moved to the 35th floor to smaller, less expensive quarters. Where once his empire had numbered 3,000 employees, by March fewer than 40 were left.

DeLorean also restructured the DMC board of directors. Kimmerly was taken off the board which he had been reluctant to join in the first place for fear of conflicts of interest. Over the ensuing months, DeLorean also bought nearly $600,000 worth of DMC properties – furniture, art works, cars (including Ken Dahlinger's 1955 gull-wing Mercedes Benz) – at discount prices as a gesture that he was putting his own money into the sagging corporation.

A belief that luxury cars could be sold attracted California financier Alan Blair who pulled together a private group and offered DeLorean a rescue package of $30 million. The price would be little enough for what Blair wanted: control of DMC and John DeLorean's job. DeLorean might be kept on in a public relations capacity but Blair wanted to run the revival attempt. Even as the talks began, Blair did what any sensible businessman would, or should – he ran a check on DeLorean and on the key men around him. He very quickly ran into Roy Nesseth's reputation.

'Based on what I learned, I would not be involved in anything that included a man like Nesseth.' He withdrew his offer.

The unidentified Arab head of state never appeared again either. Indeed there is no real evidence that he ever existed except in John DeLorean's imagination.

Early in March there was a new proposition, one that Sir Kenneth Cork was cautious about, but at least it sounded hopeful. Budget-Rent-a-Car of Boston, the third biggest car rental chain in the United States, approached Sir Kenneth directly. Budget was interested in 2,000 DMC-12s. Sir Kenneth knew he could not sell those cars without going through DMC – he tried and DeLorean flatly refused to surrender any of the rights enjoyed by DMC as sole distributor. He would not budge an inch on that. So a new scheme was quickly conceived: DeLorean would enter into negotiations with Budget to sell the rental company all the cars it wanted. Budget was interested in 1,000 cars immediately and another 1,000 over the next year. 'A lot of people would probably love to drive one, even if not to own one,' said a Budget representative. 'If Mr. DeLorean had been able to sell his product at a lower price, he would have sold every car he made. If Sir Kenneth feels he can let the cars go at a little less, then we should have a deal.' The idea then was that DMC would use the money to repay some of what it owed to the Belfast company – after it had paid off Bank of America.

DeLorean himself retained a sort of black gallows humour. During the week of the bankruptcy, a line of men's toiletries had been launched bearing his name. He told the *New York Post*: 'We're thinking of calling it "A scent for losers" or "A smell for those on the way down".' He also talked about moving the operation out of Belfast: 'We have an alternative site – it's in a warm, sunny clime on the Mediterranean.' This was nonsense: he no longer owned a thing in Belfast. It was all in the hands of the receivers who would never release any of it.

In the new period of austerity, DeLorean now took another action that would later cause considerable controversy among the lawyers and investigators picking over his estate. From now on all cheques in and all money paid out went through John DeLorean's personal account. His explanation for this was that he needed tighter financial controls. It also made him interested in economizing, perhaps for the first time since the Northern Irish had come up with money. For the rest of his corporate days, John DeLorean had a tight-fisted attitude toward expenditures – he never used the Concorde again.

On Monday March 1, DeLorean met Budget president Morris Belzberg to discuss the delicate three-cornered deal. Cork could not authorize DeLorean to negotiate about the sale of the cars already financed by Bank of America. But title to some of the remaining cars was far from clear. 'There were numerous instances of "double-dipping",' said J. Bruce McWilliams, DeLorean vice-president in charge of sales in the final days, in an article he wrote for *Car and Driver* in October 1982. 'In effect, dealers had paid for cars but had not received them, and their money had been used to keep operations going. Not surprisingly, banks as well as dealers take a dim view of double-dipping. As cases of it became known, good grey institutions such as the Bank of America, Security Pacific, and GMAC summarily shut off floor-plan arrangements with DeLorean dealers, a devastating new blow to the company. Even if the Bank of America could be paid the $20 million owed to it and cars could be released from the depots for sale, the whole financial systems for selling to dealers would need rebuilding, and there were no immediate funds available to pay back those who had been double-dipped.'

However, as DeLorean and Belzberg sat down to discuss the details of a deal, there was optimism. 'We think we can put together an agreement,' said Belzberg, 'but if we are going to it has to be in a week or two at the latest.' No deal was possible without Bank of America endorsement. It soon became clear that the money raised on the Budget deal would first have to go to the Bank, which was holding out for its pound of flesh. Sir Kenneth would have to get in line.

While DeLorean and Belzberg bargained, things were falling apart rapidly in the rest of the organization. The number of DeLorean dealers was quickly reduced. At one point it had been 345, but by the end of February it was 285 and falling. In Belfast creditors were filing suits, or going broke themselves. C.P. Trim, a Northern Irish company set up by DeLorean and NIDA specifically to supply the car project, now appointed a receiver itself. At one stage it had provided 400 sets of interior and seating trim each week. It had already halved its workforce in January. Now it closed with the loss of another 113 jobs. Most of the creditors, however, were desperately trying to keep the factory going – their only hope of getting any money back.

Earl Hansen was the general manager of American Auto Inc., a subsidiary of Pasha Industries Inc. of California, which specialized in security and shipments and which processed the DeLorean cars imported on the east coast through Wilmington, Delaware. He met the ships bringing the cars in, supervised their unloading, saw them safely through customs, and then transported them to Dick Brown's quality assurance centre at Bridgewater, New Jersey. His duties did not stop there, however. Because of the arrangement with Bank of America whereby it lent DMC $33 million and in return had a written security interest in the stock of DMC-12 cars in the U.S. (except for the last 1,000 which had been shipped without financing), Hansen's operation also had a regulatory aspect. When a car was to be shipped to a dealer, DMC would send an order to Hansen, a letter of release from the Bank of America would follow immediately, and the car would go off to the dealer. That way the Bank made sure it got its money at the same time the car was moved. It was a simple and effective operation – until the first week of March.

The day after DeLorean opened his talks with Budget, Hansen received orders from 280 Park Avenue to ship 14 cars out of the Bridgewater facility, but no letter of release came from Bank of America. Hansen was well aware of the problems DeLorean was having and had no intention of breaking the strict terms of the agreement which stated that Pasha and AAI 'agree to recognize Bank of America's security interest in the vehicles'. No letter of release, no vehicles. He ordered Fran Clark, his manager at Bridgewater, not to release anything.

The next day, however, Bill Mahr, one of the few DeLorean executives remaining at the Park Avenue office, turned up at Bridgewater. Those 14 cars must be released. Clark was taken aback, but he knew his orders. He called California, seeking guidance from Headquarters. George Pasha III gave it to him: don't release those cars. Bill Mahr finally went away grumpily. But at seven that evening he was back. This time he brought with him two armed private security men. These men, he told Clark, would stay on the premises to secure it. Clark's Pasha men were already doing that. Now there were two sets of guards, each eyeing the others warily. Clearly, something was about to break.

The next day it did. Oskar Stutz of the Bank of America National Trust and Savings Association passed the news on to George Pasha: DMC was in default. It had missed its payment on an outstanding balance of $18 million, the commitment from its dealers had fallen below the level of the Bank of America's credit agreement and all cars should now be held to the benefit of the Bank of America, as specified in Pasha's contract.

Hansen was at the Bridgewater facility all that day. All cars now belonged to Bank of America and in effect Pasha had changed sides: DeLorean was no longer a client. They were now working for Bank of America. No cars were to leave the site without Bank of America approval.

It was a long tense day, the DeLorean staff and the Pasha men walking around each other carefully.

It was nine that evening when Bill Mahr turned up again, this time accompanied by four 'unidentified associates' in the staid language of Hansen's later affidavit, or four 'armed thugs' according to Dick Brown's second hand description. Mahr demanded 15 cars, one more than the original 14. Hansen refused.

Hansen picked up the phone to call George Pasha and began to dial. A hand slammed down on his, forcing the receiver back into its cradle. Hansen could scarcely believe it. 'Call the cops,' he told one of his security guards. 'No,' said one of the DeLorean men. 'Not from here. This is DeLorean property. You can't use the phones.' The guard went round the corner and used a public phone. In the meantime Hansen tried to prepare documentary proof of his position. Again he was stopped. 'The DMC personnel, along with the two armed security personnel they had installed the day before, also prevented me from utilizing the office's telecopy equipment to receive copies of Pasha's lease agreement with DMC and of the notice of default,' said Hansen in his affidavit.

The local police arrived soon afterwards. Mahr told them that Hansen and all other Pasha personnel had been dismissed by DMC and had no right to be there. Hansen was stuck without a copy of Pasha's lease agreement or of the Bank of America's notice of default, so he had no documents proving his right to be there. The police, perplexed by what was clearly a complex situation, finally sided with DMC and asked the Pasha people to leave.

Hansen asked Fran Clark to hang around outside and watch what went on. If the DeLorean people were going to take some cars, he wanted to know where they went. It did not take long. By 10.30 p.m., the men inside started loading. They took 15 cars, with Clark following at a safe distance. They didn't go far – just twelve miles. To John DeLorean's Bedminster estate.

In California, Dick Brown was suddenly hearing about it. A few minutes later, George Pasha called. He had learned that a similar raid was planned at the Santa Ana facility. 'You've got to be kidding,' gasped Brown. Pasha was not. 'I'll handle it,' said Brown. He called his people at Santa Ana and told them what was happening. 'Call the police. I'll be there in 30 minutes.'

By the time Brown arrived the police were there. 15 minutes later a car arrived containing four armed men who tried to get in. But the police were there in force and this time they were stopped. Brown was then called to the phone. It was Roy Nesseth telephoning from Peacock Alley, a fashionable promenade in New York's Waldorf Astoria Hotel. 'Hey, Brown,' he started, 'if you want to continue living and if you want your wife and children to stay healthy, you'll cooperate.'

Brown handed the phone to a police officer, but he was shaken. A few minutes later he was again called to the phone. This time it was Tom Kimmerly, who was also at Peacock Alley.

'What are you doing there?' he demanded of Brown.

'I'm trying to straighten out this ruckus at the quality assurance centre,' said Brown reasonably.

'Well, you are not supposed to be there,' said Kimmerly.

'Why not?'

'Because you were fired!'

'Nobody's advised me I was fired.'

'You don't have to be advised,' said Kimmerly.

'I don't know what you guys are up to,' said Brown. 'But I certainly don't want any part of it.' He handed the phone to the police officer.

On Friday, the day after the Bridgewater incident, DeLorean and Brown talked on the telephone. Brown wanted confirmation of what Kimmerly had told him the night before – that he was fired. Yes, DeLorean told him, he was. He explained that the takeover of the cars was all a misunderstanding, but 'he provided no coherent explanation of the incident,' said Brown in his sworn affidavit for the Bank of America's action. 'Based upon my observation of the operation of DMC and of the behavior of Nesseth and Kimmerly, I do not believe that (these) events ... could have taken place without the knowledge and consent of ... John Z. DeLorean.'

Brown was now gone, and Bruce McWilliams, a mild, bespectacled, bald man who knew Dewey and Collins and who ignored their advice not to join DeLorean, suddenly found himself shoved into Brown's place. On Friday, according to McWilliams, 'DeLorean asked me to pack my bags for California.' The only thing that stuck in his memory about that meeting was DeLorean's statement 'that Roy Nesseth would accompany me and that he would take care of any dirty work'. DeLorean told him, 'Roy is mean. There are people with mean streaks that may surface from time to time, but Roy is different – he enjoys being mean.'

McWilliams found the office in chaos when he got to Irvine. 'Events in previous weeks had traumatized the staff. There had been numerous firings, dire predictions of events to come by the management, even a staff party at which Big Roy was burned in effigy. One was reminded of the apprehensions of Berliners as the Russian tanks drew nearer.'

While McWilliams started sorting out the immediate disaster areas – thousands of warranty claims had piled up, amounting to $1.5 million, all systems and services such as the computer operation were a shambles – Nesseth began dealing with the creditors. He used a combination of threats, evasion and hard bargaining, much to the consternation of the staff. Now many of them drifted away, or were fired.'There was no money, none at all,' said McWilliams in his article for *Car and Driver*. 'We were flat broke, even running out of necessities such as coffee, stamps and envelopes. The cleaning service was a creditor and had packed up, and offices became grungy, restrooms smelly. We owed the city of Irvine $330 for water, but they didn't cut their supply because we would have become a health hazard. In order to participate in Los Angeles's Auto Expo, we had to borrow exhibit cars from dealers because we no longer owned any. Shrubbery was carried to our stand at the show from the executive offices.'

3

In the autumn of 1981, Dick Brown had donated to the government two DMC-12s that could not be brought up to sale quality for its research programme on safety. In September they had been sent to the Dynamic Sciences track in Phoenix to be outfitted with air bags and testing dummies and crashed at speeds above the 35 mph minimum for passenger cars in the United States.

Until that moment, there had been absolutely no government inspection of the safety or emission control or fuel efficiency numbers provided to DOT or other agencies by DMC. Contrary to what most citizens believe, government safety regulators cannot test every car model that comes into the dealer showrooms. As one DOT official explains it, 'The Congress gives us just enough money for a minimum amount of testing; it costs as much as $10,000 in addition to the price of the car to crash test a car and I would rather be testing the basic models of the Chevys and Fords that millions of people drive than concentrating on limited editions such as the DeLorean.'

Besides, the DeLorean design had originated at Lotus which had an unquestioned reputation for engineering integrity.

One of the scientists present during the Phoenix crash test remembers, 'We were extremely pleased about the design of the DMC-12 cockpit and the numbers we got out of the crashes. They were among the best data we got in the entire program. If it wasn't for the fuel spills, it would have been a perfect test.'

One of the precautions the DOT testers take in crashing cars into fixed barriers is to use a fuel solvent with a highly visible red dye that makes it easy to spot any petrol spillage. To their surprise, they noticed considerable quantities of the fuel's telltale stain not only on the pavement around the car, but in the passenger compartment as well.

'We tore the car apart to find the reason. The gasoline tank was still intact and had been well placed in the front Y-area of the chassis. But we found that the electric fuel pump hung down into the tank and was held in place by two heavy rubber flanges. The heat of the day must have weakened the rubber because the impact – and you can generate up to twice the impact by going 45 mph instead of 35 mph – sent the pump moving forward and up and that raised the lid of the fuel tank and allowed the spillage,' one of the researchers stated.

The government scientists were not going to keep quiet about the fuel spillage. A report was filed in Washington. By the time the appropriate office had received the report and realized its seriousness, DMC was bankrupt.

It is likely that John DeLorean was never personally aware of the fuel spills. By this time he was trying to put together his deal with Budget. But the Bank of America was no longer interested in making things easy for him. It filed suit in federal court in New York seeking repayment of its loans and asking the court to order DMC to make 1,950 cars available to it. The bank was owed $18 million; the value of the cars at list price was nearly $50 million. But the cars were not selling, and those that were brought less than list price. The days of the early premiums had long gone.

Once again DeLorean himself remained aloof from it all, as he had from the actual building of the factory and the car. He was now holed up in a much more modest office on the 35th floor, without the panoramic views, the telescope or the space he had enjoyed in the penthouse. The art collection so painstakingly gathered by Maur Dubin was now piled up in stacks, some of it already sold. He himself remained as calm and determined as ever.

Sir Kenneth Cork had left him a chance, in fact a very good chance, of survival. Cork had sculpted an ingenious scheme, one which he was proud of and could still work if just one of DeLorean's many prospects came through with some money. It was essentially the same deal he had suggested to DeLorean before receivership, with minor refinements: a new company, DeLorean Motor Cars Limited (1982) would be formed; the factory, tooling and other equipment would be leased to it for a nominal sum. The new company would be debt-free, but it would pay off the debts of the old company when it sold completed cars.

DeLorean leaped on the plan enthusiastically. Typically, he turned it round so that it came out advantageously. 'This means that as we see it,' he wrote in the document he prepared for prospective investors, 'all the tooling, plant and equipment and learning curve having been transferred without the capital payment to the new company, the new company will be responsible for providing sufficient finance, to provide the working capital starting from a position where there is no work in progress and no finished stock, or indeed, as an empty factory. Therefore, there is in fact no purchase price.'

Cork had persuaded Jim Prior that the government should go along with the plan. And Prior agreed, not without a battle with his Cabinet colleagues. If something could be saved from the ashes, however small, then Cork's scheme was worth trying. At Dunmurry there were still 1,300 people building cars from parts already bought, mostly on credit, which would have no value unless they could be converted into cars. In those final months, DeLorean had ordered parts for a production rate of 30,000 cars a year.

DeLorean also prepared a six-year plan, showing some healthy projections. Most observers didn't give him six weeks, but DeLorean never wavered. He played with sales figures. In 1982 he could still sell 6,300 cars, he forecast. In 1983 he would introduce a turbo-charged version. By 1985 there would be a sedan as well and, by 1987, the end of his six-year plan, he would be selling 33,600 cars for revenues of nearly $1 billion and profits of $161 million. The only year the new company could lose would be year one when it would lose $1 million.

Through March and on into April he sent this plan with his accompanying glowing statement and projections to potential investor after investor. He bombarded Sir Kenneth Cork in London with news that he had at last found his man, willing to put up $30 million. Cork made the journey to New York several times, but after a while he stopped going.

Cork was astonished at the figures in the documents DeLorean was sending out. 'They have no relevance to the facts at all,' he bluntly told DeLorean, who ignored his criticisms.

Cork found something else to dislike about DeLorean's office: Roy Nesseth. And he soon noticed one intriguing little pattern: every new investor was offering the same amount of money. 'Why is it always $30 million?' he said half-jokingly to DeLorean on one occasion, flashing his renowned grin. 'Surely to God you could find the grace to vary the figure every now and again, if only for appearance sake.'

DeLorean laughed.

Nevertheless, Cork kept setting deadlines for the injection of new money. DeLorean kept missing them.

Belzberg had been a DeLorean fan: he saw DeLorean's

present plight as a personal tragedy and was keen to help. He also thought the cars would be a major attraction at his airport outlets. At the start negotiations had gone well. The Bank of America battle had soured relations for a while but they recovered. By the end of March they had arrived at a deal which was a solution to the problem of the title to the cars. Bank of America had now won its court order preventing DeLorean from selling any cars until it had been repaid. Kenneth Cork claimed the other cars belonged to the Belfast company because they had never been paid for. DeLorean denied both. Budget could not deal without having title – unless it could lease.

Then, as the deal was about to move forward, another complication arose. While negotiating to sell or lease to Budget, DeLorean and Roy Nesseth were also negotiating to sell or lease to another company: Consolidated International Corporation of Columbus, Ohio.

In London, Cork was wary to the point of scepticism. 'Frankly I would like to see the money before going too deeply into things,' he told the *Daily Telegraph*. 'Mr. DeLorean has come up with proposals before, but they don't seem to have got very far.'

Only a slight wave of hope went through the Belfast factory – there had been too many false dawns already. They were now three weeks past Cork's original deadline and they were re-signed, fatalistic. The newspapers carried conflicting headlines day by day: 'Receiver may dash last DeLorean hopes' (*Guardian*, April 21), 'DeLorean may be saved' (*Daily Telegraph*, April 23), 'Fresh hopes of buyer for DeLorean car plant' (*The Times*, April 23).

Then the Budget deal fell through, killed by the lawyers who would not allow it to go ahead unless they could guarantee the title to the cars. DeLorean himself was holding back on the Consolidated deal but it was finally going through against all his instincts. 'He really hated like hell dealing with Consolidated – regarded them as Shylock, taking their pound of flesh,' said a DeLorean executive. But he had no choice. Consolidated paid $14 million for 1,174 cars, most of it going straight to Bank of America. It did not relieve the cash squeeze, but it did mean the cars were for sale again.

Two days later, as Cork was about to close the factory, a

saviour arrived from New York. He was 38-year-old real estate magnate and financier Peter Kalikow, whose family company, H. J. Kalikow, owns several Manhattan apartment buildings and some major office buildings. Cork quickly discovered that if Kalikow wanted to invest, he would have no trouble finding the money from his own resources. He had the money all right. But would he go through with it?

It was Kalikow who set himself a deadline: May 14. 'It must be ready for signing then. Otherwise this thing could go on forever,' he told DeLorean and Cork. Kalikow had gone above the repetitive $30 million figure. He was offering $35 million. Kalikow recalls:

> I had known John for some time and known of him for longer than that. I saw him from time to time at the Boardroom and a friend of his had done some legal work for me. The friend asked if I would be interested in pursuing some type of investment. I said I would and that's how it came about.
>
> I was not a social friend at all and there was nothing that led me to believe that the company's problems were any different from what a lot of auto companies were running into at the time. I was impressed that they did so well in the period of time that they were involved in the project; that they managed to get the whole thing going with all the tooling and get a credible product on the market.
>
> The deal was put together in a short period of time but it was a comprehensive proposal as far as I was concerned. Basically it would have been an amalgamation of the companies here and it would have assured DMCL that every car sold to us would have been paid for. There would have been no problem for them – once a car was made, it would have been paid for.

Not surprisingly, Kalikow demanded majority control of DMC and John DeLorean tentatively agreed. The next step was to win the approval of the receivers. Paul Shewell flew to New York and met Kalikow.

'Shewell was very nice and polite and told me that he could not entertain my offer. We talked it over for three hours in my office. They wanted somebody to come there and bail out the place, replace their investment 100 cents on the dollar and there was just no way that I could do it that way. So I thanked him very much and that was the end of it.'

In fact the Kalikow offer would have done nothing for the receiver's position. Cork and Shewell wanted an equity investment, not just financing for the cars already made. Their interest was in trying to keep the factory going and thereby get something back for the creditors, as well as preserve jobs in Northern Ireland. Cars made would have been paid for, yes. But who paid for the cars to be made in the first place? Kalikow's offer did not help the Belfast company.

Kalikow, however, kept the deal open beyond his original deadline while DeLorean continued to wax optimistic. 'The entire arrangement will be completed by the end of May,' he announced on May 17. Two days later Kalikow pulled out.

With the Bank of America repaid $13 million of its money and now moving for its remaining $5.3 million, crisis was again looming. Both Jim Prior and Margaret Thatcher were pressuring Cork to come up with a solution or close the plant.

On Monday, May 25, Paul Shewell flew to Belfast and Dunmurry. He assembled the 1,500 workers and gave them the news. Three months of fruitless searching for backers had failed. The production line would be shut down the following week. Some 200 or so workers would be kept on for the time being to run the servicing operation for those cars already sold and to keep efforts going to sell more cars. The other 1,300 would be laid off at the end of the week. It was 'another nail in the coffin of our dying economy', said a spokesman for the joint Protestant Catholic Alliance. Shewell's statement aroused fury across the Province, expected though it was. The shop stewards at the plant talked about discrimination against Northern Ireland, and accused the government of economic withdrawal from Ulster, insisting the government was preparing the way for complete withdrawal from Northern Ireland, a move which would please no one except the IRA. Two days later they climbed a perimeter fence and started a sit-in in the factory. 'We will eat and sleep on the site for as long as is necessary,' said Sean O'Neill, the senior shop steward.

All summer long it was the same pattern. Every time Cork

was about to close the factory, there would be a new prospect. At one stage it was a consortium of British suppliers, led by Barrie Wills and Chuck Bennington, who came forward with a deal. It appealed to both Cork and Jim Prior. They found a bank – Hill, Samuel, one of the leading merchant banks in the City of London.

There was one snag. Hill, Samuel wanted its £80,000 fee up front before it would take the risk of preparing the prospectus and going ahead. And the consortium didn't have even that sort of money. Would the government pay for the prospectus? Jim Prior took the proposal all the way to Margaret Thatcher. She looked at it and said, 'It seems to me if they can't raise the fees to pay the bankers they haven't got much of a chance of raising the rest.' Another rescue bid died. Others would be raised in that spring and early summer. All came to nothing. The downhill slide picked up speed.

4

Chance continued to play a large rôle in DeLorean's fortunes. In early March another bizarre string of coincidences began to unfold, beginning in the small town of Ventura, California, halfway between Los Angeles and Morgan Hetrick's base of operations near Mojave.

Ventura Police Chief Paul Lydick began surveillance of a local resident suspected of transporting large sums of currency out of the state. A local informant had overheard the suspect brag about his currency-hauling exploits and of his contacts with a man named 'Morgan'. The surveillance spread to include several other men and led the local police to Morgan Aviation.

Lydick asked the help of the United States Customs Service and the Internal Revenue Service, and those agents quickly learned that Morgan Aviation and Morgan Hetrick were subjects of a longer-running drug probe by the strike force. The money probers and drug busters pooled resources. Rather than wait for the wily pilot to make a mistake, they decided to mount a 'sting'.

The original plan had FBI agent Benedict Tisa pose as 'James T. Benedict' and claim to be an official of the Eureka

Federal Savings and Loan Association of San Carlos, California. James Hoffman was given specific orders. He was to make contact with Hetrick and get back in his good graces. He was to convince Hetrick that the Savings and Loan official would help him with the growing problem of shifting his drug profits into legally usable cash. Hoffman was also to hint that not only was Benedict-Tisa willing to launder Hetrick's money, but he would also like a piece of a future drug deal as well.

Hoffman did as he was told. Hetrick was interested but still cautious. The net was getting tighter around him but he was far from caught.

On July 11, John DeLorean and James Hoffman met at the Marriott Hotel in Newport Beach, California. DeLorean complained to his former neighbour about his business frustrations.

What, exactly, happened next? Who moved first? Who first mentioned a drug deal? We do not yet know. But, in the stilted language of law enforcement, the strike force charged that DeLorean sought Hoffman out because he 'had a sense' of the younger man's involvement with drug trafficking and that he initiated the idea that a drug deal might generate the kind of cash he needed to save DMCL before Cork abandoned any rescue attempt.

The next event is not disputed. Hoffman told his control, DEA special agent Valestra, that John DeLorean, the big-name automobile tycoon, might be coaxed into a drug deal. Better yet, DeLorean was acquainted with prime target Morgan Hetrick. One could be used to land the other. The federal agents quickly agreed, ever mindful of the publicity value of busting a major business executive.

The agents now say the plan was changed and Hoffman was to tell Hetrick that DeLorean could be used as a source of new capital for a major coke or heroin transaction, something large enough to let banker Benedict have a piece of the action too.

In the meantime, DeLorean kept Sir Kenneth Cork and the British government searching for ways to avoid abandoning the project altogether. On August 3 Paul Shewell reported that the British investors group was asking for more time to work out a deal.

On August 9 Cork flew to New York and presented the plan to DeLorean; the investors wanted to produce a British Leyland Triumph or TR-7 type car as well as the DMC-12. Donald Lander would become chief executive of both the Belfast and U.S. operations. The investors insisted that DeLorean must be ruled out of the decision-making process before they would come in. DeLorean remained impassive. Under the agreement the receivers group had until the end of August to put their deal together. He correctly judged that they would not make it; they didn't and a 30-day extension was asked. After September 30, it would be John DeLorean's turn again to come up with a rescue plan; he had to have the money by then.

On September 4, DeLorean met Hoffman at the L'Enfant Plaza Hotel in Washington, D.C. At this meeting DeLorean was introduced to 'Mr. Vicenza': in reality Agent Valestra pretending to be a heavyweight dope distributor tied to organized crime.

While the conversation was being monitored and recorded by nearby FBI agents, DeLorean and the two men discussed, in the language of the government affidavits, 'the importation and distribution of heroin from Thailand and cocaine from South America as a means of generating large amounts of capital for the DeLorean Motor Company'. According to the transcriptions of the tapes, DeLorean agreed to supply $1.8 million to bankroll the drug buy. Vicenza-Valestra then volunteered to put up about $3 million so that the group could purchase a 220-pound load of coke. As the discussion rolled onto the government tapes, the three men agreed that Mr. Vicenza was to handle the distribution of the drugs and that DeLorean was to get most of the profits from the deal. They agreed to meet again and set the final terms.

There was no reminiscing about the Pauma Valley days when Hoffman, Hetrick and John DeLorean finally met on September 20 in a room at the Bel Air Sands Hotel in Los Angeles. The eager bank official Benedict (agent Tisa) was on hand also but most of the meeting was dominated by Hetrick who bragged about his skill as a smuggler. It was agreed Hetrick would bring in 100 kilos (220 pounds) at $50,000 a kilo, of top quality cocaine from his supply source in Colombia. Benedict was to handle the distribution of profits to DeLorean. A final meeting was set for a week later.

At about this time a most disturbing warning began to filter through the very highest levels of the Thatcher government. Highly placed United States diplomatic sources passed the word to drop any contact or any future dealings with John DeLorean. Something was up. There were no details, no mention of drugs, no hint of an arrest date. Just a word to the wise.

But Sir Kenneth was far from willing to let the DeLorean project fold. Indeed, in that final week of September it appeared as if his long search for a legitimate investor was on the verge of success. Best of all, it was a British firm that was helping to wire the deal together, a deal that could inject as much as $100 million into the enterprise. Such a major investment would not only help put the Belfast production lines back in operation and cover the cost of the cars already languishing in lots on both sides of the Atlantic, but it might also buy out the entire British government's stake – something even Jim Prior dared not hope for.

The firm involved in the negotiating with Sir Kenneth was Minet Financial Management, a branch of Minet Holdings, which was a major Lloyds of London insurance broker. Minet Financial specialized, among other things, in placing money from various British tax haven banks in the Cayman Islands and British Virgin Islands in high risk, high yield investments outside the reach of the U.K. Inland Revenue.

The framework of the proposed deal was simplicity itself. Minet's clients would lend the money directly to DeLorean Motor Company Inc., the Delaware shell which John DeLorean was now trying to transfer assets into, and which was to be the vehicle for the born-again DeLorean empire.

The $100 million would have been more than enough to rescue DeLorean. The investment could have settled the Belfast company's $30 million in creditors' debts, buy the assets of the Dunmurry plant (perhaps another $25 million), take over the inventory of cars and put the sales network back together again. This time DeLorean could have it all without the interference from NIDA and London officials, whom he now blamed for the venture's collapse.

But neither the Minet managers nor Sir Kenneth were fools. Both were aware of the weather-vane changes that could occur in negotiations with DeLorean. And Sir Kenneth would still have to persuade the Thatcher government and ultimately Parliament to ratify the deal.

So, in the flurry of telephone calls and telex messages that criss-crossed the Atlantic, Sir Kenneth and the investors imposed one condition that could not be negotiated away. If John DeLorean wanted to be part of this deal and to control the resurrection of his company, he would have to come up with a capital investment of his own by a fixed deadline. The sum required was $20 million and it would be nonrefundable if the deal failed. The deadline date was October 20.

DeLorean complained to Sir Kenneth that while he had $10 million on hand he feared he could not raise the rest. The Minet managers had an idea. The British firm had done business for some time with a small American investment bank in the Washington D.C. suburb of McLean, Virginia.

FSI Financial Services Inc. is a small firm that does about $100–$200 million a year in loan placements for individual clients. Its other distinction is that it is one of three such investment firms headed by a woman.

Jeanne Farnan is a shrewd and circumspect expert on the almost invisible threads that make up the international syndicated loan network. She was in London on another deal in the first week of October when she was asked if she could come up with a short-term loan for John DeLorean. After a day trip to inspect the Dunmurry plant, Farnan said she would return to Washington and try.

The last meeting involving the drug ring planners took place on September 28 at the Bonaventure Hotel in Los Angeles – again in a room that was monitored and recorded by the agents. Discussing the deal were Hoffman, DeLorean and Vicenza-Valestra who told DeLorean that sales from the coke buy could gross more than $50 million. As payment for fronting the $3 million in seed money, Vicenza said he wanted a 50 percent interest in DeLorean Motor Company. DeLorean's voice is heard agreeing. He later called Hetrick to see if the project could be hurried up. Talk of a heroin deal was finally dropped because, as Vicenza-Valestra explained, it might take five weeks after delivery before profits could be realized. DeLorean didn't have that kind of time. In early October, Hetrick left the Mojave Airport and the plan was in motion.

DeLorean returned to New York and immediately called Jeanne Farnan in Virginia to see how her loan was coming. Farnan recalls:

> It seemed to me that DeLorean almost had the pieces together when I got involved in this. He called me at home one night and we talked. I explained that it would have to be a stand-by loan for $10 million for a term of 90 days. The interest rate at that time was 12 percent and the closing fee was about two or three percent.
> The only problems we really had were with the receivers who objected to the bank where we first proposed to put the money. Finally we changed banks and then backed the loan funds with another investor's certificate of deposit. So it was a doubly collateralized loan. The money was to go to DMC Inc.

DeLorean did not haggle over the terms, nor did he ask for help on the other $10 million. 'He said he had that $10 million but he needed the rest to show the British government that he was operating in good faith,' Farnan says. 'He also did not tell me the money would be norefundable. No one told me that until after the affair was long over. You can imagine how I felt.'

In New York at the DMC offices, John DeLorean kept up his daily routine without a hint that something special was in the wind. He continued to make public statements predicting that a final investors' group plan would be put together by the end of October. There were reports that a Hong Kong investors' group was holding discussions, but DeLorean laughed when journalists pressed him for confirmation. Something's going to happen soon, he assured them. They would be the first to know.

Hetrick telephoned the Eureka bank and told Benedict-Tisa that he planned to arrive in Los Angeles on Monday, October 18, on Pan Am flight 442 from Miami. But he would only bring 25 of the 100 kilos promised. If that went well and he could get $1.8 million from the DeLorean-Vicenza partnership, the remaining 75 kilos would follow very soon.

The agents moved to close the trap.

The agents secured room 501 at the Sheraton Plaza hotel near the L.A. Airport. The room was a mini-suite, its rooms divided by a glass wall. On the other side cameras and recorders were set and manned.

At 3.55 p.m. on the afternoon of October 19, Hetrick met Benedict-Tisa at the airport and picked his luggage off the conveyor belt. By 4.20 they were in room 501 and Hetrick announced that he was ready to go. The agents were not. It was not until 7.45 p.m. that DEA agent Gerald Scotti and Vicenza-Valestra arrived and began their act as underworld drug wholesalers come to make the buy. The suitcase containing $1.8 million in cash was placed on a plexiglass coffee table in full view of the cameras. Hetrick looked at it but did not bother to count the money; the suitcase was closed and set aside.

Now it was Hetrick's turn. As the hidden cameras turned he told the agents that the cocaine was hidden in a car that would be driven to the hotel by his aide, Stephen Arrington. He called the younger man and told him to bring the car to the front entrance of the hotel lobby; the group would meet him there.

But Arrington misunderstood the message and arrived in Hetrick's own Cadillac. The cocaine was in another car. The men agreed on an impromptu plan of action – Arrington would take Scotti and Hoffman to the cocaine car and turn it over to them. Hetrick and Benedict-Tisa would go to dinner and make the transfer of funds later from Vicenza-Valestra. Convoys of agents trailed after both groups.

On the way, Arrington chatted freely with Scotti and Hoffman. He explained how the coke car – a Chevrolet Caprice – had been rigged with a lever under the dashboard to unlatch the back seat and expose the hidden cargo section. He boasted about similar jobs he had done for Hetrick and complained about the low pay he got for such dangerous work. By agreement, Arrington left the two agents with the Cadillac and went by himself to get the delivery car which was parked elsewhere in a public parking lot. Within minutes he arrived and as he stopped the Caprice, Scotti could see Arrington lean forward and pull the seat lever. The rear seat back popped forward.

'Go ahead, take a look,' Arrington told Scotti who clambered in the back and pulled the seat forward to expose a compartment full of 'multiple kilosize packages, mostly wrapped in brown wrapping paper with masking tape', as his affidavit would later recount.

The official Scotti narrative continues, in the stilted officialese of policemen the world over: 'I removed one of the packages, which I noted was marked "RCX" in blue felt-tip pen. I pierced the outer wrapper of the package with a key and took out a pinch of white crystalline powder in my fingers. By its distinctive smell and appearance, I believed this substance to be cocaine from my experience as a narcotics investigator. I exited the vehicle and gave a prearranged "bust" signal, at which time the agents and officers on surveillance effected the arrest of Stephen Arrington. I advised Arrington of his Constitutional Rights, but he declined to make any statement at that time.'

The time was 9 p.m. At 11.15 p.m. Morgan Hetrick and Benedict-Tisa had finished their meal at the posh La Cage aux Folles restaurant on La Cienega Boulevard and were leaving when the other agents closed in and made the arrest. Hetrick, too, kept silent after being read his rights.

He and Arrington were taken to the Terminal Island federal correctional facility nearby for fingerprinting and processing.

Suddenly the agents had a brief scare. No one had foreseen what Hetrick might do when he was allowed his mandatory telephone call after processing. Would he call DeLorean and warn him off? The fears were unfounded as Hetrick placed an understandably urgent call to his lawyer.

Back on the East Coast it was by now well into the morning of October 19. In McLean, Virginia, Jeanne Farnan and an aide had worked all weekend to complete the loan documents and get them off to New York by courier. Farnan had to turn round then and pack for yet another trip to London. This time she would be part of the negotiations between Sir Kenneth and the Minet managers about what to do next.

John DeLorean arrived at his Park Avenue offices at the usual time and immersed himself in the daily routine. By mid-morning the FSI loan documents were delivered and lay on his secretary's desk, unopened. When Farnan telephoned to ask if they had been signed, the secretary said she would see that DeLorean got them right away. Farnan said she would telephone back.

Just before noon she phoned again. Yes, Mr DeLorean had received the loan forms personally. They were on his desk, still unsigned. The secretary promised she would remind him to act soon because he was about to leave for Los Angeles and she did not know when he would be back. This alarmed Farnan.

She told the secretary that DeLorean must sign those forms before he left – there could be no delay. The deadline in London was only four hours away. She was leaving soon for London for talks about the company's future; there would be no future if he failed to sign those documents today. He must understand that.

An hour later John DeLorean left his office for the flight to Los Angeles, the unsigned documents still on his desk. Three FBI agents followed him to the airport and sat behind him on the plane. Sir Kenneth's final deadline passed as DeLorean was actually in the air. Whatever happened now, his company was dead. Even his drug money could not save it.

When he arrived at Los Angeles airport, DeLorean paused and made a quick telephone call back to his office. His secretary asked when he would be returning so she would have something to tell the now-frantic Jeanne Farnan. He brushed the question aside and took the other messages without comment or betraying any of the excitement he must have felt. Then he went briskly to the nearby Sheraton Plaza Hotel, to room 501. It was nearly 3 p.m. Within 15 minutes he was under arrest. The dream of John Z. DeLorean was ended. The nightmare was about to begin.

EPILOGUE

'I don't care what you say about John DeLorean, you have to give him credit for what he accomplished or nearly accomplished. He was a maverick. He took a swampy field in Northern Ireland and in two years turned it into a factory that produced a damn good car. Whatever else he did, you have to give him that.'

Implicit in the 'only results count' view of DeLorean's career is the false premise that entrepreneurial spirit today is so threatened that any person brave enough to set off on his own is justified in using any means to succeed. In fact, the past 20 years has seen a blossoming of individual business founders, men and women who have invested sweat and vision to create new economic growth. The revolution in high-technology industry is almost exclusively the work of small-shop mavericks who possess the courage supposedly monopolized by John DeLorean.

Undeniably, DeLorean began his career equipped with engineering skills that bordered on genius, plus an inexhaustible supply of energy and ambition. One can only guess with sadness at what an enormous contribution he might have made. Ironically, it is the engineer's definition of success – 'does it work?' – that points up the barrenness of his subsequent career. However high-flown was the rhetoric about his ethical car at the beginning, John DeLorean's dream car must be judged as being not even close to a success.

And consider the cost of DeLorean's dream. Hundreds of millions of dollars were thrown away on both sides of the Atlantic. Some £85 million of British taxpayers money went into the project. At the height it employed 2,500 people, which means £34,000 per job – a hugely high figure by any standards, even if those jobs had been soundly based. Since the majority of those jobs lasted less than a year, and all of them less than three, the cost becomes absurd. A dozen different Ulster businesses could have done with that money. Or think what Lotus, for example, could have done with a fraction of it.

The economic situation in West Belfast when DeLorean arrived was bad. When he left it was even worse. Roy Mason insisted that John DeLorean brought 'hope' – but hope raised and then dashed in such cynical fashion is worse than no new hope at all.

DeLorean left behind him a swathe of destroyed or damaged careers. Few of his former executives have fully regained their footing. Dick Brown is currently an executive of Avanti Inc, a small luxury car-maker whose 20-year history of success and high quality of product is the epitome of everything that the DeLorean project lacked. Brown, however, freely admits that there are many in his business life who hold his DeLorean involvement against him.

Bob Dewey says the same thing: a business deal he had fell through in 1982 when a financial backer discovered his former DeLorean involvement. He has teamed up with his old friend, Bill Collins, and they are partners in Detroit in a joint venture to produce a lightweight, fuel-efficient family camper bus, due out in 1984. Walter Strycker always retained large outside business interests and has resumed his independent venture capital business. Bill Haddad has become active again in the political and lobbying worlds – he was a major aide to New York's new governor Mario Cuomo in last year's election and is now writing a book of his own.

Others have not been so robust. Men like Gene Cafiero and Don Lander are strong enough to look after themselves. But Marian Gibson, although she has resumed her business career, still bears the scars, financial and emotional, of the lawsuits that DeLorean pursued her with long past his own arrest. Chuck Bennington does some consulting work for Lotus and others; Mike Loasby went freelance and operates out of his home in the Midlands; Shaun Harte, who moved might and main to make the project a success, found his DeLorean involvement a serious obstacle to a new career; Barrie Wills, the man who tried to organize a consortium to take over the factory, found a different route back into the car industry – he is heading

Clive Sinclair's electric car venture. Colin Pinn lost heavily financially by moving to Northern Ireland where he found difficulty selling the house into which he had sunk most of his savings – he is now back in Britain.

It is fair to say that nobody who worked for John DeLorean came out ahead at the end of the day. Gene Cafiero perhaps did best financially but he lost his options and his payments from DMC suddenly dried up when the company crashed. Kimmerly was a big earner, but he ended up in the creditors' list.

The repercussions on the lives of all those John DeLorean touched has been considerable. Friends of Colin Chapman blame the DeLorean affair for the Lotus chief's early death in December 1982. Lotus itself received a complete bill of health from later investigations, but there is still the unanswered question: how much, if any, did Colin Chapman have of that GPD money for his personal interests? The DeLorean involvement, although it kept Lotus alive through its liquidity crisis, made a most unfitting end to the career of one of the world's all-time great car engineers. Lotus in less than two years accomplished what many still credit John DeLorean with: building the car. Similarly, credit for building the factory and operation in Belfast must go to Chuck Bennington, Dick Brown, Dixon Hollinshead, Don Lander and men such as Harte, Broomfield, Wills, Loasby and Pinn. It was they who did it, every penny of it paid for with British taxpayers' money. John DeLorean averaged less than a day a month in Belfast, never spent a single night there in the last two years, took every opportunity to run Northern Ireland down in private – and never invested a cent in it.

John DeLorean got money out of the British Government with an ease that astonished all those close to him. Roy Mason gave him a £54 million package, enough to complete his project, everyone was assured. But the Conservative government gave him £30 million more. It is a shameful waste of government money – yet there has been no real attempt to ensure it does not happen again. The House of Commons all-party Public Accounts Committee announced it would hold an investigation after DeLorean was arrested; for a time this stopped officials and ministers talking to the authors, and others like us – which is what it may have been at least partly intended to do. Then, as the officials prepared their files, the Royal Ulster Constabulary announced it was pursuing enquiries of its own – in turn causing the PAC to postpone indefinitely its investigation. It is unlikely now that the PAC will ever look at DeLorean – and, at the time of writing, nothing more has been heard from the RUC. Nicholas Winterton, MP, continued to pursue his enquiries, just as DeLorean continued to pursue him. But he too was sharply discouraged, mostly by the Attorney General whose original investigation back in October 1981 was so cursory.

The truth is that neither Conservative nor Labour politicians want the full facts of the DeLorean case to come out in the open – it reflects equally badly on both of them. One of the most unfortunate aspects of this is that it means that the officials in Belfast who fought hardest to control John DeLorean have tended to get saddled with the blame. Those officials have been prevented from talking to us officially and had we not had access, from our own private sources, to most of the relevant files, we might have laid the blame at the wrong doors. As it is the reader can judge for himself who was truly at fault.

The final chapter on the DeLorean car saga and on the life of John Z. DeLorean will be many more years in the writing. Just how much money was siphoned from the various fund raisings may never be fully known, but a fair accounting probably will unfold very soon indeed.

An irony is that DeLorean may have less to fear from the criminal charges lodged against him in Los Angeles than he does from those in the bankruptcy court sitting in judgment in Detroit on the affairs of the DeLorean Motor Company. In the criminal proceedings, DeLorean could win and go free immediately; if he is convicted and sentenced, at least it will be a fixed term that eventually will be over with. But the bankruptcy proceedings could last for years.

Other people used John DeLorean to get what they wanted; that is undeniable. Those who worked for him frankly admit they saw his enormously positive public image as an asset they could use to achieve their own dreams and goals. Governments, too, bowed before that public image. Financiers ignored their duties to their clients in the race to get a piece of the DeLorean action. Politicians rushed to give him money, in order to solve their own problems. The public press – especially the American business press – bears a special guilt for its lazy gullibility in swallowing and ballooning the image of the iconoclastic, socially compassionate business maverick.

All of this is true, but it does not fully explain the enormous devastation that resulted from DeLorean's career of corporate banditry. After all, some individuals did resist his predations. There were government officials who disengaged themselves from his schemes and others who protected their constituents with determination. From the start, there were journalists who sounded a warning for all to hear that the car was a failure, a project doomed by DeLorean's avarice.

The missing ingredient, then, is John DeLorean's character. We will never know why he became the way he is. Others have overcome the frustrations of corporate life with individualism that did not become predation. It is still possible to have a vision and realize it fully and with honour, and it is still possible to get what one wants without destroying the dreams and lives of others in begetting it.

John DeLorean struck a chord twenty years ago when he railed against a philosophy of greed, insensitivity and self-enrichment – in the products offered by corporations and in the lives of individuals. In the end he became what he hated most – a parody of the General Motors he so despised.

Where the money went

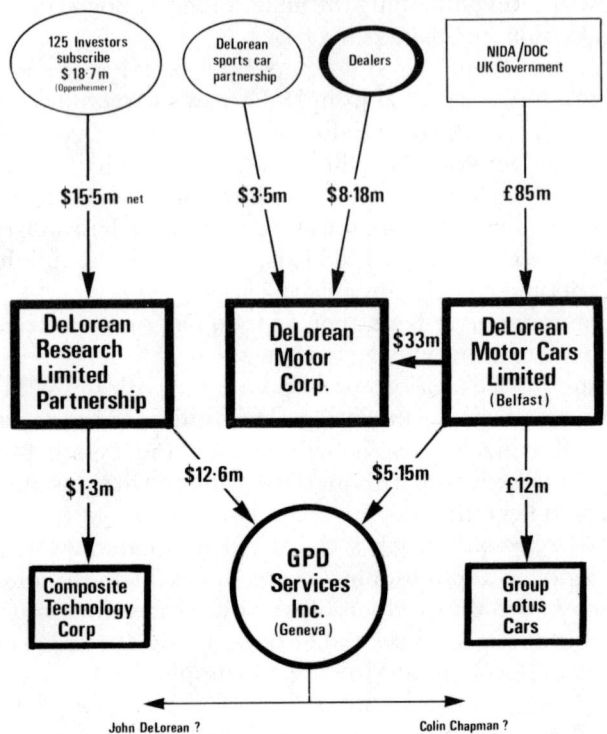

GPD Services Inc., a Panama-registered Geneva-based 'shelf' company, received $17.67 million in late 1978. All of it was apparently intended for work on the DMC-12 sports car to be done by Lotus. None of it ever got there – Lotus was paid from Belfast. Where did the GPD money go? Some $9 million can now be traced via banks in Zurich, Amsterdam and New York to Continental Illinois in Chicago which received a wire transfer from Amsterdam in the late summer of 1979. On October 2, 1979 Cristina Corp., a 100%-owned John DeLorean company (and the eventual controller of all the DeLorean interests) used $7.5 million of it to buy preferred stock in DeLorean Manufacturing Company of Detroit, which in turn used it to repay a loan from Continental Illinois. This allowed a line of credit to be transferred to Logan Manufacturing of Utah which DeLorean bought that summer. We can still only guess where the rest of it went – how much, if any, to Colin Chapman, how much to John DeLorean. At the time of DeLorean's arrest there was only $250,000 left in GPD.